THE EYE
IN THE
TRIANGLE

BOOKS BY ISRAEL REGARDIE

- What You Should Know About the Golden Dawn
- Mysticism, Psychology and Oedipus - with C.S. Hyatt and J. Marvin Spiegelman
- An Interview With Israel Regardie - with Christopher S. Hyatt
- The Complete Golden Dawn System of Magic
- The Golden Dawn Tapes - Series II
- The Eye in the Triangle
- The Tree of Life
- Energy, Prayer and Relaxation
- Geomantic Divination
- Foundations of Practical Magic
- The Sceptre of Power
- Stress Control and Relaxation
- The One Year Manual
- The Qabalah of Israel Regardie
- The Golden Dawn Tapes - Series I
- The Golden Dawn Tapes - Series III
- The Legend of Aleister Crowley
- The Tree and the Egyptian Gods
- The Lazy Man's Guide to Relaxation
- Talismans and How to Make Them
- Ceremonial Magic
- The Enochian Dictionary
- Wilhelm Reich - His Theory and Therapy
- The Teachers of Fulfillment
- Liber Nuts

CROWLEY WORKS EDITED & INTRODUCED BY ISRAEL REGARDIE

- Magick Without Tears
- The Law is For All
- Roll Away the Stone
- Regardie Narrating Crowley (Cassette Tape)
- AHA
- Gems From The Equinox
- The World's Tragedy
- The Vision and The Voice
- The Best of Crowley
- Yoga

OTHER BOOKS FROM FALCON PRESS

- Prometheus Rising - Robert Anton Wilson
- The New Inquisition - Robert Anton Wilson
- The Modern Jew in Search For His Soul - J. Marvin Spiegelman, et al
- Buddhism and Jungian Psychology - J. Marvin Spiegelman & Mokusen Miyuki
- Hinduism and Jungian Psychology - J. Marvin Spiegelman & Arwind U. Vasavada
- The Tree - J. Marvin Spiegleman
- The Knight - J. Marvin Spiegelman
- The Quest - J. Marvin Spiegelman
- The Love - J. Marvin Spiegelman
- Zen Without Zen Masters - Camden Benares
- Survival - Richard Van Praagh, M.D.
- Undoing Yourself With Energized Meditation - Christopher S. Hyatt
- This is it! It's How You Live it Now! The Endless Meditation

Inquiries into the availability of these books are welcomed by Falcon Press

THE EYE
IN THE
TRIANGLE

AN INTERPRETATION OF
ALEISTER CROWLEY
BY
ISRAEL REGARDIE

**Introduction by
Robert Anton Wilson**

**Preface by
Christopher S. Hyatt
with
Baron Peter von Gundlach**

**1986
FALCON PRESS
PHOENIX, ARIZONA 85012, U.S.A.**

International Standard Book Number: 0-941404-08-0

First Edition 1970
Second Printing 1974
First Falcon Press Printing 1982
Second Printing 1986
Third Printing 1986

Falcon Press, 3660 N. 3rd Street
Phoenix, Arizona 85012, U.S.A.

Manufactured in the United States of America

ACKNOWLEDGEMENT

The author gratefully acknowledges permission given by Hill & Wang, Inc., to reprint herein several quotations from *The Confessions of Aleister Crowley,* edited by John Symonds and Kenneth Grant, © 1969 by John Symonds and Kenneth Grant.

Reference is made to *The Confessions of Aleister Crowley* as originally published by the Mandrake Press (London, 1929-30), on pages 47, 62, 66, 107, 121, 158, 208, 209, 221, 241, 260, 274, 279, 423, 438, 440, 442, and 461.

CONTENTS

ILLUSTRATIONS

INTRODUCTION

By Robert Anton Wilson, Ph.D.

I happen to agree with Ernest Hemingway that, of all the requirements a writer needs, the most important is a built in, cast-iron, shock-proof bullshit-detector.

A writer may have seen and felt a great deal; with extreme good luck, he may even have understood what he saw and felt; but without the tool Hemingway recommended, he will never communicate efficiently.

This is especially true of writers on mysticism, who have produced more bad writing than any other single group on this planet, except for the politicians.

Ezra Pound once commented that there are two types of clarity. The first is illustrated by the sentence, "Get me two pounds of four-inch nails." The second is illustrated by, "Get me the type of Rembrandt I like." Anybody can understand the first kind of clarity; the second is clear only when speaker and hearer share a mutual universe of sensibility; but both are equally **LUCID** under ideal conditions. Most mystical writing contains neither type of clarity. Dip into Gopi Krishna or Ken Wilbur, for instance -- or into ten dozen like them -- and you will find yourself afloat in an ocean of semantic mush. Any sentence from such writers could easily be inserted into a political speech; just change "God" or "True Self" to "the government" or "the chief executive," and the general tapioca-like fog will remain the same -- vapid, rhetorical, hollow, but vaguely "inspirational" if you don't think about it.

All of which is to explain why I originally read *The Eye in the Triangle*. You see, it was recommended to me by Alan Watts, who said "It's the best book on mysticism that I've read in ten years or more."

I had been reading Alan's books for a decade and had known Alan for almost as long, and my Hemingway bullshit-detector had not yet found a sentence anywhere in his works containing **BOVINE EXCRETA.** If he recommended a book, I immediately trotted off to buy a copy. He knew what good writing was, even in the area of mysticism, where the author is, by definition, trying to unscrew the inscrutable and eff the ineffable.

I read all through *The Eye in the Triangle* in one evening and it passed the Hemingway Test with all flags flying and a band playing on the deck. There was no B.S. in it, no smog, no greasy rhetoric. It was as lucid as a cook book or a five-line objectivist poem by William Carlos Williams.

I have re-read it several times in the last twelve years -- and read it again before writing this introduction -- and I still consider it a masterpiece of exposition in one of the most difficult areas a writer can confront.

Dr. Regardie not only writes about mystical consciousness with unparalleled precision, but he has even succeeded in explaining the unique life and works of Aleister Crowley -- the most difficult, perverse, enigmatic and generally egregious individual in the whole history of occultism. Like the first books to introduce Einstein or *Finnegans Wake* or Picasso to a general audience, *The Eye in the Triangle* is an intellectual landmark, making accessible to all intelligent persons what had previously been understood only by a few. The reader can turn from this book to any of Crowley's works without being hopelessly baffled by Aleister's paradoxes, his brain-teasing riddles, his (**seemingly!**) childish jokes, and the endless dialectic between the serious things Crowley had to say and the playful way he said them.

Aleister Crowley was, in my opinion, one of the most original and important thinkers of this era -- right up there with such titans as Einstein and Joyce. Indeed, what Einstein did for physics and Joyce for the novel (and Picasso for painting, and Pound for poetry, and Wright for architecture), Crowley did for the mystic tradition. He swept aside all 19th Century barnacles and incrustations, redefined every concept, and created something that is totally contemporary with our existence as 20th Century persons.

The major intellectual discovery of our age is Relativity; that is why the general public, with intuitive accuracy, always classifies Einstein as **the** archetype of modern genius. But at the same time Albert was formulating the mathematics of Special and General Relativity, the same principle was -- synchronistically and inevitably -- being discovered/created in a dozen other fields. Anthropologists were beginning to recognize **cultural relativism,** which was a kind of Copernican Revolution of the sensibility, as it became clear that the typical reality-tunnel of Western Christian Civilization was not the only valid way to sense the Universe around us. It was from an exhibit of African art assembled by anthropologist Leo Frobenius that Picasso first saw the possibilities of organizing visual space in non-Western ways; and Frobenius also influenced the structure of Ezra Pound's *Cantos* and, through that epic, all of the poetry that is distinctly modern.

Freud and Jung were, at the same time, discovering psychological relativism, or, as I prefer to call it, neurological relativism. What any person sees in a room full of people is not just "what is really there" (which is known only to Bishop Berkeley's God) but also what that person's conditioning and complexes bring into the room **as a filter.** We are all galaxies shouting to each other over vast interstellar distances of prejudice; it is a minor miracle that we are able to understand each other even approximately. Korzybski and the General Semanticists, Garfinkle and the Ethnomethodologists, and all psychologists working in perception theory, have made this variety of relativism even more obvious than it was to Freud and Jung. Joyce's *Ulysses* mutated the novel by introducing this relativity into the very structure and style of the narrative; we never see the "real" Dublin of Berkeley's "God" in *Ulysses:* we see the Dublin that impacts on the brain of Stephen,

the Dublin that impacts on Mr. Bloom, the Dublin of the bar-
flies in Barney Kiernan's pub, the Dublin of Molly Bloom's
sleepy reveries. Each "Dublin" is equally real: that is the essence
of the Relativity Revolution.

Aleister Crowley discovered/experienced all these relativistic
reorientations in his life and expressed them in his works; thus, he
is the first truly 20th Century mystic. Crowley was reared in a
Fundamentalist Protestant sect, trained in Ceremonial Magic by
the Rosicrucian order of the Golden Dawn,* learned Buddhist
and Hindu yogas in Ceylon, climbed mountains for excitement,
and lived often amid the **avant-garde** artistic clique in Paris
(among other things, Crowley was an early champion of Rodin's
late, experimental sculpture). He also studied I Ching and Tao-
ism, experienced something of Sufism in North Africa, and was
vividly aware of Freud, Jung, Einstein and modern mathematics.
He not only learned to quantum-jump from one reality-tunnel to
another, but developed, out of traditional "magical" practices,
his own techniques for making such jumps quick and efficient.

One of his cruder exercizes, which all could profit from, was to
adopt two "opposite" personalities, such as a vegetarian pacifist
and chauvinistic militarist, key each one to a different piece of
jewelry (a talisman or ring) and change his verbal opinions, his
outer behavior, and his (more subtle) inner responses, depending
on which piece of jewelry he was wearing. It sounds childishly
simple, but the results are profound. Even physicists and anthropologists, who understand relativity better than most, could
understand it more deeply if they tried this exercize a few times.

Crowley tried, like all mystics, to abolish the ego. As Dr.
Regardie makes clear, he did not succeed in any total sense; but
those not blinded by hero-worship can easily see that this is true
of many other Illuminated and Enlightened beings. (The phrase
prima donna was coined in opera, and quickly adapted in the
other arts, but nobody deserves it more than certain Gurus and
Sages now at large in the Republic.) The ego has a seemingly
infinite phalanx of strategies for sneaking back, each time it
seems to be demolished. Crowley was always eccentric, often
outrageous on principle, and sometimes downright vicious, but he

is unique among the Illuminati in not trying to conceal such traits but, rather, in making every possible effort to ensure that disciples would never be able to sentimentally sanctify him.

"There is no sense in trying to whitewash Crowley's reputation," I was once told by Caliph Hymeneus Alpha of the *Ordo Templi Orientis* (a magical society once headed by Crowley), "Aleister spent most his life systematically blackening it."

It is a fitting part of the O.T.O. tradition that the last time I saw the Caliph giving a public lecture, he was so pie-eyed drunk as to be nearly incoherent. Crowley would have been proud of him; but I also thought of the time I saw a **Sufi Murshid** deliberately **light a cigarette!** at a Holistic Health Conference -- and of the "scandalous behaviors" of Gurdjieff, and the "blasphemies" of the Zen Masters.

What is behind Crowley's perversities involves that perennial problem of mysticism -- the necessity and the near-impossibility of abolishing the ego. The ego is not "evil;" it is an evolutionary necessity. Unfortunately, it is also very limiting: it restricts consciousness and freedom at just those points where the mystic wishes to increase consciousness and expand freedom. Crowley tackled this problem with his usual heroic and fool-hardy Total Commitment. He pushed the techniques of ceremonial magic far beyond the point most occultists dare to go; he became expert at a dozen or so varieties of Hindu and Buddhist yoga; he wrote reams and reams of "inspired" poetry -- **literally** inspired by Dionysus (booze) in many cases -- to let his unconscious gush forth; he invented many tricks like the two personalities-keyed-to-jewels mentioned before; and he experimented with more drugs more frequently than anybody in the West before the Neurological Revolution of the 1960s.

I have no doubt that Crowley got outside the normal constrictions of ego -- way outside -- many, many times. I accept the reports in his diaries that he learned to achieve **dhyana** (the trance of unity) fairly regularly and easily, and occasionally got beyond even that to **Samadhi** (the state, known only to advanced Oriental adepts and students of quantum physics, where it makes sense to say that existence and non-existence are the same.) Meanwhile, he developed and nurtured a hierarchy of separate selves, each with its own functions and levels of awareness; Dr. Regardie is especially helpful in distinguishing these separate entities and explaining which of them were responsible for which of the books and behaviors that emanated from the physical body called "Aleister Crowley."

Meanwhile, the primordial Crowley ego lurked deep in the imprinted brain circuits and crept back at every opportunity. Aleister played games with it, at times; indulged it when he was in the mood; and had a dozen gimmicks to get rid of it (temporarily) whenever he needed more consciousness and more freedom than an ego allows. An undated note by Nietzsche** says:

The task? To see things as they are. The means: to look through hundreds of eyes, across many peoples.

Every great artist attempts this; it is the goal of mysticism. It is the only way to escape the constricted, mechanical and ultimately stupid limitations of the primate ego. Crowley succeeded well enough and often enough to rank among the giants of our century, and he expressed what he had learned in terms of the Relativism which every educated person these days must accept. His wonderfully funny but often unfair diatribes against the great mystics of the generation before him, or those of his own generation who had not yet grasped Relativity, are over-stated, yes; but no more so than the polemics that were going on at the same time between the modernists in dozens of other fields and those who were trying to preserve the obsolete Victorian worldview.

Read Ezra Pound fulminating against those who wanted modern poems to sound like Victorian poems; or Frank Lloyd Wright howling against those who wanted modern buildings to look like Renaissance buildings; or Count Alfred Korzybski denouncing those who are trying to preserve Aristotelian logic in a non-Aristotelian scientific age; and you will begin to understand

Crowley's invectives against those spiritual traditions that did not understand that we have entered a New Aeon.

DO WHAT THOU WILT SHALL BE THE WHOLE OF THE LAW -- the most "infamous," the most (deliberately) shocking, and the most often misunderstood of Crowley's axioms -- is his way of placing Relativity at the heart of his system. We all have a hierarchy of selves, whether or not we are as conscious of this as Crowley and whether or not we develop each of them as he did. Out of this hierarchy a "resolution of forces" (as it would be called in physics) can emerge, if one is true to one's total psyche and does not tailor everything to the tyranny of the socially conditioned mechanical ego. This one force that is resultant of all inner selves is the True Will, in Crowley's sense. One can never go wrong by following it, even though it is different for each person. These differences are given by evolution, as Crowley knew, and cannot be permanently crushed by any kind of tyranny, of the Church, or the State, or of that herd of contented COWS who define "acceptable taste." If nature wanted us to be replicable units, we'd be ants, not primates.******* That is the meaning of Crowley's second favorite slogan, **EVERY MAN AND EVERY WOMAN IS A STAR.**

Crowley was always true to that inner "governor" -- that hidden star in every human psyche -- and followed it without flinching. It made him always the funniest, sometimes the brightest and occasionally the most abominable man of his generation. Equal fidelity to the True Will can make one person a great chef, a second a mediocre but happy accountant, a third a genius in music; genetics (and darker aspects of destiny) along with social conditioning, make up the forces that average-out to True Will.

As the great Sufi teacher, Hazrat Inayat Khan writes:********

> **However unhappy a man may be, the moment he knows the purpose of his life a switch is turned and the light is on . . . If he has to strive after that purpose all his life, he does not mind so long as he knows what the purpose is. Ten such people have much greater**

> **power than a thousand people working from
> morning till evening not knowing the pur-
> pose of their life.**

This is Crowley's doctrine of the True Will, and it is why he claimed his system would produce "geniuses." A genius is simply a person who has found his or her purpose (True Will) and is no longer swept about by every wind of circumstance.

To conclude, I would like to give an example of Crowley's "obscurity." which is also an instance of his astonishing humor, and explains a great deal that still puzzles people who have studied his work for years and still can't understand **him** as a man. I refer to a verse in *The Book of Lies* (falsely so called), Chapter 70, paragraph 6, "But FRATER PERDURABO is nothing but an EYE; what eye none knoweth." Frater Perdurabo is Crowley himself, or at least the Crowley who wrote *The Book of Lies*. But what eye? Crowley's official commentary is unhelpful: "Paragraph 6 states a fact unsuited to the grade of any reader of this book."

However, if one is persistent, one eventually finds elsewhere in the book that all the eye symbols refer to the Eye of Hoor and one is advised to seek further light in Crowley's *Liber 777*. Hunting through that complex of Qabalistic tables, the mystery is finally solved. The Eye of Hoor, among other things, means the anus.

The fact that was unsuited to the grade of any reader, but which Crowley was careful to put on record for the discerning and persistent student, is that he knew he was an ass-hole. (Of course, there is even a deeper, alchemical joke here, but I leave something to the reader's own efforts.)

Robert Anton Wilson
San Francisco
March 1982

*Be on the lookout for *THE COMPLETE GOLDEN DAWN SYSTEM OF MAGIC* by Israel Regardie -- enlarged and containing new information concerning the G.D. system, Falcon Press, Winter, 1982.
**Quoted in *THE NEW NIETZSCHE*, ed. by David Allison, Delta, 1977.
***For a complete analysis of "us" primates see *PROMETHEUS RISING* by Robert Anton Wilson, Falcon Press, Fall, 1982.
****MASTERY THROUGH ACCOMPLISHMENT*, Sufi Order Publications, New Lebanon, N.Y., 1978.

PREFACE

By Christopher S. Hyatt
with Baron Peter von Gundlach

While it is difficult to find more to say about Dr. Regardie's monumental work, I find it necessary to repeat a conversation which I had with him a few weeks ago concerning the *The Eye in the Triangle*. During our talk Dr. Regardie suggested that the *Eye* should be considered the "integrating" factor between psychology and mysticism. What this illustrates, if I may borrow from Leary's eight circuit model as elucidated by Robert Anton Wilson in his forthcoming book *Prometheus Rising*, is that while magick and other occult strategies tune in and enhance circuits five through eight, psychology and in particular transformation psychotherapies are essential for healing and altering the four lower circuits.

Nothing should be sacred about our character or personality. Crowley realized this and through "objective" means attempted to "undo" himself at the most personal level. Crowley became a laboratory of mind-body-ego experimentation and while to some he seemed obscure or mad the facts remain that he attempted to accomplish legitimate self-change through the "scientific" means at hand.

The purpose of the great work is to **Become More Than Human,**

THE EYE IN THE TRIANGLE

and this does include altering the "sacred cow" which we all hold so dear (**our habits, values and character also know as soft-ware**); that is, if our interest in the Great Work is more than arm chair amusement. Our beloved -- personality and character -- is often nothing more or less than a random collection of input data accumulated from the information [or dis-information] of Mother, Father, Teacher, Culture, Friends, Religion and History. This airy fluid entity, which often causes us more pain and misery than it is worth -- is called "self" -- the furthest thing from True Will, [the goal of the Great Work], yet we defend it daily and are more "willing" to die for it, than anything else we own.

This airy gaseous entity, this something which we **DID NOT** even create is our greatest obstacle to finding our True Will.

The Ego must lose its sacred position in our hierarchy of value. Crowley realized this and while not totally successful, he cannot be blamed or labeled a failure. A fact often forgotten is that few were around at that time with the insight, knowledge and dedication to magick who could honestly guide Crowley through the morass of his neurosis and character flaws. Neither Freud himself, Reich, nor any other of the "great" men received a full course of treatment. It is ironic that most innovators of brain change techniques do not benefit from their discoveries.

For Crowley, Magick is brain change Willed. To quote him:

> **". . . our ceremonial magic fines down then to a series of minute, though of course empirical, physiological experiments, and who so will carry them through intelligently need not fear the results."***

Obscurity has many purposes one of which is the breaking of SET, that is the way our brains put the universe together. Magick and occultism strive to alter -- undo -- and loosen the restrictions of our unwilled SETS so that we can open higher circuits. An additional armament for the occultist is a psychotherapeutic technique which can aid in this goal without having to buy the metaphysics of its underpinnings. Everyday psychology per se, can't openly admit rebellion against the culture which nurtures it.

When it does, such as the case of Wilhelm Reich, the consequences are disastrous.

Magick then is a practical science of higher brain change. It opens and evolves the higher circuits of the magician's brain, and becomes the advancing edge of the evolutionary growth of mankind.

However, Regardie emphasizes repeatedly, all too often on deaf ears, that magick is not enough. Certain parts of the brain are not changed by magick and in many cases the practice of magick hides, obscures and sometimes potentiates further character rigidity and disorder. This fact in itself implies some other form of practical work necessary to accomplish the goal of revealing the True Will (becoming your own programmer). Crowley was a living example of this over-sight; yet his genius recognized this on occasions.

Crowley in my opinion is damned and feared by many not because of his explicit sexuality, for who is not aware or involved with the sexual revolution in one form or another. Another explanation of why he is so severely condemned is his drug use, yet Leary and others have surpassed Crowley with this form of experimental brain change. Still another is his hatred of the Christian Tunnel Reality. Yet, some book stores handle the Satanic Bible, while refusing to handle Crowley. Why should this be? One possible explanation is that Crowley stood for, and still stands for the overthrow of our sacred personalities and the System which feeds on these rigidities and fears. He laughed, pitied and ridiculed the "whole human condition", while striving to free himself and mankind from Silly Gods and Foolish Devils. (In other words he cast the spell of relativity in the face of the Self-Erected Gods of Authority.) Unlike Gurdjieff who was after the same result as Crowley, A.C. flashed his truth (threw it right in our face and rubbed our nose into it) publicly without any sense of apology or "good taste". Baron von Gundlach suggests that Crowley would have enjoyed the following aside:

The real meaning of GOD [G.O.D.] is ---- the Gatherer Of Data.

Crowley did just that -- gathered data on everything and anything, then poetically and audaciously flung his DATA about for
all to see.

With better scientific models Crowley will start making sense
to more people who have been put off by his obscurity, style,
manner, and openness. **"Breaking Set"** is the spirit of Crowley.
Psychological Set Theory defines set as the predetermined way
we have at looking at the World. Set, funny enough, is the "evil"
god of Egypt, who killed his brother Horus. Horus, the new aeon
symbol, is opposed by the rigidities of the past (Set).

Set is restriction and for Crowley's "morality" restriction is
"evil", whether it be the restrictions and rigidities of our own
conditioning and prejudices or those of an entire culture and
civilization. For some this may make his best known statement
**DO WHAT THOU WILT SHALL BE THE WHOLE OF
THE LAW** a bit clearer. This statement was never intended to
be a license to behave unconsciously or robotically. In order to
follow Crowley's law you must first break set, that is undo your
conditioned reflexes and "create" an "I" who first has a Will and
second can follow that WILL. This is the prerequisite to his
famous often mis-applied statement.

Crowley stood for the Undoing of that conditioned, set, rigid
self, so that Thy True Will could be done. I attempt in my book
*Undoing Yourself With Energized Meditation and Other Devi-
ces* to provide more or less scientific techniques to accomplish
this end; recalling his goal, "The Aim of Religion, The Method of
Science".

Regardie clearly emphasizes the "flaws" in Crowley's personality not allowing the reader to fall into the Set of Hero Worship or
vilification. Hero worship should only be regarded as a technique, a method of transferring the power and energy which has
been automatically placed in other programmers (teachers, parents, and alike) and their thought structures, to a New Programmer [a Set Breaker] who has the knowledge, the desire and
the ability to break the mechanism of Hero worship fully and
finally at the right time. All legitimate systems which have higher
brain change (enlightenment) as its goal harbor and employ this

"secret" key, including some schools of psychotherapy. However, most psychotherapies address themselves to the adjustment of the person to a social-moral base. Crowley was not about to *adjust* to any system he loathed. This would have meant restriction, the prime "evil" of Crowley's Order.

He would have required an amoral therapy, one which would have freed him from his own latent anxieties, fears, and compulsions. This could have been accomplished by some Reichian or neo-Reichian therapy, but of course Reich's theory would have been severely scrutinized and its blind social, cultural and philosophical prejudices seized and destroyed by Crowley's wit, insight and genius.

Crowley would have surely benefited by Reich's techniques, and it is most interesting that Crowley's secretary Regardie, became an expert in Reichian and neo-Reichian therapy, providing an important bridge between Magick and Psychology. We salute Israel Regardie for this monumental effort, which has provided illumination, reason and insight for those of us who are involved with the Great Work. I would like to close with a quote from Crowley:

> "... all the symbols are interchangeable for each containeth in itself its own opposite. And this is the great Mystery of the Supernals that are beyond the Abyss. For below the Abyss contradiction is division. But above the Abyss contradiction is Unity. And there could be nothing true except by virtue of the contradiction that is contained in itself..."**

CHRISTOPHER S. HYATT
with BARON von GUNDLACH
APRIL 11, 1982
LOS ANGELES

THE BOOK OF THE GOETIA OF SOLOMON THE KING, by Aleister Crowley, Ram Importer, New York, 1970.
**THE VISION AND THE VOICE*, by Aleister Crowley, Edited by Israel Regardie, Sangreal, Texas, 1972.

FOREWORD

There is a time to speak and a time to remain silent. For me, the time has come now to raise my voice in the interest of clarifying the record of Aleister Crowley. He was one of the greatest mystics of all time, although a very complicated and controversial person.

He has too long suffered from misrepresentation and vilification at the hands of uninformed biographers. It is time finally to set the record straight. This must be done, not merely out of regard for the man himself, but even more importantly, because of the profound effect he has had on thousands of readers, and will yet have on countless thousands more.

John Symonds, his major biographer, evinces throughout his narrative a totally contemptuous attitude towards Crowley. This hostility altogether invalidates his attempt at biography. His book *The Great Beast* could have been excellent since every opportunity in the world was given him through access to diaries and a mass of hitherto unpublished material. Crowley had appointed him executor of his literary estate, and because of this, Symonds had a unique opportunity to set the record straight once and for all. However his personal prejudices got in the way. His writing is cynical, showing no glimmer of insight or the slightest trace of sympathy.

"Crowley was not a great poet," he wrote, "although he wrote a few good poems . . . . The dominating effect is one of insincerity." He goes on to assert that "in most of his verse there are rarely found those strains which result from a surrender to the poetic moment; instead, he mainly harnessed his talent to his occult interests and personal obsessions which are unsuitable for poetry."[1]

Charles R. Cammell thinks otherwise. His book *Aleister Crowley, the Man, the Mage, the Poet* is a far more telling piece of work. Referring to the three volumes of *Collected Works,* which incidentally is a very early publication, he wrote: "These Works were for the most part poetical, and comprised a mass of poetry which for variety, versatility, range of mood, matter and manner, had absolutely no peer or counterpart in the literature of our time."[2] He also presented a more accurate picture of Crowley as a mystic, though the edge is taken off his otherwise fine presentation by a tendency to moralize, which scotomized him to certain well-ascertained facts. Were one able to combine this volume with that of Symonds, one could form a more adequate conception of the complexity as well as creativity of this man of genius.

He is clearly not a poet to be sneered at, this man who could pen the following from *The World's Tragedy:*

Hear then! By Abrasax! The bar
Of the unshifting star
Is broken—Io! Asar!
My spirit is wrapt in the wind of light;
It is whirled away on the wings of night,
Sable-plumed are the wonderful wings,
But the silver of moonlight subtly springs
Into the feathers that flash with the pace
Of our flight to the violate bounds of space.
Time is dropt like a stone from the stars:
Space is a chaos of broken bars:
Being is merged in a furious flood
That rages and hisses and foams in the blood.

See! I am dead! I am passed, I am passed
Out of the sensible world at last.
I am not. Yet I am, as I never was,
A drop in the sphere of molten glass
Whose radiance changes and shifts and drapes
The infinite soul in finite shapes.
There is light, there is life, there is love, there is sense
Beyond speech, beyond song, beyond evidence.
There is wonder intense, a miraculous sun,
As the many are molten and mixed into one
With the heat of its passion; the one hath invaded
The heights of its soul, and its laughter is braided
With comets whose plumes are the galaxies
Like winds on the night's inaccessible seas. . . .

Or, the mystic who could write tenderly in *The Book of
Lapis Lazuli:*

I await Thee in sleeping, in waking. I invoke Thee no
more; for Thou art in me, O Thou who hast made me a
beautiful instrument tuned to Thy rapture.

Yet art Thou ever apart, even as I.

I remember a certain holy day in the dusk of the
year, in the dusk of the Equinox of Osiris, when first I
beheld Thee visibly; when first the dreadful issue was
fought out; when the Ibis-headed One charmed away
the strife.

I remember Thy first Kiss, even as a maiden should.
Nor in the dark by-ways was there another; Thy kisses
abide.

Or, again, in *The Book of the Heart Girt with a Serpent:*

Weary, weary! saith the scribe. Who shall lead me to
the sight of the Rapture of my master?

The body is weary and the soul is sore weary and
sleep weighs down their eyelids; yet ever abides the sure
consciousness of ecstasy, unknown, yet known in that
its being is certain. O Lord, be my helper, and bring me
to the bliss of the Beloved.

All day I sing of Thy delight. All night I delight in
Thy song. There is no other day or night than this.

The poet-mystic who could write the following in *Aha!* is
surely one to be reckoned with:

Even so. And One Supreme there is
Whom I have known, being He. Withdrawn
Within the curtains of the dawn
Dwells that concealed. Behold! He is
A blush, a breeze, a song, a kiss,
A rosy flame like Love, his eyes
Blue, the quintessence of all the skies,
His hair a foam of gossamer
Pale gold as jasmine, lovelier
Than all the wheat of Paradise.
O the dim water-wells his eyes!
There is such a depth of Love in them
That the adept is rapt away,
Dies on that mouth, a gleaming gem
Of dew caught in the boughs of Day!
. . . .
　　Had I a million songs,
And every song a million words,
And every word a million meanings,
I could not count the choral throngs
Of Beauty's beatific birds,
Or gather up the paltry gleanings
Of this great harvest of delight!
Hast thou not heard the words aright?
That world is truly infinite. . . . . . .

In my wanderings I came
To an ancient park aflame
With fairies' feet. Still wrapped in love
I was caught up, beyond, above
The tides of being. The great sight
Of the intolerable light
Of the whole universe that wove
The labyrinth of life and love
Blazed in me. Then some giant will,

> Mine or another's, thrust a thrill
> Through the great vision. All the light
> Went out in an immortal night,
> The world annihilated by
> The opening of the Master's Eye. . . .

His definition of poetry in the Preface to *The City of God* stems from the deepest beliefs of his life, and compares well with any similar essay:

> Poetry is the geyser of the Unconscious.
> Poetry is the intelligible musical expression of the Real whose mirror is the phenomenal Universe.
> Poetry is the Hermes to lead the "soul" Eurydice from the murk of illusion to the light of Truth; "and on Daedalian oarage fare forth to the interlunar air."
> A living poem must effect a definite magical excitement—exaltation in the hearer or reader, similar to the experience of "falling in love at first sight" with a woman. Analysis and argument cannot convince, and may inhibit the reaction, which is above emotion and reason.
> The reception of a poem, being a ritual Magical initiation, suffers no interruption. . . . .

Daniel P. Mannix's *The Beast* which first appeared in one of the men's sport magazines is a pathetic piece of hack-writing, largely a rehash of the Symonds biography but not nearly as well done. I would prefer to ignore this book but since it has appeared in a paperback edition, it is guaranteed a circulation in the thousands. Mannix is completely without comprehension of what Crowley aspired to, and apparently knows his writing only at second hand, which is not good enough for critical evaluation. If he were "a superior American sports writer" as the blurb on the back of the pocket edition indicates, then it would have been far better had he stuck to sports reporting.

On page 22 of that book, Mannix refers to me as follows:

"The mysteries of the Golden Dawn have since been published by Mr. Israel Regardie, formerly secretary of the Order, and now a psychologist in California. The Mysteries take up seven thick volumes and I've waded through most of them."

In these few lines, he has made several errors. At no time had I been the secretary of the Golden Dawn, nor had I ever held any office in that Order. I had served as Crowley's secretary for some years, but this was a generation or more *after* he had severed his own connection with the Order. Nor was I a psychologist *per se,* though I had taken four years of chiropractic training in New York and psychoanalytic training of many hundreds of clinical hours in London, New York and Los Angeles. Ultimately I came to practice, within the confines of the chiropractic profession, a manipulative form of psychotherapy based on the work of Wilhelm Reich. These facts would have been easy for Mannix to verify had he made even the slightest effort. Finally, my book *The Golden Dawn* was published in four volumes, not in seven as he states.[3]

It seems to me then that if Mannix, referring to me, could make this many mistakes within a few lines, his views about Crowley expressed in over a hundred pages are very much open to question. He does not recommend himself as an apostle of accuracy.

Finally, there is Gilbert Highet, a radio commentator who has "captured a wide, literate audience during recent years," according to the blurb on the back of his book *Talents and Geniuses* (New York, Meridian Books Inc., 1959). It also avers that he "here displays his varied interests, his wit, and his erudition in discussions of topics ranging from Bach to Zen Buddhism."

Highet offers an essay on Crowley which begins with a review of Somerset Maugham's *The Magician.* From this he concludes that Crowley was not a *fake* as some people have been led to believe, but a *failure.* In opposition to

Christianity, which is essentially sex-negative, Crowley had wished to establish a solar-phallic religion (a felicitous phrase borrowed from Jung's *Psychology of the Unconscious).* He had in mind a type of worship which would be rooted in man's deepest biological and spiritual needs. Highet says this kind of religion obviously has not succeeded in spreading to any extent—therefore Crowley has failed.

Superficially, this comment is valid. Nevertheless we have to remember that the early preaching of the Gospels was not a startling success for a considerable time. Actually some scholars wonder if it ever really succeeded in making anything but the most trivial impact on the everyday lives of most people. It took centuries of violence and bloodshed to convert the masses to Christianity. Crowley has been dead less than a score of years. Who can estimate how many hundreds or even thousands of people have been influenced in one way or another by his writing? There is no solar-phallic church to spread his gospel. But it is not impossible that time may take care of this too. Stranger things have happened![4]

Highet then continues his irrational criticism of Crowley by stating that "he was a failure. . . . He poured forth an interminable torrent of bad poetry, meaningless prose, and amateurish drawings and paints."

If they are meaningless to Highet, it only exposes his own prejudice. In a later essay on Zen, he is able to explore the subject with some semblance of empathy and insight, but he could not approach Crowley without suspicion and perhaps jealousy, because Crowley was a far greater writer.

"He would not study," wrote Highet presumptuously flying in the face of well-established facts, "but preferred to evoke visions and oracles from his own subconscious, which anyone can do."

I suppose this is the same kind of vicious criticism that must have once assailed William Blake, whose poetry, visions and apocalyptic writings are now integrally imbedded in

English literature—as I predict will much of the literary output of Crowley in time to come. If Highet had become acquainted with some of the contents of his own Unconscious, it might have spared him the ignominy of placing on record derogatory statements which ultimately will be his own judge and accuser. If *anyone* can evoke at will visions and oracles from the depths of his self, as Highet claims, all I can say is that this runs counter to my professional experience of more than twenty-five years. Most people are cut off from their roots in the unconscious psyche.

For these and other reasons, then, I have decided to reexamine the life of this literary and mystical genius to see if in the light of my own personal experience and understanding, it may not be possible to unravel some of the twisted skeins of which Crowley was fashioned. There are certain well-defined influences so outstanding that I fail to see why they have not been better exploited. They may not wholly explain him—any more than I think any person may be wholly explained, psychoanalysis notwithstanding. But perhaps some of his deep, underlying motivations may be evoked and scrutinized so that we can see what they are and how they affected him. Some of them are clear, and these I propose in the following pages to explore and delineate, for they seem to help us to understand what manner of man this was. For this was a man who has written immortally. We must keep that writing alive. It may be that what he did and what he wrote are vitally important to all of us. Flippancy and cynicism do nothing for him any more than they do for us. Something more is required to reveal the goals we are all striving towards.

NOTES

[1] *The Great Beast,* John Symonds, Rider & Co., London, 1951, p. 35.

[2] *Aleister Crowley, the Man, the Mage, the Poet,* Charles R. Cammell. London, Richards Press, 1951, p. 1.

[3] Now reissued in a revised and enlarged edition, bound in 2 volumes, by Llewellyn Publications, St. Paul, 1969.

[4] *The Berkeley Barb* of San Francisco, in its issue of September 4, 1969, seems determined to make Gilbert Highet eat his words, as well as to fulfil my own prediction. The illustration on the front page of that issue would have set all of Crowley's tissues ablaze.

PART ONE—THE MAN

> Yet holier than all These to me is
> LAYLAH, night and death; for Her do I blaspheme
> alike the finite and The Infinite.
> So wrote not FRATER PERDURABO but the
> Imp Crowley in his Name . . . .
> And yet who knoweth which is Crowley,
> and which is FRATER PERDURABO?
>
> *The Book of Lies*

CHAPTER ONE

Aleister Crowley

The station was noisy and rather gloomy. It possessed none of the pseudo-cathedral-like majesty that is associated with Pennsylvania Station or the Grand Central Station in New York City. The mid-October morning was cold and grey when I got off the boat-train at Gare St. Lazare. All the way from Cherbourg, surrounded by French voices and strange sounds only half-heard, I had been wondering what this moment would be like. The damp coldness in the sombre building had set up a muscular shiver, diffuse and fine, though anxiety with some degree of excitement had a good deal to do with it. Looking around the platform for a familiar face, I paused near the pile of luggage the porters were busily and loudly piling up.

"Do what thou wilt shall be the whole of the Law."

This was said in a very British voice, thin and smoothly slurring, but hardly Cockney as alleged by Calder Marshall. Then I knew—for of course I was more than familiar with the phrase. Just to my right stood a tall figure, rather heavy set, in blue-grey tweeds, plus fours. There was a cap of the same material placed very conservatively over a large head. The eyes were not big, but gleamed pleasantly over the dark bags beneath them. A light smile played around the corners of a small mouth. The handgrip, which came next, was not very firm—nor was mine, for that matter. I was very nervous, despite my clear pleasure in confronting Aleister Crowley for

3

the first time. A few months earlier I had sent him a photograph. And from a photograph in the *Equinox* I knew what he looked like. He could not be missed.

Here we were in Paris, after a desultory correspondence extending over two years. He had invited me to come over to Europe to be his secretary and to study with him. I had felt flattered. It all seemed a dream, one that could not be true for me. But here I was in this grimy station in the year 1928, the fulfilment of a long-cherished dream. Had I not just heard him greet me with the Thelemic watchwords "Do what thou wilt"?

In no sense of the term was it a dream. How it had all transpired is quite a story. Sometime during 1925 or 1926, I had attended a meeting in Washington, D.C., where I had heard a reading by an attorney from Crowley's *Part I of Book IV*—a tiny classic on the subject of Yoga practices.[1] By this time I was somewhat familiar with the standard texts on the subject, and so was in a relatively good position to appreciate some facets of Crowley's unique point of view.

The upshot was that I wrote Crowley a letter, heaven only knows what about, care of one or another of his publishers. Most of them were no longer in business. Months went by without an answer. For the time being, the matter escaped my mind.

There were more pressing matters that clamoured for attention. I had gone to Philadelphia to attend one of the art schools there, hoping that an art career was ahead of me, and I began preparations for it. Then tardily the expected letter from Crowley arrived. It was brief but pleasant. He told me to get in touch with his agent in New York City.

Immediately a letter was sent off, resulting quickly in an invitation to meet with Karl Germer in New York. Not more than a few days elapsed before I entrained one week-end for the big city to spend a very pleasant day with Germer. He was a handsome German, formerly an officer in the old

Wehrmacht. His enthusiasm for Crowley was boundless and contagious. One of the results of this early visit was that he sold me a set of the *Equinox* together with two or three other rare Crowley items. These became bedside books and textbooks for many months to come. Germer and I would meet from time to time in New York or in Washington, discussing the Great Work and Crowley's connection with it. My reading had been making me conscious of the proposal that the Great Work was dedicated to the task of the transformation of man, to the quest for self-discovery.

I liked Karl; he became a very good friend. One of the end results of this relationship was that Karl served as liaison with Crowley. Of the many threads that were interwoven in the complex skein of events and circumstances that drew me to Crowley, Germer's influence has to be noted as among the more prominent ones.

On the night in October 1928 when I set sail from New York for Paris, there was a pleasant dinner at a good New York restaurant. Present were Karl Germer and Cora Eaton, who subsequently became his wife, Dorothy Olsen (a former mistress of Crowley), my sister and myself. Conviviality was the law that night. Everyone enjoyed himself with a good dinner and good wine and good conversation, except my sister who acted as a wet blanket. But on that occasion nothing could dampen my spirits; it was a celebration of my confrontation with destiny.

All this ran through my mind rapidly while I observed him. Very quickly and easily, Crowley helped me to get my luggage together. There was no problem; customs had been cleared at Cherbourg. A taxi got us quickly to his apartment where we had coffee. While we talked, he brewed it himself in a small Cona glass apparatus--rather like what we would call a Silex coffee maker—heated by a diminutive alcohol lamp. I had never seen one before; I was impressed. Impressed by that as I was by everything else. Some four or five months later, so was an Inspector from the Surete Generale who mistook it for some infernal machine for distilling drugs. But coffee was all it brewed, coffee that was strong and black. We talked—and talked some more.

I was never aware, then or at any time during the next few years, of what other people had called his hypnotic eyes. They were warm eyes, small but friendly and alive—rather inclined to fix themselves in one position and bore in—but hardly hypnotic in any sense of the word. Those who complained that his eyes were hypnotic must have possessed a fine ability to project their own particular psychological problems on to him. One felt confronted by authority—that was something else again. It was a quality natural to his personality, shining through even when he was most relaxed and at ease.

I had the feeling that I was completely exposed. I am sure this was a feeling of my own that I projected on him. But I had no psychoanalytic background then; I had not even turned twenty-one. At that age, one could afford to be naive; projection would be natural. I felt that our conversation revealed me altogether and that I had delivered myself into his hands, lock, stock and barrel. He never took advantage of that trust or abused it—not until years later when our relationship fell apart.

It was around the time that the Mandrake Press folded up in London, thus terminating a publishing programme that had first showed every sign of being a great success. We merely drifted apart following this debacle in 1931. He was in Europe somewhere with his lady love, and I had settled down in London, temporarily serving as secretary for Thomas Burke, the novelist and short-story writer, for whom I have the warmest feelings, the most profound respect and gratitude.

At the time we parted I was studying mysticism in all its phases, branches and variations. Some of the Catholic mystics, especially St. Francis of Assisi, intrigued me enormously. I was saturating myself in the vast literature that had grown up about St. Francis. One of my dearest friends, Clare Cameron, who has written some lovely delicate things, including *Green Fields of England,* a poetic topography of the English countryside to which she first introduced me, complimented me by thinking that St. Francis and I had much in common. In my youthful vanity, 1 was very flattered. And since she called me Francis, this was the name that stuck and that later I came to adopt.

Four or five years later, after my experience with the Golden Dawn and a lengthy Freudian analysis, for both of which I can say in all humility and simplicity--thank God!--I returned home to the United States. It was with a sigh of relief as I sailed into New York harbor, after the wild storms and turmoils of the preceding hectic years, years of initiation, harassment and, I hope, growth. It was good to leave the areas where conflict had become accentuated.

I had dropped Crowley a warm note, enclosing a copy I think of one of my more recent books. Two of the earlier ones had been dedicated to him. Sometime later, an answer came from him. He both joked and reprimanded me, together with some anti-Semitic slur, about the adoption of the name Francis and he facetiously called me "Frank." I am afraid I did not take it lightly. It would have been wiser to have accepted his chiding--and to have let the whole matter fall back into oblivion where it belonged. His slurs struck a raw nerve. Among my weakest character traits at that time was a sensitivity to criticism, valid or invalid. It still abides with me, though the passing years have attenuated it considerably. But in those days I was inclined to be more hot-headed than I am now, so that I retorted as nastily as I thought he had chided me. I did not keep a copy of the letter I wrote him, but my memory has kept vividly alive the stupid opening of that bitter rejoinder of mine.

I should remind the reader that his baptismal name was Edward Alexander Crowley. In his late teens or early twenties, after reading Shelley whom he came to love, he rejected his Christian names for all but legal purposes, adopting for regular daily usage the name Aleister. Knowing this, I addressed him with a ridiculous diminutive of his name, intending to sting him deeply. Apparently I did!

"Darling Alice,
       You really are a contemptible bitch! . . . . " etc.

He never forgave me for this insult. There was no direct letter in response. He was altogether through with me. But some weeks later, several of my friends and correspondents, including many people whom I had not met but who knew of me through my books, received an anonymous letter. My vilest character traits and attributes, as perceived by Crowley, were there delineated at scurrilous length. Crowley had struck again! In his own inimitable way—in the projection of his own character traits.

This anonymous letter circulated far and wide during that Fall of 1937. It has recently (1969) turned up again bearing the postmark of Barstow, California, mailed by some unknown personal enemy. In order to deprive this and other character assassins of any further ammunition, as well as to exorcise the ghost that they may feel they can evoke at any moment, I have decided to publish Crowley's scurrilous letter in its entirety. It may then be understood why I remained silent for so many years, divorced wholly from the occult movement, before coming to Crowley's rescue with a rational biography—which in all fairness he deserves. It would not be decent to let this opportunity slip by, and let the world continue in its belief that Symonds' horrible account is veridical.

   Israel Regudy was born in the neighborhood of Mile End Road, in one of the vilest slums in London.

Of this fact he was morbidly conscious, and his racial and social shame embittered his life from the start.

"Regardie" is the blunder of a recruiting sergeant in Washington on the occasion of his brother enlisting in the United States Army. Regudy adopted this error as sounding less Jewish. "Francis" which he has now taken appears to be a pure invention.

About the year 1924 he began to study the work of, and corresponded with, Mr. Aleister Crowley. He put up so plausible an appeal that the latter gentleman paid his passage from America and accepted him as a regular student of Magic.

Apart from his inferiority complex, he was found to be suffering from severe chronic constipation, and measures were taken to cure him of this and also his ingrained habit of onanism.

The cure in the latter case was successful, but Regudy abused his freedom by going under some railway arches and acquiring an intractable gonorrhoea.

Mr. Crowley supplied him with shelter, food and clothing for over two years, and was ultimately able to get him a good job as Book-keeper and Secretary to a firm of publishers.

Regudy betrayed, robbed and insulted his benefactor.

For some years his life was somewhat obscure, but he seems to have been wandering for the most part around the West of England as a vagrant, existing on the charity, according to some accounts, of various elderly women; according to others, of some obscure religious orders.

His studies in the Qabalah and Magic enabled him to ingratiate himself with Dion Fortune, who picked him out of his misery and helped him in every possible way.

He betrayed, robbed and insulted his benefactress.

Being now a little more on his feet, he was able to move about more freely, and soon managed to scrape acquaintance with a middle-aged lady occupied in varieties of "healing" by massage and other devices. He switched over to this form of human activity, and made considerable sums of money. He was thus able to betray, rob and insult his benefactress, go over to

America, and start a quackery of his own.

It took me a long time to forgive him for this disgusting bit of self-projection. It is only within the last few years, that my admiration for him as a great mystic has triumphed over my resentment and bitterness, enabling me to put aside my contempt for the nasty, petty, vicious louse that occasionally he was on the level of practical human relations. It is this and only this change of mind that has enabled me finally to begin this book.

But this anecdote, and the reproduction of this scurrilous letter sanctified by his anonymity, demonstrates at least a couple of things. Whenever he wished to attack anybody, he portrayed them in terms of his own character traits. However badly Symonds has mauled original source-material, this one fact is fairly well portrayed. Since he had been maligned often enough in his life-time, Crowley was fairly familiar with the technique of character-assassination and vilification.

Secondly, it is clear that he was not a man to be trifled with. Years of living by his wits as an adventurer had whittled off any useless psychological tissue--and he could play dirty. Perhaps there might be some validity to a few of the alleged escapades which place him in a rather dishonorable stance.

On a previous page, I spoke of a visit from an inspector of the Surete Generale. There is quite a story to this, and I believe I am the only person alive to-day who can really elucidate what happened.

In order to join Crowley in Paris, it was necessary for me to obtain both a passport from the U. S. State Department and a visa from the French Consul in Washington, D. C. where I was living at the time. I was still not quite twenty-one years of age, and so legally a minor. My father was supposed to have given his written consent for both of these diplomatic instruments of travel. Meanwhile I had told my parents nothing of Crowley, and not much more about my consuming interest in mysticism. Since I had been attending Art School, I simply told them that I had been invited to study painting with an English artist in Paris. With this explanation, they agreed to my departure, giving me the necessary document for the passport office.

However, I found it a nuisance to explain every step to be taken. When it came time to obtain the French visa, I typed a letter as though from my father and appended his signature. In other words—I compounded a felony; in addition to lying I forged his signature.

I thought nothing of it at the time. I was jesuitical in intellectual attitude; the end justified the means. Now I had both the passport and the visa—and everything was in order for the trip abroad to come face to face with Destiny.

While all of this was happening, one of my several sisters—who for this narrative will be signified by Nosey Parker, since this does describe some of her characteristics—had glanced through my set of the *Equinox*. There she had read, without the slightest degree of comprehension, Crowley's brilliant essay *Energized Enthusiasm*. It dealt with the invocation of Dionysius, Aphrodite and Apollo, which he translated colloquially as the worship of wine, women and song, and it did deal with sex among other things. To her puritanical mind this was rather horrible.

She had a history of what I would now consider a severe anxiety hysteria. She was emotionally and physically ill a great deal of the time, and her neurosis had gradually resulted in her discovery of the world of diet, nutrition and health. Had she given her psychic health as much attention as she did to calories, proteins and vitamins, we would all have been better off. Her prudery also found moral support in the lunatic fringes of the occult where sex was anathema. She made everyone's life her personal business, was a holy terror in her relations with the rest of the family.

Shocked beyond belief upon discovering that Crowley had written about sex in his own inimitable way, she became infected with what Wilhelm Reich calls the Emotional Plague. In a jocular vein, Crowley had written elsewhere that there would be no clear thinking on the subject of sex, continence and erotology until it was clearly understood "as being solely a branch of athletics." He wrote rather pragmatically "let the student decide for himself what form of life, what moral code, will least tend to excite his mind . . . . It is a purely practical code, of no value in itself." But these rational approaches had no meaning for her.

Her prurience being further excited by a recent Sunday Hearst smear of Crowley—she had only one recourse. High-handedly, without consulting me or anyone else, she marched off to the French Consul to beg him to deny me a visa to visit France. A visa had been granted she was told, and nothing further could be done at this end. She must have given the French consul a full run-down of the Crowley story as perceived through the dark scotoma of her hysteria, and it must have been a lurid story indeed. The French consul promised to refer the matter back to Paris for investigation.

Thus it was that some three or four months after I had arrived in Paris, the inspector from the Surete Generale came to see what kind of wicked monster this man Crowley was. The sinister coffee-brewing gadget evidently spurred him on to make a more complete investigation. In this process, he excavated a crop of vicious journalism of the Horatio Bottomley-cum-William Randolph Hearst variety, and the fact that five years earlier Mussolini had expelled Crowley from Italy on grounds of purely political expediency. He also discovered that Crowley had written in America about 1917 what appeared to be pro-German propaganda. This is a fascinating story in itself and has been described very well by P. R. Stephensen in his *Legend of Aleister Crowley*.[2] It was further found that Crowley was, at least nominally, the

British head of the Ordo Templi Orientis—a German Rosicrucian society. Possibly the Surete Generale did not recognize the difference between an occult and a political organization, and so it came to the idiotic conclusion that Crowley was a paid German spy.

In the meantime, two other minor events need reporting. Just prior to my arrival, Crowley had notified the police that Miroslava, a former mistress, had stolen some money from him. Some weeks after my arrival in Paris, I was the bearer of a letter from Crowley to the police headquarters in the 16th arrondisement announcing that it was all an error, that he had found the money and that the whole matter should now be dismissed—and would they issue a *carte d'identite* for his secretary, the bearer of this note. My limited high school French was altogether inadequate for carrying on a conversation with a most disinterested police official—so the matter of my registration lapsed and came to nothing.

When the Surete Generale matter finally came to a head six months after my leaving the United States, brought to a boiling climax by complaints from a public relations man whom Crowley had dismissed, all hell broke loose. *Refus de Sejours* were handed out in March to Crowley for being a German spy and a dope addict, to his current mistress Marie de Miramar who later became his wife, and to me both for being associated with him and for not possessing a valid *carte d'identite*. As a matter of practical politics, Crowley became ill forthwith so that he was enabled to stay on in Paris to find out what really was involved, while de Miramar and I were promptly expelled. We were not permitted to land in England (despite the fact that I had been born in London). We were considered, as colleagues of Crowley, "undesirable aliens," and were put back aboard the Channel steamer. Eventually we wound up in Brussels to wait for Crowley's arrival.

This expulsion was for me guilt by association. In those days, so massive was my sense of culpability, that I felt as profoundly ashamed of the *refus de sejour* as if I had actually been guilty of the most heinous crimes. My emotional anguish at that time was considerable. I am glad at last to be able to write about it. It gives the silly matter a chance to be aired—altogether apart from the fact that it puts on record the true facts relative to Crowley's expulsion from Paris.

Nosey Parker's fears and guilts had set into operation a complex chain of events which she could not have foreseen. Her intentions may have been good; but so were those of the Inquisitors who condemned men to burn at the stake in order to save their immortal souls. This is characteristic of the carriers of the Emotional Plague. My own life was complicated unnecessarily for years by this concatenation of events—and so was that of everybody else who was connected with Crowley at that particular time.

During the period that I stayed with him and served as his secretary, there was a nightly session after dinner—almost a routine or ritual—of chess-playing. After a while I came to loathe the game. It took me many years before I was able to return to it again for pleasure. Crowley not only enjoyed the game, he was a competent player. In addition, it was one of his contentions, which at that time was quite unintelligible to me, that by playing chess with someone, he was able to obtain a fairly clear picture of how he operated psychologically. Some people play a cautious game, others are more reckless in their expenditure of pieces. Some start out with a flair, and wind up after a dozen moves not knowing what they want to do or where they want to go or how to do it. Still others reach their best performance only towards the end of the game, after they are through probing their opponent's defenses and aggressive tactics. These attitudes are basic to the individual's general functioning, and operate in most areas of his life.

He would often take one of the books written by the great chess masters, and patiently play out on the board before him the game described in the text. He would analyze the game played, attempting to see if there were justification for the conclusions reached by the writer, and how, were he playing the game, he might be able to improve upon it. Very often he would give me a piece or two to make the game more interesting; he would play minus a Knight or Bishop, sometimes even without a Queen. Most of the time he won, and on those rare occasions when I did beat him, it was only because, I am quite sure, he let me win.

On the occasions when Gerald Yorke would come over from England, or down from London after we moved to Knockholt in Kent, we would set up two boards. Crowley would play both of us simultaneously, going from one board to another, and would beat us both.

The feat, however, at which I marvelled then, and still do, was his blindfold chess. He would make himself comfortable in a big chair, where he would smoke very expensive cigars when he had them, or a big pipe filled with perique or latakia tobacco. This effectively put up a choking smoke screen. Through this he could be dimly perceived warming a large *balon* of brandy in his hands, rolling it, smelling its bouquet, and sipping it gently with all ceremonial art.

Yorke and I would be well away from him, or behind him, with a board in front of each of us. Yorke would call out "Pawn to King 4" and Crowley, having built up an imaginary chessboard in his mind, would respond with the appropriate move. When it was my turn to open and move, I would call out "Pawn to Queen 4" or whatever opening I had decided upon. Sometimes I would make it different from Yorke's only in the hope that Crowley might thus become confused. But no! He was able to keep the imaginary picture of both boards quite distinct. More often than not he was able to beat us both.

In those early days in Paris, an occasional gust of anxiety would well up within me. Long before I had left the United

States, I had read the trashy Hearst newspaper "exposés" of
Crowley. And while I had refused steadfastly to believe this
wretched yellow journalism, the seeds of doubt had been well
planted. Therefore, in trepidation, I half-expected some kind
of homosexual advance from him. In point of fact, nothing
of this kind ever occurred.

One week-end in the winter of 1928-29, Yorke took the
boat-train over from London for a conference with Crowley.
Yorke and I never had a great deal in common. There were
only occasional distant-friendly chats. Our only bond of
union was our common interest in Crowley, otherwise we
would never have met.   But I do recall, on one occasion
when he let his hair down or I did, and we mutually
confessed our latent apprehensions about the possibility of
"the old boy," as we familiarly called him, trying some
homosexual monkey-tricks with either one. We were both
relieved to find out that we shared this anxiety. Sharing
anxiety, like guilt, thins it out, making its burden more
tolerable. And we were even more relieved that nothing really
had transpired.

I came to have a great deal of respect for Crowley because
of his liberal sexual attitudes. He has never been, within the
realm of my personal experience, the "wild man" that one of
his recent biographers depicts with some enthusiasm.

John Symonds, the author of *The Great Beast*, implied
that Crowley seduced every young man who made contact
with him. This may sometimes have been true. But there
were innumerable exceptions. I rather fancy that where Allan
Bennett was concerned, there were never any homosexual
relations, although Allan lived with him in London for well
over a year. Crowley always had a galaxy of girls in and out
of the apartment. Apparently Allan was celibate either by an
act of will or as a consequence of his inhibitions, I know not
which. I feel rather certain no homosexuality transpired
between them.

That Crowley did have homosexual components is indisputable. His book *The Bagh-i-Muattar*, which I have not seen in over thirty years or so, is devoted to homosexuality. The subject intrudes itself into even his loftiest type of devotional, mystical writing. There are poems scattered throughout a dozen books, which are frank confessionals of sexual experiences with men and boys.

Whatever may be involved here, is counter-balanced by his heterosexuality. This bisexuality is characterized by infidelity and promiscuity. It seemed as if he were incapable of maintaining a single sexual attachment for any length of time without complicating it with another. He made no secret of this. In this respect, he was true to the command given him in one of his prophetic books, "Veil not your vices in virtuous words."

I am also reminded of a piece of counsel Crowley gave me in Paris. We were discussing the obvious fact of my timidity. It was his considered opinion that I should for the time being relinquish all my interests in mysticism, to walk and work my way around the world to familiarize myself with every conceivable vice. This same idea was once given him, for he expressed it in a prose-poem he wrote around 1907, "Go thou unto the outermost places and subdue all things. Subdue thy fear and thy disgust. Then—yield!"

I did not do this. Now, many years later, and being able to look back more or less objectively on this incident, I still am glad I did not accept this advice. However, I am now able to perceive what he had in mind. I think his insights were superb, but his techniques for dealing with neurotic problems were woefully inadequate. Undoubtedly he had a recognition of what today I would call the character armor, the sum total of all the defense-mechanisms which imprison the psyche in a closed cognitive system or shell. The motive here would be to get rid of the inhibiting armor. Practical familiarity with vices would, in my estimation, only have heightened the already existent sense of guilt, and so in the end would have thwarted every possibility of inner freedom. A better recommendation would have been psychotherapy of one kind or another. But he knew little psychotherapy then, and I knew less. Several years had to elapse before I was fortunate enough to be guided into psychotherapy.

And yet one cannot dismiss without due reflection anything that this man has said. For example, in one of his later books, he has elaborated considerably the essential viewpoint of the counsel he once gave me. He wrote:

> The Magician should devise for himself a definite technique for destroying "evil." The essence of such a practice will consist in training the mind and the body to confront things which cause fear, pain, disgust, shame and the like. He must learn to endure them, then to become indifferent to them, then to analyze them until they give pleasure and instruction, and finally to appreciate them for their own sake, as aspects of Truth. When this has been done, he should abandon them if they are really harmful in relation to health or comfort. Also, our selection of "evils" is limited to those that cannot damage us irreparably. E.G., one ought to practice smelling assafoetida until one likes it; but not arsine or hydrocyanic acid. Again, one might have a liaison with an ugly old woman until one beheld and loved the star which she is; it would be too dangerous to overcome the distaste for dishonesty by forcing oneself to pick pockets. Acts which are essentially dishonourable must not be done; they should be justified only by calm contemplation of their correctness in abstract cases.
>
> Love is a virtue, it grows stronger and purer and less selfish by applying it to what it loathes; but theft is a vice involving the slave-idea that one's neighbor is superior to oneself. It is admirable only for its power to develop certain moral and mental qualities in primitive types, to prevent the atrophy of such faculties as our own vigilance, and for the interest which it adds to the "tragedy, Man."[3]

It is clear then that Aleister Crowley was a strange man. He embodied in himself quite overtly and unashamedly all those drives and tendencies that are concealed and latent in most of us. Credit has to be accorded him for psychological experimentation—not with laboratory animals, but with himself as the subject. As a result of this, he discovered that our current socially acceptable attitude towards man is a mass of ill-digested dogmas and irrational beliefs that have been foisted on us unthinkingly down through the centuries. Though a timid shy person in his boyhood and earlier years, he transformed himself in a variety of ways through the application of his own individual methods, even though some of these may not be to our liking. But, like many teachers and wise men long before him, he found that perhaps the only keyword that is literally true of man is *transformation*—if he will.

Capable of the highest devotion and idealism, he also indulged in the most grotesque debauchery. Spitefulness and pettiness seemed at times second nature. While his courage and fearlessness were second to none, I still recall on one occasion when I awakened him from an after-lunch nap to answer the telephone. Startled, he jumped off the couch with a look of the most abject terror on his face.

He was possessed of a wonderful sense of humor. At times it was gross and Rabelaisian; at others very warm and gentle. His humor and leg-pulling stemmed from an exuberance that would have rivalled a five-year-old's. He loved playing pranks. But it always startled him, so vast was his naivete, when people did not always realize that they were pranks.

I love the story told by P. R. Stephenson in *The Legend of Aleister Crowley*. It concerns Epstein's monument to Oscar Wilde which was to be placed on exhibition in the Pere la Chaise cemetery in Paris. It was, until the police discovered that Epstein had sculpted genitals on the statue in a very prominent manner. Crowley always condemned the English for their bourgeois attitudes and blue-stocking morality, but he had not counted on the French. The police refused to permit the monument to be unveiled. There was a decided furor. Ultimately a compromise was effected. A metal butterfly had to be affixed to the offending part, thus rendering Oscar Wilde pure and noble.

Secretly, at dead of night, Crowley unveiled the statue by a stratagem "in the interests of art." He smuggled the butterfly out of Paris and the country. When he got back to London, he marched triumphantly into the Cafe Royal with the metal butterfly serving as a cod-piece over evening dress. We are told there was a great sensation.

Crowley was well-known in this haunt of the bohemians of that time. Periodically he would disappear here. Then, after a time, he would dramatically re-appear, the picture of vigorous health and radiance, energy literally pouring from him—marked contrast to the soft, pale flabbiness of the usual habitues of this Cafe.

Then there is the delightful story given by Nicholas Heron (Prediction Annual, 1964):

"Please tell me," an earnest and well-meaning lady once asked Aleister Crowley, "what school do you think would be best for my daughter?"

Crowley had endured her conversation with commendable patience for some while, and could hardly have been used to questions of this kind. However, he rose nobly to the occasion.

"Madame," he replied gravely, "send her to Radclyffe Hall."

Miss Radclyffe Hall, Heron hastens to add, was the author of a book called *The Well of Loneliness*, the Sapphic theme of which made it a literary sensation of the time.

I learned soon after arriving in Paris, that Crowley had a mistress. I half-way expected this, but only half-way; for in my hypocritical state of pseudo-innocence of those far-off days, I did not let myself dwell on such awful moral possibilities. So I accepted her, whom Symonds calls Miroslava. She was short, pudgy, and, from my vantage point of today, the most unlikely person to be Crowley's mistress. But such were the facts!

One Saturday night, within the first weeks of my stay there, she invited me to go to a movie with her. I agreed with some alacrity. I desperately needed a change—a change to an old familiar pattern, a haven of refuge, a kind of security from all the new, disconcerting events that were transpiring in the Crowley menage.

What the movie was I do not recall now. It was just prior to the advent of the talkies. But I know I did enjoy it, and she was very friendly and almost convivial. After the movie, we went to a nearby cafe for some coffee, or perhaps a drink. There to my sincere astonishment, she informed me that she was not going to return to Crowley. It never dawned on me to ask her why, or to discuss the matter with her at all. At this moment of writing, I would very much like to have known her attitude and her motives for leaving him. But in a very matter-of-fact prosaic way, I promised I would convey her message to Crowley.

On my way back to my hotel, I had the cab stop at the apartment on Avenue de Suffren, where I found him still up, reading, as usual, detective stories. When I informed him what had happened, his eyebrows raised a little—the one on the right more perhaps than the one on the left—and then he murmured:

"The Lord hath given. The Lord hath taken away. Blessed be the name of the Lord."

And that was the end of that!

By an indirect association route, this reference to detective stories reminds me of an altogether different kind of experience which revealed yet another side of Crowley. By his own admission, he had a broad streak of real spitefulness.

There was a curious chap named Aloysius Comet who used to come down from London to visit with Crowley, when we were living in Kent. Crowley found him interesting for a while. Comet could play chess moderately well, which Crowley appreciated tremendously at the time, for he was undergoing one of his recurrent attacks of phlebitis which kept him confined to the house. Comet was also a fairly good raconteur, and loved to talk about a prominent symptom of his masochistic neurosis, flagellation. Crowley thought him altogether amusing, though rather pathetic.

One day, while playing chess with Crowley, Comet admitted having just contracted a common venereal disease. He blushed while talking about it, thus confessing to a profound sense of guilt. It was like feeling dirty and unbathed most of the time, as he put it. At first, he took a gentle ribbing from Crowley who said: "Don't worry about it. It's no worse than a cold in the head!"

At this time Crowley was an inveterate reader and connoisseur of detective stories. He devoured them voraciously, partly because much of the time he was bored. Another reason was that he had once essayed a series of detective stories himself, patterned after an idealization of himself—a sleuth named Simon Iff.

In one of the stories he had just finished reading, there was a character named Badcock—a perfectly good and legitimate English name.

Whenever Comet turned up in Knockholt—which was quite often, for he was a disciple of sorts and knelt devotedly at the feet of the Master—he was called Badcock. It was always "Badcock, this!" and "Badcock, that!" He was given this nickname both when alone or whenever there were other people visiting Crowley. The master thought it was enormously funny. He delighted in embarrassing and humiliating Comet in front of friends, first by using the fictional name, and then by referring facetiously to the malady which Comet had contracted.

To expose Comet was extraordinarily cruel. The poor fellow flushed and perspired freely, no doubt wishing for the ground beneath him to open up and swallow him whole. I once glanced at him sympathetically, but he could only lower his eyes. Eventually, in spite of his masochism, he could no longer stand this spitefulness and lack of consideration and disappeared. Crowley had thought it all a great joke!

In contrast, I remember vividly one incident where he showed a considerable degree of empathy, of concern, of not wishing to hurt tender feelings. When I joined him in Paris, I was timid and callow and naive. So far as my personal appearance was concerned, there could be no criticisms, save one minor though very obvious detail, which Crowley did not miss.

One day, while he was dictating some letters to me, he asked me to take one letter but to omit the opening line "Dear so and so." I should add that while in the United States I had procured a Stenotype, a shorthand machine, and a text-book dealing with the system, and had taught myself how to use it. Within a few months I had acquired a workable speed of well over a hundred words per minute.

I was seated. with the Stenotype on the table in front of me, looking at times at Crowley, or permitting my eyes and my attention to wander around the room while writing more or less automatically. He began to dictate to the unnamed correspondent, but towards the end of the letter, in the last paragraph, he added quite nonchalantly, something to the effect that you might consider examining your fingernails more closely. Other people do, and judge you accordingly. An occasional manicure might prove more than useful, etc., etc.

In my stupidity and absent-mindedness, I had typed all of this down, never once realizing that he was doing this for my sake, and that he had not wished to hurt my feelings by calling attention to the fact that my fingernails were not well cared for, and that the general appearance of my hands could be improved. It did not occur to me until some years later that this had been a device he had used to help me.

On the basis of the John Symonds biography and what he had read years ago in the yellow press, a friend of mine recently suggested that Crowley was altogether pathological, a schizophrene. Admittedly, there can really be no doubt of the presence of some kind of pathology. But after due consideration as to what name we should give it, I hardly know. Diagnosis can be too slick, too easy.

I do not believe that a schizophrene is capable of the tremendous self-discipline and mental training that Crowley embarked upon. A little later I wish to describe and define some of this training that Crowley employed. Long hours devoted to meditative exercises, the hard grind of pranayama, intellectual study, and other forms of the strictest self-training which are evidenced in so many of the things that he wrote—are certainly not the way of the schizophrene. Nor is mountain-climbing, or big-game hunting, or exploring! However misguided Crowley may have been at times, I doubt if his self-probing had left untouched many levels of his unconscious psychic functioning.

Masochism is plainly indicated in the following piece of rhetoric quoted by Symonds from one of Crowley's very early diaries:

> I am to Thee the harlot, crowned with poison and gold, my garment many-coloured, soiled with shame and smeared with blood, who for no price but of wantonness have prostituted myself to all that lusted after me, nay who have plucked unwilling sleeves, and with seduction, bribe and threat multiplied my stuprations. I have made my flesh rotten, my blood venomous, my nerves hell-tortured, my brain hag-ridden. I have infected the round world with corruption.

But just as one swallow does not make a summer, neither does this by itself make Crowley into a masochist. For one thing, his capacity for sheer pleasure, adventure and excitement was too vast.

Another viewpoint is possible about this "ecstasy of abasement" as Crowley referred to it in another place. Things are not always what they seem. What may superficially seem to us like masochism, has for the mystic another value entirely different. We would be ill-advised to ignore altogether this testimony. For as the mystic is more and more subjected to the transforming nature of the Light, he is often plunged into an acute awareness of the inadequacy and utter vileness of the lower or "natural" self. As Evelyn Underhill expressed it, the greatest of the contemplative saints were increasingly aware of their own abasement as they approached the unitive state. The true lover of the divine is alternately abased by his supreme unworthiness and by his good fortune. There are moments when, just as he is sure that the banner over him is Love, so is he equally sure that there yet remains an ineradicable selfhood staining the radiance of eternity.

Therefore in contrast to the masochistic self-abasement in a writing he called *The Book of The Heart Girt with a Serpent,* Crowley wrote immediately following it:

> But I have burnt within thee as a pure flame without oil. In the midnight I was brighter than the moon; in the daytime I exceeded utterly the sun; in the byways of thy being I flamed, and dispelled the illusion.

The compulsive neurotic may be capable of sticking at any task for a long period of time, at small details and dull routines for years on end. But in all of this mechanical work there is no trace of creativity. His creative urges would have been lost and submerged in the neurotic need for compulsive thinking and acting. Spontaneous behavior is altogether beyond him. A mystical experience of any kind would destroy him utterly, because it would render his defensive compulsiveness quite meaningless. And this is a far cry from Aleister Crowley.

There always remains the psychiatric waste-paper-basket item - the constitutional psychopath. Crowley's apparent lack of conscience and lack of adaptability to the real world around him might warrant such a diagnostic label—at first sight only, however. An examination of his history discloses a very sensitive youth, conscience-ridden indeed, who slaved and laboured to discipline himself to get rid of every vestige of this conscience which he came altogether to despise as a relic of the Christian faith which he had rejected. So much of his behavior is understandable simply in terms of revolt. And what first appears to be a rigid lack of adaptability is soon perceived to be exactly the opposite. A man, infinitely flexible, but resolute—determined to resist to the bitter end and to fight to the death what he considered to be the foul symptoms of a dying and decadent culture.

There is no single label that can apply to this multi-faceted personality. He was entirely too creative, vital, spontaneous. A different set of standards has to apply if we are to subsume him under the restrictions of a petty nosological term.

What kind of man did he consider himself to be? In a late book dealing with the Tarot cards, Crowley selected one card, the Prince of Wands, as an avenue for self-description. It is interesting to compare this vision of himself with the biographical items that have already been detailed.

The moral qualities appropriate to this figure are swiftness and strength. But he is sometimes inclined to act on impulse; sometimes easily led by external influences; sometimes, especially in trifles, a prey to indecision. He is often violent, especially in the expression of an opinion, but he does not necessarily

hold the opinion about which he is so emphatic. He
states a vigorous proposition for the sake of making it.
He is in fact very slow to make up his mind thoroughly
on any subject, but always sees both sides of every
question. He is essentially just, but always feels that
justice is not to be attained in the intellectual world. His
character is intensely noble and generous. He may be an
extravagant boaster, while slyly laughing both at the
object of his boast and at himself for making it. He is
romantic, especially in matters of history and tradition,
to the point of folly, and may engineer "stunts" or play
elaborate practical jokes. He might select some
inoffensive nobody, and pursue him for years with every
weapon of ridicule, as Swift tormented the unhappy
Partridge, all without the least animus, ready to give the
shirt off his back, should his victim be in need. His sense
of humour is omnivorous, and may make him a
mysterious figure, dreaded without reason by people
who actually know nothing about him but his name—as
a symbol of Terror. This is due to the influence of the
last decan of Cancer upon this card.

One of his greatest faults is pride; meanness and
pettiness of any kind he holds in infinite scorn. His
courage is fanatically strong, and his endurance
indefatigable. He is always fighting against odds, and
always wins in the long—the very long—run. This is
principally due to his enormous capacity for work,
which he exercises for its own sake, "without lust of
result"; perhaps his haughty contempt for the world at
large—which however co-exists with profound and
ecstatic respect for "every man and every woman" as "a
star"—is responsible for this.[4]

Even when a young man, Crowley's life was characterized
by a sense of an unfulfilled duty, a mission yet to be
performed. He was a most ambitious young man. Whether it
was a call to spiritual vocation as it were, or a paranoid
manifestation of incipient ego disease, should be
discussed—but not here. There are many poems of his,
written at early dates—long before the dictation of *The Book*

of the Law and its date of April 1904—which clearly indicate
this ambition. For example:

I SWEAR

I swear by all the stars that stream
Through all the lofty leaves of night:
I swear by the tremendous towers
That cross Granada's vale of flowers:
I swear by their impending gleam,
The Sierra's snowy swords of light!

By all the cruel and cold despair
That Christ hath brought upon the land
By Mary and the false blind beastly
Lies of the prudish and the priestly:
By God and death and hate I swear
That man shall rise, shall understand.

I swear by this my lucid Eye,
By all the freedom I have won,
That men shall learn to love and doubt,
Put faith and slavery to the rout,
And eagle-pinioned even as I
Soar to the splendour of the sun![5]

Some biographers have wondered just what it was that
burned within Crowley, forcing him to become a
teacher—altogether independently of the injunctions of *The
Book of the Law*[6] in which he was commanded to teach.

The term Crowleyanity was an invention of the late
General J. F. C. Fuller, one of the most powerful and
important of all Crowley's disciples. In the opening years of
the twentieth century, Crowley used a fictitious business
name—the Society for the Propagation of Religious Truth—to
publish his *Collected Works* and other of his writings. He
offered a prize of £150 for the best essay on his works, to be
used by the Society to advertise its publications. Of all the

essays submitted, that of Fuller's struck Crowley most favorably. They became fast friends for many long years.

Fuller's essay was published under the title of *The Star in the West*. It was an ambitious, flamboyant, and extravagant panegyric dedicated to Crowley's extant writings. Therein he coined the phrase Crowleyanity. It never really "took," despite the fact that an occasional reviewer or critic would pick it up for mention once every so often.

But the teaching compulsion existed altogether apart from and previous to Fuller's coined phrase. It was part of his psychic structure. As I perceive the facts, Crowley's father, first a Quaker, became an itinerant Plymouth Brethren advocate and "preacher." He would travel here and there, challenging the religious beliefs of whomsoever he encountered. In effect, he tried to undermine their current religious attitudes in order to turn attention to God, as interpreted by him and the Plymouth Brethren. Crowley felt that his father was magnificently eloquent, "speaking as he did from the heart. But, being a gentleman, he could not be a real revivalist, which means manipulating the hysteria of mob psychology."

Crowley himself speaks of his attachment to and admiration for his father. There is enough available data to suggest that an identification ensued.

It sufficed to motivate Crowley unconsciously to imitate his father and to become a religious teacher. This is not the entire story by any manner of means, but it certainly is one of the very powerful determinants in this man's history.

Because the Plymouth Brethren believed the Bible to be literally inspired by God, no change of a letter, a word, or any part of it would be tolerated. They never accepted the Revised Version of the Bible. All the original wordings had a divine sanction and meaning. Even this dogmatic attitude became incorporated into Crowley's subsequent views. For in *The Book of the Law*, which is the dominant creation in Crowley's whole life, it was written "Change not so much as the style of a letter." There are many other parallels.

Though he identified himself with his father and thus acquired the sense of a mission, and though he altogether rejected Christianity, the basic attitudes operated throughout whatever occult-religious philosophy he came to adopt or gradually to develop. It would be interesting to trace out, in the various strata of his voluminous writings, some of the basic views of the Plymouth Brethren whom he detested so completely. I am quite sure that such an investigation would be both illuminating and rewarding.

So far as his need to teach was concerned, it is clear on the basis of ample evidence that it antedated both *The Book of the Law* and *The Star in the West*. It became part and parcel of his structure as a result of his identification with his evangelist father. This one fact played a dominant role in his entire life-span, giving significance to a great deal that otherwise would have very little meaning.

There are two excerpts from his manifold literary productions that ought to be quoted here. More than almost anything else, they are indicative of what he came to stand for and what he came to teach. They express the quintessence of his unique philosophical and religious point of view. Though these two excerpts were not specifically written to stand in direct relation to one another, nevertheless it will be evident that there is a necessary connection between them. The second one entitled "The Rights of Man", based of course on *The Book of the Law*, is the necessary sequel to the first more rhetorical one which I have entitled "Credo." The first is abstracted from a fairly late ritual of his which he called "The Ritual of the Mark of the Beast."

CREDO[7]

I also am a Star in Space, unique and self-existent, an individual essence incorruptible; I also am one Soul; I am identical with All and None. I am in All and all in Me; I am, apart from all and lord of all, and one with all.

I am a God, I very God of very God; I go upon my way to work my will; for I have made matter and motion for my mirror; I have decreed for my delight that Nothingness should figure itself as twain, that I might dream a dance of names and natures, and enjoy the substance of simplicity by watching the wanderings of my shadows. I am not that which is not; I know not that which knows not; I love not that which loves not. For I am love, whereby division dies in delight; I am Knowledge, whereby all parts, plunged in the whole, perish and pass into perfection; and I am that I am, the being wherein Being is lost in Nothing, nor deigns to be but by its Will to unfold its nature, its need to express its perfection in all possibilities, each phase a partial phantasm, and yet inevitable and absolute.

I am Omniscient, for naught exists for me unless I know it. I am Omnipotent, for naught occurs save by Necessity my Soul's expression through my will to be, to do, to suffer the symbols of itself. I am Omnipresent, for naught exists where I am not, who fashioned space as a condition of my consciousness of myself, who am the centre of all, and my circumference the frame of mine own fancy.

I am the All, for all that exists for me is a necessary expression in thought of some tendency of my nature, and all my thoughts are only the letters of my Name.

I am the One, for all that I am is not the absolute All, and all my all is mine and not another's; mine, who conceive of others like myself in essence and truth, yet unlike in expression and illusion.

I am the None, for all that I am is the imperfect image of the perfect; each partial phantom must perish in the clasp of its counterpart; each form fulfilling itself by finding its equated opposite, and satisfying its need to be the Absolute by the attainment of annihilation.

Following is the second excerpt. It is predicated on the metaphysical formula from *The Book of the Law* to express the basic facts of his religious beliefs:

> Do what thou wilt shall be the whole of the Law.
> > There is no god but Man.
> Man has the right to live by his own Law.
> Man has the right to live in the way that he wills to do.
> Man has the right to dress as he wills to do.
> Man has the right to dwell where he wills to dwell.
> Man has the right to move as he will on the face of
> > the Earth.
> Man has the right to eat what he will.
> Man has the right to drink what he will.
> Man has the right to think what he will.
> Man has the right to speak as he will.
> Man has the right to write as he will.
> Man has the right to mould as he will.
> Man has the right to paint as he will.
> Man has the right to carve as he will.
> Man has the right to work as he will.
> Man has the right to love as he will, when, where and
> > with whom he will.
> Man has the right to die when and how he will.
> Man has the right to kill those who would thwart
> > these rights.[8]

NOTES

[1] Recently reprinted, along with Part II, in *Book Four* by the Sangreal Foundation of Dallas, Texas, and distributed by Llewellyn Publications, St. Paul, Minn.

[2] Currently being reprinted and soon to be released by Llewellyn Publications, St. Paul, Minn., with new material by Israel Regardie.

[3] *Magick*, The Master Therion, Paris, 1929, p. 339. Now reprinted as *Magick in Theory and Practice*, Aleister Crowley, Castle Books, New York.

[4] *The Book of Thoth*, The Master Therion, O.T.O., London, 1944, p. 153. Reprinted in 1969 by Shambala Publications, Berkeley, Calif.

[5] *Konx Om Pax*, Aleister Crowley, Boleskine, 1907, p. 104.

[6] *The Book of the Law*, reprinted, in part, in *The Complete Magick Curriculum of the Secret Order G.∴B.∴G.∴*, Louis T. Culling, Llewellyn Publications, St. Paul, 1969.

[7] *Magick*, Paris, 1929, p. 335.

[8] *Liber Oz*, London, 1939.

Regardie,
when he first met Aleister Crowley in October, 1928.

RÉPUBLIQUE FRANÇAISE

PRÉFECTURE DE POLICE

CABINET DU PRÉFET

Sous-Direction Administrative

SERVICE DES ÉTRANGERS

Paris, *4 – 8 MARS 1929* 92

REFUS DE SÉJOUR

Nº *56 587*.

M *Regardie Israel*

né le *17 11 1907*

à *Londres*

de nationalité *américaine*

demeurant *11 avenue de Tiffran*

objet d'un refus de séjour par *Dec Minist du*

5 Février 1929

est mis en demeure de quitter le territoire français à la date du

9 Mars 1929

Aucune autorisation de déplacement ne lui est accordée, hormis

celle de se rendre à *l'Étranger*.

Le présent avis lui tiendra lieu de pièce d'identité jusqu'à son

départ en remplacement des pièces régulières qui lui ont été retirées.

Pour le Préfet de Police :

f du Service des Etrangers,

Le présent avis devra être retiré des mains de l'intéressé à son départ de
France, par les autorités de police de la gare frontière ou du port d'embarquement,
et devra être retourné au Service Central des Cartes d'identité, 7, rue Cambacérès.

Refus de Sejour
Expulsion order from France.

Aleister Crowley
As he appeared just about the time of joining the Golden
Dawn.

CHAPTER TWO

Frater Perdurabo

"Long hast thou dwelt in darkness. Quit the night and seek the Day!"

Almost more than anything else in his entire life, these exhortations shaped the seventy-two year life of Aleister Crowley—poet, mountaineer and occultist. It was in 1898, sponsored by a man who was destined to be one of his closest friends and his most intimate colleague for years, that he was initiated into the Hermetic Order of the Golden Dawn. It was here that he first heard those solemn words, which he took with the utmost seriousness. From that moment, with only a few years characterized by a minimal interest in the occult, he was a dedicated mystic enquiring into the secrets of the Universe. And in that year he chose the magical motto of *Perdurabo* "I will endure unto the end," thus assuming the character of Frater Perdurabo who challenged the unknown with a passion and fervor that was peculiar only to him, as he sought to attain to the very highest.

The essence of this spiritual viewpoint which dominated his entire life is expressed so well in one of his early books:

O my God! Use Thou me again, alway. For ever! For ever! . . . .
O my God! Thou art my little pet tortoise!
Yet Thou sustainest the World-Elephant.
I creep under Thy carapace, like a lover into the bed of his beautiful; I creep in, and sit in Thine heart, as

cubby and cosy as may be.
    Thou shelterest me, that I hear not the trumpeting of
that World-Elephant.[1]

That he was moved as profoundly as he was, is in part
explicable by a curious piece of psychological preparation.
Just previously he had written a famous mystic writer, A. E.
Waite, for counsel. In reply Waite urged him to read a certain
book which spoke of a hidden community of Light, an
invisible and interior Sanctuary whose sainted members
watched over the welfare of mankind. Since he was in a
psychological quandary, a spiritual impasse, he had fervently
aspired to and wished to be admitted to their School. When
therefore he was invited to join the Golden Dawn, he came to
use this Order, consciously or otherwise, as a screen on which
to project his aspirations.

    In this sequence, *The Cloud Upon the Sanctuary* by Karl
von Eckartshausen and the Hermetic Order of the Golden
Dawn have been the two major influences of Crowley's
life-time. Resulting from these two specific contacts, there
were two other secondary influences operating within the
framework of the Golden Dawn that further helped to shape
the plastic, pliable psychological material that made up
Aleister Crowley in his early twenties. And this shaping
stayed with him until the day he died.

    The two men who affected profoundly his growth and
development as an individual were members of the Order.
One was his sponsor in the Golden Dawn, the other was one
of its more brilliant members whom he met after having been
admitted as a member himself.

    The first was George Cecil Jones, a chemist who lived in
Basingstoke, where Crowley used to visit often in order to
tap Jones' brains. Crowley subsequently used Jones as
authority in the formation of his own Order and as
imprimatur on his official publications. He is often referred

to by the initials of his Order mottoes, Frater V.N. and D.D.S. Crowley exalted Jones to sainthood in order to justify his own exalted position. Just what Crowley thought of Jones, and his influence, is best described by Crowley himself in a letter which serves as epilogue and dedication to "Eleusis", the last essay in his *Collected Works:*

November 18, 1906

MY DEAR ION,—I address you by the unfamiliar title in giving you, a man self-damned, God knows how unjustly, as the author of the phrase, "I am not an appreciator of poetry, and I have no Keats," these volumes. For the matter thereof is already in great part yours and as such cannot be given. The rest I offer because it is hardly possible to close definitely, as I do now, a period of many years' work, without reflecting upon that period as a whole. And, when I do so, I find you at the beginning like Ladas or Pheidippides of old, running—ready to run on until you achieve the goal or your heart burst; but you are among a crowd. I join you. Eight years ago this day you, Hermes, led me blindfold to awake a chosen runner of the course. "In all my wanderings in darkness your light shone before me though I knew it not." To-day (one may almost hope, turning into the straight) you and I are alone. Terrible and joyous! We shall find companions at the End, at the banquet, lissome and cool and garlanded; companions with a Silver Star or maybe a Jewelled Eye mobile and uncertain—as if alive—on their foreheads. We shall be bidden to sit, and they will wreathe us with immortal flowers, and give us to drink of the seemly wine of Iacchus—well! but until then, unless my heart deceives me, no third shall appear to join us. Indeed, may two attain? It seems a thing impossible in nature. May it not be that—near as the resounding roar of the viewless spectators sounds to our dust-dimmed ears—there stands some awful opposer in the way, some fear or some seduction? Why do you grip that bar in your left hand? Does not this loincloth irk my limbs?

We should have shaved our heads before the race—the curls are moist and heavy! Why did we cumber ourselves with sandals? Long ere now our feet would have grown hard. Well, if my heart bursts, it bursts; you must give these volumes to the young athletes, that they may learn wherefore I failed—wherefore it was given unto me to run thus far. For, if I have put nothing else therein, most surely that is there.

Aleister Crowley

The other man was Allan Bennett who, years later, became a Buddhist monk with the name of Ananda Metteya (the Pali for Maitreyananda, as he is known in other passages), and played a considerable role in the Buddhist movement in Ceylon and Burma. Right after Crowley's induction into the Order, he came to live with Crowley in a flat in Chancery Lane, there teaching him everything he knew about the Order methods. Together they experimented widely, studying intensely for over eighteen months.

When Crowley first met him, Allan had been living in a cheap tenement on the South bank of the Thames, in Southwark or Lambeth. There were financial difficulties, so he must have been grateful when Crowley invited him to come and stay with him. He was a mathematician and a man of science, a specialist, so Crowley avers, in the phenomenon of electricity. Allan was also a profound student of the Hindu and Buddhist religio-philosophy of which he had as it were an inborn understanding. Crowley describes him as tall with a stoop produced by his sickness, chronic bronchial asthma. "His head, crowned with a shock of wild black hair, was intensely noble; the brows, both wide and lofty, overhung indomitable piercing eyes. The face would have been handsome had it not been for the haggardness and pallor due to his almost continual suffering."

That there were neurotic antecedents is made very plain, both by some of Crowley's descriptions in his *Confessions,*

and by the account given by Cammell, from which I
extrapolate the following:

"This man (Allan Bennett) must indeed have had a
remarkable personality. Born in 1871, and having when a boy
lost his father, he was brought up by his mother in the
Catholic faith. This he had renounced at the age of sixteen on
discovering, according to Crowley, the physiological facts
concerning childbirth."[2]

If he did not know the facts of life at sixteen, we can only
infer clinically that since he was not stupid, his psychological
defense-mechanisms were massive indeed. The kind of
inhibiting armor that he had need to develop would of
necessity produce the most devastating psycho-somatic
symptoms.

There is an early poem dedicated to Allan entitled *The
Hermit's Hymn to Solitude.* It begins with the laudatory
Buddhist proem "Namo Tasso Bhagavato Arahato
Sammasammbuddhasa," "Hail unto Thee! The Blessed One,
The Perfected One, the All-Enlightened One!" And then he
wrote:

> Venerable Lord and Best of Friends: We, seeing the
> cycle in which Maha Brahma is perhaps more a drifting
> buoy than ourselves, knowing that it is called the
> walking in delusion, the puppet show of delusion, the
> writhing of delusion, the fetter of delusion, are aware
> that the way out of the desert is found by going into the
> desert. Will you, in your lonely lamaserai, accept this
> hymn from me, who, in the centre of civilization, am
> perhaps more isolated than you in your craggy fastness
> among the trackless steppes of your Untrodden Land?
>
> Mightiest Self! Supreme in Self-Contentment!
> Sole Spirit gyring in its own ellipse;
> Palpable, formless, infinite presentment
> Of thine own light in thine own soul's eclipse!
> Let thy chaste lips
> Sweep through the empty aethers guarding thee

(As in a fortress girded by the sea
The raging winds and wings of air
Lift the wild waves and bear
Innavigable foam to seaward), bend thee down,
Touch, draw me with thy kiss
Into thine own deep bliss,
Into thy sleep, thy life, thy imperishable crown!
Let that young godhead in thine eyes
Pierce mine, fulfil me of their secrecies,
Thy peace, thy purity, thy soul impenetrably wise.

Close association also played a decisive role in moulding Crowley's intellectual attitudes where Oriental mysticism was concerned. For through Ananda Metteya he became exposed to Hinduism and Buddhism, to yoga and tantra practices of every kind. From then on, the whole of his literary output is filled with the most profound insights into the doctrines of Sorrow, Change and Impermanence, the three characteristics fundamental to the beliefs of the Theravadin Buddhists.

Here again the dialectic approach presaged in the Golden Dawn came to operate. For against this Buddhist set of three characteristics, as they are called, Crowley arrayed as logical antimonies Sat, Chit, and Ananda—Being, Consciousness and Bliss—the three characteristics of Atman, the Self, in Hinduism. Their transcendence is possible only in the expansion of consciousness, the mystical experience, as he himself discovered after having lived through a period in which this conflict produced the most profound mental anguish. It was resolved ultimately in a series of spiritual events which are the high-water marks of his life.

However far-fetched it may seem at first sight, the only other person from the last century I can compare Crowley with is Sri Ramakrishna. Not always gentle and kind perhaps as we are told Ramakrishna was, but like him capable of experimenting with every known form of religious and mystical technique in existence. Expansion of consciousness by any method or means—meditation, magical exaltation, drugs, and sexual exhaustion—were all tried by Crowley separately or in combination.

For example, from a brilliant essay entitled *The Psychology of Hashish*,[3] the following excerpts indicate briefly the kind of thinking of which he was capable in this direction:

> My travels in India had familiarized me with their systems of meditation and with the fact that many of the lesser Yogis employed hashish (whether vainly or no we shall discuss later) to obtain Samadhi, that oneness with the Universe, or with the Nothingness, which is the feeble expression by which alone we can shadow that supreme trance . . . . Meditation therefore annoyed me, as tightening and constricting the soul. I began to ask myself if the "dryness" was an essential part of the process. If by some means I could shake its catafalque of Mind, might not the Infinite Divine Spirit leap unfettered to the Light . . . . Let it not be imagined that I devised these thoughts from pure sloth or weariness. But with the mystical means then at my disposal I required a period of days or of weeks to obtain any Result . . . . If only, therefore, I could reduce the necessary period to a few hours! . . . .
>
> This was my hypothesis . . . . "Let me see whether by first exalting myself mystically and continuing my invocations while the drug dissolved the matrix of the diamond Soul, that diamond might not manifest limpid and sparkling" . . . . and then, of course, I remembered that this ceremonial intoxication constitutes the supreme ritual of all religions . . . .
>
> It may be useful here to distinguish once and for all between false and real mystical phenomena; for in the previous sections we have spoken of both without distinction. In the "astral visions" the consciousness is hardly disturbed; in magical evocations, it is intensely exalted; but it is still bound by its original conditions. The Ego is still opposed to the non-Ego; time is, if

altered in rate, still there; so, too, is Space, the sort of Space we are all conscious of. Again, the phenomena observed follow the usual laws of growth and decay.

But all true mystical phenomena contradict these conditions.

In the first place, the Ego and the non-Ego unite explosively, their product having none of the qualities of either. It is precisely such a phenomenon as the direct combination of Hydrogen and Chlorine. The first thing observed is the flash; in our analogy, the ecstasy or Ananda (bliss) attending the Dhyana. And as this flash does not aid us to analyse the Hydrochloric acid gas, so the Ananda prevents us by startling us from perceiving the true nature of the phenomenon. In higher mystic states, then, we find that the Yogi or Magician has learned how to suppress it . . . . The new consciousness resulting from the combination is, too, always a simple one. Even where it is infinitely complex, as in Atmadarshana or the Vision of the Universal Peacock, its oneness is the truer of these two contradictory truths . . . .

Among the several factors apart from the Golden Dawn that determined the course Crowley was to take, were the tenets of the Plymouth Brethren. This was a religious fundamentalist sect dedicated to Biblical literalism. This was the religion of his boyhood, his parents going to marked extremes to make sure that he was a good Christian. This, coupled with the rationalistic free-thinking of Ingersoll and Bradlaugh, plus other sceptics with whom he became acquainted while at Cambridge, became woven inextricably into the syncretistic fabric of the religio-philosophic system he elaborated from the basic Golden Dawn doctrine.

His total and undying hatred of Christianity is really no mystery. It becomes intelligible to the point where anyone with sensitivity and compassion can have much sympathy with his point of view. All that is required is to gain some familiarity with the historical antecedents of his attitude.

His family, as I have said, belonged to the Plymouth Brethren, a religious group that developed antagonism to the Church of England and so split off, having as the main item of their faith biblical literalism. This was their rock, and this their guide-line through the stormy seas of life. No matter how one might call attention to the seeming contradictions of one section of the Bible as compared with another, these people developed a profound interpretative skill enabling them to justify their behavior at any one moment in terms of a specific chapter and verse.

That their behavior differed from their theory, they were well aware of. But they could justify it scripturally in terms of another specific chapter and verse. Crowley amusedly asks, in an imaginary conversation "Shall I buy railroad stocks?" and the answer would be "No!" The Bible does not mention railroads. "But would it be good business, the opportunity presenting itself, if I picked up some at a good price?" Yes, would be the answer, because "Whatsoever thy hand findeth to do, do it with all thy might." In other words, they had you coming or going.

The home situation presented insoluble conflicts to this boy. His father, previously a Quaker, was a devout member of the Plymouth Brethren. He loved to challenge people, wherever they happened to be, on basic questions of faith and their role in life. His mother was equally fanatic, though less well-informed. She played a dominant role in the development of whatever his neurosis was, and in one form or another entered symbolically into all his mystical writing.

In the Introduction to *The World's Tragedy*,[4] he wrote:

> My whole soul cramped; society denied me; books debarred me, with the rare exception of Scott, Ballantyne, and some of Dickens, with a few even worse!
> To illustrate the domestic principles of literary criticism:

I was forbidden David Copperfield because of "Little Em'ly." Emily being my Mother's name, I might cease to respect her. For the same reason she proscribed the Bab Ballads, recommended by a rash tutor, because "Emily Jane was a nursery maid!" Coleridge's *Ancient Mariner* was condemned because of the water-snakes whom he "blessed" unaware; snakes being cursed in Genesis!

He lived in a spiritual, social and intellectual vacuum. It left its distorting mark on him for ever.

Mother, in moments of exasperation no doubt, would call him "a beast." With his knowledge of the Bible, it did not take too long for him to find out about the Beast of The Book of *Revelation,* the Beast who was Anti-Christ. He ultimately identified himself with that Beast, without question aided and abetted by his mother.

When he came to revolt against Christianity with all the venom and brilliance that he could muster, there could be no alternative but that he had to ally himself with those forces that ran counter to the stupidities his mother stood for. So he *became* the Beast. And since *Revelation* counted the number of the Beast and found it to be 666, the number of a Man, he turned all his Qabalistic and numerological skill in later years to finding this number in any meaningful word or motto that came his way.

His father died when he was about eight years of age. So he and mother went to live with a maternal uncle Tom Bishop.

Crowley really had little criticism of his mother, save that she was not too bright and had religious monomania, which perhaps began in what he was inclined to call the 'hysteria of widowhood.'

The uncle was another story. Crowley has described him as a sexual degenerate, a bully, a liar, and everything vile. There is an *Obituary* in *Equinox VIII,* where Crowley fantasied

about the death of Uncle Tom, describing him as the most
grotesque hypocrite of all time. In the blue *Equinox,* there is
a review by Crowley of a book *Evolution Criticized* written
by this Uncle. Crowley really rolls up his sleeves and goes to
work to show the kind of vicious creature Uncle Tom was,
using every bit of the invective and vitriol that was in him.

In the *Confessions,* the matter is put very succinctly:

> No more cruel fanatic, no meaner villain, ever walked
> this earth. My father, wrong-headed as he was, had
> humanity and a certain degree of common-sense; he had
> a logical mind and never confused spiritual with material
> issues. He could never have believed, like my uncle, that
> the cut and colour of "Sunday clothes" could be a
> matter of importance to the Deity. Having decided that
> faith and not works was essential to salvation, he could
> not attach any vital importance to works. With him, the
> reason for refraining from sin was simply that it showed
> ingratitude to the Saviour. In the case of the sinner, it
> was almost a hopeful sign that he should sin
> thoroughly . . . .

It should be clear, then, that he did not like his uncle, and
since Tom Bishop was a devout Christian, it requires no great
psychological acumen to realize the simple identification that
followed. Tom Bishop = Evangelical = Christianity = Christ.
If the first item of the equation were hated, then the last
clause would elicit the same reaction.

*"I did not hate God or Christ, but merely the God and
Christ of the people I hated,"* Crowley added simply but
significantly in the *Confessions.* (Italics are mine.) He has
been more misunderstood and misquoted in this connection
than almost anyone else I have known.

But again, one swallow does not make a summer. His
whole boyhood at school was tainted by the smug morality
(or immorality) of the Plymouth Brethren. He was so
emotionally traumatized in those formative years that the

psychologist might well wonder that he grew into any kind of productive adult at all.

In the Introduction to *The World's Tragedy*—a tremendously passionate indictment of Christianity—he gives some part of the boyhood history which led to his total adult rejection of Christianity. The introduction is subdivided into several sections, one being *A Boyhood in Hell.* It opens with:

> The Rev. H. d'Arcy Champney, M.A. of Corpus Christi College, Cambridge, had come out of sect.
> He had voted at the Parliamentary elections by crossing out the names of the candidates and writing: "I vote for King Jesus."

With this brief description, one can well imagine what this fanatical crackpot was, and what kind of school he conducted for the sons of the faithful in Cambridge. Crowley had to stop the narrative at this juncture to utter a vehement and vitriolic curse that has all the bitter earmarks of an ancient Biblical denunciation.

The school may have been good enough from the academic point of view, good enough to have satisfied the examiners. But morally and physically, it must have been a diabolical engine of destruction and corruption. I have heard similar accounts from patients who were sons and daughters of ministers. I doubt if the general public even now will believe this.

"We were told that 'the Lord had a special care of the school, and brought to light that which was done in darkness' etc. etc. *ad nauseam.* 'The instrument was on this occasion so-and-so, who had nobly come forward, etc. etc.' In other words hypocrisy and sneaking were the only virtues." This might well be one of the several dynamic factors that forced Crowley in his prime to the conclusion that Christianity is a slave religion, whose virtues are hypocrisy, lying, sin and guilt. He was thoroughly conditioned to this end.

"For instance," he goes on to narrate with bitterness, "a boy named Glascott, with insane taint, told Mr. Champney that he had visited me (12 years old) at my mother's house during the holidays"—true so far, he had—"and found me lying drunk at the bottom of the stairs. My mother was never asked about this; nor was I told of it. I was put in 'Coventry', i.e.: nor master nor boy might speak to me, or I to them. I was fed on bread and water; during work-hours I walked solitary around the playground. I was expected to 'confess' the crime of which I was not only innocent, but unaccused."

If he subsequently came to call himself "Alastor, the Spirit of Solitude, the Wanderer of the Wastes" we have in the above anecdote one of the several emotional determinants which we must surely consider as involved in his solitariness.

Admittedly, this is but one of many factors. We must never forget however that all true mystics come to consider themselves as basically homeless and without root on earth. "The foxes have holes, the birds of the air have nests, but the Son of Man hath no place to lay his head." Zimmer, in his *Philosophies of India*, has a beautiful footnote (p. 461) confirmatory of this attitude: *"Parahamsas:* the Vedantic ascetics, roaming through the world in homeless freedom, are compared to wild swans, or ganders; for these are at home in the trackless lofty sky as well as in the waters of the lakes of the land, just as saints are at home in the formless sphere devoid of attributes as well as in the garb of the human individual, seemingly moving among us in the phenomenal sphere of bondage."

This severe, ridiculous and criminal punishment went on for a term and a half. "Physically I broke down. The strain and the misery affected my kidneys, and I had to leave school altogether for two years."

There were other accusations levelled against him: that he had tried to corrupt one of the boys named Chamberlain, which he denied. We can really believe Crowley in this denial, for later he never attempted in any way to conceal his basic homosexual interests and activities. If this story had been factual, I am sure he would have been the first to admit it and glory in it.

Another accusation was that once he "had strolled up to a group of boys in the playground who were indeed holding" a *mock* prayer-meeting. One of the boys, seeing him coming, invited him in with "Brother Crowley will now lead us in prayer." On this occasion, Aleister was too wary and walked away. "But instead of doing what a wise boy would have done; gone straight to the head and accused them of forty-six distinct unmentionable crimes, I let things slide." He made up for this neglect in his adulthood, when he always accused someone first of the most awful moral defects.

The boys who had invited him to the mock prayer-meeting now hurried off by themselves to the Head, complaining that Crowley had tried to lead them away from Jesus!

The routine on Sunday at this School would have been enough to have given anyone the willies. "Morning prayers and sermon (about 45 minutes). Morning 'Meeting' (1½ to 2 hours). Open-air preaching on Parker's Piece (say one hour). Bible reading and learning by heart. Reading of the few books 'sanctioned for Sunday' (say 2 hours). Prayer-meeting (called voluntary, but to stay away meant that some sneak in the school would accuse you of something next day (say 1 hour). Evening prayer and sermon (say 30 minutes). Preaching of the Gospel in the meeting room (1½ hours). Ditto on Parker's Piece (say one hour). Prayer before retiring (say ½ hour)."

If this would not result in the development of total hatred and rejection of any religion, I do not know what would. As one reads and ponders over this early history of Crowley, one wonders if his denunciations are vehement enough! And that would be true not only of Christianity to which he was subjected, but had it been Judaism or Islam, the conclusion would have to be the same. I have had Jewish and Moslem patients whose religious indoctrinations were not dissimilar to this one of Crowley's and they came to hate their religion with a similar fervour.

Crowley's health suffered in boyhood, and since he had to be out of school for a long time, his family provided tutors for him. Most were from Cambridge, and they had to be Plymouth Brethren, or overtly religious zealots, for the family to hire them. One of the tutors, while in charge of his morals and liberal education, aided and abetted Crowley in extinguishing street lamps. When a policeman pounced on the boy, the tutor forsook him and fled.

"I was always being watched for signs of masturbation, and always being warned and worried about it. It says something of human innocence that after four years of this insane treatment I was still absolutely ignorant, though on fire in every nerve to learn the practice that people made so much fuss about."

Here, Crowley is psychologically naive. This may have been human innocence, but it also indicates severe neurotic repression. While the Plymouth Brethren must be held accountable for some part in this, there are other determinants which I propose to explore later. Among these should be mentioned his incestuous strivings for his mother, which appear surreptitiously in his writings. If this deduction is valid, such strivings would have had to be vigorously repressed because of religious training, and anchored in the deepest levels of his unconscious.

Another tutor profoundly involved with missionary work tried to initiate Crowley into sodomitic practices. "I knew exactly what he was doing, as it happened. I let him go as far as he did, with the deliberate intention of making sure on that point."

Again he wrote: "They sent me to Malvern, where my weakness made me the prey of every bully . . . . Sodomy was the rule at Malvern; my study-companion used even to take money for it. I cunningly used my knowledge of the fact to get away from the school . . . . They sent me to Tonbridge; my health broke down; partly, one may say, through what would have been my own fault or misfortune if I had been properly educated." A scribbled note in the margin of Crowley's own copy of *The World's Tragedy* states simply that he "caught the clap!"

He was sent here, and sent there. More tutors and misery and torture, until finally "they sent me to Cambridge. I found myself my own master, and settled down to lead a righteous, sober and Godly life; and to make up for lost time in the matter of education.

"Outside purely scholastic subjects, they had taught me to fight, to love the truth, to hate oppression,—and by God! I think they taught me well."

So, if here and there, in this story of Aleister Crowley who became mystic and mage and poet, it is said that he thoroughly hated Christianity, perhaps it will now be understood why.

He was not content merely to hate Christianity impotently. When he was on a retirement somewhere in New Hampshire around 1917, he came across a copy of George Bernard Shaw's *Androcles and the Lion*. In an introduction to this book Mr. Shaw was unwise enough to write about his own socialistic interpretation of Christ. This roused Crowley's ire because, first of all, he knew the Bible backwards and forwards, which Mr. Shaw did not. Second, he rejected Shaw's interpretations which, so he claimed, were not based on the intrinsic evidence of the Bible, which he thereupon quoted at great length. Third, he knew the East at first hand—Mr. Shaw did not. Finally, he was familiar at first hand with the mystical experience and with mystical literature, without which nothing about Jesus makes sense. And this Mr. Shaw was not. The result was that as his ire increased, his literary impulse mounted so that critical notes multiplied until—lo! and behold! he had written an anti-Christian text that he entitled *The Gospel According to St. Bernard Shaw.*

The basic motive may have been his early boyhood loathing of Christianity. But the book itself comprised sound scholarship, sober reasoning and marshalling of historical fact, and an interpretation which only in recent years has acquired another kind of corroboration.

The following is a fair example of the general attitude of criticism adopted in this Gospel:

> "Jesus" is a composite figure of several incompatible elements. There is therefore no "he" in the case. The Gospels are a crude compilation of Gnosticism, Judaism, Essenism, Hinduism, Buddhism, with the watch-words of various sacerdotal-political cults, thrown at random into a hotch-potch of distorted legends of the persons of the Pagan Pantheon, and glued with a semblance of unity in the interests of sustaining the shaken fabric of local faiths against the assaults of the consolidation of civilization, and of applying the cooperative principle to businesses whose throats were being cut by competition.

It is too bad that this book has never been published except in private mimeographed form. It would be far better received today than fifty years ago!

He also became well-versed in philosophy. In fact, the greater part of his own system represents a dynamic and dialectical reconciliation between the opposing philosophies of the Hindu Advaita on the one hand and the Buddhist Anatta doctrine on the other. This Oriental philosophical conflict became recapitulated for him in the more recent Occidental opposition of Berkeley's idealism and Hume's scepticism. *Liber Os Abysmi* on page 291 of this book demonstrates clearly this attitude and the practical use to which he put this philosophical conflict.

The intellectually lazy, the merely uninformed or the sexually lame and halt will find little in his writings to appeal to them. Far too many demands will be made upon what they know and what they are intrinsically.

NOTES

[1] *Liber VII vel Lapidis Lazuli.* Chapter II, vv 6-9, London (no date, but probably about 1909). Reprinted in *The Holy Books*, Sangreal Foundation, Dallas, Texas, 1969.

[2] *Aleister Crowley*, C. R. Cammell, London, Richards Press, 1954, p. 40.

[3] *The Equinox*, Vol. I, No. III, p. 36 ff. See also *Roll Away The Stone* Llewelly, St. Paul, 1968.

[4] *The World's Tragedy*, Paris, 1910.

PART TWO—NEOPHYTE

The Voice of my Higher Self said unto me: Let me enter the Path of Darkness and, peradventure, there shall I find the Light. I am the only Being in an Abyss of Darkness; from an Abyss of Darkness came I forth ere my birth, from the Silence of a Primal Sleep.

And the Voice of Ages answered to my Soul: I am He who formulates in Darkness—the Light that shineth in Darkness, yet the Darkness comprehendeth it not.

Neophyte Ritual, G. D.

CHAPTER THREE

The Golden Dawn

Beyond all other mundane events it was the influence of the Hermetic Order of the Golden Dawn that shaped Aleister Crowley's life. Once exposed to its Qabalistic system of grades and philosophy, its magical practices and ceremonies, he was never the same.

William Butler Yeats had also been an initiate of this organization, and at one time a dedicated and very active member. As Virginia Moore in *The Unicorn* ably indicated and at some length, Yeats was able to leave the Order behind him, more or less, first to study spiritualism and then to immerse himself in Oriental thought. It is true that some of his poetry and visionary writings show a trace of the Golden Dawn. But it is a weary and cautious one, not a dominant one. His later writing gives little indication of it at all, even though Virginia Moore has tried valiantly but I think vainly to prove its continued influence.

This is hardly true of Crowley. From 1898 when he entered the Order, to 1947 when he died, it was an ever-present ferment in one form or another. There can be no understanding of Crowley as a person, no realization of what he strove for, unless this basic fact be grasped and understood. For this reason, the Golden Dawn will have to be recreated in detail, and its history and philosophy presented here for consideration. I propose to show how much of what he so lavishly created had its dark roots in the Order. These

59

roots were developed, changed and expanded, but they are the same roots to which he was exposed long ago.

There are many versions of the Order's origin—some of them good, others wholly unreliable. There is first of all my own version in *My Rosicrucian Adventure*. Crowley's *History Lection* is well-written and quite reliable, save that it places him in an exalted position while reducing others to small importance. *The Temple of King Solomon*, a serial narrative written by the late General J.F.C. Fuller under Crowley's supervision, and running through the different numbers of the *Equinox* is invaluable for its detailed information. The patriarchal Arthur Edward Waite, only a couple of years before his death wrote a fair biography *Shadows of Life and Thought*. In it, he dealt at some length with the Golden Dawn, giving a few less known facts, but in a rather derogatory manner, as though it were of little value and served an insignificant role in his life. The truth is that he too was enormously indebted to the Order in a variety of ways.

One of the most complete recent accounts, however, is Virginia Moore's *The Unicorn*. This purports to be a biographical study of William Butler Yeats, and his search for reality. She has done a great deal of unravelling of some of the confused strands comprising the historical perplexities found in the later history of the Golden Dawn. She is partial of course to Yeats. In some places she is over-dramatic, admittedly in the cause of good writing. In so doing, however, she needlessly becomes very critical of and unfriendly to Crowley.

For example, relative to a magical diary that was kept by Crowley, she wrote that many of his statements are suspect, "being intertwined with absurd talk about a Secret Ring entrusted to his keeping by the Masters, a Secret Tibetan Bell of Electrum Magicum with a striker of human bone, and Crosses of Blood inflicted on the breast; and the whole lot must be thrown out of court."

I will not let the whole lot be thrown out of court. She has her own case to plead for Yeats, and she does this magnificently. But in pleading for Yeats, she has shown a prejudice towards and lack of discrimination about Crowley.

I was about eighteen years of age when I first read the document she refers to, *John St. John*, a diary written by Crowley to cover a short retirement.[1] In this record he attempted to show that expansion of consciousness is possible in a more or less restricted period of time by the use of well-defined meditative and magical methods. He did mention, it is true, the ring and a Tibetan bell, as she has indicated. But he also mentioned eating oysters, drinking wine, having sexual intercourse, playing billiards, posing for a portrait, and a number of other things. What she did not perceive, which struck me so forcibly even in my adolescence, was that when Crowley began to speak or write of the spiritual experience which dawned on him towards the end of the retirement period, his entire attitude and language changed. His pompousness, rhetoric, and braggadocio disappeared. Instead, he wrote simply:

> When therefore I had made ready the chamber, so that all was dark, save for the Lamp upon the Altar, I began as recorded above, to inflame myself in praying, calling upon my Lord . . . . And the Chamber was filled with that wondrous glow of ultraviolet light self-luminous, without a source, that hath no counterpart in Nature unless it be in that Dawn of the North. . . . Then subtly, easily, simply, imperceptibly gliding, I passed away into nothing. And I was wrapped in the black brilliance of my Lord, that interpenetrated me in every part, fusing its light with my darkness, and leaving there no darkness, but pure light. Also I beheld my Lord in a figure and I felt the interior trembling kindle itself into a Kiss—and I perceived the true Sacraments—and I beheld in one moment all the mystic visions in one; and the Holy Grail appeared unto me,

and many other inexpressible things were known of me . . . .

At 10.0 arrived at Brenner's studio, and took the pose. At once, automatically, the interior trembling began again, and again the subtle brilliance flowed through me. The consciousness again died and was reborn as the divine, always without shock or stress . . . . Having gone back into the life of the world—yet a world transfigured!—I did all my little work, my little amusements, all the things that one does, very quietly and beatifically. At 10:30 the rapture began to carry me away; yet I withstood it and went on with my game of Billiards, for politeness' sake. And even there in the Café du Dome was the glory within me, and I therein; so that every time that I failed at a stroke and stood up and drank in that ambrosial air, I was nigh falling for that intense sweetness that dissolved away the soul. Even as a lover that swoons with excess of pleasure at the first kiss of the beloved, even so was I, oh my Lord Adonai! Wherefore I am come hither to my chamber to inflame myself in praying at the Altar that I have set up. And I am ready, robed, armed, anointed . . . .

This observation must provide me with the occasion to insist that this excerpt from Crowley's *John St. John* is typical of the man. This theme, more than anything else I know with the possible exception of sex and love, pervades and permeates everything he wrote and did. I could almost use the phrase "God-intoxicated" in reference to him. If the other theme with which he was preoccupied is asserted to be a more frequent one in his literary output, all I can say for the moment is that he identified the two topics in a most extraordinary way. The ecstasy of sex he considered akin to the ecstasy of spiritual experience. It is the same Ananda, as the Hindus would term it, operating through the physical channel. For example, there is the following excerpt from his *Confessions* where he discussed the result of his visit to a Hindu Temple:

One of the great sights of South India is the great Temple of the Shivalingam. I spent a good deal of time in its courts meditating on the mystery of Phallic worship. Apologists ordinarily base their defense on a denial that the lingam is worshipped as such. They claim correctly enough that it is merely the symbol of the supreme creative spiritual force of the Most High. It is perfectly true, none the less, that barren women circumambulate it in the hope of becoming fruitful. I accepted this sublimation gladly, because I had not yet been healed of the wound of Amfortas: I had not got rid of the shame of sex. My instinct told me that Blake was right in saying: "The lust of the goat is the glory of God." But I lacked the courage to admit it. The result of my training had been to obsess me with the hideously foul idea that inflicts such misery on Western minds and curses life with civil war. Europeans cannot face the facts frankly, they cannot escape from their animal appetite, yet suffer the tortures of fear and shame even while gratifying it. As Freud has now shown, this devastating complex is not merely responsible for most of the social and domestic misery of Europe and America, but exposes the individual to neurosis. It is hardly too much to say that our lives are blasted by conscience. We resort to suppression, and the germs create an abscess.

The Order issued its own historical lecture,[2] some of it veridical and some of it fanciful. "The Order of the Golden Dawn," it stated, "is an Hermetic Society whose members are taught the principles of Occult Science and the Magic of Hermes. During the early part of the last century, several eminent Adepti and Chiefs of the Order in France and England died, and their death caused a temporary dormant condition of Temple work." This official lecture, however, made no attempt to indicate what occurred in that hiatus, and how it was bridged, and by whom. A wide gulf exists.

This history continues:

Prominent among the Adepti of our Order and of public renown were Eliphas Levi the greatest of modern French magi, Ragon, the author of several books of occult lore; Kenneth M. Mackenzie, author of the famous and learned Masonic Encyclopaedia; and Frederick Hockley possessed of the power of vision in the crystal, and whose manuscripts are highly esteemed. These and other contemporary Adepti of this Order received their knowledge and power from predecessors of equal and even of greater eminence. They received indeed and have handed down to us their doctrine and system of Theosophy and Hermetic Science and the higher Alchemy from a long series of practised investigators whose origin is traced to the Fratres Roseae Crucis of Germany, which association was founded by one Christian Rosenkreutz about the year 1398 A.D. . . .

The Rosicrucian revival of Mysticism was but a new development of the vastly older wisdom of the Qabalistic Rabbis and of that very ancient secret knowledge, the Magic of the Egyptians, in which the Hebrew Pentateuch tells you that Moses the founder of the Jewish system was "learned," that is, in which he had been initiated.

What is the function of this Qabalistic interpretation of religion? This magic of which both The Golden Dawn and Aleister Crowley speak? If I say its goal is illumination or the expansion of consciousness, not much at first may be gleaned from that. Yet "being brought to the Light" is a most apt description of the high goals of the system. It *is* the Great Work. There is no ambiguity in the concept of the Order Rituals as Crowley found them towards the close of the nineteenth century. The theme permeates the entire work from Neophyte to Adeptus Minor, and beyond.

"Down through the ages of recorded history," wrote Willis W. Harman in a recent essay in *Main Currents* (Vol. XX, I, p. 5 *et seq*) "various groups, from the ancient Gnostics to the modern Theosophists, within the Hindu, Buddhist, Moslem and Christian traditions alike, have insisted that man has far vaster potentiality for knowledge, and hence power over his fate, than he ordinarily dreams of as possible. They have claimed that it is possible to *know*—in a way that is completely different from the mere accumulation of facts—man's essential nature and his true relationship to the creative force behind the universe, and wherein his fulfilment lies—that is, what it is he values most highly when the meaning of life is clearly seen. For this knowledge men have followed religious teachers and joined secret societies. They have willingly submitted to the travails of elaborate initiation procedures and training for years in various yoga and meditation techniques. They have practiced fasting, flagellation and austerity . . . . Among them all the experience of *gnosis,* of direct perception and knowledge, has been the most highly prized of all human experiences."

What he learned from the Golden Dawn, Crowley adopted as his own set of magical standards—as when he says that the next step for every man is "the knowledge and conversation of the Holy Guardian Angel." The motives for the use of this rather archaic language he explains at great length in the *Equinox* as part of a discussion about the term "Augoeides":

> Lytton calls him Adonai in "Zanoni", and I often use this name in the note-books. Abramelin calls him Holy Guardian Angel. I adopt this:
> 1. Because Abramelin's system is so simple and effective.
> 2. Because since *all* theories of the universe are absurd it is better to talk in the language of one which is patently absurd, so as to mortify the metaphysical man.
> 3. Because a child can understand it.
> Theosophists call him the Higher Self, Silent Watcher, or Great Master. The Golden Dawn calls him the Genius. Gnostics say the Logos. Egyptians say Asar-Un-Nefer . . . .

There are historical antecedents in his life for the use of such archaic language, and in his autobiography Crowley calls attention to one significant episode:

> He remembers its general appearance, and that of the little family group. A porter, staggering under a heavy trunk, slid it suddenly off his back. It missed crushing the boy by a hair's breadth. He does not remember whether he was snatched away, or anything else, except his father's exclamation: "His Guardian Angel was watching over him." It seems possible that this early impression determined his course in later life when he came to take up Magick; for the one document which gripped him was "The Book of the Sacred Magic of Abramelin the Mage," in which the essential work is "To obtain the Knowledge and Conversation of the Holy Guardian Angel."

The experience of the rising of the Light in both vision and waking state is common to mystics of every age and of every people. Most of the experiences recorded by William James in his *Varieties of Religious Experience* mention this as one of the outstanding stigmata, shall I say, of the mystical experience. It must be an occurrence of the greatest significance in the treading of the Path because it appears always and everywhere as unconditioned. It is an experience which defies definition, as well in its elementary flashes as in its most advanced transports. No code of thought, philosophy or religion, no logical process can bind or limit it. Always it represents, spiritually, a marked attainment, a liberation from the perplexities and turmoils of life, and from nearly every psychic complication. As Jung once expressed it, it "thereby frees the inner personality from emotional and imaginary entanglements, creating thus a unity of being which is universally felt as a release." It is the attainment of spiritual puberty, marking a significant stage in growth.

Symptomatic of this stage of interior growth is the utter

transformation that comes over what previously appeared to be "the Chaos, the Darkness, and the Gates of the Land of Night", to use a Golden Dawn ritual phrase. While man is assumed into godhead, and the divine spirit is brought down into manhood, a new earth and a new heaven make their appearance. It is the development of a totally new outlook. It is the redeeming point of view; familiar objects take on a divine radiance illumined by an internal spiritual light.

In his book *Centuries of Meditation,* Thomas Traherne gives a beautiful description of the rapture of the inner personality and its reaction when it is freed by the mystical experience from all entanglements with the outside world. He says:

> The corn was orient and immortal wheat, which never should be reaped, nor was ever sown. I thought it had stood from everlasting to everlasting. The dust and the stones of the street were as precious as gold; the gates were at first the end of the world. The green trees when I saw them first through one of the gates, transported and ravished me, their sweetness and unusual beauty made my heart leap, and almost mad with ecstasy, they were such strange and wonderful things. The men! O what venerable and reverend creatures did the aged seem! Immortal Cherubim! And the young men glittering and sparkling angels and maids, strange seraphic pieces of life and beauty. Boys and girls tumbling in the street, and playing, were moving jewels . . . . I knew not that they were born or should die. But all things abided eternally as they were in their proper places. Eternity was manifested in the Light of Day, and something infinite behind everything appeared.

It is to effect this exaltation and expansion of the consciousness to the Light, that the magical system of the Golden Dawn, as well as Crowley's own reformulation of that Order, exists. The function of every phase of its work, the avowed intention of its principal rituals, and explicit statement of its teaching, is to assist in the discovery of that unity of being which is the inner self, the higher and divine Genius. Not only does the system imply this by its ritualistic movements and axiomata, but there are clear and unmistakable passages where these ideas are given unequivocal expression.

The whole object of Magic and mystical training "is by the intervention of the symbol, ceremonial and sacrament, so to lead the soul that it may be withdrawn from the attraction of matter and delivered from the absorption therein, whereby it walks in somnambulism, knowing not whence it cometh nor whither it goeth." Moreover in the same ritual, celebrated at the autumnal and vernal equinoxes, the Chief Adept officiating recites an invocation beseeching guidance for the newly-installed Hierophant:

"That he may well and worthily direct those who have been called from the tribulation of the darkness into the Light of this little kingdom of Thy love. And vouchsafe also, that going forward in love for Thee, through him and with him, they may pass from the Desire of Thy house into the Light of Thy presence." This is succeeded by sentences read by his two assistants: "The desire of Thy house hath eaten me up," and "I desire to be dissolved and to be with Thee."

And finally, that not the least vestige of misunderstanding may remain as to the object of this training which profoundly influenced both Yeats and Crowley and many another, let me offer one more quotation from this ritual. Referring to the upper triad of Sephiroth on the Qabalistic Tree of Life and the Temple that in old time was built on high, the speech adds, "The holy place was made waste and the Sons of the House of Wisdom were taken away into the captivity of the senses. We have worshipped since then in a house made with hands, receiving a sacramental ministration by a derived light in place of the co-habiting Glory. And yet,

amidst signs and symbols the tokens of the Higher Presence
have never been wanting in our hearts. By the waters of
Babylon we have sat down and wept, but we have ever
remembered Zion, and that memorial is a witness testifying
that we shall yet return with exultation into the House of our
Father."

Years later, in the second volume of the *Equinox*, Crowley
wrote an Editorial, in which he said:

> We perceive in the sensible world, Sorrow. Ultimately
> that is: We admit the existence of a Problem requiring
> solution . . . . Following on this we say: If any
> resolution there be to . . . the Vanity of Life and the
> Vanity of Thought, it must be in the attainment of a
> Consciousness which transcends both of them. Let us
> call this supernormal consciousness, or, for want of a
> better name "Spiritual Experience." . . . . We further
> believe that the Consummation of Spiritual Experience
> is reflected into the spheres of intellect and action as
> Genius, so that by taking an ordinary man we can by
> training produce a Master.

In yet another issue of the *Equinox*, he also wrote:

> I. The world progresses by virtue of the appearance of
>   Christs (geniuses).
> II. Christs (geniuses) are men with super-consciousness
>   of the highest order.
> III. Super-consciousness of the highest order is obtainable
>   by known methods. Therefore, by employing the
>   quintessence of known methods we cause the world
>   to progress . . . .

This excursion into theory is motivated only by the wish
to clarify the essence of what is called the Great Work. This is
the core of the Golden Dawn and, regardless of all later
excesses and exaggerations, the heart of Crowley as well.

The historical account circulated within the Golden Dawn is merely one source of information. Another is a slender highly informative booklet entitled *Data of the History Of the Rosicrucians* which was published in 1916 by the late Dr. William Wynn Westcott. There we find the following statement: "In 1887 by the permission of S.D.A., a continental Rosecrucian Adept, the Isis-Urania Temple of Hermetic students of the G.D. was formed to give instruction in the mediaeval Occult sciences. Fratres. M.E.V. with S.A. and S.R.M.D. became the chiefs, and the latter wrote the rituals in modern English from old Rosicrucian manuscripts (the property of S.A.) supplemented by his own literary researches."

These statements narrate the beginning of the Hermetic Order of the Golden Dawn—an organization which has exerted a greater influence on the development of occultism since its revival in the last quarter of the nineteenth century than most people realize. Its membership was recruited from every circle of life, including physicians, psychologists, clergymen, artists, philosophers and poets. Humble men and women from every level of society have drawn inspiration from it.

As an organization, it preferred always to shroud itself in an impenetrable cloak of mystery. No matter how many vague rumors circulated about it and its whereabouts, it came to be very difficult to join. Waite himself narrates sarcastically that his first application was rejected—which he was informed was a customary procedure—and it was only after a period of time that he re-applied, to be accepted. Its teachings and methods of instruction were stringently guarded by various penalties attached to the most awe-inspiring obligations in order to ensure secrecy. So well have these obligations been kept, with one or two exceptions, that the general public knows next to nothing about the Order, its teaching, or the extent and nature of its membership. It is common knowledge that Arthur Machen, Florence Farr, Algernon Blackwood and many other writers, actors and actresses were members—including as mentioned William Butler Yeats. The latter has written circuitously about it, apparently bound by his initiatory oaths, and has said little that made sense. Waite was not afraid to give names in his biography *Shadows of Life and Thought.* And Virginia Moore in *The Unicorn* also gives names, based on the extensive research she undertook to write her book on Yeats.

It is evident then that some of its members were prominent and intelligent people—not the usual occult nit-wits some critics have been prone to suspect.

With regard to the mottoes given in Dr. Westcott's statement above, it is necessary that we give them a little attention in order to unravel, as far as may be possible, the almost inextricable confusion which has characterized every previous effort to detail rationally the history of the Order. M.E.V. was the motto chosen by Dr. William Robert Woodman, an eminent Freemason of the last century. *Sapere Aude* and *Non Omnis Moriar* were the two mottoes used on various occasions by Dr. Westcott, an antiquarian, coroner by profession and an occult scholar.

S.R.M.D. or *S. Rhiogail Ma. Dhream* was the magical motto of Samuel Liddell who, later, under the influence of Gaelic fantasies and aspirations, expanded the name to MacGregor Mathers. During the period when Crowley recognized Mathers as his Chief, he wrote a poem:

THE ROSICRUCIAN

A sa Majesté Jacques IV d'Ecosse. *

I see the centuries wax and wane.
I know their mystery of pain,

---

*Supposed to have escaped from Flodden and become an Adept; to have reappeared as the "Comte de St. Germain," and later (so hinted Mr. S.L. Mathers) as Mr. S.L. Mathers. (A.C.)

The secrets of the living fire,
The key of life: I live: I reign:
For I am master of desire.

Silent, I pass amid the folk
Caught in its mesh, slaves to its yoke.
Silent, unknown, I work and will
Redemption, godhead's master-stroke.
And breaking of the wands of ill . . . .

Aloof, alone, unloved, I stand
With love and worship in my hand.
I commune with the Gods; I wait
Their summons and I fire the brand.
I speak Their Word: and there is Fate . . . .

I sit, as God must sit: I reign.
Redemption from the threads of pain
I weave, until the veil be drawn.
I burn the chaff, I glean the grain;
In silence I await the dawn.[3]

Mathers was the translator of three mediaeval magical
texts: *The Greater Key of King Solomon*, *The Kaballah
Unveiled* (which consisted of certain portions from Knorr
Von Rosenroth's Latin rendition of the Zohar, prefixed by a
lengthy introduction of some erudition), and *The Book of the
Sacred Magic of Abramelin the Mage*. Within the framework
of the second Order, he employed the Latin motto *Deo Duce
Comite Ferro*. I am under the impression that where the dual
mottoes of Westcott and Mathers are concerned, one was
chosen for use in the Golden Dawn, the so-called outer or
exoteric organization, and the second for use in the inner or
Rosicrucian Order.

S.D.A. was the abbreviation of the motto *Sapiens
Dominabitur Astris*, chosen by a Fraulein Anna Sprengel of
Nuremberg. Such were the four actors on this occult stage,
the *dramatis personae* of the commencement of the Order.

What the actual events were that culminated in the authorization of the Order remain unclear, even to this day. There are so many conflicting stories, the truth is almost impossible to discover. At any rate, so far as England is concerned, we must seek for its origins in the Societas Rosicruciana in Anglia. This was an organization formulated in 1865 by eminent Freemasons, some of them claiming Rosicrucian initiation from Continental adepti. Among those claiming this initiation was one Kenneth MacKenzie, a Masonic scholar and encyclopaedist, who purported to have received his at the hands of a Count Apponyi in Austria. The objects of this Society which confined its membership to Freemasons in good standing, were "to afford mutual aid and encouragement in working out the great problems of Life, and in discovering the secrets of nature; to facilitate the study of the systems of philosophy founded upon the Kaballah and the doctrines of Hermes Trismegistus."

Dr. Westcott also remarks that today its members are "concerned in the study and administration of medicines, and in their manufacture upon old lines; they also teach and practise the curative effects of coloured light, and cultivate mental processes which are believed to induce spiritual enlightenment and extended powers of the human senses, especially in the directions of clairvoyance and clairaudience."

In *The True History of the Rosicrucians*, Waite was bitingly critical of everything and everybody except his own execrable literary style and his own obscure brand of mysticism. "He who lives by the sword shall perish by the sword." When Crowley came to full term and published his own periodical the *Equinox*, issue after issue contained scathing diatribes and virulent attacks on Waite. His obscure literary style especially came in for constant lampooning. I cannot feel too sad about this; it was poetic justice!

Chief among these critical essays and book reviews is one

that should not be allowed to lapse in the oblivion of
forgotten things. It is an essay entitled *The Dangers of
Mysticism,* dedicated to A. E. Waite, based on one piece of
Waite's writing, and it quotes Waite in a variety of different
ways.

> A curious idea is being sedulously disseminated, and
> appears to be gaining ground, that mysticism is the
> "Safe" Path to the Highest, and magic the dangerous
> Path to the Lowest.
> There are several comments to be made on this
> assertion.   One may doubt whether anything worth
> doing at all is free from danger, and one may wonder
> what danger can threaten the man whose object is his
> own utter ruin. One may also smile a little grimly at the
> integrity of those who try to include all Magic under
> Black Magic, as is the present trick of the Mystic
> Militant here on earth . . . .
> But apart from this question, it is by no means
> certain that the formula is as simple as it seems . . . . We
> find a modern journalist who has done more than
> dabble in mysticism writing, "This mystic life at its
> highest is undeniably selfish"; . . . . We find another so
> sensitive that the mention of his name by the present
> writer induces an attack of epileptic mania; if such are
> really "united with" or "absorbed in" God, what of
> God? . . . . The mystic is solitary and shut up, lacks
> wholesome combat . . . . There is an exaggerated awe, a
> solemnity of diction, a vanity of archaic phrases, a false
> veil of holiness upon the unclean shrine. Stilted
> affectation masquerades as dignity; a rag-bag of
> mediaevalism apes profundity; jargon passes for
> literature; phylacteries increase about the hem of the
> perfect prig, prude, and Pharisee . . . . Corollary to this
> attitude is the lack of all human virtue . . . .
> The Magician is not nearly so liable to fall into this
> fearful mire of pride as the mystic; he is occupied with
> things outside himself, and can correct his pride. Indeed,
> he is constantly being corrected by Nature . . . . The
> greatest magician, when he acts in his human capacity,

acts as a man should. Unselfishness is very often his long suit. Just this the mystic lacks. Trying to absorb the lower planes into the higher, he neglects the lower, a mistake no magician could make . . . .

Christ, at the height of his career, found time to wash the feet of his disciples; any Master who does not do this on every plane is a Black Brother. The Hindus honour no man who becomes "Sannyasi" (nearly our "hermit") until he has faithfully fulfilled all his duties as a man and a citizen. Celibacy is immoral, and the celibate shirks one of the greatest difficulties of the Path . . . . Beware of all those who shirk the lower difficulties; it's a good bet that they shirk the higher difficulties too . . . .

Let him remember that an ounce of honest pride is better than a ton of false humility, although an ounce of true humility is worth an ounce of honest pride; the man who works has no time to bother with either. And let him remember Christ's statement of the Law "to love God with all thy heart, and thy neighbour as thyself."

This, then, is one of Crowley's commentaries on Arthur Edward Waite. It is a valid criticism; but beyond that it exemplifies Aleister Crowley.

The first Chief of this English Rosicrucian Society, its Supreme Magus so-called, was one Robert Wentworth Little, who is said to have rescued some old German rituals from a certain Masonic storeroom, and it was from certain of those papers that the Society's rituals were elaborated. He died in 1878, to be succeeded by Dr. William R. Woodman. Both Westcott and MacGregor Mathers were prominent and active members of this august Masonic body. In fact, the former became Supreme Magus upon Woodman's death, the office of Junior Magus being conferred upon Mathers.

A legend has it that Westcott once discovered in his library a series of cipher manuscripts. In order to decipher them he enlisted the aid of MacGregor Mathers. It is also said that this

library belonged to the Rosicrucian Society, and that those
cipher manuscripts were among the rituals and documents
originally rescued by Robert W. Little from Freemason's
Hall.

Other accounts suggest that Westcott found the
manuscripts on a bookstall in Farringdon Street. Further
legends claim that they were discovered in the library
inherited from Frederick Hockley, who died in 1885.
Whatever the origin of these mysterious cipher manuscripts,
when eventually deciphered they gave the address of a
Fraulein Anna Sprengel who purported to be the Rosicrucian
Adept. Here was a discovery which naturally was not to be
neglected. Its direct result was the transmission of
authorization to Woodman, Westcott and Mathers to
formulate in England a semi-secret occult organization. It was
to employ an elaborate magical ceremonial and Qabalistic
philosophy as parts of a comprehensive scheme of spiritual
discipline. Its foundation was designed to include both men
and women on a basis of perfect equality, in
contradistinction to the traditional Masonic policy of the
Rosicrucian Society. Thus, in 1887, the Hermetic Order of
the Golden Dawn was established. Its first English
temple—Isis-Urania, was opened in the following year.

In his autobiography, Waite elaborates considerably on
this:

> Westcott himself had assured me years previously (1)
> that there was a name and address among the "Cipher
> Mss", (2) that he wrote to Fraulein Sprengel, the person
> named, and (3) that he received answers. This
> notwithstanding, it has to be remembered (1) that the
> alleged Ciphers de-code in English and not in German;
> (2) that the allocation of Tarot Trumps Major to the
> Hebrew Letters, and therefore by inference to the Paths
> on the Tree of Life, is of French invention; and (3) that
> the Ciphers otherwise bear no mark and carry no

suggestion of German origin. It looks as though, after all these travellings, everything remains in suspense on the Rituals of the Golden Dawn . . . If it happened that he (Kenneth MacKenzie) was telling the truth, it is not impossible that this multifarious person, who is known to have talked once at least with Eliphas Levi and to have left behind him some serious Enochian documents, may have produced the G.D. Ciphers, in part from his recollection of German Grade experiences, and in part from his inventive resources . . . .

I conclude—with almost utter detachment over the whole subject *(This is one of Waite's pet phrases and means but little—I.R.)* (1) that the G.D. Ritual notes were produced well after 1870—perhaps even ten years later, (2) that they were not the work of Westcott, Woodman and Mathers; (3) that it is unsafe to challenge their remote German connections . . . . (4) that the original Isis-Urania Temple may have started work in London with a tacit recognition of the fact on the part of some not dissimilar institution existing previously in German; (5) that it was never authorized officially; (6) that it was not under any German or Continental obedience; (7) that it was not responsible to anything but its own Official Headship; (8) that a pretended Warrant which was exhibited to Neophytes was no better than a solemn mockery; (9) that the Rite laid claim, by implication and otherwise, on remote antiquity; (10) that it was to this extent a mountebank concern; (11) that it was described invariably as governed by a Triadic Headship; (12) that when Dr. Woodman passed away the vacancy caused by his death was never filled, to the expressed and unexpressed dissatisfaction of several older Members.

So much for Waite! And so much for that part of the history!

As to what happened after the inauguration of Temple work here, we have little record. On the basis of records left by a Dr. R. Felkin, and corroborated by Waite, we know that half-a-dozen Temples were instituted in various parts of the

British Isles. Crowley's account written many years later, continues the historical theme in these words:

> After some time S.D.A. died; further requests for help were met with a prompt refusal from the colleagues of S.D.A. It was written by one of them that S.D.A.'s schemes had always been regarded with disapproval but since the absolute rule of the Adepts is never to interfere with the judgment of any other person whomsoever—how much more, then, one of themselves, and that one most highly revered!—they had refrained from active opposition. The Adept who wrote this added that the Order had already quite enough knowledge to enable it or its members to formulate a magical link with the adepts. Shortly after this, one called S.R.M.D. announced that he had formulated such a link, and that himself with two others was to govern the Order . . . . We content ourselves, then, with observing that the death of one of his two colleagues, and the weakness of the other, secured to S.R.M.D. the sole authority . . . .

Some of this may require elucidation. In 1891, after a few days' illness, Dr. Woodman died, leaving the management of the Order to Westcott and Mathers. Evidently these two Masons carried on fairly well together for about six years, for the Order flourished. Exactly why Westcott withdrew from the Order, for this is the next major occurrence, is difficult to discover.

Several accounts are extant; we may take our pick. One version has it that he accidentally left some of the Order manuscripts in a portfolio bearing his signature in a cab, and the driver upon finding them turned them over to the authorities. Since Westcott was by profession a coroner in East London, the medical authorities strongly objected to one in an official capacity being even remotely connected with anything that savoured occult. It was suggested to him, therefore, that he withdraw from the Order or resign his post as coroner. He chose to resign from the Order. Yet again, others suggest that it was simply a personal quarrel that led to the parting of the ways with the autocratic Mathers—quite a likely story.

Waite's biography hinted at something more, but what it was we may never know for he has since died. However, intimations of what was involved may be gleaned from other directions. We may be able to piece them together in what was evidently a fantastic tale.

One of the scissors-and-paste books that Waite wrote in his early journalistic days was entitled *Devil Worship in France*. Even he admits that it was "a newspaper craze of the moment, and was done in uttermost haste. It bears the marks throughout." In other words he acknowledged himself as an opportunist anxious to make hay while the sun shone over a current scandal, or for some ready cash. We would do well to remember this self-evaluation.

The book concerned a Leo Taxil and a mock conspiracy of his to match French Masonry with the Roman Catholic Church in France. "It was he who created Diana Vaughan, a 'Palladist' of perfect initiation, Grand Mistress of the Temple of Occult Freemasonry and Grand Inspectress of the New and Reformed Palladium, having its headquarters at Charleston, U.S.A., under the supreme pontificate of Albert Pike." This is Waite's account in *The Brotherhood of the Rosy Cross*. The Palladins were said to be descended from the Templars. Like the Ordo Templi Orientis, which Crowley later headed in England after authorization from Theodor Reuss, the German head, it taught a species of sex-magic. A woman named Diana Vaughan was involved in this whole weird affair—"wealthy, beautiful and highly placed, the Palladian Diana was a lineal descendant of Thomas Vaughan" the English occultist.

A scandal was brewing both in Paris and London, with poor Westcott caught in the middle. He had given his consent for his name to be used in the reformulation of the Order of the Palladins. Waite attempted to blow the whole thing sky-high by stating it was a lie, and that there never was a Diana Vaughan.

A friend of mine however has a Palladin charter on which appear the signatures of Leo Taxil as Secretary, Westcott as Grand Commander, and Diana Vaughan as Inspector General! Accusations and denials were rampant at the time, though all we inherit is confusion. The result of all of this was that Mathers forced Westcott into the background of the Order, perhaps to avoid a more open airing of his alleged connections with the infamous Leo Taxil and the scandalous Palladins. Thus Mathers reigned supreme. But in doing so, we are told he became an autocrat within the Order.

Between Mathers and Crowley there were more than casual resemblances. Both were men of athletic physique, fascinated by high-sounding titles, inventing a Gaelic lineage for themselves, but at the same time convinced of their high spiritual calling. Mathers often quoted from the ritual "There is no part of me which is not of the Gods" and this became part of his general attitude towards life. This hardly sounds like cynicism; rather it inspires respect and admiration. Where others saw nothing both these men beheld angels, portents and other high omens. For example, one of Crowley's self-imposed obligations for the grade of Magister Templii is "I will interpret every phenomenon as a particular dealing of God with my soul." This is a serious undertaking. Their dress, speech, and daily behavior merged with the content of their psychic world. It is a pity no one has written a biography of Mathers. From the stray references to him here, there and everywhere, "his was a fantastic life, full of magic, learning and madness," says Symonds.

So it would seem that just as Crowley was a difficult person to maintain relations with—by his own confession he had no use for moral responsibility; a phrase denoting inhibition and repression—we might assume that Mathers was equally difficult. He was a dictator, and not a benevolent one. Some of the more independent Order members who dared to differ or argue with him about the governance of the Order were promptly expelled. Pride and egotism were intrinsic parts of his character structure, as they were with Crowley, and both suffered thereby. I fancy that Mathers became a model for Crowley, however unconsciously, of what a magician should be, and that Crowley patterned his own life accordingly.

"In 1890," Symonds tells us, "MacGregor Mathers was earning his living as the curator of the Museum of Frederick J. Horniman, M.P., at Forest Hill. In 1891, the appointment ceased. He had had a quarrel with Horniman and had been dismissed. Fortunately, Horniman's daughter, who had been a fellow student at the Slade Institute with Mathers' wife, Nina Bergson, gave him £443 a year, and on this he went to live in Paris."[4] He preferred to live there, where he engaged among other things in research in the Arsenal Library. He discovered a magical manuscript which he translated into English with the title *The Sacred Magic of Abramelin the Mage*. This we shall hear more about throughout this narrative. It is another important determinant in the Crowley history.

While walking in the Bois de Bologne one day, meditating on this book and matters connected with the governance of the Order, Mathers claimed triumphantly that he was approached by three men. He asserted that these were Adepts belonging to the hidden or Secret Third Order, and therefore belonged to that category of men described in *The Cloud Upon the Sanctuary*. Apparently, so he claims, they had materialized themselves, and in that tense emotional and spiritual atmosphere of psychical phenomena, confirmed him in the sole rulership of the Order. This piece of information he promptly conveyed to the members in London. He stated specifically that in this manner he had been enabled to forge a link between the second or Rosicrucian Order and the Third Order of the Secret Chiefs.

In a manifesto addressed to the Adepti of the Second Order in 1896, Mathers asserted:

> As to the Secret Chiefs with whom I am in touch and from whom I have received the wisdom of the Second Order which I communicated to you, I can tell you nothing. I do not even know their Earthly names, and I have very seldom seen them in their physical bodies . . . . They used to meet me physically at a time and place fixed in advance. For my part, I believe they are human beings living on this Earth, but possessed of terrible and superhuman powers . . . . My physical encounters with them have shown me how difficult it is for a mortal, however "advanced," to support their presence . . . . I do not mean that during my rare meetings with them I experienced the same feeling of intense physical depression that accompanies the loss of magnetism. On the contrary, I felt I was in contact with a force so terrible that I can only compare it to the shock one would receive from being near a flash of lightning during a great thunder-storm, experiencing at the same time great difficulty in breathing . . . .

On the strength of this alleged occurrence, he demanded absolute loyalty and obedience from every member, naming himself as a chosen vessel. Those who refused to send a written statement of voluntary submission to him were either expelled from the Order or degraded to a lower rank. This may not seem important to us today, but to anyone who had invested the Order and its grades and teaching with energy and inner significance, it could be a disheartening experience.

In the meantime, dissatisfaction with the autocratic leadership of Mathers was growing. No clearcut reasons are given for this, but evidently this restlessness had been growing along with Mathers' ego. It has been suggested that he was guilty of innumerable magical tricks of an irresponsible nature which brought disrepute to him and to the Order. Another group claimed that he sought and obtained publicity by staging Egyptian rites and ceremonies in Paris. Others, more romantically inclined, and Crowley and Cammell belong in this category, asserted that his English translation of the Abramelin book was a powerful magical act which attracted to him forces of evil so terrible that he was prostrated by them. Virginia Moore also confirms that the "threat of publication of this short-cut to 'the knowledge and conversation of the Guardian Angel or Higher Self' seemed enough to stir up the demons. Mathers suffered accident after accident bicycling on the Auteuil roads. Soon he was forced to walk." I presume her attitude here reflects that of Yeats.

Dr. Felkin presents a more rational view—that it was simply spiritual pride and love of power which so gained the ascendancy that sooner or later there had to be difficulties in his interpersonal relations. Nobody would put up with his egotism. Consciously or not, Crowley has repeated almost all of Mathers' dramatic stances, down to the last detail, the egotism, the public Rites, and the forging of the link with the Secret Chiefs.

Though claiming unquestioned leadership and refusing to appoint two other members to fill the vacant posts of co-Chiefs, Mathers had offered to the vanity of the more advanced members of the Second Order, additional grades in the path of adeptship and even more esoteric teaching. These apparently were not forthcoming. The spiteful response from the disillusioned Adepti, whose vanity was thus outraged, was that he had neither the knowledge nor the grades to impart. Further unpleasant bickering drew from Mathers the retort that he was certainly not going to waste either his grades or his knowledge on such hopeless duffers as they were. In any event, he was Chief—and they could take it or leave it!

A virulent quarrel was thus developing. Though for some

years it had fermented beneath the surface, it finally culminated in a group of fifty or sixty of the Adepti forming a powerful combination to expel Mathers.

Just before this happened, Florence Farr who had been appointed by Mathers to run the London Temple while he spent his time in Paris, decided for reasons of her own to vacate her office. Mathers refused to accept her resignation. He feared she might form a schismatic combination to work under Westcott, and this he would not permit. It was in this letter, dated the middle of February 1900, that he made the astonishing statement that Westcott had never been at any time in touch with Fraulein Sprengel in Nuremberg. And then he sprang a bombshell—that Westcott had "either himself forged or procured to be forged the professed correspondence between him and her."

Poor Florence Farr! This hit her very hard. She was stunned by this accusation of dishonesty and forgery levelled against Westcott who seemed a very unlikely person to engage in such activities. "It was testified further," wrote Waite in his biography, "that he, Mathers, was compelled under oath, as if against his will, to maintain this imposture on his own part. The answer of Westcott to this charge did not admit its accuracy but pointed out—in almost tremulous terms—that his witnesses were dead and that he would therefore remain neutral."

Florence Farr then formed a Committee of Seven within the Second Order to investigate the allegations. She asked Mathers for his own sake and that of the Order to produce proof of the accuracy of these statements. They argued—since it was upon the authority of this alleged correspondence that the Order was founded—that the historical position of descent from mediaeval Rosicrucian sources would collapse should it be proven that the correspondence had been forged. This viewpoint was not wholly valid, for while Mathers had accused Westcott of never having been in touch with Fraulein Sprengel, he had never denied having himself been in constant communication with her. A lengthy correspondence followed between the Committee and Mathers. Mathers refused unconditionally to acknowledge the authority, or even the existence, of the Committee, nor would he produce proof of any kind to substantiate his claim that Westcott had forged Second Order communications.

The evidence appears to be overwhelming against Westcott having forged documents. His character structure would not permit such an act. "I knew Westcott moderately well," testifies Waite in the autobiography, "and—amidst all his follies and pretensions—I do not believe that he was the kind of man who would have forged documents." This view was shared by Crowley.

Knowing Crowley's tendencies, it always came as a surprise to me when he spoke well of a man. There are only a handful of people whom he has not at some time or other maligned. It was one of his psychological symptoms to project massively, to use a psychoanalytic cliché. Whatever his own problems or disagreeable personality traits were, these he projected on to someone else.

For example: many years ago, in the mid-twenties, before I went to Paris to serve as his secretary, I wrote him from the States asking his opinion of a Theosophical lecturer I had known for some time. It happens that this man really was of unblemished character. Perhaps the only criticism that one could voice about him was that he was a dedicated Theosophist, a zealot, a sincere fanatic. Crowley's reply was that this man was a Were-wolf, lived off wealthy women, and something else equally vile that I now have forgotten. At the time, this opinion disturbed me enormously. I had had little exposure to psychoanalysis, and no experience of Crowley as a person other than as a writer, and was generally green and naive. It took many years of growing up—on the couch as well as off it—before I was able to recognize clearly this piece of Crowley pathology.

To come back to this theme, it is a pleasant respite from mud-slinging to read in one of the *Equinoxes*:

> I wish expressly to dissociate from my strictures on Mathers Brother Wynn Westcott his colleague; for I have heard and believe nothing which would lead me to doubt his uprightness and integrity. But I warn him in public, as I have (vainly) warned him in private, that by retaining the cipher MSS. of the Order, and preserving silence on the subject, he makes himself an accomplice in, or at least an accessory to, the frauds of his colleague. And I ask him in public, as I have (vainly) asked him in private, to deposit the MSS. with the Trustees of the British Museum with an account of how they came into his possession; or if they are no longer in his possession, to state publicly how he first obtained them, and why, and to whom, he parted with them.
>
> I ask him in the name of faith between man and man; in the name of those unfortunates who, for no worse fault than their aspiration to the Hidden Wisdom, have been and still are being befooled and betrayed and robbed by his colleague under the aegis of the respectability of his own name; and in the Name of Him, who, planning the Universe, employed the Plumb-line, the Level and the Square.

No good purpose can be served by enlarging upon the muddy events which immediately followed. The history of the Order is so confused at this juncture, and the rumours which have come down to us so chaotic and contradictory that it has proved impossible to extricate the truth from the debris of slander, abuse and recrimination.

It would seem that Mathers on his part expelled the rebels who then formed a schism, which they re-named The Stella Matutina. On the other hand, it was also held by Waite that Mathers was expelled by a large majority of the members. He was left with only half a dozen staunch adherents, including Crowley at first, with whose assistance, moral and financial, he continued his Temple in Paris.

Since we are tracing the history of the Order to show Crowley's connection with it, and to show how at least its names and titles and ideology were appropriated by him when he came to form his own Order, it is now necessary to back-track and fill in some of the gaps in the narrative.

NOTES

[1] *Equinox, Vol. I, No. 1*, p. 132 (Supplement)

[2] *The Golden Dawn*, Israel Regardie, St. Paul, 1969, Vol. I, p. 16.

[3] *Collected Works*, Vol. I, p. 207.

[4] *The Great Beast*, John Symonds, p. 31.

CHAPTER FOUR

Revolt

The unpleasantness that was brewing in the Order and which came to a head with the open Revolt had many causes, obviously. One of them must have been Crowley serving as the catalyst. Virginia Moore lists five of the possible factors that could have led to the quarrel in the year 1900:

1. Was Yeats indignant because Mathers had "deserted" to Paris, leaving Florence Farr as deputy?

2. Had Yeats with other members resented the fact that they had waited for years for so-called higher grades?

3. Had the London group bitterly resented the pledge of personal obedience to Mathers under penalty of expulsion?

4. Were Mathers' titles such as the Comte de Glenstrae causes of irritation?

5. Was it because of Crowley who had been befriended by Mathers?

When Crowley had applied to the Temple authorities in London to be advanced to the Adeptus Minor grade, he was refused. The ruling Chiefs were well within their rights to refuse advancement to anyone. This was their privilege. However, there were personal feelings involved here—and some of these were felt by Yeats, reflected by Virginia Moore in her book.

The ruling Chiefs did not like Crowley, his attitudes, his behavior, or anything about him. They wanted nothing to do with him, directly or indirectly. His egotism was just

89

beginning to show, and he was sowing his wild oats with a fine degree of abandon, caring nothing for the notoriety which attended it. Or, if he did care, it must have been with pleasure and little else. Periodically in his youth he would adopt outrageous pseudonyms, believing them to be romantic. For example, he attempted to live incognito in London with the inconspicuous name of Count Vladimir Svareff. The London Adepti, hearing of this and other of his exhibitionist escapades, could hardly be pleased.

Crowley had assumed that the Adepti of Isis-Urania were just jealous of his rapid progress through the outer Order, as he had egotistically assumed that Yeats was jealous of his poetry. These assumptions are not altogether true. Anyone who had memorized the so-called knowledge lectures—a mass of disconnected Qabalistic and occult knowledge, plus the Hebrew alphabet—could be advanced as rapidly as he wanted through the outer Order. Only in a couple of grades was there assumed to be a waiting period, and this for only a few months. So I gather it was a clashing of personalities—at first!

After the London group had rejected him, Mathers accepted Crowley's application for initiation into the Second or Rosicrucian Order, inviting him to come to Paris for the ceremony. This was simply equivalent to Mathers openly expressing his contempt for the members in London.

Many years ago, when I first began to investigate this matter, I observed in my book *My Rosicrucian Adventure,* that:

> It was towards the close of 1898, just prior to the Revolt, that Aleister Crowley was introduced to the Order by Frater Volo Noscere (George Cecil Jones), receiving his Neophyte initiation at Mark Mason's Hall. It was clear, soon after he had joined, that here was a highly gifted young man, and that in many ways, though unrestrained and undisciplined, his was a

powerfully magical personality. From Capt. J.F.C. Fuller's verbose and flamboyant account in the *Equinox,* we gather that Crowley was advanced through the grades of the Order quickly, and assimilated the routine knowledge without the least difficulty. Those grades which were not formally separated by automatic delays, were taken at the rate of one a month, and succeeding ones at the prescribed intervals of three, seven, and nine months.

This must provide the occasion for me to declare that this was routine progress. It did not carry with it the implication that one had to be a great magician to get the grades quickly. This was the inference made by Fuller about Crowley. It is not true. It is undeniable that he brought into the Order his own genius. He had read widely on occult subjects, and evidently had been exposed to bits of the Qabalah, alchemy, etc. Under those circumstances, the knowledge lectures posed no great difficulty. Probably he was already familiar with the material. If not, he could have memorized it in a couple of hours.

When, many years later, I became a member of the Stella Matutina, which was nothing but the Golden Dawn re-christened by the schismatic group, I followed pretty much the same procedure. It did not mean, in my case, that I was gifted beyond all others. I had been interested for almost ten years in the Qabalah and Theosophy, comparative religion and mythology, and in philosophy and psychology. I had already written two books, *A Garden of Pomegranates* and *The Tree of Life.* These were, incidentally, symbolical of my having severed the umbilical cord that tied me to Crowley, and were dedicated to him. They also served to provide a concise introduction to the far more profound but scattered writings of Crowley. It was on the basis of *The Tree of Life*, that I was invited to join the Order.

The fact that Crowley sailed through the grades of the

Outer Order quickly did not carry with it *per se* the evident piece of flattery that he was already a great magician of whom the other members of Isis-Urania were completely jealous.

It was likely that, by this time, he was behaving like a young man about town. In Cambridge, he had learned to throw off the yoke of the Plymouth Brethren with the inhibitions that his mother had foisted on him. And he took full advantage of the freedom that Cambridge afforded him. We may assume that he disseminated with vigour the knowledge of his escapades, as part of his rebellion against the familial and religious yoke.

It is also likely that some of the members of Isis-Urania belonged to the old school of occultism, and were straight-laced. They did not believe an Adept should drink, fornicate, have fun and raise hell—which was what Crowley was doing with enthusiasm. He liked it. He was developing a handsomely scandalous reputation, winning the disapproval of some of the Adepti, who felt that they were not running a reformatory for delinquent boys. Perhaps they feared that one bad apple might spoil the whole barrel.

People who employ such a compulsive morality are actually terrified at the emotional and instinctual possibilities latent within them. Unconsciously, they have imprisoned themselves in a meshwork of highly complex defense-mechanisms which block all possibility of spontaneous behavior. This network functions as an armor, both on the psychological level as inhibitions, and on the somatic level as muscular tensions and visceral dysfunctions. Anyone who is capable of operating relatively freely, without the intervention of the armor, would awaken their hostility and resentment. Such a person would represent all that they have hated and feared. He would be a threat which could undo all they have managed through a lifetime to repress.

Freud encountered this, as the history of psychoanalysis

indicates. Wilhelm Reich was victimized by the same set of forces. Crowley too was subjected to this, first at the hands of the London adepti, and then by the general public. Certainly, he aided and abetted them by his lack of discrimination, and by his urges towards exhibitionism. Nobody would have bothered him, had he kept his private business to himself. Journalists found him an ideal victim for their own latent aggressiveness, and took advantage of every opening he gave them. He was a good target for them, since he was a threat also to their own precarious neurotic equilibrium.

By the time Crowley had taken his Portal grade, a preliminary to the Adept degree, the Revolt as already described was in full swing. The wisdom and authority of Mathers was doubted, challenged and repudiated. Crowley was barred from further advancement in the London group despite the deliberate warning contained in Mathers' manifesto: "What I discountenance and will check and punish whenever I find it in the Order is the attempt to criticize and interfere with the private life of members of the Order . . . . The private life of a person is a matter between himself or herself and his or her God."

Whether Mathers was impressed by the latent promise of Crowley's personality with its energy and enthusiasm, or whether he decided upon his next step to show contempt for the ruling Chiefs of Isis-Urania Temple, we do not know. Both may be true. Crowley was invited to Ahathoor Temple in Paris where he was initiated into the Second Order, receiving the grade of Adeptus Minor.

While on this subject, I should register a curious fact. Upon receiving the Neophyte degree, and thus being received into the Outer Order of the Golden Dawn, he chose the magical motto of *Perdurabo*, "I will endure unto the end." Several other members had adopted a second motto after having entered the Second Order of the Roseae Rubeae et Aureae

Crucis.

For example, Westcott's mottoes were *Non Omnis Moriar* and *Sapere Aude*. Mathers had already selected *S. Rhiogail Ma Dhream* and *Deo Duce Comite Ferro*. We would surmise, under these circumstances, that Crowley would feel obliged to select a second motto also.

This procedure differed somewhat from the one followed during the period when I was a member. It was neither demanded nor expected. For my motto for the Neophyte Grade, I had selected *Ad Majorem Adonai Gloriam—Adonai,* the Crowley term for the Higher Self or the Holy Guardian Angel, replacing Dei in the old Jesuit motto. For the 5=6 Adept degree, I retained the same motto.

I mention this because there is a slight mystery here, to be explored more fully later.

Crowley has never overtly revealed what his motto for the Adept Minor grade was. He is far from reluctant about naming his other mottoes for the higher grades. For example, he chose, for the 6=5 grade, the motto *Ol Sonuf Vaorsagi*—three words opening one of the Angelical Keys of the Enochian system, meaning "I reign over you." The first few lines of that Key read: "I reign over you, saith the God of Justice, in power exalted above the Firmament of Wrath: in whose hands the Sun is as a Sword and the Moon as a through-thrusting fire:"

For the grade of 7=4, he used *Ou Mh,* [1] which is the Greek for "No, definitely no!" After he had crossed the Abyss and acquired the grade of 8=3, his motto was *Vi Veri Universum Vivus Vici,* the Latin for "In my lifetime I have conquered the universe by the force of truth." Years later, when he made himself a Magus 9=2 in the United States, he chose the motto *To Mega Therion,* meaning both The Master Therion and The Great Beast.

Since the 5=6 grade is essentially a degree with Christian symbolism, I suspect he chose a title with a definite Christian implication. His revolt against the Plymouth Brethren was still in process but not complete at that time. Some of his early poetry indicates that he could use the name Christ without getting outraged or nauseated, or merely contemptuous as was the case later. Again, quoting Virginia Moore in *The Unicorn*, when she comments on Crowley's assertion that he took the Order with absolute seriousness right from the start, "But Yeats thought that from the beginning he took it wrong. For all his mouthing of the word "Christ," Christianity seems never to have penetrated."[2]

Of the last statement there can be no doubt whatsoever. He rejected it wholly—at least on a conscious level. Nor does Yeats' testimony mean very much here. But his observation about Crowley's mouthing the word "Christ" is meaningful in this connection. For it may confirm my thesis that his 5=6 motto did contain a Christian referent. Only later, as he rebelled more and more vigorously, and acquired more scholarly and occult material with which to rebel, must he have felt ashamed and impelled to hide from others the Christian nature of his early aspirations. This will be explored more fully later.

When the news got around in London that Mathers had initiated Crowley, it served only to inflame the differences which were now openly separating Mathers from his erstwhile followers. It also aggravated the bitter hatred which the Order members bore and still bear for Crowley to this day. Crowley did nothing to placate this group. He even went so far as to apply to them for the lecture and knowledge material to which, theoretically, he was now entitled. Of course he was refused. To Florence Farr, Yeats and other members he was *persona non grata*. To quote Virginia Moore, he was "a show-off, a charlatan, and perhaps a black magician." This latter was ridiculous—because at that stage he was merely in the throes of learning a bit about magic, and could hardly be accused of debasing what little practical knowledge he was acquiring.

It was customary among the sanctimonious blue-stockings of that time to call anyone a "black magician" who had rational attitudes about sex, and who believed that a natural sex life was an intrinsic part of every-day living.

Crowley did not take these accusations lying down. He promptly notified Mathers of what was going on. Mathers thought the Order members were mad. This led to the correspondence between Mathers and Florence Farr, previously noted, in which it was alleged that Westcott was a forger and Mathers, by high authority, was the sole head of the Order.

To Crowley's credit, it must be conceded that when open revolt did break out, at least he did side with Mathers, and immediately offered both his purse and his services to his Chief in Paris. About a week after this, he wrote in his diary:

> D.D.C.F. accepts my services, therefore do I rejoice that my sacrifice is accepted. Therefore do I again postpone the Operation of Abramelin the Mage, having by God's Grace formulated even in this a new link with the Higher, and gained a new weapon against the Great Princes of the Evil of the World.

One might question whether Crowley had ulterior motives in this act of loyalty. I would fancy that at that time he had only a good deal of admiration for and gratitude to Mathers for aiding him when Isis-Urania rejected him. Certainly he had no respect for the people in Isis-Urania who had scorned him. It was logical therefore to expect him to side with Mathers.

When a meeting was arranged by Mathers with the rebels in London, Crowley acted as Mathers' plenipotentiary. From the diplomatic point of view this was not very wise; there was already too much bad blood between the two factions, and the appointment of Crowley was not going to mollify anyone. But it gave Crowley a wonderful opportunity to be the exhibitionist. For this dramatic occasion, he dressed in the fantastic garb of a Highland chieftain, with kilt, dirks, and tartan, concealing his face with a heavy black mask. Mathers in large part was responsible for this masquerade, but we can be sure that Crowley never objected in the least to it. Apart from anything else, he made himself a laughing stock in London, making it difficult for anyone to take him or his mission seriously.

Not only did the rebels of Isis-Urania not take him seriously—they threw him out. This led to legal actions and a good deal of newspaper publicity which did no-one any good—except Crowley. The notoriety was food for his burgeoning egotism. He seemed to thrive on publicity. Good or bad notices made no difference—so long as he was noticed. "Every knock is a boost" would almost apply in his instance.

Crowley's description of his encounter with the London Adepti written by General Fuller in *Equinox III* is an extraordinary story with many quotations from letters written by Mathers, and brief excerpts from Crowley's own diaries at that time. However it is such a hodge-podge of confused issues and vague scandal that it is difficult to make sense of it. Some of it is sufficiently amusing and psychopathological as to make it worthwhile to disentangle one or two of its confused skeins.

A little background is necessary to reveal the fundamental issues. Some of it may be a bit hard to follow. There is an air of mystery, intrigue and vagueness about this encounter that makes it worth reproducing. It reminds one a little of mediaeval witchcraft, people being bound by spells and bewitched by psychic powers; one could well imagine being transported back several centuries in time.

Around the time of the Revolt, a certain Mrs. Rose Horos approached Mathers in Paris. Her husband appeared to be interested in the Egyptian Rites that were being staged publicly by Mathers, even promising to finance them on a wider scale. Mathers came to acknowledge Mrs. Horos as an initiate of some status, and gave her confidences and "top secret" papers and documents of the Order. Exactly why he was fooled in this way is not at all clear. It was stated in defense of Mathers that Mrs. Horos was able to repeat to him a certain conversation he had had years previously when visiting Madame Blavatsky at Denmark Hill, and the repetition of this scrap of conversation impressed him tremendously. Anyway, it was a sad piece of deception, and an unhappy acknowledgement on the part of Mathers. It indicated his gullibility and his lack of insight into character.

Mrs. Horos and her husband were soon discovered to be sex perverts, whatever this may have meant. Nor was this all, for it is alleged that they were responsible for the theft from Mathers of a complete set of Order documents. Subsequently when the immoral activities of these two people attracted the attention of the police, they were arrested. In December 1901, at their trial, the Order was given unpleasant and unmerited publicity by being associated with these two unsavoury characters.

A couple of months before this, Mathers had addressed a letter from Paris to the editor of *Light*, but it was not published until January 11, 1902. In this letter Mathers protested "against the shameful and utterly unauthorized use of its name (The Golden Dawn) for their own abominable and immoral purposes by the execrable couple calling themselves 'Mr. and Mrs. Horos'." He went on to say, "I have yet to learn how, when, where and from whom she obtained the knowledge of that Order, which she then certainly possessed. She was also acquainted with the names and addresses of several of the members, notably of those belonging to the discordant category."

At the time Crowley was appointed envoy to London, Mathers warned him that Mrs. Horos was a "vampire of remarkable power." This is Fuller's account in the *Equinox;* that is to say, one who "uses sexual love as a bait to catch her victims by." Afraid that Mrs. Horos might take over the command of the London Order, Mathers warned Crowley to use cold steel and the MacGregor tartan against her if he was ever threatened. This might be one of the reasons Crowley was attired so fantastically as a Highland chief when he attempted to seize the London Temple. It was theoretically to protect himself against Mrs. Horos. In passing, we might note that this misguided woman would have had greater need to protect herself against Crowley who really needed no such magical accoutrements as those recommended by his superior. Seduction would never have harmed *him.*

It was further asserted by Mathers that she was a financial fraud, perhaps because having promised to finance some of his publicly conducted Rites she never fulfilled that promise, and that her husband was but a victim of her vampirism, a sort of soulless maniac, possessing unexpected and demoniacal strength when inspired by her. Mathers thought her motive was hostility against the Order, himself, and the Great Work. Most of the London adepti felt that if she were a fraud who had deceived their Chief, he too must be a fraud.

When Crowley got to London, he went to visit two more friendly Adepti—and this is where the fun started. On the way, the headlights on the cab (paraffin or carbide in those days) caught fire, and a cab-horse got scared and bolted with him in the cab. During a social visit with one of the Sorores, the fire in her home would not burn—Mathers had predicted this phenomenon as an indication of the active witchcraft of the Horos couple. Another set of psychic phenomena followed. The rose cross given him by Mathers began to fade and lose color; it whitened. Unlikely as it may seem, a rubber raincoat caught fire when it was nowhere near an open flame. At other places, fires that should have burned were not anxious to do so. All of these and other psychic phenomena were taken as direct evidence of the malignant magic either of the Horos couple, or of enemies within the ranks of the Order. You can take it for what it is worth!

When the Horos nonsense had subsided, the members of Isis-Urania still continued their revolt. As their first magical gesture of independence, they changed the name of the Order to the Stella Matutina. Ruled for a year by a committee of twelve, they came to realize that this was far from satisfactory. Since, however, it had taken several years to brew and then to develop into an open gesture of defiance, the spirit which had conceived the rebellion was not to be banished at a single stroke.

Having elevated the standard of revolt by expelling their former chief, the Stella Matutina was haunted by that ghost. After inconceivable pettiness and dispute—some described bitterly by Yeats and quoted in *The Unicorn*, (and rather coldly mentioned by Waite in his biography)—the rebels were persuaded by circumstance to abandon every feature of their reform to return to the original scheme of appointing Three Chiefs to govern and lead them. Even this was later abandoned—if not officially at least in practice. A virtual autocracy similar to that enjoyed by Mathers was once more instituted, though on a lesser scale, if only because the personalities were smaller. The days of the giants were over. The revolt had really been in vain. From one point of view only, however. For it set the stage for one of the most important events in Crowley's career—his attempt to become the head of the Order.

Although Waite has some of his dates a little confused, his account in *Shadows of Life and Thought* is perhaps the best that we have so far of this transitional phase of the Order. "For a brief period," he wrote, "the Isis-Urania Temple and the Inner Order were in charge of a Moderator and Council, Westcott remaining in abeyance, there being no evidence that he resigned. At the end of about twelve months the Second Order called a meeting at Mark Masons' Hall and there elected J.W. Brodie-Innes, Dr. R.W. Felkin and Marcus Worsley Blackden to carry on the Order for a period of one year."

It should be interpolated here that Brodie-Innes belonged to the traditional occult school of interpretation within the Order. That is to say, he practised quite overtly the Golden Dawn system of ceremonial magic and occult training as laid down at the beginning. There was bound to be a clashing, if not of personalities, then of principles. Eventually both Waite and Brodie-Innes went their separate ways—which was probably best for both of them.

In this conflict, Crowley naturally came to take sides. For Waite, he had only supreme contempt, resorting to ridicule as his best weapon to express it. In later years, Brodie-Innes, in one way or another, was brought to Crowley's literary attention. Because he opposed Waite in demanding the strictest adherence to the ancient disciplines, he received Crowley's benediction and fulsome praise. Brodie-Innes was a writer of novels, amongst other things, and in the *Equinox IV* (September 1910) Crowley expressed his respect and admiration while reviewing "Morag the Seal":

> One must wish that Mr. Brodie-Innes' English were equal to his imagination. Again and again a lack of perfect control over his medium spoils one of the finest stories ever thought . . . . Not many men have imagination so delicate and—dictame!—but Mr. Brodie-Innes writes 'with authority, and not as the scribes.' Why he allows Mathers to go about saying that he is a Jesuit and a poisoner will be revealed at the Last Day. Perhaps, like us, he can't catch him. Or perhaps it is that he is contented to be a great novelist—as he is, bar the weakness of his English and an occasional touch of early Victorian prunes-and-prismism. He has every other qualification. God bless him!

One other Golden Dawn writer of this period received nothing but contemptuous notice from Crowley. Whenever there was a review of any work by Algernon Blackwood, you will there perceive venom and the most derogatory abuse to be levelled at any writer. There must have been some kind of exchange between these two men that, so far, I know nothing about.

Here I should mention that at no time does Waite mention Crowley in his biography. It could mean that Waite often wished Crowley were dead. I could not blame him were that true; the *Equinox* ridiculed him as often as it was published. But I doubt whether Waite could ever have confessed to the possibility that such avoidance is equivalent to a deathwish. Nor in this connection, does he speak of Yeats as having been involved in the reconstruction after the Revolt. In his biography, Waite mentioned Yeats but once, and that is the end of it.

As Waite has described it, he initiated the opposition to Brodie-Innes claiming the Headship of the Order. It was not merely a difference of personalities; it was based upon some difference in ideals. Brodie-Innes conducted the Temple up North, in England; Felkin kept his Temple going in Bristol; Blackden maintained another, though I am not sure where, while Waite kept Isis-Urania in London as a center for his mystical Christian interpretation of the Order teaching.

"The Mother-Temple—that of Isis-Urania—fell ultimately into my hands" wrote Waite, "and a preliminary transformation of Rituals changed the face of things." After his account of the death of the three original founders, Waite continues: "In 1914 I put an end to the Isis-Urania or Mother-Temple owing to internecine feuds on the authenticity of documents . . . . Of a new Rite which arose, as if from the dead ashes, there will be a word to say in conclusion; but there is no story to tell, either by myself or another. May that most sacred centre give up no outward form."

I was told that its rituals were changed and elaborated into verbose and interminable parades of turgidity. It is not difficult to imagine this when one examines some of Arthur Edward Waite's writing which can only be compared to someone speaking with a hot potato in his mouth. It is practically unintelligible. And if this characterized his mystical interpretation of the Order teaching—it is sad!

Formerly united by a single fraternal bond under one head, there were now several Temples being conducted by different groupings of men. So thoroughly had the central unity of the Order broken up that each of these Temples appointed its own set of Chiefs, considering itself by these gestures an autonomous occult body. Thus began the downfall of organized magical instruction through the semi-esoteric channels of the Hermetic Order of the Golden Dawn. An amusing sidelight on human nature is disclosed by the fact that in one of the Obligations retained by the schismatic groups, there still remains the original clause: "Do you further undertake not to be a stirrer up of strife, of schism, or of opposition to the Chiefs?"

The stage was thus set for the *coup de grace* which was later administered by Crowley. This was done in a number of ways, all amounting to the same thing. He ultimately gave meaning to the Revolt and turned it to his own advantage. By siding with Mathers he had acquired, in his own mind, prestige. He was now on the side of the Chiefs, the Secret Hidden Community of the Elect, and they would be bound to notice him and use him for their own divine ends.

It became his assumption that the Order was no longer governed by real Chiefs. Mathers had fallen from grace, whether because of the publication of Abramelin or some other factor. In having thus fallen, he was no longer able to initiate in any real sense of the term. In that case, Crowley was not bound by oaths. He had not perceived that if

Mathers had fallen from grace and was no longer capable of truly initiating, then he himself had not really been initiated. In any event, he would never have felt obligated by any oath.

After the Horos scandal, Crowley and Mathers parted more or less on good terms. Legend has it that Crowley had some growing doubts about Mathers, but if so, he kept them pretty much to himself, and went about his business. He travelled abroad for years, explored, climbed mountains, got married, practised Yoga, and visited his old friend Allan Bennett in Ceylon. Shortly afterwards, in 1904, there occurred the second most important event in Crowley's life, the dictation of *The Book of the Law*. More will be said about this later.

As a result of this book, he wrote Mathers to the effect that the whole Golden Dawn system was abrogate, and that he, Crowley, had been designated by the Secret Chiefs to head the Order. In other words, he was deposing Mathers from his own miniscule Order remnant. Mathers doubtless ignored this as a piece of braggadocio from the young upstart whom he had once mistakenly befriended.

It was in the spring of 1909 that Crowley began to issue his periodical, the *Equinox*, the plan being to issue every March and September, for five years, one large volume containing, in abridged and edited form, the abrogated Golden Dawn Rituals and some new material written by Crowley.

At this juncture, I feel compelled to question a statement by certain Order members that Crowley did not obtain the full Order teaching. Some of these denials are entirely too vehement. First of all, from a close study of Crowley's literary output there can be no question but that he did obtain his Adeptus Minor grade from Mathers after the London group refused to advance him. Secondly, in *Equinox II*, it was written, perhaps by Fuller, that: "so ardent was he in his search after knowledge that he even went so far as to invoke Mercury by obtaining access to and copying the 5=6 rituals and knowledge lectures belonging to Frater F.L. saying to himself 'All for knowledge, even life, even honour, All!' "

Never forget that Mercury is the god who rules over thieves and liars!

Finally, even if these facts were untrue, we have but to recall that he was the intimate friend of George Cecil Jones and Allan Bennett, both advanced members of the grade of Adeptus Minor. Both of these gentlemen coached and trained him so that he benefitted by their knowledge and wide experience. Whatever knowledge these Fraters had received from the Order documents was certainly given to Crowley, whatever may have been the means fair or foul by which he obtained that teaching. And while he did not publish it in its detailed entirety, he reproduced enough of it to convince anyone who knows anything of the Order methodology that Crowley possessed full knowledge.

To return to the *Equinoxes,* according to an advance notice, Volume III was scheduled to contain the ceremony of the Grade of Adeptus Minor, the most important as well as the most beautiful of all the grade rituals employed by the Golden Dawn. As might have been expected, Mathers learned of this proposal. We could even assume that Crowley deliberately wrote him to that effect. Had Mathers ignored the matter, very few people would have learned anything of the Golden Dawn, or, for that matter, of the *Equinox*. But in order to prevent the open dissemination of the Rituals he had written, Mathers immediately instigated legal proceedings, an action which gave a vast amount of publicity to Crowley as well as to the Golden Dawn and to Magic.

The hearing promptly came before the Court, delaying the appearance of the third volume of the *Equinox*. Evidently the Court was sympathetic to the case of Mathers, for an injunction was granted. Crowley lodged an appeal at once, and with a display of wit and dry humor, the Court of

Appeals set aside the injunction, thus paving the way for the immediate distribution of the *Equinox*.

The result was that most of the daily newspapers carried long sensational articles on the recent case and on so-called Rosicrucian teaching. Some also reproduced a number of the diagrams used in the grade ceremonies for didactic purposes. Even the design painted on the lid of the Pastos or Tomb of Christian Rosenkreutz achieved a certain degree of notoriety. The upshot was that Crowley managed to get a great deal of free publicity. And being an exhibitionist he gloated over the fact. The Revolt had paid off—for Crowley, but not for anybody else.

There must have been a kind of destiny to all these proceedings. No one at any earlier period could have foretold that there would be a revolt, or that it would go hardly with Mathers, or that in the end the catalyst who had precipitated the conflicts would emerge victorious—if only for a little while. The mills of God grind slowly indeed, but they do grind exceeding small.

NOTES

[1] Another New Testament Greek scholar has just told me that this phrase may also mean "Not yet!"

[2] *The Unicorn*, Virginia Moore, New York, MacMillan, 1954, p. 159.

CHAPTER FIVE

Prologue

It was the autumn of 1898. Crowley had gone to Switzerland for winter sports and mountain-climbing in which he had become thoroughly adept, and in which he had begun to acquire some reputation. While in Zermatt, he met an Englishman named Julian Baker, who happened to be a chemist, though at the time Crowley was not aware of that fact. If he had been, he might have been more careful of his speech—and then the whole course of his destiny would have been altered. While walking back with Baker to the hotel, Crowley began presumptuously to expound the principles of alchemy. He really knew nothing about it, but for a year or so before this he had read widely on every phase of occultism available to him.

Why he had read in this area of occultism is a story by itself best told in his own words in his biography:

> Having won freedom, he had the sense not to waste any time in enjoying it. He had been deprived of all English literature but the Bible during the whole of his youth, and he spent his three years at Cambridge in repairing the defect. He was also working for the Diplomatic Service, the late Lord Salisbury and the late Lord Ritchie having taken an interest in his career, and given him nominations. In October 1897, he was suddenly recalled to his understanding of the evils of the alleged "existing religion" and experienced a trance, in which he perceived the utter folly of all human

ambition. The fame of an ambassador rarely outlives a century. That of a poet is almost as ephemeral. The earth must one day perish. He must build in some material more lasting. This conception drove him to the study of Alchemy and Magick. He wrote to the author of *The Book of Black Magic and of Pacts*, a pompous American named Arthur Waite, notorious for the affectations and obscurities of his style, and the mealy-mouthed muddle of his mysticism. This nebulous impressario, presenting an asthmatic Isis in the Opera "Bull-Frogs", had hinted in his preface that he knew certain guarded occult sanctuaries wherein Truth and Wisdom were jealously guarded by a body of Initiates, to be dispensed to the postulant himself to partake of their privileges. Mr. Waite recommended him to read a book called *The Cloud on the Sanctuary*.

This account of how Crowley happened to turn to mysticism is relatively worthless. All we can say honestly and simply is that the awakening *comes*. There is no certain method, no stereotyped set of stimuli or patterns, no standard set of responses. But when it is there, when it does come, the individual is never the same. It is rather like being brought to the Light, in the ritualistic sense, except that this is no ritual. It occurs in the most natural, and, in one sense, the most unsought way.

But he did take Waite's advice, and procure the book. It was destined to play an important part in his life. The author, Karl von Eckartshausen, wrote of an invisible or Secret Assembly of Saints or Adepts who "saw by their own inward light." Not a part of any church or secular organization, they remained apart, watching over and directing the destinies of the world. It is to be supposed that Crowley wanted above all to be noticed by them, to be their servant or messenger, or even to become one of them. This provocative theme is implicit in everything he thought, wrote or did, particularly after he had achieved a series of initiatory visions in the North Sahara desert in 1909.

In order to clarify the effect of Eckartshausen upon him, it would be well to give several quotations from *The Cloud* so that we may more readily divine what moved this young man so deeply:

> The great and true work of building the Temple means, in other words, to develop in us the interior sensorium, or the organ to receive God . . . . The most exalted aim of religion is the intimate union of man with God; and this union is possible here below; but it can only take place by the opening of our inner sensorium, which enables our hearts to become receptive of God. . . .
>
> A more advanced school has always existed to which the deposition of all science has been confided, and this school was the community illuminated interiorly by the Saviour, the society of the Elect, which has continued from the first day of creation to the present time; its members, it is true, are scattered all over the world, but they have always been united by one spirit and one truth; they have had but one knowledge, a single source of truth, one lord, one doctor, and one master, in whom resides substantially the whole plenitude of God, who also alone initiates them into the high mysteries of Nature and the Spiritual World . . . .
>
> This community possesses a school, in which all who thirst for knowledge are instructed by the Spirit of Wisdom itself; and all the mysteries of God and of nature are preserved therein for the children of Light . . . Herein is the School of the Prophets and of all who search for wisdom; it is in this community alone that truth and the explanation of all mystery is to be found. It is the most hidden of communities, yet it possesses members gathered from many orders; of such is this School . . . .
>
> Anyone can look for the entrance, and any man who is within can teach another to seek for it; but only he who is ripe can arrive inside . . . . He who is ripe is joined to the chain, perhaps often where he thought

least likely, and at a point of which he knew nothing
himself . . . . There are methods by which ripeness is
attained, for in this holy communion is the primitive
storehouse of the most ancient and original science of
the human race, with the primitive mysteries also of all
science.

Being intense, passionate, and still idealistic, Crowley was
impressed enough by this message to yearn deeply for leads
of one kind or another that might bring him to the School of
this Hidden Community of Saints. And yearning, he would
assume every stray contact to be *the* one that would bring
him to it. So, when Julian Baker, impressed by this young
man's sincerity and aspiration, promised to introduce him to
someone in England who could help him, one can understand
what transpired within him. It was the answer to the deepest
prayer of his heart.

Baker kept his promise. Through him Crowley was
introduced to George Cecil Jones, another chemist, and an
advanced member of the Order of the Golden Dawn.

As soon as Crowley found out that Jones really
understood something of what he was seeking he "went
down to Basingstoke, where he lived, and more or less sat in
his pocket. It was not long before I found out exactly where
my destiny lay," he said in his autobiography.

In that book, he also stated that Jones who was a
Welshman possessed a fiery but unstable temper, was the son
of a suicide, "and bore a striking resemblance to many
conventional representations of Jesus Christ. His spirit was
both ardent and subtle. He was very widely read in Magick;
and, being by profession, an analytical chemist, was able to
investigate the subject in a scientific spirit."

This is the kind of man that Crowley could understand.
From that day onward, a close, intimate relationship
developed with all sorts of overtones and undertones that
have not yet been fully or clearly delineated. In 1906-07 when

Crowley reached the very heights of spiritual experience, after having travelled all over the world experimenting with a host of mystical techniques, he found that George Cecil Jones had undergone similar experiences.

Jones was impressed with Crowley and for this reason agreed to sponsor Crowley's application to the Order. Unlike Waite's, Crowley's was accepted the first time. And thus it was in 1898, in a private house in the West-end of London, the initiation occurred which, directly as well as indirectly, influenced the remaining years of his life.

Poet he was, and explorer and mountaineer too—but all of these areas served thereafter mainly as channels for the expression of his mysticism. And the Golden Dawn served as the starter and the focus of all his subsequent ideas and inner experiences. It was the fulfillment of his noblest dream that followed hard upon his inner awakening and which took form and substance from the Eckartshausen vision of the Secret Community and its school.

It was the rule in the Order for the newly inducted Candidate to adopt a new name, usually couched in Latin, Hebrew or Greek. In the ritual of the 0=0 grade, the Hierophant intones "I give permission to admit . . . . . , who now loses his name and will henceforth be known among us as . . . . . . "

I suppose the intent is similar to the christening process. The adoption of the new name represents an ideal to which the individual will labor and aspire for the rest of his life. The new name is the beginning of a new consecrated life. Crowley has never indicated why he chose the name Perdurabo, and what was the ideal behind it, save to give us the translation "I will endure unto the end."

A decade later, after he had tasted many kinds of spiritual exaltation, he could write—with subtle Qabalistic manipulations of his motto—"for enduring unto The End, at The End was Naught to endure." But even though there was literally a cipher (zero) at the end of the name Perdurabo, his egotism remained intact to the end of his days, inflated despite the promise of his verbal manipulations.

It is interesting to note that even in the selection of this magical motto, there was the intrusion—however unconscious—of his early religious training among the Plymouth Brethren. For in Mark 13:3-37 there appears: " . . . but say whatsoever is given you in that hour, for it is not you who speak, but the Holy Spirit. And brother will deliver up brother to death, and the father his child, and children will rise up against parents and have them put to death; and you will be hated by all for my name's sake. *But he who endures to the end will be saved.*"

There are at least two psychological determinants here. The first relates to his latent hostility toward his mother. The second one is that he was not only going to be saved, for this was inculcated as part of his early training, but he was going to be the leader at the head of the column "when the saints go marching in." Salvation, however, was the end.

Once Crowley had become a member of the Order, he met the second most important spiritual contact of his life. This was Allan Bennett, an Adeptus Minor of the Inner Order. They rapidly became dear and abiding friends. Bennett moved in with Crowley, sharing the latter's flat in Chancery Lane, and collaborated in a work of exploration, experimentation, and magical research unequalled anywhere or by anyone in a long time. There is a sonnet for Bennett in an early book:

> O Man of Sorrows: brother unto Grief!
> > O pale with suffering, and dumb hours of pain!
> > O worn with Thought! thy purpose springs again
> The Soul of Resurrection; thou art chief
> And lord of all thy mind; O patient thief
> > Of God's own fire! What mysteries find fane
> > In the white shrine of thy white spirit's reign,
> Thou man of Sorrows; O, beyond belief!

> Let perfect Peace be with thee; let thy days
>   Prosper in spite of thine unselfish soul:
>   And as thou lovest, so let Love increase
> Upon thee and about thee; till thy ways
>   Gleam with the splendour of that secret goal
>   Whose long war grows the great abiding peace.

Days, weeks and months they worked together, these two zealots, poring over manuscripts and magical books. They must have made talismans, amulets, and god-forms, and painted all the symbols of the Order in full color as required by the regulations. Ceremony after ceremony of every conceivable kind they must have performed. Divinatory processes, of geomancy and above all Tarot, were taught him by Allan who used the motto *Yehi Aour*, "Let there be Light." Bennett must also have taught him the art of skrying in the spirit vision, travelling clairvoyance, investigating symbols, their meanings known or not, so that their true significance could be divined. He must have given Crowley a good training in Qabalistic processes too. There is an essay or two of his remaining which indicates profundity and depth of insight. It was an invaluable training for Crowley—one too that is at the bottom of the very real skill he came to have in practical occultism.

However, there was something else that must have had a far-reaching effect on him. And that was Allan's bronchial asthma. I imagine the damp, wretched English climate did nothing to alleviate this condition. At that time, there was no psychotherapy of the depth variety. About the only recourse then for the relief of chest congestion was drugs. Opium, morphine, chloroform and cocaine were some of the drugs used by Bennett, and while they did tend to relieve for varying periods of time the asthmatic spasms, eventually they also produced narcosis—bringing an end to his efficiency for the time being.

One interesting facet of this is that years later Crowley also developed asthma. By that time, other drugs had been discovered which were more prompt and somewhat more effective than those used by Bennett. But relief at best was still only temporary. He suffered a good deal from it, especially when smoking as he did that dark perique tobacco by the continuous pipeful, which could only aggravate the already grossly irritated condition of his bronchi.

In 1919, after his return to Britain from the United States where he had lived during World War I, his asthma still bothering him, an English physician prescribed heroin as a medication to relieve the bronchial spasms. From that day on, he was "hooked." There were long periods when he broke the habit and was free. But, rationalize as he might on the basis of the injunctions in *The Book of the Law* to take foaming wines and strange drugs, he became an addict, pure and simple. Despite the enormous will that he had developed, he was relatively impotent in the face of the drug. The realization that he was "hooked" must have been humiliating to a degree, though I doubt if it was very noticeable to anyone but himself.

Curiously enough, about the time I parted company with Crowley in 1932, I began to suffer from asthma too. It came out of the blue, and its occurrence shocked me tremendously, for I had never had it before. For quite a while, I never suspected that this difficulty in breathing was asthma. At that time I was undergoing considerable emotional stress and strain.

I remember meeting Dion Fortune, a very competent writer on Qabalah and allied subjects, who conducted an Order of her own derived from the Golden Dawn and its magical knowledge. Some time after I had met her around 1933, she and her husband graciously invited me to spend a week-end with them in the King Arthur country near Glastonbury. It was then that I developed a really splendid bout of asthma which confined me to bed for the entire week-end. Her husband, a very fine and competent physician, treated me with medications and so helped me to recover. They were very kind people, and I am grateful.

A few years afterwards, when I had returned to New York, I maintained a regular correspondence with another English writer who conducted a little occult group. It was from him, who also suffered from asthma, that I learned of a theory that somehow asthma is an occupational disease of occultists and mystics. I wonder!

Ephedrine and epinephrine inhalers helped me tremendously, but the stimulus they both gave to the heart during the period of administration would often lay me low. A recent electro-cardiogram showed a now healed posterior infarction. I must once have had a silent coronary. Later, I was introduced to the anti-histamines which were certainly more effective in producing relief, but in addition they induced drowsiness and lethargy. Ultimately, this and other factors led to my undergoing psychotherapy.

The first round was Freudian analysis, and it gave me relief for long periods of time, but under stress the wheeze tended to return in full force. Years afterwards, I returned for another cycle; that helped still further. Finally, I was introduced to Reichian vegetotherapy, and after much hard work, emotional anguish and the passage of time, I was cured and have had little asthma since.

This has served to give me insight into what bothered Bennett and Crowley. Crowley's biography does not tell us what Bennett did for a living—as far as that goes, we learn very little about the man. We do know that he was penniless, and came to live with Crowley, acting in effect as his instructor in magic. If he had no financial resources, he must have been thoroughly insecure in our particular social environment, altogether apart from the more dynamic and historical factors lying in the background of his life. After he had completed his role of acting as guru to Crowley, he went to Ceylon to become a Buddhist monk. Under these circumstances, his financial insecurity would not bother him very much. That was part of the social context of a monk. In the West, however, it is a different story, one that must have embarrassed him a great deal.

Altogether, from the stormy antecedents of Crowley's life, we do know that he worked his way successfully through a small fortune, and wound up just before the first World War practically penniless. Among his few remaining assets was a large stock of books on poetry which he had published at his own expense, but they were not liquid enough to be of much immediate service to him. From then on he had to live by his wits, an adventurer. They were very precarious years, right to the end of his life. He must have experienced tremendous anxieties, though he dared acknowledge these only on rare occasions, as if by accident.

It is my contention that rather than being due to the repression of hostility or aggressiveness, asthma is essentially a symptom of fear and insecurity. The asthmatic is a fearful person. Usually his early training forbids his acknowledging this. Thus the fear is kept repressed. We do know from Wilhelm Reich that in order for any set of feelings to be blocked off, many sets of muscles have to be in a state of tension. In other words, we block or repress not only with our minds, but with our bodies, with our muscles. Fear can be characterized by taking a full inhalation, then holding the breath while staring forward with eyes wide open. This characterizes the asthmatic; he cannot let go of his air. He cannot relax. He dare not let his chest or anything else go, for then he would be confronted by the unacknowledgable fact that he is anxious.

This is easy to see where Crowley is concerned. He was an insecure and frightened youngster as his biography shows. When he found a new way of life, the old fear was never really discharged, regardless of the occasional foolhardiness of his behavior. His exhibitionism, his devil-may-care attitudes and his apparent courage were largely compulsive defense-mechanisms which adequately concealed the fear. It remained repressed. But under stress, which was a concomitant of his entire life, it emerged as asthma.

Neither Crowley nor Bennett, I would say, really had the courage—regardless of the depth of their meditations and magical work—to face up to the basic fact that they were anxious people. Anxiety-ridden men who were over-compensating for, but not eradicating, the worm of fear eating at their vitals. Sad to say, even the Order teaching gave them grounds for the continuation of their repressions. It exhorted "Fear is failure, and the forerunner of failure. Be thou therefore without fear. For in the heart of the coward, virtue abideth not!"

The association with Allan had another very important sequel. I have already indicated that he used drugs to assuage his sufferings from asthma. In doing so, he must have discovered that some of them had a distinct effect on the mind. They expanded consciousness, and produced a simulacrum of the mystical or religious experience. "There exists," he came to believe, "a drug whose use will open the gates of the World behind the Veil of Matter."

Crowley was determined to find this drug. Once Allan had imparted to him the rudiments of his pharmacological knowledge about their effect, he decided to experiment himself with opium, cocaine, ether and hashish. At first he had no difficulty in getting these drugs. The Dangerous Drugs Act was not passed in England until 1920.

He has written about this extensively, and some of his finest writing deals with penetrating analyses of ether and hashish as aids to meditation, and as chemical devices to catapult the psyche headlong into the mystical experience. He contended, among other things, that if the Neophyte could taste the glory and the ineffability of his goals by means of an introductory dose of hashish, he would then be willing to embark upon a life-long program of self-discipline to make the divine an intrinsic part of his being.

It is a pity that he didn't live long enough to learn directly of the vast amount of scientific research that is today being conducted with regard to lysergic acid (LSD). Not only has this drug, and other psychedelic agents, been employed to provide insights into the common mental diseases, but the subjects of creativity and mystical experience have also come within the purview of people who, under other circumstances or with other tools, might never have been exposed to considerations of this type. There is an extensive literature dealing with this, much of it on a high level of insight and interpretation.

I am thinking specifically of a brilliant neuro-psychiatrist whom I had known casually for some years. He was a neo-Freudian. Had I suggested to him ten years ago that a topic of such philosophical profundity as religious mysticism could ever have appealed to him, I am certain he would have laughed at me. However, since he has been exposed to lysergic acid—both having administered it professionally as part of a psychotherapeutic regimen for patients, and having taken it himself out of curiosity—his whole attitude has undergone a tremendous metamorphosis.

Nor should we forget one of the more popular books that once made an enormous impression on the general public, evoking wide interest—Aldous Huxley's *Doors of Perception*. It would be worth a great deal to make some comparisons with this book and a Crowley essay like *The Psychology of Hashish*. [1] I can assert that Crowley loses nothing in the comparison. Actually he showed depths of understanding, based on his vast experience with meditation and mystical states, that had not yet dawned on Huxley. In the early days, however, of his association with Allan Bennett, he was just beginning to learn of the possibilities of this approach.

We must return to his awakening and to the Golden Dawn.

Captain Fuller's account in *Equinox II* of Crowley's progress
through the grades of the Golden Dawn is very useful. Above
all, it provides dates. Since it must have been written under
Crowley's supervision, it must have met with Crowley's
approval to have been published in the *Equinox*. It is
therefore reliable, on that score. It provides abundant insights
into Crowley's attitudes toward these matters. Fuller
approaches this topic with enthusiastic and florid writing,
somewhat exaggerated perhaps, but very interesting. Let me
give an example of how Fuller approaches rhetorically
Crowley's first interests in the Great Work:[2]

> Deeply read in poetry, philosophy and science, gifted
> beyond the common lot, and already a poet of brilliant
> promise; he suddenly hurries from out the darkness like
> a wild prophetic star, and overturning the desks and the
> stools of the schoolmen, and casting their pedagogic
> papilla from his lips, escapes from the stuffy cloisters of
> mildewed learning, and the colleges of dialectic
> dogmatics, and seeks, what as yet he cannot find in the
> freedom which in his youthful ardour appears to him to
> live but a furlong or two beyond the spires and gables of
> that city of hidebound pedants which had been his
> school, his home, and his prison.
> Then came the great awakening. Curious to say, it
> was towards the hour of midnight on the last day of the
> year when the old slinks away from the new, that he
> happened to be riding alone, wrapped in the dark cloak
> of unutterable thoughts. A distant bell chimed the last
> quarter of the dying year, and the snow which lay fine
> and crisp on the roadway was being caught up here and
> there by the puffs of sharp frosty wind that came
> snake-like through the hedges and the trees, whirling it
> on spectre-like in the chill and silver moonlight. But
> dark were his thoughts, for the world had failed him.
> Freedom had he sought, but not the freedom that he
> had gained . . . .

The story, as I have already quoted it in part in Crowley's own words, is that at midnight on December 31st, 1896 in Stockholm, he was somehow awakened to the knowledge that he possessed a magical means of becoming conscious of and satisfying a part of himself which previously he had not been aware of. "It was an experience of horror and pain, combined with a certain ghostly terror, yet at the same time it was the key to the purest and holiest spiritual ecstasy that exists. At the time, I was not aware of the supreme importance of the matter. It seemed to me little more than a development of certain magical processes with which I was already familiar, it was an isolated experience, not repeated until exactly twelve months later, to the minute."

The second mystical experience brought him to the realization of the transient quality of everything, the Buddhist *Anicca*, impermanence.

He yearned for a more lasting medium of expression, some field of activity where accomplishment might not fade so rapidly, and where high achievement would persist for a rather longer period of time.

During this set of reflections and meditations "my animal nature stood rebuked and kept silence in the presence of the immanent divinity of the Holy Ghost; omnipotent, omniscient, and omnipresent, yet blossoming in my soul as if the entire forces of the Universe from all eternity were concentrated and made manifest in a single rose."

He was in Stockholm at the time of this mood of introspection. And as he walked, brooding, pondering over this problem, it came to him that he would have to seek his goals in an altogether different area. And so it was that he began to read in mysticism, occultism, and allied fields.

But what intrigues me about this inner prompting to find his way in the area of mysticism, is that it does not really seem to be the Vision of Universal Sorrow, as later on he came to call it. It was indeed a high perception of the transient quality of things. But it appears as if he were motivated by some ego-fulfilling need—an eccentricity which more than almost anything else has been one of the most malignant urges of his whole life.

This fact does not invalidate all that Crowley did; it does not denigrate the whole man. There was much more to Crowley than this—infinitely more. The variety, depth and multiplicity of his writing prove this. But while pleading his cause, I must not fail to recognize and name motives that appear to be present and active. It is important to be honest and fair with him and his work.

In his autobiography—which he called his autohagiography—he has likened himself to a Buddha in his role as the *Logos Aionos*, as the Word of the New Aeon. He goes so far as to call attention to some of the ancient legends that there are three signs on the physical body which are indicative of Buddhahood. Crowley, writing of himself in the third person, "was remarkable from the moment of his arrival. He bore on his body the three most important distinguishing marks of a Buddha. He was tongue-tied, and on the second day of his incarnation a surgeon cut the fraenum linguae. He had also the characteristic membrane, which necessitated an operation for phimosis some three lustres later. Lastly he had upon the centre of his heart four hairs curling from left to right in the exact form of a Swastika."

Whether he was serious or not, is difficult to determine in this particular area. He had a rich sense of humor that occasionally ran away with him. He loved to pull the legs of his devotees and the general public. This, and his vanity, gave him a lot of trouble.

However, before we dismiss this topic with levity, I should remind the reader that in Tibet, such a phenomenon as a "living Buddha" is recognized—and they have colloquial terms for it, one of them being a *tulku*. According to Madame Alexandra David Neel, in her occult travelogue *With*

Mystics and Magicians in Tibet:

> " . . . the reincarnation of the *tulkus* cannot astonish
> people who believe in a transmigrating ego. According
> to that view, we all are *tulkus*, for the *self*, now
> embodied in our present form, cannot but have existed
> previously in other forms. The only peculiarity with
> *tulkus* is that they are reincarnations of remarkable
> personalities, that they sometimes remember their
> previous lives and are able, at the time of death, to
> choose and make known the place of their next birth
> and their future parents . . . . In learned Tibetan circles,
> they are considered, for all practical purposes, as real
> reincarnations of their predecessors and the formalities
> regarding their recognition have been devised
> accordingly.
>   "Living Buddha" is a current appellation given by
> foreigners to lamas *tulkus*. Now, in spite of the many
> books on Buddhism which have been published in
> Western languages, there still remain a large number of
> Westerners who take the word Buddha for a proper
> noun: the name of the founder of Buddhism. To these
> people, the words "living Buddha" convey the idea of a
> reincarnation of Gautama the historical Buddha.
>   There is no Tibetan, even among the most ignorant
> villages of herdsmen, who entertains such a false
> view . . . .

But, as the legend goes, what finally pushed Gautama on
the Path was his satiety in the palace of his father, and the
unexpected confrontation with poverty, disease and death on
the occasion when he stole away for a few hours from the
oriental luxury of the palace. Sir Edwin Arnold describes this
dramatic situation in *The Light of Asia* in a far different way:

> " . . . The veil is rent
> Which blinded me! I am as all these men
> Who cry upon their gods and are not heard,
> Or are not heeded—yet there must be aid!

For them and me and all there must be help!
Perchance the gods have need of help themselves,
Being so feeble that when sad lips cry
They cannot save! I would not let one cry
Whom I could save! How can it be that Brahm
Would make a world and keep it miserable,
Since, if, all-powerful, he leaves it so.
He is not good, and if not powerful,
He is not God?—Channa! lead home again!
It is enough! mine eyes have seen enough!

This is quite a different story. The motives seem entirely different, or at least appear to be on the surface. But this could be the result of the poetic idealization by Sir Edwin Arnold and the long Buddhist tradition. Its origins may have been no nobler than Crowley's. Time changes a lot of concepts, raises some high, and dashes others to the ground.

Whatever the drives were that impelled Crowley towards the investigation of mysticism—a religious experience, a profound sense of personal insecurity, or emotional problems—his whole being responded to them with vigor. This was a time of tremendous inner turmoil. Someone has written that "the spiritual anguish of man has no cure but mysticism." Whoever wrote that phrase hit the nail right on the head where Crowley was concerned. He was experiencing anguish all right, and his instincts turned him in the right direction for the cure.

Once pushed nothing could stop him. He read omnivorously and studied constantly. He developed the habit of following every reference and lead in one book to wherever it might take him. A casual reference, when pursued, led in a totally different direction, to other authorities and to other texts. Consequently in a relatively short period, he had acquired more than a passing familiarity with some of the principal items of literature within this broad area. He had acquired a background well on its way to being encyclopedic. It was this intellectual equipment that he brought with him into the Golden Dawn.

In time, Crowley developed a very interesting attitude toward the initial motivating factors that impelled any student toward the Great Work. These varied from person to person and were manifold. One student would aspire because he had an inferiority complex. Another because he desired power over women, or wished to increase his sexual potency. Still another was vaguely interested in comparative religion or philosophy—or was engaged actively in breaking away from the faith in which he had been bred as a child. Regardless of the motive, any one of these students would have been accepted by Crowley without any question. That is to say, he would never overtly challenge the original motive that instigated the search.

His own motives were interesting. They were far from what some of his critics have foolishly imagined. Cupidity, greed, the need for disciples, these have been but a few of the motives attributed to him. All, in fact, are wrong.

It was his belief that once a student was actively engaged in real work, not merely speculating on an idle intellectual level, he would sooner or later obtain results. No matter how vague or slight the initial results, one enormous sequel would follow. The prime motive would undergo modification.

Crowley once said that if a man wanted to begin the study of Magic because he wished to evoke a demon to kill his enemy, that would be all right too. For the student would soon discover the hierarchical structure of the world of magic. That is to say, the demon in question could not be controlled or ordered until the student had made contact with the entity immediately superior. And this entity could only be beseeched to function in terms of *his* superior—and so on. Very shortly, then, the student would be constrained to invoke, in a direct line, the God or spiritual force ruling over all such operations. In that case he would have to unite his consciousness with that of the God. By that time, so many

transformations in consciousness would have taken place,
that the original malefic intent would have disappeared and
been replaced by other more worthy and higher aspirations.

In other words, the initial motives or goals are soon
discarded, to be replaced by nobler ones. In one of the
so-called holy books, *Liber LXV*, there is a beautiful parable
which expresses this very well:

> Behold! The Abyss of the Great Deep. Therein is a
> mighty dolphin, lashing his sides with the force of the
> waves.
> There is also an harper of gold, playing infinite tunes.
> Then the dolphin delighted therein, and put off his
> body, and became a bird.
> The harper also laid aside his harp, and played infinite
> tunes upon the Pan-pipe.
> Then the bird desired exceedingly this bliss, and
> laying down its wings became a faun of the forest.
> The harper also laid down his Pan-pipe and with the
> human voice sang his infinite tunes.
> Then the faun was enraptured, and followed far; at
> last the harper was silent, and the faun became Pan in
> the midst of the primal forest of Eternity.
> Thou canst not charm the dolphin with silence, O my
> prophet.

There is yet another important reference to the ideals and
goals that draw one to the Great Work, in a chapter entitled
Pilgrim-Talk in *The Book of Lies:*

> O thou that settest out upon The Path, false is the
> Phantom that thou seekest. When thou hast it thou shalt
> know all bitterness, thy teeth fixed in the Sodom-Apple.
> Thus hast thou been lured along That Path, whose
> terror else had driven thee far away.
> O thou that strideth upon the middle of The Path, no
> phantoms mock thee. For the stride's sake thou stridest.
> Thus art thou lured along That Path, whose
> fascination else had driven thee far away.

O thou that drawest toward the End of The Path, effort is no more. Faster and faster dost thou fall, thy weariness is changed in Ineffable Rest.

For there is no Thou upon That Path; thou hast become The Way.

Thus he came into the Order to receive the Neophyte degree. Not much has been written on ritual by psychologists to provide illumination for the layman. There are technical books, but these are mostly for the professionals in psychology, anthropology and sociology. About the only one who had something of value to contribute in this sphere was Jung who, in *The Secret of the Golden Flower*, explained that "magical practices are the projections of psychic events which, in cases like these, exert a counter-influence on the soul, and act like a kind of enchantment of one's own personality. That is to say, by means of these concrete performances, the attention or better said the interest is brought back to an inner sacred domain which is the source and goal of the soul. This inner domain contains the unity of life and consciousness which, though once possessed, has been lost and must now be found again."

Some writers on psychedelic drugs are the only others who throw any light today on the nature of mystical experience. For example, Harman in *Main Currents*, previously mentioned, wrote: "Use of the psychedelic agents offers some confirmation of the testimony of mystics that there are dimensions of human experience which lie beyond ordinary consciousness, yet which can be consciously tapped."

And in another part of this essay we read: "The action of the consciousness-expanding drugs gives the person access to hitherto inaccessible psychic material, facilitates thinking and feeling in unfamiliar ways, allows perception of himself and the world about him in an unhabitual manner, and makes it possible for him to re-examine his basic beliefs and values in the light of such new data."

Although the Golden Dawn never recommended the use of any such consciousness-expanding drugs—this was Crowley's contribution based upon his personal experiences with Allan Bennett—nevertheless the above would amount to a fair statement of its beliefs. It would modify the above statement only to the extent of substituting the phrase "the action of the consciousness-expanding drugs" with the more acceptable notion of "the action of traditional magical routines." And though these latter might be objected to by conventional institutions as being "artificial aids to spirituality or enlightenment" this could equally be argued of liturgy, religious symbol, meditational techniques, fasting, or asceticism.

NOTES

[1] See my book *Roll Away the Stone* (Llewellyn Publications, St. Paul, 1968) which reprints Crowley's essays and reviews the use of drugs and other psychedelic agents in the mystical experience.

[2] *Equinox*, Vol. I, No. II, p. 233.

[3] *Magic and Mystery in Tibet*, A. David-Neel, University Books, New York, p. 115.

CHAPTER SIX

Initiation

On that fateful night in the middle of November, 1898, this twenty-three year old poet found himself clothed in a black gown, shod in red slippers, hoodwinked—a narrow mask over his eyes—and bound thrice around his waist with a white cord. From the ante-chamber in a house in Great Queen Street, he was ushered past the sentinel into the large room which served as a Temple by an officer known as the Hegemon whose "office symbolizes those higher aspirations of the soul which should guide its action." As he passed through the doorway, blind-folded, it is not difficult to imagine his anxiety, suspense and anticipation.

He must have been thoroughly keyed up. Was this not the fulfillment of all his dreams? Was he really being inducted into the august presence of those sublime beings of whom von Eckhartshausen had written? It was almost too good to be true that within a few months after having read the book, as Waite had recommended, he was entering into that sacred school. But it *was* true.

As he groped through the darkness, he heard a voice slowly intone: "I give permission to admit Aleister Crowley who now loses his name and will henceforth be known among us as Perdurabo." It was the Hierophant who gave this permission, an officer standing on the dais, whose station "is on the Throne of the East in the place where the Sun rises, and I am the Master of the Hall, governing it according to the

Laws of the Order, as He whose Image I am, is the Master of all who work for the Hidden Knowledge."

Even for the cynical and hardboiled, it is a moving experience. I personally approached this after many years of study. There was always the hope I might be able to undergo an initiatory experience of this kind. True, in fantasy one tends to over-evaluate this beforehand so that perhaps one comes to expect too much from it. Even so, it becomes an emotional experience heightened by anticipation, passion, aspiration to the highest, the noblest ideals.

It must have been so with Crowley, for he was a passionate and vigorous young man capable of the highest ideals and the most lofty aspiration. What must he have felt when, after having passed well within the portals of the chamber, he heard a sonorous voice calling, "Inheritor of a Dying World, arise and enter the Darkness. The Mother of Darkness hath blinded him with her Hair. The Father of Darkness hath hidden him under His Wings. His limbs are still weary from the wars which were in Heaven." Being a poet and a Biblical student, he could respond to fine language with an inner thrill.

There was something in the air too. It was contributed by something other than the words of the ceremony, however elevating and ennobling they might be. In one of the expository documents of the Golden Dawn, Mathers addressed each participating officer in these words:

> Thus should he act. Let him remember what particular God he represents. Exalting his mind unto the contemplation thereof, let him think of himself as a vast figure, standing or moving in the likeness of that God, colossal, his head lost in the clouds, with the light flashing round it from the head-dress of the God—his feet resting upon the Earth in darkness, thunder and rolling clouds, and his form wrapped in flashes of lightning—the while vibrating the Name of the God.

> Thus standing, let him endeavour to hear the voice of
> the God whom he represents and of the God-forms of
> the other officers as previously explained.
>
> Let him speak, then, not as if unto an assembly of
> mortals but as to an assembly of Gods. Let his voice be
> so directed as to roll through the Universe to the utmost
> confines of space. Let the Candidate represent unto
> him, as it were, a world whom he is beginning to lead
> unto the knowledge of its governing Angel. As it is
> written "The lightning lighteneth out of the East and
> shineth even unto the West, even so, shall the coming of
> the Son of Man be."

Crowley was purified with water and, within the
undulating waves of incense-laden air, was consecrated with
fire—twice, a third time, and a fourth. He was paraded
around the Temple, halted with peremptory challenges, and
given a momentary glimpse, when the hood-wink was raised
for a fraction of a second, of brightly gowned figures with
cowls and sceptres, swords and banners, intoning memorable
passages. "Light dawning in Darkness is thy Name, the Light
of a Golden Day." There were prayers such as "Look Thou
with favour on this Neophyte who now standeth before
Thee, and grant Thine aid unto the highest aspirations of his
soul."

In this dramatic atmosphere, it is not impossible for a
powerful inner experience to occur. The setting is right, and
if the candidate has been sufficiently prepared by life and
living that the awakening is due, there can be the sudden
flash of light which is the harbinger of wonderful things to
come. I am reminded of a remarkable passage in a little book
by Mabel Collins:[1]

> Look for the flower to bloom in the silence that
> follows the storm; not till then.
> It shall grow, it will shoot up, it will make branches
> and leaves and form buds, while the storm continues,
> while the battle lasts. But not till the whole personality

of the man is dissolved and melted—not until it is held by the divine fragment which has created it, as a mere subject for grave experiment and experience—not until the whole nature has yielded and become subject unto its higher Self, can the bloom open. Then will come a calm such as comes in a tropical country after the heavy rain, when Nature works so swiftly that one may see her action. And in the deep silence the mysterious event will occur which will prove that the way has been found. Call it by what name you will, it is a voice that speaks where there is none to speak—it is a messenger that comes, a messenger without form or substance; or it is the flower of the soul that has opened.

When Symonds tries to deal with this type of possibility, his own contempt exudes—probably self-contempt more than anything else—which makes him incapable of dealing with the Crowley story honestly. From the first page of his book to the last, he wrote in a half-mocking mood, and whether he was aware of it or not, this meant that he was hardly objective and capable of dealing with obvious facts. His narrative was colored by whatever his own frustrating life experiences were.

For example, Symonds wrote: "In spite of its high sounding title, the Golden Dawn met in uninspiring back rooms in Chelsea and the central area of London." Where else could they have met? Would Symonds have had them conduct their ceremonies in Westminster Abbey? Personally I think that might have been rather wonderful—and moving. But where for the love of God, where else?

"Those who could, paid their few shillings contribution for stationery, rent, and out-of-pocket expenses." That is one indication that it was not organized to exploit people like some fraternal organizations that Symonds could name. It functioned somewhat on a humanitarian level—though it could well be criticized for not demanding a decent fee or dues for its offices. And I should remind Symonds that in the first century of this era, the newly converted Christians met in dark caves and catacombs, and dingy little buildings, far less impressive than a backroom in Chelsea.

"Crowley described his first meeting with the members of the Order, among whom were Arthur Machen, the writer, and Florence Farr, the actress, as a bit of a shock—they were such an assemblage of non-entities." Here Symonds is aping or merely repeating Crowley's own contemptuous attitudes. Arthur Machen, William B. Yeats, Brodie-Innes, Algernon Blackwood and others of this type are not exactly non-entities. Crowley may not have admired them—any more than they him—but they were people who were actively engaged in the business of living and earning well-deserved literary reputations. His own egotism must have been so vast that unless his genius were instantaneously recognized and eulogized, his response was likely to be derogatory.

So in this Temple in the backstreets of Chelsea, where he received his Neophyte degree, he was being moved in strange and subtle ways. Unconscious archetypes, to be Jungian, were being activated by the ceremony and every bit of him was in an uproar. For the Hierophant coming down from the dais in the East, while holding the banner and a sceptre, declaimed, as Crowley's hoodwink was being removed:

"Inheritor of a Dying World, we call thee to the Living Beauty. Wanderer in the Wild Darkness, we call thee to the Gentle Light. Long hast thou dwelt in Darkness. Quit the night and seek the day."[2]

It might not be the kind of language that Symonds cares for particularly, but it is far better prose than he has ever written.

Apart from the dramatic acceptance of the oath and obligation of the Order this is the crowning moment of the ceremony. One is moved in ways that one hardly understands. Too much is going on—within as well as without.

The Kerux, a kind of sentinel, personifies the reasoning faculties. He is the officer who leads the candidate accompanied by the Hegemon to the various stations in the Temple. He is the intelligent part of the mind, functioning in obedience to the Will; the Qabalistic *Ruach*. This role was occupied on that fateful night by George Cecil Jones. And in that role, he was pointed to by the Hierophant who addressed Crowley: "In all thy wanderings in darkness, the Lamp of the Kerux went before thee, though it was not seen by thine eyes. It is the symbol of the Light of the Hidden Knowledge."

The higher part of the mind, the aspiring, sensitive and intuitive consciousness, the *Neschamah*, is represented by the Hegemon who ever seeks the rising of the Light, while the active conscious will of man is signified by the Hiereus, the guardian against evil. The Hierophant, in this initial ceremony of Neophyte, acts on behalf of the higher spiritual Self, that divine Self which too rarely, if ever at all, we become aware of. It is the essential state of enlightenment, this interior Self, Osiris glorified through trial and perfected by suffering, which is represented by the Hierophant on the dais. He is ordinarily seated on the throne of the East in the place of the rising Sun, and with but two or three exceptions never moves from that abode in the Temple.

As the Order system teaches, the everlasting abode of the higher Self is in that supernal sanctuary of the Tree of Life, above the abyss, the higher sanctuary which is ever guarded from chaos by the flaming sword whirling every way on the borders of the Abyss. From that high spiritual stronghold it gazes down upon man, evolved for the object of providing it with experience—involved in neither its struggle nor its tribulations, yet, from another paradoxical point of view, suffering acutely thereby. And seldom does that Genius leave its palace of the stars except when, voluntarily, the lower self opens itself to the higher by an act of sincerest aspiration or self-sacrifice. Only then is the descent of the Light within the heart and mind made possible.

Thus when the Hierophant leaves the throne of the East, he represents that Higher Self in action, and as Osiris he marks the active descent of the supernal splendor; for he utters, while leaving the dais with wand uplifted, "I come in the Power of the Light. I come in the Light of Wisdom. I come in the Mercy of the Light. The Light hath healing in its wings."

And having brought the Light to the aspirant, he then returns to his throne on the dais, as though that divine Genius of whom he is the Temple symbol and agent awaited the deliberate willed return of the aspirant himself to the everlasting abode of the Light.

In one of the commentaries to this ceremony, Mathers observed that "The higher Self remains in the station of Harpocrates, and at this point, the spirit-vision should see a gleaming white triangle formulated over the Candidate's head . . . . As he passes the Hierophant's throne the red Calvary Cross is astrally formed above the astral White Triangle on his forehead, so that so long as he belongs to the Order, he may bear that potent and sublime symbol as a link with his Higher Self and as an aid in searching out the forces of the Divine Light—if he will." These are the symbols of the Golden Dawn, the cross above equilibrating the white triangle below.

In the A.A., the reformulation of the Order that Crowley engineered in the year 1909, the symbol of the Third Order, the Silver Star with the eye therein (the symbol of spiritual discernment and Samadhi), was formulated astrally on the forehead of its initiates. The theory is that initiation puts its stamp for ever on each candidate. Were one sufficiently clairvoyant he would be able to perceive that particular symbol glowing in the field of that candidate.

It may have distressed Crowley to have such an elevating

episode in his initiatory ritual followed by the usual bourgeois clap-trap of secret societies, the signs and grips, and so forth. But years later, when he was in a position to reconstruct rituals of initiation for the Order of Templars of the Orient, he also included such trivia. For he came to realize, as did those who had written the Neophyte ritual of the Golden Dawn, that these too have their place, and all are explained in terms of the quest for Light.

The various groupings of officers and their ritual movements are not haphazard meanderings but are given a good deal of significance. At the altar, for example, the three principal officers form about the candidate a Triad, representing again the supernal Light of the higher Self, and these are represented by the same number of circumambulations. The white cord bound thrice about the waist has reference to a similar set of ideas, the binding of the lower by the higher. Even the symbols on the altar are indicative of the rise of the Light—they are the cross and triangle already mentioned. Despite the fact that the whole of this intricate symbolism can hardly be realized by the candidate at the time of his initiation, its intrinsic virtue as a body of suggestion is such that unconsciously it is perceived to function as a catalytic agent.

From one point of view, the officers employed in these Rituals represent the psychic projections Jung refers to in *The Secret of the Golden Flower*. They represent, even as figures in dreams do, the different aspects of man himself, personifications of abstract psychological principles inhering within the human organism. Through the admittedly artificial or conventional means of a dramatic projection of these spiritual principles in a well-ordered ceremony, a reaction is induced in consciousness. This reaction is the awakening from a dormant condition of those hitherto latent faculties represented objectively by the officers. It can be called suggestion, substituting one obscurity for another. The magical philosophy would not object to the notion that suggestion only stimulates or awakens, in this instance, what is already present or in a state of latency.

Without the least conscious effort on the part of the aspirant, an involuntary current of sympathy is produced by this dramatic delineation of psychic events which may be sufficient to accomplish the intrinsic purpose of the ceremony or ritual. The aesthetic appeal to the imagination of the candidate—quite apart from what could be called the inner working of the trained officiants—stirs to renewed activity the life of the inner domain. And the entire action of this type of dramatic initiatory ritual is that the soul may discover itself whirled in exaltation to the heights, and during that mystical elevation receive the rushing forth or the descent of the Light. This latter was expressed within the Order as Konx Om Pax.

A great deal depends on the status or readiness of the Candidate. If he is otherwise prepared by inner growth, by the maturity that is exacted by life itself, if he has been endowed by right of birth with the appropriate sensitivity and artistic imagination, then the initiation may provide the spur to a series of internal changes that can result in illumination. And this, after all, is the final goal of mysticism and the initiatory system of the Golden Dawn.

In this preliminary ritual which actually foreshadows all other formulae and magical processes, Crowley heard for the first time that phrase which was to play such a vital part in all his later thinking. "There are two contending forces and one always uniting them." And again: "Unbalanced power is the ebbing away of Life. Unbalanced Mercy is weakness and the fading out of the Will. Unbalanced Severity is cruelty and the barrenness of Mind." This philosophical dialectic became an intrinsic part of his final philosophy. It was supported and supplemented by visionary experiences, but the essence of it is the same. In 1909, when he was obtaining the visions of the Thirty Aethyrs of the Enochian system, he was told: "All the symbols are interchangeable, for each one containeth in itself its own opposite. And this is the great Mystery of the Supernals that are beyond the Abyss, for below the Abyss, contradiction is Unity. And there could be nothing true except by virtue of the contradiction that is contained in itself."

Norman Brown in his book *Life Against Death*, wrote eloquently that psychoanalysis, mysticism, poetry, the philosophy of organism, etc., are a miscellaneous concoction. However, common to all is a mode of consciousness that can be called dialectical, thus an activity of consciousness struggling to circumvent the limitations imposed by the formal-logical law of contradiction. Acceptance of the substantial identity of poetic logic and dream logic completes the connection between poetry and dialectic.

With the great initiation over, he experienced one of his first and greatest disappointments with the Order. If he had not been so furious he might have been plunged into the depths of despair, as only a poet can. He fully expected to be made the recipient of great truths and deep mysteries that had never before been revealed to the profane. All the books he had thus far read had indicated there was something beyond, had hinted at dark possibilities and high promises that could be opened to him if all went right.

Instead, he was told that before he could be advanced to the next grade, he would be given an examination on certain material which would be furnished him, and which he should study. This was not at all unreasonable, but to his chagrin and consternation, instead of unspeakable mysteries, he was handed the Hebrew alphabet and a few Hebrew words from the Qabalah.

What a let-down! He had been familiar with these prosaic facts for a long while. There was nothing new—or secret—about any of this. Anyone could run across these items of information, and a great deal more, in books readily available to any student, altogether apart from initiates of the Order. He raved and ranted angrily. Both Jones and Baker tried to reason with him, explaining that as time went on, and as he proved himself, he would be given more advanced material. What he had received was routine data that was automatically given to the newly received and initiated neophyte. When he had proven himself capable to the authorities, then would be the time to receive other kinds of data. This undoubtedly relaxed him somewhat, for he went on studying, furiously as was his habit. In those days his energies were high, nigh on inexhaustible. There is no question at all as to the fact that whatever he did, he did it with intensity. He could not do anything in a half-hearted way. His whole soul was thrown compulsively and whole-heartedly into it. In a month, he must have taken the examination, passed successfully, and so was permitted to take the next grade in December 1898.

The five grades that follow hard upon the Neophyte ceremony to which he had just been admitted are of an entirely different order. The basic theme of the Neophyte ritual is being "brought to the Light." In other words its thesis is illumination, the mystical experience. Right at the start of his career in the Golden Dawn, this was the message vouchsafed to him. Later rituals re-affirmed it.

In between, however, were the elemental grades relating to Earth, Air, Water and Fire. Their object is the awakening of the unconscious archetypes, the elemental bases of what must develop into the instrument of the higher. Awakened, and integrated into the circle of the Self, they are to be consecrated to the Great Work that they may become worthy vehicles for the indwelling of the Light. First, however, it was necessary that they be awakened. For until¹ their presence is divined, their transmutation cannot be accomplished. In symbolic form and pageantry, the ceremony of each grade calls forth the "beings" or forces that comprise that particular element. And as a steel placed in close proximity to a magnet receives some degree of its magnetism, and comparable to the electrical phenomenon of induction, so the presence of power induces power. Contact with the appropriate type of elemental force produces an identical type of reaction within the bio-psychological sphere of the Candidate. It is thus that growth and advancement proceeds.

Speeches of the several officers deal almost exclusively with knowledge pertaining to that grade and element. Excerpts from some Qabalistic texts and ritual fragments of the ancient Mysteries do much towards producing an impressive atmosphere.

The element offered for the work of transmutation in the Grade of Zelator, 1=10, is the earthy part of the Candidate. The ritual symbolically admits him to the first rung of the mighty ladder whose heights are lost in the Light above. The first rung is the lowest sphere of the conventional Tree of Life of the Qabalah—*Malkuth*, the Sanctum Regnum. To it is ascribed the first grade and the element of Earth.

So it was that as Crowley was ushered into the Temple, again blindfolded, again keyed up with anticipation, he heard ominously: "Except Adonai build the house, their labor is but lost that build it. Except Adonai keep the City, the Watchman waketh in vain ... " It is this that stamps the ritual throughout.

Furthermore, he was exhorted "Prepare to enter the Immeasurable region." And so he did. He was ceremonially conducted, as symbolical of this entry into those higher regions of the mind—to three stations, the first two being those of Evil and the divine Presence. At each of these stations, the Guardians rejected his progress at the point of a sword. Strongly, they urged him in his unprepared state to return whence he came. There was a great deal to be done before he could progress. His third attempt to go forward placed him in a balanced position, the path of equilibrium, the Middle Way, where he was received. And a way was cleared for him by the Hierophant, who again represented the celestial Soul of things. He then uttered a beautiful and moving speech:

> Tetragrammation placed Kerubim at the East of the Garden of Eden and a Flaming Sword which turned every way to keep the Path of the Tree of Life, for He has created Nature that Man being cast out of Eden may not fall into the Void. He has bound Man with the Stars as with a chain. He allures him with Scattered Fragments of the Divine Body in bird and beast and flower, and He laments over him in the Wind and in the Sea and in the birds. When the times are ended, He will call the Kerubim from the East of the Garden and all shall be consumed and become Infinite and Holy.

During this journey to the different stations in the Temple, the stability of Earth was established within him, that eventually it might prove an enduring temple of the holy spirit.

Virginia Moore has a very fine paragaph in this connection:[3]

> " . . . all (the elemental rituals) use symbolism from Egypt, Palestine, and Greece; all quote the ancient Mysteries, as well as the Old and the New Testament; all underscore the necessity of balancing the opposites of an essentially dualistic world; all speak of demons as the "reversals" of angels, and as examples of that evil, which, as imbalance, is ultimately redeemable; all rest heavily on the Cabala, stressing its great central image of the Tree of Life as formed by the Ten Sephiroth—the Tree up which crawls the Serpent of Nature connecting but not touching the Sephiroth, and down which, through the Sephiroth, shoots the lightning of the Spirit; all "deal" with the twenty two trumps of the Tarot, as symbolizing the twenty two "paths" on that

Tree; all cite the various forms of the Cross—Fylfot, Calvary, Greek, Tau, Qabalistic, Ansata, and Rosicrucian; all make use of the four Kerubim, four cardinal points, four elements, and four Enochian Tablets with their "angelic language"; all summon to a high standard of conduct; all see the Trinity as not only Father, Mother, and "child", that is Kether, Binah and Chokmah, but also as the archetypal idea—"the threefold creative idea operating in all things"; all praise God magnificently, using His "Secret Names"; all speak of men as potential gods, meaning something higher than human or "matter-bound", though far beneath God their Maker; all say that becoming consciously "gods" constitutes the Great Work; and all cry with a loud cry "Quit the material and seek the Spiritual."

All of this material provided a central pivot around which the young initiate Crowley could organize the vast mass of comparative religious and mythological material he was now collecting. The pivot was the Tree of Life of the Qabalah, with its ten Sephiroth and twenty-two connecting paths. Some years after this, when his thinking had crystallized, he was able to formulate the notion that these items of the Tree could be likened to a filing cabinet with ten main jackets. In these jackets could be classified different kinds of knowledge, unified on the basis of a common basic numerical scheme.

The Book 777 has for its primary object the construction of a magical alphabet.

One of the greatest difficulties experienced by the student—a difficulty which increases rather than diminishes with his advance in knowledge—is this: he finds it impossible to gain any clear idea of the meanings of the terms which he employs . . . . Let us suppose for a moment that by some miracle we obtain a clear idea of the meaning of the word. The trouble has merely begun, for there immediately arises the question of the relations of one term to the others . . . .

The system of the Qabalah . . . is perfectly sound. We

can easily discard the dogmatic interpretations of the Rabbins. We can refer everything in the Universe to the system of pure number whose symbols will be intelligible to all rational minds in an identical sense. And the relations between these symbols are fixed by Nature . . . .

Such are the nature of the considerations that led me to adopt the Tree of Life as the basis of the magical alphabet. The 10 numbers and the 22 letters of the Hebrew Alphabet, with their traditional and rational correspondences (taking into consideration their numerical and geometrical interrelations), afford us a coherent systematic groundwork sufficiently rigid for our foundation and sufficiently elastic for our superstructure.

Fine! But to what end, all of this?

Glorious, glorious, glorious art Thou, O my lover supernal, O Self of myself.

For I have found Thee alike in the Me and the Thee; there is no difference, O my beautiful, my desirable one! In the One and the Many have I found Thee; yea, I have found Thee.

The Zelator initiation conferred upon him an honorific title *Pereclinas de Faustis*, Wanderer in the Wilderness, and taught him the prayer of the Earth spirits:

O Invisible King, Who, taking the Earth for Foundation, didst hollow its depths to fill them with Thy Almighty Power. Thou whose Name shaketh the Arches of the World, Thou who causest the seven metals to flow in the veins of the rocks, King of the seven lights, Rewarder of the subterranean workers, lead us into the desirable Air and into the Realm of Splendour.

We watch and we labour unceasingly, we seek and we hope, by the twelve stones of the Holy City, by the buried Talismans, by the Axis of the Lodestone which passes through the centre of the Earth—O Lord, O Lord,

O Lord! Have pity upon those who suffer. Expand our hearts, unbind and upraise our minds, enlarge our natures . . . .

Thou Who hidest beneath the Earth in the Kingdom of Gems, the marvellous Seed of the Stars! Live, reign, and be Thou the Eternal Dispenser of the Treasures whereof Thou hast made us the Wardens.

Before he took the next grade of 2=9, in January 1899, there was a month in which to study the usual knowledge lectures. These I have reproduced in their entirety in the first volume of *The Golden Dawn*. They are not very inspiring, mostly didactic and traditional material to commit to memory. There was little, again, to which he had not already been exposed. Some alchemical information was given, not of great consequence, mostly Qabalistic interpretations of archaic symbols; meaningful in a study of some primitive texts, but boring if you have already worked out some significance to them. Additionally, there was some basic material about the seventy-eight Tarot cards and their attribution to the Tree of Life. To this material, he became very attached at once, perhaps because by this time he was studying *sub rosa* with Allan Bennett and had learned some of the more profound usages of the system.

One of the very last books he published before he died, nearly a half a century later, was *The Tarot of the Egyptians*. It demonstrated little of his old sparkle. The fires were indeed dying down. But—apart from the splendid art work of Lady Frieda Harris who has managed to catch the magnificent spirit of his interpretations of the cards with clarity and beauty—the whole book is predicated on this basic Tarot information bequeathed him from the Golden Dawn. It had been digested, assimilated, incorporated into his very being, illuminated by his own vast spiritual experience, integrated with everything else that he had acquired in the meantime. It had thus been transformed in a manner that neither he, nor his Golden Dawn teachers, could have foreseen at the time he was taken through these grades towards the close of the nineteenth century.

I am fond of his penetrating essay on the relations existing between the student and the cards themselves, found in the above-named book. He wrote:[4]

> It now being established, at the conclusion of the essay, that the cards of the Tarot are living individuals, it is proper to consider the relations which obtain between them and the student.
>
> Consider the analogy of a debutante at her coming-out ball. She is introduced to seventy-eight grown people. Assuming her to be a particularly intelligent girl, with a very high social education, she may know all about the position and general characteristics of these people. This, however, will not imply real knowledge of any one of them; she will have no means of saying how any one will react to her. At most, she can know only a few facts from which deductions may be made.
>
> The position of the student of the Tarot is very similar. In this essay, and in these designs, is given an analysis of the general character of each card; but he cannot reach any true appreciation of them without observing their behavior over a long period; he can only come to an understanding of the Tarot through experience. It will not be sufficient for him to intensify his studies of the cards as objective things; he must use them; he must live with them. They, too, must live with him. A card is not isolated from its fellow. The reactions of the cards, their interplay with each other, must be built into the very life of the student.

The grade after the Earth ceremony is called Theoricus, 2=9, and is referred to the ninth Sephirah on the Tree of Life, *Yesod*, the Foundation. To it are attibuted the sphere of the operation of Luna and the element Air. Crowley found it had an altogether different atmosphere and feeling from the earlier Earth ritual. Here again he was conducted to various stations around the Temple, after first having sworn to maintain secrecy as before, with the "Powers of Air" witnessing his solemn pledge. Here the robed guardians of the quarters wore symbolic masks, forcing him to halt here and there to learn basic formulae.

> The Priest with the Mask of Osiris spake and said: "Thou canst not pass the Gate of the Eastern Heaven unless thou canst tell me my Name." Thou art Nu, Goddess of the Firmament of Air. Thou art Hormaku, Lord of the Eastern Sun.

And so on, from station to station, from mask to mask, from symbol to symbol. These names and ideas never left him. During the year 1904, when *The Book of the Law* came to be written down, Nu is described in beautiful devotional terms that must have carried a great deal of unconscious meaning for him. Symonds, I think it was, made the statement that in Crowley's system Nu or Nuit corresponds in a general way to the Virgin Mary of the Roman Catholic Church. There might be some validity to this, for he was able to get involved emotionally and spiritually with this concept as with almost nothing else:

> Now, therefore, I am known to ye by my name Nuit . . . . Since I am Infinite Space, and the Infinite Stars thereof, do ye also thus . . . . Then the priest answered and said unto the Queen of Space, kissing her lovely brows, and the dew of her light bathing his whole body in a sweet-smelling perfume of sweat: O Nuit, continuous one of Heaven, let it be ever thus; that men speak not of Thee as One but as None; and let them speak not of thee at all, since thou art continuous!

In this Theoricus ritual, he was given the honorific title of *Paroais de Rejectis*, brought from among the Rejected, which carries with it an extensive mythology relating to the cornerstone which the builders rejected. Furthermore, he heard another of the important exhortations that are present in one or the other of the Order rituals:

> The Fan, Lamp, Cup and Salt represent the four elements themselves whose inhabitants are the Sylphs, Salamanders, Undines, and Gnomes. Be thou, therefore, prompt and active as the Sylphs, but avoid frivolity and caprice. Be energetic and strong as the Salamanders, but avoid irritability and ferocity. Be flexible and attentive to images, like the Undines, but avoid idleness and changeability; be laborious and patient like the Gnomes, but avoid grossness and avarice. So shalt thou gradually develop the powers of thy soul.

Too bad he did not take this counsel more to heart!

The peroration of the ritual is the Prayer of the Sylphs which, in part, I give here since it contains some beautiful verbal imagery:

> Spirit of Life! Spirit of Wisdom! Whose breath giveth forth and withdraweth the form of all things: Thou, before Whom the life of being is but a shadow which changeth, and a vapour which passeth: Thou, Who mountest upon the clouds, and Who walkest upon the Wings of the Wind. Thou, who breathest forth Thy Breath, and endless space is peopled: Thou, Who drawest in Thy breath, and all that cometh from Thee, returneth unto Thee! Ceaseless Motion, in Eternal Stability, be Thou eternally blessed! . . . .
> Let the Ray of Thy Intelligence and the Warmth of Thy love penetrate even unto us! Then that which is volatile shall be fixed; the shadow shall be a body; the spirit of Air shall be a Soul; the Dream shall be a thought. And no more shall we be swept away by the Tempest, but we shall hold the Bridles of the Winged Steeds of Dawn. And we shall direct the course of the Evening Breeze to fly before Thee!

Once more the new knowledge lectures proved no insuperable problem, for he sailed through them without the slightest difficulty, and so was ready for the next grade. In February of that same year, 1899, he was taken through the next grade, that of Practicus, 3=8, attributed to the element Water, and the planet Mercury. The greater part of this ritual seemed obscure to him at first, consisting as it did of quotations from *The Chaldean Oracles*—turgid, ponderous, but sonorous and employing titles from the Samothracian mysteries, like Axieros the first Kabir, Axiokersos the second Kabir, and Kasmillos the Candidate.

Moreover, in this grade, he was introduced to the first of two diagrams, the second being exhibited in the following grade of 4=7, which summarized most of the Golden Dawn philosophy. The honorific title of *Monoceris de Astris* the Unicorn from the Stars, was given him, and in a paper supplementary to the usual knowledge lectures, he was informed:

> Learn first, O Practicus of our ancient Order, that True Equilibrium is the basis of the Soul. If thou thyself hast not a sure foundation, whereon wilt thou stand to direct the forces of Nature?

Some have thought it too bad this did not affect him more. It might have saved him a lot of the excesses of his later life, and it could have shown him that perhaps exhibitionism and equilibrium are poles apart.

However, there is an extenuating circumstance which should be mentioned. Though he concealed it passionately, as though it were a mask of shame, he had been a very shy and timid boy. Grown to adulthood, his neurotic characteristics appeared, superficially, to have been eliminated. I am far from sure that they were. As part of his attempt to achieve some kind of equilibrium, he may have overcompensated and developed some aggressive, devil-may-care attitudes, and the overt exhibitionism I have spoken of. Perhaps this was his interpretation of equilibrium. If so, it caused him a lot of trouble.

At the close of this Practicus ritual, he heard the usual peroration, this time the prayer of the Undines:

> Terrible King of the Sea, Thou who holdest the keys of the cataracts of Heaven, and who enclosest the subterranean Waters in the cavernous hollows of Earth. King of the deluge and of the Rains of Spring. Thou who openest the sources of the rivers and of the fountains; Thou who commandest moisture which is, as it were, the Blood of the Earth, to become the sap of the plants, we adore Thee and we invoke Thee . . . .
> Lead us into the true life, through intelligence, through love! Lead us into immortality through sacrifice, that one day we may be found worthy to offer unto Thee, the Water, the Blood and the Tears, for the Remission of Sins! Amen.

Briefly, the powerful symbolism of this grade was summarized for him by the position on the altar of the principal Order emblems so arranged that "the cross" was placed "above the triangle of the waters." This also indicated the immediate task ahead of the candidate.

The diagrams, as I have indicated, take on a peculiar meaning, and though their theme apparently is Biblical in nature, accompanied by explanations in a curious phraseology consonant therewith, they are nevertheless highly suggestive. They contain the rudiments of a profound psychology.

The diagram called *The Garden of Eden* depicted a personified representation of the three fundamental principles in man. Each of these is apparently separate, functioning independently on its own plane without cooperation with either the higher or lower. Principally, it represented man in the now departed morning of the race, in the primary rounds of evolutionary effort when self-consciousness had not yet been awakened and when peace and harmony prevailed both within and without by right of heritage rather than through the price of personal labor. The diagram appeared in the Water grade of Practicus, since Water is a fitting symbol of this placid peace. At the summit of the diagram stands the Apocalyptic woman clothed with the Sun of glory, crowned with the twelve stars, and the moon lying at her feet. Her symbolism pertains to the supernal essence of mind, representing thus the type and symbol of the glittering Augoeides, the *Neschamah*. "It is," remarks Jung, describing an analogous conception in *The Secret of the Golden Flower*, "a line or principle of life that strives after super-human, shining heights."

Now compare this interpretation with the actual dynamic experience that Crowley achieved around 1909, when, with Victor Neuburg as his companion, he walked through North Africa, obtaining the psycho-spiritual material which later became incorporated in his book *The Vision and the Voice:*

> We are come unto a palace of which every stone is a separate jewel, and is set with millions of moons.
> And this palace is nothing but the body of a woman, proud and delicate, and beyond imagination fair. She is like a child of twelve years old. She has very deep eyelids, and long lashes. Her eyes are closed, or nearly closed. It is impossible to say anything about her. She is naked; her whole body is covered with fine gold hairs, that are the electric flames which are the spears of mighty and terrible Angels whose breast plates are the scales of her skin. And the hair of her head, that flows down to her feet, is the very light of God himself .... The Seer is lost in wonder, which is Peace ....
> This is the Daughter of the King. This is the Virgin of Eternity. This is She that the Holy One hath wrested from the Giant Time, and the prize of them that have overcome Space. This is She that is set upon the Throne

of Understanding. Holy, Holy, Holy is her name, not to be spoken among men. For Kore have they called her, and Malkah, and Betulah, and Persephone .... This is She that hath bedecked her hair with seven stars, the seven breaths of God that move and thrill its excellence. And she hath tied her hair with seven combs, whereupon are written the seven secret names of God that are not known even of the Angels, or of the Archangels, or of the Leader of the Armies of the Lord.

Holy, Holy, Holy art thou, and blessed be thy name for ever, unto whom the Aeons are but the pulsings of thy blood ....

At the base of the tree, in the diagram, stands Eve, the Nephesch, who, in opposition to the divine Feminine, stands for the "dark, earth-born, feminine principle with its emotionality and instinctiveness reaching far back into the depths of time, and into the roots of physiological continuity," says Jung. But here is Crowley's subsequent interpretation of her:

> Let not the Magician forget for a single second what is his one sole business. His uninitiated "self" (as he absurdly thinks it) is a mob of wild women, hysterical from uncomprehended and unsated animal instinct; they will tear Pentheus, the merely human king who presumes to repress them, into mere shreds of flesh; his own Mother, Nature, the first to claw at his windpipe! None but Bacchus, the Holy Guardian Angel, hath grace to be God to this riot of maniacs; he alone can transform the disorderly rabble into a pageant of harmonious movements, tune their hyaena howls to the symphony of a paean, and their reasonless rage to self-controlled rapture ....

Between the two female figures stands Adam, supported by the fundamental strength of Eve, the *Ruach* or Ego not yet awakened to a realization of its almost infinite power and potentiality. From the larger point of view, he represents mankind as a whole, unawakened, still struggling to achieve mental and spiritual freedom—man, the sleeping giant. In the personal sense, he represents the individual candidate on the Path, just prior to the awakening of the "sleeping dogs" within his being.

Beneath these three figures sleeps a coiled many-headed dragon, silent, unawakened, still. None is aware of that latent power, titanic and promethean, coiled beneath, the active magical power centered in man, the libido, neutral, neither good nor evil in itself, but able to activate whatever it is directed towards.

Three months now elapsed, the longest wait so far between grades, and a very long time for the impatient Crowley. Yet, he was still busy, being disciplined by Allan Bennett, so that the passage of time was almost unnoticed. With Allan's training, the taking of the Order grades was a mere formality, confirming officially what had been occurring outside the confines of the Order. But in May 1899, he took his examination on the theoretical material, and so was permitted to be advanced to the grade of Philosophus, 4=7. This grade was attributed to the element of Fire and the planet Venus.

After the customary oath, he was again confronted by officers assuming the Masks of Gods. They barred his way, intoning those wonderfully sonorous passages from ancient texts.

> I have said Darkness of Darkness—are not the Countenances of Darkness fallen with Kings? Do the Sons of the Night of Time last for ever? And have they not yet passed away? Before all things are the Waters and the Darkness and the Gates of the Land of Night . . . .

Following these again are some vigorous dynamic passages from the Bible, which properly intoned, can make one's blood turn cold. They must have done this to Crowley, for later he wrote many poems incorporating these ideas and phrases.

> Curse ye Meroz, saith the Angel of the Lord—curse ye bitterly, the inhabitants thereof, because they came not to the help of the Lord—to the help of the Lord against the mighty. The River Kishon swept them away—that ancient River, the River Kishon. O my soul, thou hast trodden down Strength! .... The Lord thundered through the Heavens and the Highest gave forth His Voice—hailstones and flashings of fire! He sent out His arrows and scattered them. He hurled His lightnings and destroyed them ....

Crowley was poet and mystic enough, even in those early years, to thrill to these rhetorical passages. When he came to full term as a mystic, he realized that it is not so much the content of the prayer or invocation which is effective, as the intensity the candidate or the celebrant can bring to it. In fact, on one occasion in 1906 when *in extremis* he recited "From Greenland's icy mountains"—for him, at that moment, it became effective. So long as one can *inflame* oneself in praying, working up as it were an inner frenzy of enthusiasm, that emotional intensity can be counted on to hurl the soul over the precipice of everyday compulsive "normality" into a purely noetic spiritual area, above the conflict-laden mind.

After having conferred upon him the honorific title of *Pharos Illuminans,* Illuminating Tower of Light, he heard the last of the so-called Elemental prayers:

> Immortal, Eternal, Ineffable and Uncreated Father of all ... help us, Thy children, whom Thou hast loved since the birth of the Ages of Time! .... O Thou Flashing Fire, there Thou illuminatest all things with Thine Insupportable Glory, whence flow the ceaseless streams of Splendour which nourish Thine Infinite Spirit .... Thou hast created us as a third Order in our

Elemental Empire. There our continual exercise is to praise and to adore Thy Desires; there we ceaselessly burn with eternal aspirations unto Thee, O Father! O Mother of Mothers! O Archetype eternal of Maternity and Love! O Son, the Flower of all Sons! Form of all Forms! Soul, Spirit, Harmony and Numeral of all things! Amen!

And so this fourth grade of Philosophus carried Crowley one step further along the Path. The elements encountered were principally of a Watery nature where the connecting pathways were concerned, and Fire for the Sephirah or grade itself. These elements were of an identical nature to those of the preceding grade, but here their order and power were quite reversed. Previously the Water was predominant. Now the Fire rages and whirls in lurid storm, with water only as the complementary element in which it may manifest, and in order that due equilibrium may be maintained. These two are the primary terrestrial elements which intelligently controlled and creatively employed, may lead eventually to the restoration of the Golden Age. By their transmutation a new paradise may be recreated from the darkness and chaos into which it had formerly fallen. For the Light may not legitimately be called forth upon man nor dwell within him, until chaos has been turned into equilibrium of complete realization and enlightenment. And until order has been restored to the lower elements of his earthy kingdom, neither peace nor inner security may be his lot.

In *Post-cards to Probationers*, Crowley attempted to deal with this problem in the later days of the *Equinox*, in a slightly different way, for the benefit of his own students. He advised them:

I. Man being a finite being, he is incapable of apprehending the infinite. Nor does his communion with infinite being (true or false) alter this fact.

II. Let then the student contradict every vision and

refuse to enjoy it; first, because there is certainly another vision possible of precisely contradictory nature; secondly, because though he is God, he is also a man upon an insignificant planet.

Being thus equilibriated laterally and vertically, it may be that, either by affirmation or denial of all these things together, he may attain the supreme trance.

The large diagram of *The Fall* that was shown him was similar in some ways to that depicted in the previous grade. It is really a continuation of the theme. As the peace of Eden was shown before, now in the grade of Philosophus the power of Fire is shown to have called forth catastrophe. Years afterwards, in his book called *Magick*, Crowley was able to observe that "the aspirant on the threshold of initiation finds himself assailed by the complexes which have corrupted him, their externalization excruciating him, and his agonized reluctance to their elimination plunging him into such ordeals that he seems (both to himself and to others) to have turned from a noble and upright man into an unutterable scoundrel."

These are the experiences and events which occur to every aspirant when initiation forces the realization upon him, through the activation of the latent contents of his own psyche, that "all is sorrow." In fact, the existential criterion or hall-mark of successful initiation is the occurrence of these or similar experiences. It is comparable to the common observation that when good psychotherapy is being practised, the analysand must be practically consumed with anxiety. If none is present, the psychotherapy is not being effective. The whole universe, under the stimulation of the magical elements and the interior analysis, seems to tumble like a pack of cards crazily about one's feet. This is the *solvé* half of the alchemical *solvé et coagula* formula. Analysis must precede synthesis. Corruption is the primitive base from which the pure gold of the spirit is drawn. So far as the nature of the environment and the creative power of the personal self permits, the task implied by the *coagula* formula is to assemble the discrete elements of the seif, and remould them nearer to the heart's desire.

The hydra-headed Dragon formerly coiled under the Tree, in this diagram has usurped its former position. Its several horned heads wind their way up into the very structure of the Tree of Life. This kind of activity gives rise to a new Sephirah called *Daath*. It is the child of Wisdom and Understanding, the conjunction of *Chokmah* and *Binah* on the Tree—knowledge. It refers to the symbolic sphere formed within or above the *Ruach*, the mind, by means of experience, and this assimilated becomes transmuted into intuition and insight. Fundamentally, however, it is the ascent of the Dragon, or, if you wish, the obsession of the personality by a welling up of the contents of what was hitherto unconscious which first renders *Daath* a possibility.

Lured downwards by the tree of knowledge (and we would do well to remember in what sense the Bible speaks of the verb "to know") towards the "darkly splendid world wherein continually lieth a faithless depth" Eve, the lower self, ceases to give support to Adam. She has yielded to the awful fascination of the awakening psyche. Far easier is it to fall than to climb to the distant heights. Yet the Fall is catastrophic only from one point of view. The awareness of the rise of the Dragon endows man also with the consciousness of power—and power is life and progress. The dragon is the symbol of the enemy to be overcome, as well as, when eventually conquered, the great prize to be won at the end. This is the theme constantly expounded by Jung; he is worth reading on this score.

The significance of all this is to point to a higher type of consciousness, the beginning of a spiritual rebirth. It acts as a self-evolved link between the higher Self at peace in its supernal place, and the human soul, bound by its fall to the world of illusion, fear and anxiety. But until that self-awareness and acquired knowledge are turned to higher and initiated goals, sorrow and anxiety are the inevitable results. In other words, it will not do for the Adept to be cut off from his roots. He must unite all the component parts of his mind-body system and integrate every element on the Tree, his own organism. He must develop by use, the titanic forces of his unconscious psyche so that they may become as a powerful but docile beast whereon he may ride. The personality must be reorganized on an entirely new basis. Every element therein demands equilibration so that illumination ensuing from magical work may not give rise to fanaticism and pathology instead of Adeptship and integrity. Balance is required for the accomplishment of the Great Work. "Equilibrium is the basis of the soul."

Therefore the four grades of Earth, Air, Water and Fire plant the seeds of the microcosmic pentagram, and above them in the Portal ceremony the Crown of the quintessence is added so that the elemental vehemence may be tempered, and that all may work together in balanced disposition.

These grades are therefore an important and integral part of the work of initiation, despite hostile criticism. To compare them, however, with those which precede and follow, is symptomatic of intellectual confusion of function. It is rather as if one said that milk is more virtuous than Friday! Yet similar comparisons in magical and mystical matters are constantly made without exciting ridicule. Different categories may not be so compared. The purpose of the Neophyte ritual is quite distinct from that of Zelator, and it is mistaken policy to compare them. What could be asked is whether the Zelator and the other elemental grades really accomplish what they purport to do. The concensus of experience is on the whole that they do—though perhaps some have questioned it where Crowley's magical career is concerned. I am still unconvinced that most of his critics are right—nor on the other hand can I altogether accept his own evaluations.

One of the last injunctions proferred him towards the end of the Philosophus grade was:

> To study thoroughly the Mysteries which have been unfolded to your view in your progress from the humble position of Neophyte, so that yours may not be the merely superficial knowledge which marks the conceited and ignorant man, but that you may really and thoroughly understand what you profess to know, and not by your ignorance and folly bring disgrace on that Order which has honoured you so far.

Well—now he had seven months to wait before he could be advanced to the next degree. Waiting, for his impetuous make-up, was a torment. But he kept himself busy. Fuller tells us that right after this degree, he met MacGregor Mathers for the first time.

For Crowley, this man was without question a very important person. In his *Confessions*, Crowley wrote that he thought Mathers was a scholar and a gentleman, and without doubt a magician of extraordinary ability. "He had that habit of authority which inspires confidence because it never doubts itself. A man who makes such claims as he did cannot be judged by conventional codes and canons. Ordinary morality is only for ordinary people." Much of this feeling about Mathers was without question what he felt about himself and his own mission. "The whole of Mathers' conduct," he went on to say, "might have been in the nature of a test. It might have been his way of asking the Adepts whether they had the power of concentrating on the spiritual situation, of giving up for ever all their prejudices."

Then, following the above remarks, he comes to the *piece de resistance*, without which little of Crowley's behavior is intelligible. "Anyhow, as far as I was concerned, Mathers was my only link with the Secret Chiefs to whom I was pledged."

During the waiting period referred to above, Crowley was travelling the length and breadth of the British Isles looking for a house suitable for magical work, for a retirement. In November 1899, he found one in Scotland.

We have to recall that for some eighteen months Allan Bennett had come to live with him in his apartment where, together, they had labored hard at every phase of magic. Allan had been a good teacher, so that, in reality, long before Crowley received his Portal degree in December 1899 he was a fairly well experienced magus. This was around the time when Allan was enabled to leave England. The cold, damp climate was too much for him. He was on his way East, to Ceylon. Teacher and student met again there, much later, but essentially this was the end of the relationship. It had been good for both of them.

NOTES

[1] *The Light on the Path*, Mabel Collins, Adyar, Theosophical Publishing Co., 1936, p. 22.

[2] All quotations from the initiatory rituals are from *The Golden Dawn*, Vol. II, St. Paul, Llewellyn Publications, 1969.

[3] Virginia Moore, *op. cit.*, p. 142.

[4] *The Book of Thoth*, Aleister Crowley, London, O.T.O., 1944, This book has recently been reprinted by Samuel Weiser, New York, 1969, and also by Shambala Publications, Berkeley, Calif., 1969.
Though the sparkle was indeed gone, I must modify my earlier reactions now that I have had the opportunity to re-read the book (November 1969). In order to appreciate its profundity and philosophic splendor, one needs to compare it with other books dealing with the same subject.
I am thinking of one particularly, that was written by an eminent authority on the Tarot. It is indeed a good piece of work, and for the beginner I assert that there is none better. But to compare this, or any other, to Crowley's *Book of Thoth* is like comparing a fourth grade arithmetic book with a treatise involving fourth-dimensional mathematics.

CHAPTER SEVEN

"I Am The Heart . . ."

The grades of the Order were attributed to the ten Sephiroth of the Qabalistic Tree of Life. Each one of these Sephiroth is joined by a series of connecting pathways, each of which has to be symbolically traversed in the grade ceremonies. Thus there are several pathways leading to Tiphareth, the central Sephirah on the Tree, to which the Adeptus Minor ritual is allocated. One of the most significant pieces of furniture or equipment in this latter ritual is the Vault of the Adepti, where, according to legend, Christian Rosenkreutz had been interred.

The so-called Portal ritual precedes this Adeptus Minor or 5=6 ritual, and follows after the four elemental grades. It provides the peak of the pentagram, representing the fifth element Ether or Akasa. It has no place, *per se*, on the Tree of Life, as do the other elemental grades. It is an artificial construct enabling the Order to draw together several so-far-disconnected strands of thought and symbolism, to integrate them for future use in the 5=6 ritual. The Portal ritual, therefore, represents an introduction to an integrative process, a glimpse into the work of the Second or Rosicrucian Order.

One of the strands of thought to be tied together is the pentagram. There has to be a fifth point. The truncated pyramid is another analogous symbol, the four sides referring to the four elements, and the flat top referring to Ether. In the Enochian system, especially, was this symbolism extensively employed. Briefly, the Portal grade is an artifact—but a useful one. Thus it is called the Ritual of the Portal of the Vault of the Adepti—a long and impressive title—especially when the Candidate was given the full treatment: Lord of the Paths of the Portal of the Vault of the Adepti!

The ceremony itself was equally impressive and colorful. All of the officers were clad in Second Order regalia, brightly colored robes and capes. The rubric describes the Chief Adept as wearing a White cassock, yellow shoes, red cloak of the Hierophant, yellow and white nemyss or head-dress, the Second Order Rose-cross symbol on a yellow collar, the sceptre of five elemental colors, and surmounted by a pentagram; a white lamp and brazier and candle were also part of the equipment. All five officiating officers were clad in robes of brilliant hue.

The formulae employed in this ceremony are totally different from those preceding. Some scholars believe that the four main elemental rituals have some root in tradition. However, this Portal ritual shows signs of being an artifact, and so reveals most clearly the handiwork of Mathers. Be that as it may, it did convey a set of ideas and feelings to the Candidate, and managed to bridge the two Orders, the Golden Dawn in the Outer and the Roseae Rubeae et Aureae Crucis.

Here was Crowley, in the last few weeks of the year 1899, being admitted to the Second Order—or at least to the Portal grade which was the outskirts of the hidden city. Once more there was the customary pledge never to reveal the secrets of the Order; not to use his knowledge for evil; to regard all of the knowledge imparted as a sacred trust; to exercise brotherly love, charity and forebearance towards all the members of the Order; and finally not to be a stirrer up of strife, of schism, or of opposition to the Chiefs.

Did he keep any single clause of this obligation?

The Ritual in many ways resembled all those preceding, the Candidate being escorted here and there, challenged, questioned, advanced and challenged again. In addition to the Diagrams already mentioned, another was shown—Pan, attributed on the Tree of Life to Capricorn and the Path of *Ayin*, a Hebrew letter which when spelled out in full is the word meaning an Eye. One formal speech described it thus:

> " . . . the gross generative powers of nature on the material plane, and is analogous to the Pan of the Greeks and the Egyptian Goat of Mendes (the symbol of Khem). In certain aspects, this Key represents the brutal forces of nature, which to the unbelieving man only obscure and do not reflect the luminous Countenance of God. It also alludes to the sexual powers of natural generation . . . he represents the gross and materialized Elemental Forces of Nature . . . He is the eternal renewer of all the changing forms of Creation in conformity with the Law of the All-Powerful One (Blessed be He) . . .

Rather prosaic and bourgeois on the whole! But in Crowley's hands, or rather under the transcendental impact of the illuminations which shook him through and through during the year 1907, when *The Book of Lapis Lazuli* came into being, it prompted an introductory entitled *The Prologue of the Unborn:*

> Into my loneliness comes—
> The sound of a flute in dim groves that haunt the uttermost hills.
> Even from the brave river they reach to the edge of the wilderness.
> And I behold Pan.
> The snows are eternal above, above—
> And their perfume smokes upwards into the nostrils of the stars.
> But what have I to do with these?
> To me only the distant flute, the abiding vision of Pan.

On all sides Pan to the eye, to the ear;
The perfume of Pan pervading, the taste of him
utterly filling my mouth, so that the tongue breaks
forth into a weird and monstrous speech.
The embrace of him intense on every centre of pain
and pleasure.
The sixth interior sense aflame with the inmost self of
Him.
Myself flung down the precipice of being
Even to the abyss, annihilation.
An end to loneliness, as to all.
Pan! Pan! Io Pan! Io Pan!

He was never content with merely the letter and form of
his instruction. For him theory counted little, constant
practice meant much more. By means of both Yoga and
magical practices he was enabled to experience
transcendental, mystical states in which he *became* what
previously had been mere verbiage.

During the American period, he wrote *The Hymn to Pan*
which most writers on Crowley are more prone to seize upon
as typical of him and his attitudes towards Pan. Most of these
writers are not familiar, apparently, with *The Prologue of the
Unborn,* which is infinitely better writing, and of far higher
inspiration than the other.

In this connection, I think it is also prudent to consider
another piece of his much later writing illuminating his point
of view:

"The Devil" is, historically, the God of any people
that one personally dislikes . . . . This serpent, Satan, is
not the enemy of Man, but He who made Gods of our
race, knowing Good and Evil. He bade "Know Thyself!"
and taught Initiation. He is "the Devil" of the Book of
Thoth, and His emblem is Baphomet, the Androgyne
who is the hieroglyph of arcane perfection. The number
of His Atu is XV, which is *Yod He,* the Monogram of
the Eternal, the Father one with the Mother, the Virgin

Seed one with all-containing Space. He is therefore Life and Love. But moreover his letter is *Ayin,* the Eye; he is Light, and his Zodiacal image is Capricornus, that leaping goat whose attribute is Liberty . . . .

He is the Open Eye of the exalted Sun, before whom all shadows flee away; also that Secret Eye which makes an image of its God, the Light, and gives it power to utter oracles, enlightening the mind.

Thus, he is Man made God, exalted, eager; he has come consciously to his full stature, and so is ready to set out on his journey to redeem the world. But he may not appear in this true form; the Vision of Pan would drive men mad with fear. He must conceal himself in his original guise.

He therefore becomes apparently the man that he was at the beginning; he lives the life of a man; indeed, he is wholly man. But his initiation has made him master of the Event by giving him the understanding that whatever happens to him is the execution of his true will.

In the succeeding phases of the Portal grade, he was shown other large charts and diagrams, illustrative in symbolic form of the basic philosophical notions of the Order. One of these elaborated in alchemical language the vision of Nebuchadnezzar, as the Hiereus enjoins him:

> Thou art this head of Gold. Thy head represents in thee the dominion of the Divine ruling over the rest of the body. The silver is the world of the heart, the brass is the material passion, the iron is the firm purpose, and the feet, part of iron and part of clay, are the mingled strength and infirmity of the natural man. And the Stone made without hands is the Eternal Stone of the Wise, which will become the Mountain of Initiation, whereby the whole Earth shall be filled with the knowledge of God.

In another section of the ritual, the same officer

recommends: "While the Wheel revolves, the hub is still. Seek ever then the centre, look from without to within." Apparently, Crowley did just this, for years later in one of the extraordinary visions of the North Africa series known as *The Vision and the Voice,* the wheel re-appears. In the twentieth Aethyr, so-called, he saw:

> The dew that was upon the face of the stone is gone, and it is become like a pool of clear golden water. And now the light is come into the Rosy Cross. Yet all that I see is the night, with the stars therein, as they appear through a telescope . . . . Now behind the angels are archangels with trumpets. These cause all things to appear at once, so that there is a tremendous confusion of images. And now I perceive that all these things are but veils of the wheel, for they all gather themselves into a wheel that spins with incredible velocity. It hath many colours, but all thrilled with white light, so that they are transparent and luminous. This one wheel is forty-nine wheels, set at different angles, and has forty-nine concentric tyres at equal distances from the centre. And wherever the rays from any two wheels meet, there is a blinding flash of glory. It must be understood that though so much detail is visible in the wheel, yet at the same time the impression is of a single, simple object.
>
> It seems that this wheel is being spun by a hand. Though the wheel fills the whole Aire, yet the hand is much bigger than the wheel. And though this vision is so great and splendid, yet there is no seriousness with it, or solemnity. It seems that the hand is spinning the wheel merely for pleasure, it would be better to say amusement . . . .
>
> And all the rays of the wheel stream out at me, and I am blasted and blinded with the light. I am caught up into the wheel. I am one with the wheel. I am greater than the wheel . . . .
>
> And now it is the dance of Shiva. I lie beneath his feet, his saint, his victim. My form is the form of the God Ptah in my essence, but the form of the god Seb in

my form. And this is the reason of existence, that in this dance which is delight, there must needs be both the god and the adept. Also the earth herself is a saint, and the sun and the moon dance upon her, torturing her with delight . . . .

The formality and verbiage of the Mathers ritual had now become transcendental experience for Crowley. This is *gnosis*!

Again, ritually, the Chief Adept reminds him of the dialectical nature of the Great Work:

Let this remind you once more, that only in and by the reconciliation of opposing forces is the Pathway made to the true occult knowledge and practical power. Good alone is might and Truth alone shall prevail. Evil is but weakness and the power of evil magic exists but in the contest of unbalanced forces, which in the end will destroy and ruin him who hath subjected himself thereto . . . .

Now he was in the Inner Order finally, in the Portal only—but in the Inner Order nonetheless. He had the long honorific title of *Hodos Chamelionis*, and Lord of the Paths of the Portal. But, permission or no, and secret or no, he was almost as fully equipped magically as were most of the initiating officers.

Bennett had been a superb teacher. No wonder Crowley was thoroughly devoted to him, and spoke so glowingly of him for the rest of his life. Even when Allan became a Buddhist monk, no enmity sprang up between these two men. Crowley could not accept Buddhism, once he had become completely indoctrinated and saw its weaknesses. But his eventual rejection of Buddhism did not alienate him from Allan.

Nine months, the period of human gestation, was the period of time demanded by the Order as the interval between the Portal grade and that of Adeptus Minor. This brings us to September 1900.

The revolt was now in full swing, as already described earlier. The London group wanted nothing to do with him. Allan was no longer in England, having gone to Ceylon to see if the warm soft climate there might suit him better and be more kind to his bronchial asthmatic condition than the damp and cold of the "old gray land."

Crowley had gone to Paris, where Mathers had invited him to receive the 5=6 degree. He went with elation and exalted anticipation, for he had projected some of his own headstrong idealism on his Chief. While he realized that the grade would give him little that Jones and Bennett had not already imparted to him, receiving the degree from Mathers would go far towards legitimizing these accomplishments. Now no one would be able to question who and what he was so far as the Order was concerned.

Having obtained the Portal degree, with its implication of completing and fulfilling all points of the pentagram—one would have thought then that the task of initiation—from the ceremonial viewpoint—was at an end. Apparently, however, the metaphysical theory here is somewhat more involved. Even in actual practice, to activate the five elemental bases within the personality is not the sole work. The Temple may be ready—but there is no god within. The Adeptus Minor degree lays down and completes in ceremony what the 0=0 degree only intimates, that the whole man is not merely a healthy, naturally functioning animal or elemental man. He is certainly all of this—but something more. All kingdoms of nature are incorporated within his structure, which must then be sanctified by the operation of the Higher Self. It is this that makes the God-man—and this is the goal of the Great Work.

So Crowley set about finding a name or motto that would express his aspiration to the highest. Perdurabo was all right for the Outer Order, but at this moment he needed a name which would be more fitting in the Rosicrucian Order in which he was about to be initiated.

Traditionally, the Rosicrucians were Christians of the Reformation—mystics, alchemists, occultists, but always Christians. The founder of the Order, according to the *Fama Fraternitatis,* was Christian Rosenkreutz. Many critics had already assumed this name to be a pseudonym, a symbol. All initiates of the Order similarly assumed pseudonyms to express their quest in the Path towards enlightenment.

Crowley's later anti-Christian fervor no doubt led him to eliminate and totally destroy any obvious clue that might lead one to discover the Christian intent of his motto for the 5=6 grade. He was not very proud of his earlier Christian zeal. He could not take the more mature view that a youth can be forgiven for every extravagance. Advancing years and maturity give one the right to take a benign stand where the excesses and extravagances of earlier life are concerned. Somehow Crowley could never attain this benign stand relative to the hated religion of his mother and the Plymouth Brethren, which was anathema to him. *Thus every reference to the Second Order name he adopted appears to be blotted out almost beyond hope of recovery.*

However, I propose that there are two or three clues that, pieced carefully together, may give us a hint as to his motto. It may well have fitted his aspirations and ideals in September 1900 in Paris, when he was but 25 years of age. One can be tremendously mature intellectually—as his essays undoubtedly prove. Emotionally, he was vital, strong, impetuous, outgoing—but so immature.

One of the rituals to which either Jones or Bennett had introduced him was The Preliminary Invocation of the Goetia, as he called it, or the Bornless Ritual. The earliest record discovered of this is in a work entitled *Fragment of a Graeco-Egyptian Work Upon Magic* by Charles Wycliffe

Goodwin, M.A., published in 1852 for the Cambridge Antiquarian Society. Reprinted in the late 1800's by E. Wallis Budge in his *Egyptian Magic*, it became popular among the members of the Golden Dawn. Crowley appropriated it, reprinting it as a proem to his *Goetia*, which he had paid Mathers to translate for him.

Symonds mocks Crowley rendition of the important phrase in the first line of the ritual. He claims it should be "The Headless One" instead of "The Bornless One." But Symonds ought to know that in many languages "head" and "beginning" are synonymous and may be used interchangeably. "The Headless One" might be rendered as "The One without a beginning" or even more concisely as "The Bornless One."

The closing paragraph of the ritual is as follows:

I am He, The Bornless Spirit! having sight in the feet, Strong, and the Immortal Fire!
I am He! the Truth!
I am He! Who hate that evil should be wrought in the World!
I am He! that lighteneth and thundereth;
I am He, from whom is the Shower of the Life of Earth;
I am He, whose mouth ever flameth;
I am He, the Begetter and Manifester unto the Light;
I am He; the Grace of the World!
'The Heart Girt with a Serpent' is my name!

This ritual, like so many other things from the early Golden Dawn days, played a tremendous part in his development. From it, in the Cefalu days—that is in the early 20's, he compiled and developed *Liber Samekh*. This is a complex interpretation of the many barbarous names of evocation in this ritual and provides a rubric for its operation and an essay concerning its goals. This ritual always meant a great deal to him, especially the line in italics. He had used it

for twenty years, in small retirements as in great magical
retirements. It was through this ritual during the China walk
that he achieved the more spectacular of his
results—spectacular in the sense of mystical experiences. It
was his own personal invocation, and has become identified
with him.

Around 1907, he wrote an inspired prose-poem that he
called *Liber LXV*. The enumeration of 65 is that of the
Hebrew word Adonai, which carries with it the meaning of
the higher Self, or the Holy Guardian Angel as he preferred
to call it. The sub-title of the book was significantly *The
Book of the Heart Girt with a Serpent*. In other words, one
of the lines in the Bornless Ritual which early in his magical
life was so meaningful to him became the title of this
devotional mystical text. Its opening lines are:

> *I am the Heart; and the Snake is entwined*
> *About the invisible core of the mind.*
> Rise, O my snake! It is now the hour
> Of the hooded and holy ineffable flower.
> Rise, O my snake, into brilliance of bloom
> On the corpse of Osiris afloat in the tomb!
> O heart of my mother, my sister, mine own,
> Thou art given to Nile, to the terror Typhon!
> Ah me! but the glory of ravening storm
> Enswathes thee and wraps thee in frenzy of form.
> Be still, O my soul! that the spell may dissolve
> As the wands are upraised, and the aeons revolve.
> Behold! in my beauty how joyous Thou art,
> O Snake that caresses the crown of mine heart!
> Behold! we are one, and the tempest of years
> Goes down to the dusk, and the Beetle appears.
> O Beetle! the drone of Thy dolorous note
> Be ever the trance of this tremulous throat!
> I await the awakening! The summons on high
> From the Lord Adonai, from the Lord Adonai!

Here is enshrined the essence of the mystical philosophy of

Yoga, relating to the raising of the serpent-power, the Kundalini. This is conceived as the magical energy coiled in the base of the spine. When it can be moved upwards to the spiritual centers above the head, illumination occurs and with it Moksha, freedom from this world of illusion and delusion, and from the necessity of incarnation in this vale of tears.

Around 1901, he had written a poem called *Invocation*. It is in a volume entitled "Oracles" published around 1905, consisting of previously unpublished poems dated from 1886 to 1903. It carries with it the subtitle, *The Autobiography of an Art*. In this long poem *Invocation*, which incorporates a great deal of Golden Dawn knowledge, there occur these significant lines:

> I am the Heart of Jesus girt about
> With the swift Serpent.

In *The Temple of the Holy Ghost* published in 1901, right after his 5=6 initiation, is a poem entitled *The Athanor*. I quote it only because it shows that he could still use the word Christ in a sincere devotional way:

> O thou, mine angel, whom these eyes have seen,
>   These hands have handled, and this mouth has
>   kissed!
> O thou, the very tongue of fire, the clean
>   Sweet-scented presence of a holier Christ!
> Listen, and answer, and behold! My wings
> Droop, O thou stronger than the immortal kings!

Since we know that Crowley later came to regard *Liber LXV*, with one or two other works of the same period, to be in a different category from everything else he had written, and since he regarded *Liber Samekh* as the invocation *par excellence* of the Holy Guardian Angel, these two lines written very early must be most meaningful. They were written during the Golden Dawn period, that is before 1901.

While he was still rebelling against mother and her distortions of Christianity, and studying Ingersoll, Bradlaugh and James G. Frazer, together with Buddhism, Hinduism and Yoga, his total rejection of Christianity had not yet been fully developed. It was an interim period. He could still use Christian words and phrases without actually becoming outraged, as later.

For the time being, I will assume that these words "I am the Heart of Jesus girt about with the swift Serpent," whatever they were when put in good Latin, became his magical motto for Adeptship. They were part of the most important magical ritual of his Adeptship, and Christian enough to conform to the Christian mysticism of the 5=6 grade. I can well imagine Mathers greeting Very Honoured Frater "Heart of Jesus" after having conferred upon him the 5=6 degree!

So our young adept, with a natural Christian bias approached the central core of the Golden Dawn initiatory system with devotion and aspiration. He was prepared for an inner rebirth.

He recalled one of the knowledge lectures where Mathers had written:

> Remember that there is hardly a circumstance in the rituals even of the First Order which has not its special meaning and application, and which does not conceal a potent magical formula. These ceremonies have brought thee into contact with certain forces which thou hast now to learn to awaken in thyself, and to this end, read, study and re-read that which thou hast already received. Be not sure even after the lapse of much time that thou hast fully discovered all that is to be learned from these. And to be of use unto thee, this must be the work of thine own inner self, thine own and not the work of another for thee, so that thou mayest gradually attain to the knowledge of the Divine Ones.

The theme of this 5=6 Ritual is simple, elevating and dramatic. Its essence is:

> Buried with that Light in a mystical death, rising again in a mystical resurrection, cleansed and purified through him our Master, O brother of the Cross of the Rose. Like him, O adepts of all ages, have ye toiled. Like him have ye suffered tribulation. Poverty, torture and death have ye passed through. They have been but the purification of the gold. In the alembic of thine heart, through the athanor of affliction, seek thou the True Stone of the Wise.

Even the themes of the two previous diagrams of the Garden of Eden and the Fall are continued in this grade. Escorted into the Vault, the aspirant is shown the lid of the tomb of Osiris, the Pastos wherein was buried Christian Rosenkreutz, and on that lid is a painting which brings fulfillment to the narrative begun before.

It is divided into two sections. The lower half of the painting depicts a figure of Adam, similar to his presentation in the grade of Practicus, though here the heads of the dragon are falling back from the Tree. It shows the Justified One, the illuminated Adept, by his immolation and self-sacrifice rescuing the fallen kingdom of his natural self from the clutches of an outraged eros. Above this, as though to show the true nature behind the deceptive appearance of things, is illustrated a noble figure of majesty and divinity, described in the Ritual by quotations from the Scriptures.

> And being turned I saw seven golden light-bearers, and in the midst of the Light-bearers, one like unto the Ben Adam, clothed with a garment down to the feet, and girt with a golden girdle. His head and his hair were white as snow, and his eyes as flaming fire; his feet like unto fine brass as if they burned in a furnace. And his voice like the sound of many waters. And he had in his right hand seven stars, and out of his mouth went the

Sword of Flame, and his countenance was as the Sun in his strength.

It is to effect this redemption of the personality, to regenerate and transmute the enormous power of the red dragon, and attempt to bring the individual to some realization of his potential godhead, that is the object of the Adeptus Minor ceremony. It indicates the psychological solution of the anima problem. "Arise! Shine! For thy Light is come!"

This is why he had come to Paris, why he had accepted Mathers' invitation. Four officers officiated at Ahathoor—with Mathers as the Chief Adept, clothed in a gorgeous blue and purple robe, with a winged sphered wand. At the opening of the ritual, he was not present in the fore part of the Temple—being, according to the terms of the rubric, in the Vault of the Adepts. But two other officers, one wearing red and orange, the other yellow and rose pink, were there with the Candidate's sponsor who was called Hodos Chamelionis, clad only in nemyss, white gown, and yellow shoes. Immediately upon entry, Crowley was challenged. He was then coached to read out all his grades and qualifications, and "by virtue of these honours and dignities, I now come to demand my reception and acknowledgment as an Adeptus Minor of the 5=6 grade of the Second Order."

This may have been all right in the Portal grade with its lengthy honorific titles, but for this high degree it would not do at all. The answer to his demand for initiation could well have served Crowley as a lesson for the rest of his life. One has only to open the blue *Equinox,* for example, apart from other of his writings, to read the full pompous listing of his Masonic honours and dignities and grades and degrees. It availed him nothing.

O Aspirant! It is written that he who exalteth himself

shall be abased, but that he who humbleth himself shall
be exalted, and that blessed are the poor in spirit for
theirs is the Kingdom of Heaven. It is not by
proclamation of honours and dignities, great though
they may be, that thou canst gain admission to the
Tomb of the Adepti of the Rose of Ruby and the Cross
of Gold, but only by that humility and purity of spirit
that befitteth the aspirant unto higher things.

I wish to do Crowley justice where insight into his own
problems is concerned. It may seem at times that his egotism
played havoc with him without any awareness on his part.
Yet—as I have previously intimated, there were few areas of
his psyche that he had not investigated. This assumption is
confirmed in one of his book reviews, where he hid some of
his most profound comments and philosophical conclusions.
In *Equinox III* (published in the Spring of 1910), he has a
review of a book entitled *John Dee* written by Charlotte Fell
Smith. It is signed by one of Crowley's innumerable
pseudonyms, Edward Kelly. John Dee was Queen Elizabeth's
astrologer, and Edward Kelly was his colleague and
clairvoyant collaborator. It is one of Crowley's contentions
that in a former life he was Sir Edward Kelly. Be that as it
may, the last paragraph of the review is illuminating,
touching on Crowley's enlarged ego:

For one thing I do most seriously take blame, that
my training was too strong for my power to receive
spiritual truth. For when the Holy Angels came to
instruct me in the great truths, that there is no sin, that
the soul passes from house to house, that Jesus was but
a man, that the Holy Ghost was not a person, I rejected
them as false. Ah! have I not paid bitterly for this error?
Still, the incarnation was not all loss; not only did I
attain the Grade of Major Adept, but left enough secret
knowledge in an available form to carry me on for a
long while. I am getting it back now; with luck I'll be a
Magister Templi soon, *if I can only get rid of my giant*

personality. (Italics are mine—I.R.) You may say, by the
way, that this is hardly a review of a book on my old
master, silly old josser! Exactly; I never cared a dump
for him. He was just a text for my sermon then; and so
he is now.

Edward Kelly

So he was ordered to return to the ante-room. There he
was to divest himself of all the sashes, medallions, and
insignia with which he had been clothed. It was a pretty piece
of symbolism—the divesting of the self of all pride and
vanity—but, alas, only symbolism. In the Ordo Templi
Orientis, when he came to reformulate the old German rituals
himself, Crowley coped more realistically with this ego
problem by having the candidate strip himself not only of
vestments and adornments, but of all his clothing, to appear
amongst his fellows stark naked. Pride *is* abashed—for few
human figures are that beautiful to-day, to tolerate being
seen in all their nakedness.

He was told, after he had knelt and prayed, and been
conducted back into the Temple:

> Think not, O Aspirant, that the trial of humility
> which thou hast passed was ordained but to jest with
> thy feelings. Far from us be any such design. But it was
> intended to point out to thee that the truly wise man is
> but little in his own eyes, however great his attainments
> may appear to the ignorant, and that even the highest
> intellectual achievements are but as nothing in the sight
> of the Lord of the Universe . . . .

When he had risen to his feet, the same officer cautioned
him:

> Despise not sadness and hate not suffering, for they
> are the initiators of the heart . . . . Slander not and revile
> not. If thou canst not praise, do not condemn . . . . Bear
> with one another and forgive one another, even as the

Master hath said.

Oath-taking time was an important sector of each ritual. But on this occasion it was an even more impressive experience than before, one calculated to cut through the petty facade of intellectualism and evoke a deep emotional response. In the Temple, toward the West, stood a large Cross on a raised dais. Crowley was led quietly and slowly to the dais, and backed against the cross. His arms were passed through running nooses, and a loose cord was bound about his waist and feet. Though the rubric says "two Adepti stand on either side to support him," and though Virginia Moore overdramatizes this part of the ritual to depict Yeats' great perseverance and nobility of spirit, there was really no need for this. The candidate stood on his own feet, with arms extended at either side, supported actually by the rope nooses. The long, serious pledge was recited after the invocation of an Angelic force *Hua* "that thou mayest invisibly place thy hand upon the head of this aspirant in attestation of his obligation."

The Sephiroth of the Qabalistic Tree are ten in number. In this ceremony, the clauses of the Obligation were one for each Sephiroth.

More or less in its entirety, I quote the Adeptus Minor obligation, sworn on the Cross, because the basic theme will reappear many times during this history. On several critical occasions in his life, Crowley bound himself with further obligations, essentially re-statements of this particular oath, for specific ends and for specific purposes.

> 1. *Kether.* I, Frater "Heart of Jesus girt about with the swift Serpent," a member of the Body of Christ, do this day spiritually bind myself, even as I am now bound physically upon the Cross of Suffering.
> 2. *Chokmah.* That I will to the utmost lead a pure and unselfish life, and will prove myself a faithful and

devoted servant of this Order.

3. *Binah.* That I will keep secret all things connected with the Order and its Secret Knowledge, from the whole world, equally from him who is a member of the First Order of the Golden Dawn as from an uninitiated person, and that I will maintain the Veil of strict secrecy between the First and Second Orders.[1]

4. *Chesed.* That I will uphold to the utmost the authority of the Chiefs of the Order . . . .[2]

5. *Geburah.* Furthermore, that I will perform all practical work connected with this Order in a place concealed and apart from the gaze of the outer and uninitiated world . . . .

6. *Tiphareth.* I further promise and swear that with the Divine Permission I will, from this day forward, apply myself to the Great Work—which is, to purify and exalt my Spiritual Nature so that with the Divine Aid, I may at length attain to be more than human, and thus gradually raise and unite myself to my Higher and Divine Genius, and that in this event I will not abuse the great power entrusted to me.

7. *Netzach.* I furthermore solemnly pledge myself never . . . . to debase my knowledge of practical Magic to purposes of evil and self-seeking . . . .

8. *Hod.* I further promise to support the admission of both sexes to our Order, on a perfect equality, and that I will always display brotherly love and forbearance towards the members of the whole Order, neither slandering nor evil-speaking nor repeating nor tale-bearing, whereby strife and ill-feeling may be engendered.[3]

9. *Yesod.* I also undertake to work unassisted at the subjects prescribed for study in the various practical grades from Zelator Adeptus Minor to Adept Adeptus Minor, on pain of being degraded to that of Lord of the Paths of the Portal only.

10. *Malkuth.* Finally, if in my travels I should meet a stranger who professes to be a member of the Rosicrucian Order, I will examine him with care before acknowledging him to be such. Such are the words of

this my Obligation as an Adeptus Minor, whereunto I
pledge myself in the Presence of the Divine One, and of
the Great Avenging Angel Hua, and if I fail herein, may
my Rose be disintegrated and my power in Magic cease.

With this oath in mind, consideration of his so-called
Abramelin oath and the later oath in Mexico to pursue the
concentration training of Oscar Eckenstein, will indicate the
source of their origin. These are further examples of the
theme basic to this study of Crowley—that *all* his work, in
one way or another, is predicated on the curriculum of the
Golden Dawn. *All his work is a direct continuation of the
Golden Dawn tradition.*

Still immolated on the Cross, he then saw the Second
Adept unsheath a dagger. With this dagger, first dipped in
wine in a chalice, the Adept traced Christ's stigmata: the
brow: "There are Three that bear witness in Heaven; the
Father, the Word, and the Holy Spirit, and these three are
one . . . " Then the feet with: "There are Three that bear
witness on earth; the Spirit, the Water, and the Blood, and
these Three agree in One." For the right hand: "Except ye be
born of water and the Spirit, ye cannot enter the Kingdom of
Heaven . . . " And for the left hand: "If ye be crucified with
Christ, ye shall also reign with Him."

After the taking of the Pledge, he was removed from the
Cross. Then the history of the Rosicrucian Order, largely
extrapolated from the mediaeval *Fama Fraternitatis* was
narrated. There was method in the madness, and method in
the procedure, as Crowley by now was quite familiar. He had
already become familiar with the old Rosicrucian classics and
with the essentials of the ceremony, because he had in some
manner appropriated the rubric and studied it long before he
came to Paris.

As the Second Adept narrated: "When the tablet was

forcibly wrenched away, it pulled with it a large stone which thus partially uncovered a secret door," he drew back a dark curtain revealing the door to the Vault itself. At this juncture, another officer ordered Crowley out to wait in the anteroom. This was to permit the opening of the Vault and the preparation of the Chief Adept, in this case Mathers. He had been sitting quietly in the Vault, out of sight, listening intently to the first part of the Ceremony. And if he acted in terms of the Rubric he himself had written, he was doing a great deal with his trained imagination—summoning to the Temple and the Vault the beings and forces appropriate to the grade.

Once Crowley was out of sight, Mathers was assisted into the Pastos of Christian Rosenkreutz. This is really a large wooden box or coffin, brightly painted with several designs and symbols. It was placed in the middle of the Vault, a seven-sided chamber. On each side were painted symbols representing the Sephiroth, the planets and alchemical principles in bright color with their flashing complements. It has to be seen to be appreciated. Once in the Pastos, a small round table or Altar was rolled over it, so that at first sight only the implements on the altar were visible. Inscribed on the circular altar were versicles that once had meaning for Rosenkreutz:

"A.G.R.C.—Ad Gloriam Roseae Crucis

"A.C.R.G.—Ad Crucis Roseae Gloriam.

"Hoc Universi Compendium Unius Mihi Sepulchrum Feci—Unto the Glory of the Rose Cross I have constructed this Tomb for myself as a Compendium of the Universal Unity."

Within the next circle were written: "Yeheshua mihi omnia—Jesus is all things to me." In the center were the four Kerubic animals of the prophet Ezekiel's vision, with other appropriate sentences.

Again there was a prayer or Invocation—and the Golden Dawn had some very beautiful ones—after which the Aspirant was marked afresh with the stigmata. Then he was instructed to say, while holding a cross in his hands: "In and by that Sign, I demand that the Pastos of our Founder be opened, for my victory is in the Cross of the Rose." Two of the officers rolled aside the circular altar, opened the lid—and behold! There was Mathers, eyes closed, clad in his brilliantly colored regalia, dramatically reciting:

> Buried with that Light in a mystical death, rising again in a mystical Resurrection, cleansed and purified through Him our Master, O Brother of the Cross and the Rose. Like Him, O Adepts of all ages, have ye toiled. Like Him have ye suffered tribulation. Poverty, torture and death have ye passed through. They have been but the purification of the Gold. In the alembic of thine heart, through the athanor of affliction, seek thou the true Stone of the Wise.

There was a dramatic exchange of sceptres and other ceremonial implements to facilitate the process of identification, and again Crowley was told to leave the Vault for the final point of the Ritual. But before he was conducted out, he was again reminded of the spiritual dialectic that had obtained throughout all phases of the Order:

> Quit then, this Tomb, O Aspirant, with thine arms crossed upon thy breast, bearing in thy right hand the Crook of Mercy and in thy left the Scourge of Severity, the emblems of those Eternal Forces betwixt which the equilibrium of the Universe dependeth; those forces whose reconciliation is the Key of Life, whose separation is evil and death . . . .

A dramatic ritual of this kind actually induces a species of

identification. There is a *participation mystique*. All other
things being equal—sincerity, preparation, sensitivity and an
active, artistic imagination—the candidate finds himself swept
along with the movement of the ritual. No deliberate
conscious effort on his part actually is required. Given the
skill on the part of the officers in making their movements
and speeches, and assuming that the ritual is well-written, and
granting that the Candidate is capable of illumination, he is
lifted out of himself into an altogether different mode of
operation. It is as though the customary frame of mind, what
Wilhelm Reich has called the character-armor, were
overthrown momentarily and another level of consciousness
made operative. This armor is nothing more than the total
network of psychoanalytic defense-mechanisms organized
together to form a cognitive system, designed to shield a
vulnerable mind. The Ceremony—temporarily or
otherwise—shatters this network, leaving the vulnerable mind
wholly open to the higher.

Crowley—being a poet, and very sensitive—was profoundly
moved when he saw Mathers, no longer in the Tomb, but
standing in the East, arms extended, intoning biblical
passages intertwined with phrases from other sacred books.

> I am the Resurrection and the Life. He that believeth
> in Me, though he were dead, yet shall he live. And
> whosoever liveth and believeth in Me, shall never
> die . . . . I am the First, and I am the Last. I am He that
> liveth and was dead, and behold! I am alive for
> evermore, and hold the keys of Hell and of Death . . .

Both of the other officers knelt down West of the Altar
with Crowley, while Mathers continued:

> For I know that my Redeemer liveth, and that He
> shall stand at the latter day upon the earth. I am the
> Way, the Truth and the Life. No man cometh unto the

Father but by Me. I am the Purified. I have passed through the Gates of Darkness unto Light. I have fought upon Earth for Good. I have finished my Work. I have entered into the Invisible. I am the Sun in his rising. I have passed through the hour of cloud and of night. I am Amoun the Concealed One, the Opener of the Day . . .

Following hard upon the invocation of "Let the White Brilliance of the Divine Spirit descend" Crowley was acknowledged as an Adeptus Minor of the Order. He was asked to rise, standing on his own feet. All three officers then participated directly, touching him with their sceptres, saying:

Be thy mind opened unto the higher. Be thy heart a centre of Light. Be thy body the Temple of the Rose Cross.

In effect, this was the end of the ceremony, though there were some technical and pedagogic considerations which, from the dramatic point of view, were anti-climactic.

Whatever the effect of the ritual upon him—and we know it was considerable—a great deal of his poetry written after this date concerns itself profoundly with these themes. For example, among the titles of his books published not long after are *Mysteries, Lyrical and Dramatic* (1898) where we find a prophetic sonnet entitled *Perdurabo:*

Exile from humankind! The snow's fresh flakes
Are warmer than men's hearts. My mind is wrought
Into dark shapes of solitary thought
That loves and sympathises, but awakes
No answering love or pity. What a pang
Hath this strange solitude to aggravate
The self-abasement and the blows of Fate!
No snake of hell hath so severe a fang!

> I am not lower than all men—I feel
> Too keenly. Yet my place is not above,
> Though I have this—unalterable Love
> In every fibre. I am crucified
> Apart on a lone burning crag of steel,
> Tortured, cast out; and yet—I shall abide.

The Temple of the Holy Ghost published in 1901 evinces even more specifically the Golden Dawn influence. In *The Neophyte*, he wrote:

> So, I am here. My brows are bent in prayer;
> I kneel already in the Gates of Dawn;
> And I am come, albeit unaware,
> To the deep sanctuary; my hope is drawn
> From wells profounder than the very sea.
> Yea, I am come, where least I guessed it so,
> Into the very Presence of the Three
> That are beyond all Gods. And now I know
> What spiritual Light is drawing me
> Up to its stooping splendour. In my soul
> I feel the Spring, the all-devouring Dawn,
> Rush with my Rising. There, beyond the goal,
> The Veil is rent!
>   Yes: let the Veil be drawn.

Once again, in *The Evocation,* a long poem showing the direct effect of the practical study with Allan Bennett in the magical arts, we read:

> My left hand seeks the lamen. Once again
>   Fearless I front the awful shape before me,
> Fearless I speak his Name. My trembling brain
> Vibrates that Word of Power. I cry amain:
>   "Down, Dweller of the Darkness, and adore me!
> I am thy Master, and thy God! Behold
> The Rose of Ruby and the Cross of Gold."

There is another sonnet *The Rose and the Cross:*

Out of the seething cauldron of my woes,
  Where sweets and salt and bitterness I flung;
  Where charmed music gathered from my tongue,
And where I chained strange archipelagoes
Of fallen stars; where fiery passion flows
  A curious bitumen; where among
  The glowing medley moved the tune unsung
Of perfect love: Thence grew the Mystic Rose.

Its myriad petals of divided light;
  Its leaves of the most radiant emerald;
Its heart of fire like rubies. At the sight
  I lifted up my heart to God and called:
How shall I pluck this dream of my desire?
And lo! there shaped itself the Cross of Fire!

The fourth section of this book is called *The Holy of Holies*. Here is poem after poem of mystical import. When it was reprinted years afterwards in *The Collected Works,* the editor annotated these. The notes themselves are a mystical education, showing to what extent Crowley had assimilated the Order symbolism and teaching, and how easily it flowed out in his creative work. One of them, *The Palace of the World,* describes at length the banishing ritual of the Pentagram, to which is added the footnote, undoubtedly Crowley's: "Those who regard this ritual as a mere device to invoke or banish spirits, are unworthy to possess it. Properly understood, it is the Medicine of Metals and the Stone of the Wise."

The Athanor shows to what extent the 5=6 had activated his very soul. This theme is the one that permeates every bit of his later writing:

For spiritual life and love and light
  Climb the swayed ladder of our various fate;
The steep rude stair that mocks the hero's might,
  Casts off the wise, and crumbles with the great.
Yet from the highest crown no blossom fell,

Save one, to bring salvation unto Hell.

O angel of my spiritual desire!
　O luminous master of the silver feet!
O passionate rose of infinite white fire!
　O cross of sacrifice made bitter-sweet!
O wide-wing, star-brow, veritable lord!
O mystic bearer of the flaming sword!

O brows half seen, O visionary star
　Seen in the fragrant breezes of the East!
O lover of my love, O avatar
　Of the All-One, O mystical High Priest!
O thou before whose eyes my weak eyes fail,
Wonderful warden of the Holy Grail!

Tanhauser, Argonauts, and *Orpheus* are long epics, tedious
taken as a whole, but containing many delicate and lovely
poems, an occasional divine line—and floating all the way
through is the Golden Dawn.

In *Oracles* again there are many items that reflect practical
familiarity with the magical formulae that were given him by
the Order. One is called *The Invocation*. It was also selected
for inclusion in *The Oxford Book of English Mystical Verse.*
The footnote appended to it in the *Collected Works* says
"Versified from the Manuscript called Shin of Shin in Z-2."
Z-2 was a manuscript of magical formulae given to advanced
members of the Zelator Adeptus Minor Grade in the
Hermetic Order of the Golden Dawn. I shall have need to
refer to this manuscript later, in the Mexican episode:

O self Divine! O Living Lord of Me!
Self-shining flame, begotten of Beyond!
Godhead immaculate! Swift tongue of fire,
Kindled from that immeasurable light
The boundless, the immutable. Come forth,
My God, my lover, spirit of my heart,
Heart of my soul, white virgin of the Dawn,
My Queen of all perfection, come thou forth

From thine abode beyond the Silences
To me the prisoner, me the mortal man,
Shrined in this clay; come forth, I say, to me,
Initiate my quickened soul; draw near
And let the glory of thy Godhead shine
Through all the luminous aethers of the air
Even to earth, thy footstool; unto me
Who by these sacred invocations draw
The holy influence within myself
To strengthen and to purify my will
And holy aspiration to thy Life.
Purge me and consecrate until my heart
Burn through the very limits of the veil,
And rend it at the hour of sacrifice
That even the secret pillar in the midst
May be made manifest to mortal eyes . . . .

        O thou Starlight face,
And crowned diamond of my self and soul,
Thou Queenly Angel of my Higher Will,
Form in my spirit a more subtle fire
Of God, that I may comprehend the more
The sacred purity of thy divine
Essence! O Queen, O Goddess of my life,
Light unbegotten, Scintillating spark
Of the All-Self! O holy, holy Spouse
Of my most godlike thought, come forth! I say,
And manifest unto thy worshipper
In more candescent fulgours! . . . .
       . . . .

For I invoke thee by the sacred rites
And secret words of everlasting power:
By the swift symbol of the Golden Dawn
And all its promise, by the Cross of Fire,
And by the Gleaming Symbol: by the Rose
And Cross of Light and Life, the holy Ankh,
The Rose of Ruby and the Cross of Gold.
By these I say, Come forth! my holy Spouse,
And make me one with thine abundant ray

Of the vast ocean of the unmanifest
Limitless Negativity of Light
Flowing, in Jesus manifest, through space,
In equilibrium, upon the world
Illumined by the White Supernal Gleam
Through the red Cross of Calvary: Come forth
My actual Self! Come forth, O dazzling one,
Wrapped in the glory of the Holy Place
Whence I have called thee: Come thou forth to me,
And permeate my being, till my face
Shine with the light reflected, till my brows
Gleam with thy starry symbol, till my voice
Reach the Ineffable: Come forth, I say
And make me one with thee; that all my ways
May glitter with thy holy influence,
That I may be found worthy at the end
To sacrifice before the Holy Ones . . . .
. . . .

O crowned with starlight! Winged with emerald
Wider than Heaven! O profounder blue
Of the abyss of water! O thou flame
Flashing through all the caverns of the night,
Tongues leaping from the immeasurable
Up through the glittering Steeps unmanifest
To the ineffable! O Golden Sun!
Vibrating glory of my higher self!
I heard thy voice resounding in the Abyss:
"I am the only being in the deep
Of Darkness: let me rise and gird myself
To tread the path of Darkness: even so
I may attain the light. For from the Abyss
I came before my birth; from those dim halls
And silence of a primal sleep! And He,
The Voice of Ages, answered me and said:
Behold! for I am He that formulates
In darkness! Child of Earth! The Light doth shine
In darkness, but the darkness understands
No ray of that initiating light!"
. . . .

Leave me not alone,
O Holy Spirit! Come to comfort me,
To draw me, and to make me manifest,
Osiris to the weeping world; that I
Be lifted up upon the Cross of Pain
And sacrifice, to draw all human kind
And every germ of matter that hath life,
Even after me, to the ineffable
Kingdom of Light! O holy, holy Queen!
Let thy wide Pinions overshadow me!

I am, the Resurrection and the Life!
The Reconciler of the Light and the Dark.
I am the Rescuer of mortal things.
I am the Force in Matter manifest.
I am the Godhead manifest in flesh.
I stand above, among the Holy Ones.
I am all-purified through suffering,
All-perfect in the mystic sacrifice,
And in the knowledge of my Selfhood made
One with the Everlasting Lords of Life.
The Glorified through Trial is My Name.
The Rescuer of Matter is My Name.
I am the Heart of Jesus girt about
With the Swift Serpent! I, Osirified
Stand in this Hall of Twofold Truth and say:
Holy art Thou, Lord of the Universe!
Holy art Thou, whom Nature hath not formed!
Holy art Thou, O vast and Mighty One!
O Lord of Darkness and O Lord of Light!
. . . .

I see the Darkness fall as lightning falls!
I watch the Ages like a torrent roll
Past me: and as a garment I shake off
The clinging skirts of Time. My place is fixed
In the abyss beyond all Stars and Suns,
I AM, the Resurrection and the Life!
. . . .

In the fourth part of *Orpheus,* he has used much of the
mystical teaching of the East, together with that of the
Golden Dawn. Some of the free renderings from the Egyptian
Book of the Dead are very well done, as:

> For I am Yesterday, and I
>   To-day, and I tomorrow, born
> Now and again, on high, on high
>   Travelling on Dian's naked horn!
> I am the Soul that doth create
>   The Gods, and all the Kin of Breath.
> I come from the sequestered state;
>   My birth is from the House of Death.
> Hail! ye twin hawks high pinnacled
>   That watch upon the universe!
> Ye that the bier of God beheld!
>   That bore it onwards, ministers
> Of peace within the House of Wrath,
> Servants of him that cometh forth
> At dawn with many-coloured lights
>   Mounting from underneath the North,
> The shrine of the celestial Heights!
>
> He is in me, and I in Him!
>   Mine is the crystal radiance
> That filleth aether to the brim
>   Wherein all stars and suns may dance.
> I am the beautiful and glad
>   Rejoicing in the golden day.
> I am the spirit silken-clad
>   That fareth on the fiery way.
> I have escaped from Him, whose eyes
>   Are closed at eventide, and wise
> To drag thee to the House of Wrong:—
>   I am armed! I am armed! I am strong! I am strong!
> I make my way: opposing horns
>   Of secret foemen push their lust
> In vain: my song their fury scorns;
>   They sink, they grovel in the dust.

Hail, self-created Lord of Night!
Inscrutable and infinite!
   Let Orpheus journey forth to see
   The Disk in peace and victory!
Let him adore the splendid sight,
   The radiance of the Heaven of Nu:
Soar like a bird, laved by the light,
   To pierce the far eternal blue!

. . . .

NOTES

[1] This is the clause that quite clearly Allan Bennett broke in becoming Crowley's teacher before the latter had been formally inducted into the Second Order.

[2] Those who expelled Mathers obviously violated their Oaths on this particular score—as did Crowley also.

[3] Many of the London Adepti obviously violated this clause of the Oath.

PHOTO BY ARNOLD GENTHE, N.Y.

Baphomet XI O.T.O.
Supreme and Holy King of Ireland, Iona, and all the Britains
that are in the Sanctuary of the Gnosis

Grand Master of the Knights of the Holy Ghost
Grand Master of the Knights of the Temple
Custos of the Illuminati in the United States of America
Etc., Etc., Etc.

PART THREE MAGUS

Therefore, O Ananda, be ye lamps·unto yourselves. Be ye a refuge to yourselves. Betake yourselves to no external refuge. Hold fast to the truth as a lamp. Look not for refuge to any one beside yourselves.

Buddha.

CHAPTER EIGHT

Mexico

Aleister Crowley had arrived. This initiation into the 5=6 grade definitely marked his full entry into the Second Order. Now he was an Adept! He realized, however, he was on a plateau. Allan had departed for Ceylon, both for his health and to study Buddhism and Yoga.

There must have been a big emptiness in Crowley's heart. Little mention is made in his diaries of his relationship with Jones at this stage; but whatever that relationship was, it did not exert much pressure on him to remain in England. When the Revolt first broke out, he left Boleskine, renouncing his opening efforts to do the Abramelin operation to offer his services to Mathers. There did not seem much point in going North again.

Under ordinary circumstances the procedure for the newly initiated Adeptus Minor would be to settle down for some serious study, richly larded with hard work. A curriculum was given every newly arrived initiate, detailing all phases of the practical work to be accomplished. With concentrated effort and a good deal of leisure time, this could be sailed through in five years perhaps, though for most people I would say enough is there to keep them busy for the rest of their lives.

It should be remembered however that Crowley had completed most of this work when he had been studying with Allan. He had the boundless energy to devote most of his time to every minute detail and chore demanded by the Great Work. Money was no problem; his inheritance had taken care of that so there were no difficulties put in the way of his concerted striving to complete the work. At the end of this particular year, there was still much to do—to become adept in the use of these practical magical methods of the Order. He was quite willing to proceed and to complete the appointed task, but—he was restless. Too much had been happening, and there was nothing at Boleskine to anchor him to a single spot where he could complete the task ahead of him.

While he was in Paris for the initiation he had met some friends of McGregor Mathers who had just returned from a trip to Mexico. Their description of the country intrigued him. There were some high mountains he could climb. The climate seemed warm and sunny. And the people, he was told, were friendly and uncluttered with the rush and phony values of his native England. So why should he not go?

He made arrangements with an old friend to join him later in Mexico for some mountain climbing. It was good-bye to England, and then the boat to New York.

Before dealing at length with the Mexican episode of his life, there are two matters to discuss. There is the Adeptus Minor curriculum which I want to quote at length, so that it will be clearly understood that this matter was not of a mere dilettante dabbling in occultism, but Crowley's dedication to and reorganization of his inner life. The other episode deals with the means whereby he managed to get Allan Bennett off to the warmth of the East, thus saving Allan's life.

As mentioned earlier, Crowley had inherited a considerable fortune. He could easily have given Allan enough money for the journey to Ceylon. This he did not do. Whatever rationalizations were given, they mean little.

Crowley and Jones went about this business of helping Allan by a circuitous route; they decided to perform a magical operation. It was their determination to "evoke to visible manifestation" one of the "beings" described in the *Goetia,* a mediaeval textbook of Magic. Crowley had become acquainted with a Latin manuscript of this text, and had given Mathers a sum of money to translate it into English. In this book there was a description of an entity by the name of Buer, described as follows: "He appeareth in Sagittary, and that is his shape when the Sun is there. He teaches Philosophy, both Moral and Natural, and the Logic Art, and also the Virtues of all Herbs and Plants. He healeth all distempers in man, and giveth good Familiars." Another classification has him ruled by Mercury, the god of Aesculapia, the healing God.

Be that as it may, the ceremony of evocation was decided upon and in due time completed. Crowley's description of it, extrapolated from *Magick Without Tears,* is most interesting:

I was wide awake, keyed up, keenly observant at the time.

The temple was approximately 16 feet by 8, and 12 high. A small "double-cube" altar of acacia was in the centre of a circle; outside there was a triangle in which it was proposed to get the demon to appear. The room was thick with the smoke of incense . . . .

As the ceremony proceeded, we were aware that the smoke was not uniform in thickness throughout the room, but tended to be almost opaquely dense in some parts of it, all but clear in others. This effect was much more definite than could possibly be explained by draughts, or by our own movements. Presently it gathered itself together still more completely, until it was roughly as if a column of smoke were rising from the triangle, leaving the rest of the room practically clear.

Finally, at the climax of the ritual—we had got as far as the 'stronger and more potent conjuration'—we both saw, vaguely enough, but yet beyond doubt, parts of a quite definite figure. In particular, there was a helmet suggesting Athene (or, horror! Brittania!), part of a tunic or chlamys, and very solid footgear. (I thought of the 'well-greaved Greeks'.) Now this was very far from satisfactory; it corresponded in no wise with the appearance of Buer which the Goetia had led us to expect. Worse, this was as far as it went; no doubt, seeing it at all had disturbed our concentration. (This is where training in Yoga would have helped our Magick.) From that point it was a wash-out. We could not get back the enthusiasm necessary to persist. We called it a day, did the banishings, closed the temple, and went to bed with our tails between our legs.

(And yet, from a saner point of view, the Operation had been a shining success. "Miraculous" things began to happen; in one way and another the gates opened for Allan to migrate to less asthmatic climes; and the object of our work was amply attained.)

So much for the ceremony itself. On the plane of interpersonal relations, it appears that Crowley had called upon an old flame of his, a girl whose husband was in India, telling her that she had the chance of doing a completely unselfish, unfettered act. He asked her for a specific sum of money saying "I have private reasons for not using my own money in this matter." She agreed, giving him the money. This, apparently, Crowley turned over to Allan (who obviously must have known nothing about it), as his steamship fare abroad.

Symonds reported the incident as "Over twenty years later, when Crowley's name had become familiar to the world, this incident was published in *The Sunday Express.* He came under the notice of the police in 1900, when he stole £200 from a widow with whom he cohabited; the woman, however, refused to prosecute."

Symonds comments that the year is right for it was then that Crowley entrained for Scotland after having seen Allan leave England for the Orient.

But there are a couple of facts that are worthy of consideration.

John Bull, a weekly English periodical edited by Horatio Bottomly, had long pandered to the hypocritical English public with the printing of juicy scandalous stories about Crowley. Eventually, this Bottomley was sentenced to seven years' penal servitude for fleecing the same public.

A paper called *The Looking Glass* published by Mr. F. de Wend Fenton, also indulged in the same kind of pernicious libellous writing about Crowley. Soon after this, Fenton was arrested and fined for sending pornography through the mail.

I do not know what happened to James Douglas who wrote several scurrilous pieces of vilification of Crowley in *The Sunday Express.* It would not surprise me in the least if he came to no good end.

What then of Symonds' reporting?

Crowley had been generous with Allan. The latter during a difficult economic cycle came to live with him for well over a year, with Crowley footing all the bills without complaint. Their relationship was a remarkably close one. I do know that Allan was one of the few people Crowley never bitterly attacked at any time in his life. He would have done anything within his power for Allan. Whatever his weird motives were for not directly advancing Allan the money with which to go East, I doubt strongly if there is the least validity to the story of stealing money from a former flame.

Not that I believe Crowley was simon pure. Mine is not blind hero worship. As I have previously intimated, there was a broad streak of viciousness and cruelty in the man. Moral responsibility meant little to him. That he has indulged in blackmail, as Cammell has stated, would not surprise me in the least. He was quite capable of this and many other things too. But the above description of the money incident does not ring true to me.

Let me insist again on the paradoxical nature of this man Crowley. He was no "saint" in the conventional prosaic sense of the word, however true it may be on another level. I have had one experience, at the least, which showed up a thoroughly despicable trait in his character. I have described this in the first chapter.

Allan did get away to the East. That was the primary thing for Crowley. And whether the money came indirectly through the evocation of Buer or directly through a former mistress, the desired result was the same.

The G.D. curriculum provided for his grade remained the immediate task confronting him. Allan had introduced him to fundamental technical methods and the basic nature of the work, so that he could continue practicing without help. There was enough to keep him busy for a long while.

1. *Part One and Two. A. Preliminary*. Most of this work was study material. The student had to study, intellectually, the 5=6 obligation, the Ritual of the grade, the Qabalistic Tree of Life in full color called the *Minutum Mundum,* and a paper on the art of drawing Sigils from the Rose. Also the Hexagram and Pentagram Rituals, the basic tools of ceremonial work.

2. *Part One and Two. B. Implements.* Documents describing the construction and ceremonial consecration of the Lotus Wand, Rose-Cross Lamen, Sword and the four elemental weapons; examination of the implements as described, and arranging for a Chief to be present in the Temple during their actual consecration.

3. *Part One and Two. G. Neophyte Formulae.* This called for a close study of the Neophyte ritual and the symbolism and practical formulae involved, describing to the Chief the arrangement of the Astral Temple and the relative positions of the God-forms in it, demonstrating ability to build up any God-form required with appropriate vibratory names.

4. *Part One and Two. C. Psychic.* One of the most important phases of the Golden Dawn work, the development of Tattwa vision, or traveling clairvoyance,

known at other times as skrying in the spirit vision.

5. *Part One and Two. Divination.* On a selected question, the student had to work out in detail a Divination using Geomancy, Tarot, and Astrology. The goal here was to enhance the intuitive faculty.

6. *Part One and Two. Enochian.* The Enochian or Angelic System was the crown of the Order Work. All training systems of every kind were amalgamated and synthesized into this Enochian system. There was a great deal of detailed theoretical work connected with it.

7. *Part One. E. Talismans.* There was a theoretical and practical examination in the art of constructing talismans for specific purposes.

8. *Part One and Two. H. Consecration and Evocation.* Theoretical and practical examination on the formula of the Neophyte Ritual, based on the document Z-2.

As far as skrying in the Spirit vision is concerned, I can think of no better description or explanation of what this means than the following piece of writing by Crowley:[1]

> The Aspirant should remember that he is a Microcosm. 'Universus sum et Nihil universe a me alienum puto' should be his motto. He should make it his daily practice to travel on the Astral Plane, taking in turn each of the most synthetic sections, the Sephiroth and the Paths. These being thoroughly understood, ... he should start on a new series of expeditions to explore the subordinate sections of each. He may then practice Rising on the Planes from these spheres, one after the other in rotation . . . . It should be his aim to obtain a comprehensive knowledge of the entire Astral Plane, with impartial love of truth for its own sake; just as a child learns the geography of the whole planet, though he may have no intention of ever leaving his native land.

In another place, he offers a few additional words of

explanation which should be included here:

> *The universe is a projection of ourselves; an image as*
> *unreal as that of our faces in a mirror, yet, like that*
> *face, the necessary form of expression thereof, not to be*
> *altered save as we alter ourselves.* The mirror may be
> distorted, dull, clouded, or cracked; and to this extent,
> the reflection of ourselves may be false even in respect
> of its symbolic presentation. In that Light, therefore, all
> that we do is to discover ourselves by means of a
> sequence of hieroglyphics, and the changes which we
> apparently operate are in an objective sence illusions.
>
> But the Light serves us in this way. It enables us to
> see ourselves, and therefore to aid us to initiate
> ourselves by showing us what we are doing. In the same
> way a watchmaker uses a lens, though it exaggerates and
> thus falsifies the image of the system of wheels which he
> is trying to adjust. In the same way, a writer employs
> arbitrary characters according to a meaningless
> convention in order to enable his reader by retranslating
> them to obtain an approximation of his idea.[2]

This description of astral projection as a device to acquire
self-awareness has been substantiated to-day by the Jungian
concept of creative fantasy. Towards the close of *Two Essays
on Analytical Psychology* Jung provides examples of two
fantasies which are extraordinarily similar to the astral
travelling described here. It would make little difference
whether the technique is described as "skrying in the spirit
vision" or creative fantasy, the results appear to be
practically identical. Moreover, a whole new school of
psychotherapy is in the making, as a result of the work of an
Italian psychiatrist, Roberto Assagioli. This school has
evolved a technique of psychosynthesis which includes
"symbolic visualization." It too bears some resemblance to
the Golden Dawn technique of tattwa vision, except that it is
not yet so well developed as the latter, which is described at
some length in *The Golden Dawn, Vol. IV.*[3]

As magical training, the curriculum represents hard work.
It is evident from the diaries, and of course from all his later
practical work, that most of this material he worked through
with Allan. And what remained was left for the nine and
one-half months' residence in Mexico and later for China. In
both of these countries, he did some concentrated and
intensive work on several facets of the above schedule. He did
a little work in Mexico on one complex phase of the
Enochian system, but found he could not go very far with it.
Only later, in 1909 when he was far more mature, mentally
as well as spiritually, was he able to complete that particular
work which I have described in the chapter entitled "North
Africa."

There are not many people who can go through this
arduous training in a short period of time—or even at all. It
requires many years of serious effort, dogged persistence, and
practice in order to acquire proficiency. In effect, this is the
story of Aleister Crowley for very many years, and the story
that most biographers have neglected.

Explanatory of what he meant by Magic, I have
extrapolated the following paragraphs from a very early essay
Berashith, written when he was about 27 or so years of age:

> By meditation, I do not mean merely 'thinking about'
> anything, however profoundly, but the absolute
> restraint of the mind to the contemplation of a single
> object, whether gross, fine, or altogether spiritual.
> Now true magical ceremonial is entirely directed to
> attain this end, and forms a magnificent gymnasium for
> those who are not already finished mental athletes. By
> act, word and thought, both in quantity and quality, the
> one object of the ceremony is being constantly
> indicated. Every fumigation, purification, banishing,
> invocation, evocation, is chiefly a reminder of the single
> purpose, until the supreme moment arrives, and every
> fibre of the body, every force-channel of the mind, is
> strained out in one overwhelming rush of the Will in the

direction desired. Such is the real purport of all the apparently fantastic directions of Solomon, Abramelin, and other sages of repute. When a man has evoked and mastered such forces as Taphthartharath, Belial, Amaimon, and the great powers of the elements, then he may safely be permitted to begin to try to stop thinking. For needless to say, the universe, including the thinker, exists only by virtue of the thinker's thoughts.

When glancing through Mannix's book about Crowley, it amused me to read of his cynical denunciation of magic and allied occult fields. Symonds has a similar attitude. Only Cammell of the three is better informed. It seems extraordinary that any intelligent person today could dismiss not merely as negligible but as wholly fraud and deception the entire field of psychical research. Apart from the wide notice given to Rhine's recent work with parapsychology at Duke University—the new term for the far older psychical research—writers such as Mannix indicate that they have a psychic scotoma of massive proportions. They must never acknowledge the existence of anything that might briefly challenge the narrow view they have formed of life. A larger, wider outlook must be positively frightening to them. It is safer to ridicule, to condemn, to employ the method of *reductio ad absurdum.* This again, is the Emotional Plague described so well by Reich.

The whole area of mystical experience with its close relation to occultism and psychical phenomena is difficult for the average person to handle. He functions, by and large, as if he were only a physical organism that will perish when its day is done, and that is the end. Parapsychology has begun to impress some people with the fact that extra-sensory perception means that the organism is far more extensive than hitherto supposed. Perhaps there is an intelligence functioning above or below the surface of consciousness which is not co-extensive with the cellular structure with which it is so closely conjoined. Telepathy, clairvoyance, mediumistic phenomena, apparitions, and the whole field of psychical phenomena prove this beyond any shadow of doubt. The difficulty is that the average person is unfamiliar with it, and usually scoffs at its existence before having even investigated the vast body of literature grown up around it. To accept it, he must re-organize his own intellectual structure, and his vaguely realized beliefs.

Crowley must have left England late in the month of June, 1900, for he tells us that when he arrived in New York, at the climax of a heat wave only New York can have, he was fairly prostrated by the heat and humidity. From this he fled to Mexico City. It might have been hot there, but the elevation alone would have made it infinitely more tolerable than the concrete canyons and glass and steel towers of New York City.

There was something about Mexico—the land of sunshine and gaiety, poverty and squalor, freedom and manana—that intrigued him enormously. How else explain the fact that he stayed there for over nine months? Apart from his living in the United States for the four year War period, and his residence in Sicily for a period of a few years after the War, this was the longest period of time he stayed anywhere. And this was Alastor, the Wanderer of the Wastes, the Spirit of Solitude! In this bright dry land of sharply silhouetted hills, ancient memories must have awakened within him. During the days of high inspiration of 1907 when *The Book of Lapis Lazuli* came to be written, he penned the following:

> And Oh! the chirp of the cicada!
> I remember the days when I was cacique in Mexico.
> O my God, wast Thou then as now my beautiful lover?
> Was my boyhood then as now Thy toy, Thy joy?

Verily, I remember those iron days.

I remember how we drenched the bitter lakes with our torrent of gold; how we sank the treasurable image in the crater of Citlaltapetl.

How the good flame lifted us even unto the lowlands, setting us down in the impenetrable forest.

Yea, Thou wast a strange scarlet bird with a bill of gold. I was Thy mate in the forests of the lowland; and ever we heard from afar the shrill chant of mutilated priests and the insane clamour of the Sacrifice of Maidens.

There was a weird winged God that told us of his wisdom.

Symonds advises that once there:

"He hired a house overlooking the Alameda, the beautiful park in the centre of Mexico City, and engaged a young Indian girl to look after him and share his bed. Then he settled down to Magic . . . ."

"The City of Mexico began by irritating me intensely," wrote Crowley in his *Confessions*. "The hotel had no organized service; they didn't seem to care whether one got anything to eat or not. In fact, in the whole city, there was only one restaurant where one could get anything outside the regular local dishes. Nobody bothers about eating. The same applies to drinking, as far as the palate is concerned. People ate to satisfy hunger, and drank to get drunk. There were no fine vintages; the principal drinks were pulque, which is the fermented sap of the aloe; mescal, tequila, and aguardiente; the last being a general term applicable to any distilled spirit. In those days I was practically an abstainer, and as I had a fastidious daintiness which made me dislike trying experiments, I never even sampled any of these drinks."

For some while, he took a needed vacation from Magic, dedicating his bountiful energies to the pursuit of Venus. There were several affairs, as there always were in Crowley's life, some preposterous, others bizarre. His attraction for strange, exotic and weird women was characteristic of him; and he found them plentiful in Mexico.

Toward the end of the year, Oscar Eckenstein arrived from Europe to go mountaineering with him. In those two or three months, Crowley found he had had his fill of vacation, and was ready not merely for mountain-climbing but for serious inner development as well.

The relationship between these two men is altogether remarkable. Eckenstein is about the only man in his life besides Allan on whom he never turned. The respect and admiration he had gained for his mountain-climbing colleague and friend continued to flourish without alteration.

"Eckenstein was a man twenty years older than myself," wrote Crowley in his autobiography. "His business in life was mathematics and science, and his one pleasure mountaineering. He was probably the best all-round man in England, but his achievements were little known because of his almost fanatical objection to publicity. He hated self-advertising quacks like the principal members of the Alpine Club with an intensity which, legitimate as it was, was almost overdone. His detestation of every kind of humbug and false pretence was an overmastering passion. I have never met any man who upheld the highest moral ideals with such unflinching candour . . . . He was rather short and sturdily built. He did not know the meaning of the word "fatigue." He could endure the utmost hardship without turning a hair. He was absolutely reliable, either as leader or second man, and this quality was based upon profound and accurate calculations. He knew his limitations to a hair's breadth. I never saw him attempt anything beyond his powers; and I never knew him in want of anything from lack of foresight."

Crowley considered Eckenstein the greatest climber of his time. He regarded him both as a brother and as a father-figure whom he revered and respected. As Bennett was his guru in Magic, so Eckenstein was his master in mountaineering.

It is a curious phenomenon that all three men suffered from bronchial asthma. One of the lines of Jungian interpretation is that the wheezing of asthma is suggestive of men who are overly ambitious, who must climb too high—too much so for their own emotional and bodily comfort. It rather fits here.

To the *Sword of Song*, Crowley appended some erudite and amusing notes, explanatory of some of his more obscure references. One of these notes relates to Eckenstein, praising his friend, and libelling the Alpine Club at the same time:

> Take Oscar Eckenstein—he climbs
> Alone, unroped, a thousand times.
> He scales his peak, he makes his pass,
> He does not fall into a crevasse!
> But if the Alpine Club should seek
> To follow him on pass or peak—
> (Their cowardice, their mental rot,
> Are balanced nicely—they will not.)
> —I see the Alpine Journal's border
> Of black grow broader, broader, broader,
> Until the Editor himself
> Falls from some broad and easy shelf,
> And in his death the Journal dies.
> Ah! bombast, footle, simple lies!
> Where would you then appear in type?

Off went these two men, comrades and friends, to explore and climb the mountains of Mexico. And what a time they had! Crowley has described this at great length in his *Confessions,* and Symonds has also dealt with it, making it unnecessary for me to add anything. But what Symonds has omitted is a curious fact. Eckenstein was totally uninterested in Crowley's poetry and even less, if possible, in his magical interests. He deplored them. But one day he must have reproached Crowley and said "Why don't you learn how to discipline your mind? Why don't you learn how to concentrate? You are far too scattered, and you waste your energies."

This came as a shock to Crowley. From Eckenstein this was not the sort of thing he expected. He would have been willing to accept any criticism and advice on the technique of mountain—climbing, but this? He could not accept the fact that he was unable to concentrate. His pride was offended. After all, he had had a very good education. He had come down from Cambridge, where he had studied mathematics and the sciences, philosophy and comparative religion, literature, and was a passionately lyrical poet. Passion tends to crowd out other psycho-physical preoccupations to induce of its own accord an intense concentration.

Nevertheless Eckenstein challenged him to prove he could concentrate his mind *at will*. To his horror Crowley found he could not meet the challenge. This determined him to embark upon a training recommended by Eckenstein that would remedy this deficiency. It was his first introduction to Raja Yoga.

To Crowley, it seemed at the time that Eckenstein was a messenger. From the Chiefs of the Order? From the Community or School of Saints about whom he had read in von Eckartshausen's *The Cloud on the Sanctuary*?

For his own private information and edification, he took an oath to embark seriously upon this concentration-training, in which oath he gave a magical motto to Eckenstein. Though Eckenstein was not a member of the Golden Dawn, and would no doubt have been contemptuous of it, Crowley labelled him Frater D.A. And from that date on, in his diary writings, Eckenstein is known as Frater D.A. What these initials stand for is not known.

Dated the 22nd of February, 1901 in Guadalajara, Crowley set down his oath to practice concentration, and describes the situation in these terms:

> Now, the year being yet young, one D.A. came unto me, and spake.
>
> And he spake not any more (as had been his wont) in guise of a skeptic and indifferent man; but indeed with the very voice and power of a Great Guru, or of one definitely sent from such a Brother of the Great White Lodge.
>
> Yea! though he spake unto me words of all disapproval, did I give thanks and grace to God that he had deemed my folly worthy to attract his wisdom . . . . Under his direction, therefore, I began to apply myself unto the practice of Raja-yoga, at the same time avoiding all, even the smallest, consideration of things occult, as also he bade me . . . .

From this day forward, regardless of where they traveled or what mountain they were climbing, no matter what the situations were, two or three or more times a day, he made himself engage in this most arduous of all mental disciplines. He would take a perfectly simple or even trivial object, say a white triangle, a stick, or his Rose-cross, and force his mind to concentrate on it. He learned to be thoroughly systematic about this discipline. In front of him, would be a stop-watch, pencil and notebook. At the end of his practice period, he would record in a diary how many minutes he had attempted to concentrate, and how many times his mind wandered away. These mind-wanderings he called "breaks." He was able eventually to categorize these into several discrete groups. After about three weeks of daily exercise, he was able to record that he had concentrated for 59½ minutes, during which there were over 25 breaks. It was not very good, and he knew it.

Here this man is so paradoxical, so extraordinary. There was no occasion or event, ordinarily, which he would not seize upon as a means of expressing his egotism. This was one of his major characteristics. Whether or not it was an evidence of his essential inferiority and guilt feelings is immaterial. When however we come to examine his self-discipline in Yoga and Magic, we find no trace of self-glorification, no egotism, no exaltation. There is restraint. He just sticks tenaciously to the practices, whatever they were, and enters them honestly and simply in this diary-record.

Between January and April, 1901, whether Crowley was living in the fastnesses of the Nevada de Colima, or the Nevada de Toluca, or Amecameca, or even on the slopes of Popocatapetl, his diary shows daily entries. Each entry depicts a particular attempt to practice concentration. There is no fanfare, just the statement of the object used for meditation, the amount of time consumed, and some simple comment.

In January he attempted to visualize the ordinary Egyptian Winged globe. He then concentrated on this mental image. Total time was four minutes. Comment: The entire meditation was bad. Another day, he used a Tattva symbol. This is one of a series of coloured geometrical objects used by the Hindus to symbolize the elements. This particular symbol was a small red triangle superimposed on a standing black egg. Time was three minutes. Comment: There was no difficulty in getting the object clear; but the mind wandered.

Some weeks later, he again concentrated on the mental image of the winged globe. The time consumed was ten minutes. There were ten breaks. This did not please him, for the diary records a resolution he made at this time: "I resolve to increase my powers greatly by the aid of the Most High, until I can meditate for twenty-four hours on one object." That was a tall order—but one could expect this kind of brash resolution from a man who was no more than twenty-six or so. I wonder how many men of his or any other age could have stood the continued stress and strain of this persistent exercise.

Towards the end of April, he was able to concentrate on his Rose-cross symbol for as long as 23 minutes. with only

nine breaks. By this time he was beginning to learn something
about the process, and something about the way his own
mind worked. For he wrote, about this particular practice: "I
think breaks are longer in themselves than of old; for I find
myself concentrating on them and forgetting the primary
altogether. But I have no means of telling how long it is
before the error is discovered." At the very best, this was an
indication that his ability to concentrate was improving. It
led him to experiment in different directions. And never
forget that while all this was going on, he was leading a very
rough athletic and rigorous life. There was nothing
schizophrenic about climbing the highest mountains in
Mexico. Nor anything masochistic about his quiet dogged
persistence in the face of every obstacle and hazard.

"During this whole period of rough travel, work is
fatiguing, difficult and uncertain. Regularity is impossible, as
regards hours and even days, and the mind, being so full of
other things, seems to refuse to compose itself. Nearly always
I was too tired to do two (let alone three) meditations; and
the weariness of the morrow was another hostile factor. Let
me hope that my return here (Mexico City) will work
wonders."

His lyrical ability was not dormant during this period.
Many poems were written in Mexico City. But the most
important to my mind is one called *Assumpta Canidia,* from
which I give the last two stanzas:

> Thus wait I on the spring-forgotten shore;
>   Looking with vain unweeping eyes, for aye
>   Into the wedding of the sea and sky,
> (That do not wed, ah me!) for evermore
> Hopeless, forgetting even to aspire
>   Unto that Wisdom; miserably dumb;
>   Waiting for the Impossible to come,
> Whether in mercy or damnation dire—
>   I who have been all Beauty and all Power!—

> This is thine hour, Apollyon, thine Hour!
>
> I, who have twice beheld the awful throne;
>   And, as it were the vision of a glass,
>   Beheld the Mist be born thereon, and pass;
> I, who have stood upon the four-square stone!
> I, who have twice been One—! Woe, Woe is me!
>   Lost, lost, upon the lifeless, deathless plane,
>   The desert desolate, the air inane;
> Fallen, O fallen to eternity!
>   I, who have looked upon the Lord of Light;
>   I, I am Nothing, and dissolved in Night!

While traveling from mountain range to mountain range, he devised other sets of exercises to develop mental skills of one kind or another, to aid his meditative ability. In the year before he entered the Golden Dawn, he had come across *The Spiritual Exercises* by St. Ignatius of Loyola. In this book, the general of the Jesuits recommended the intense visualization of various dramatic scenes in the life of Christ, and meditation on them until a species of identification be achieved. Crowley devised exercises based on what he had read; they became elaborate and difficult. For example:

> I tried to imagine the sound of a waterfall. This was very difficult to get at; and it makes one's ears sing for a long time afterwards. If I really got it, it was however not strong enough to shut out other physical sounds. I also tried to imagine the 'puff-puff' of an engine. This resulted better than the last, but it caused the skin of my head to commence vibrating.

I never cease to marvel over the basic simplicity of this strange man. He experimented and adventured in these psychological and spiritual areas with a kind of indomitability that most of us have never had. I wonder how many of us could get to the point of disciplining our minds in this way, training them to behave in the way we wished them to. To teach them to concentrate and build up interior sensations like the sound of a waterfall, the taste of chocolate, the smell of a particular perfume, or what-not. There are not many who would have the patience, let alone the will-power to keep at this for more than a few weeks, or even a few days. This is one of the reasons for my great irritation when I read of criticisms from people who have no concept at all of what Aleister Crowley did, or was attempting to do. They could have absolutely no understanding of the values by which this man operated and functioned in his every-day life.

Towards the end of April, he drew up for himself a tight schedule. He had once more returned to his magical practices, which this new schedule included, as well as the concentration exercises. It was outlined as follows:

1. In the morning, the assumption of a God-form, and the Shin operation.

2. Before Tiffin. An astral projection practice.

3. In the evening. A magical ceremony of some sort, work on talismans, the Enochian tablets, etc.

In other words, the program included the whole regimen of the Adeptus Minor, a regimen which he was once more pushing very hard. Eckenstein, friend and teacher, left him sometime in April, returning to London where he immediately set about organizing and planning the next Himalaya expedition. Crowley himself made for San Francisco where he intended to get a boat for the East. He proposed to visit Allan in Ceylon for some time, and later on in the summer of 1902, to climb Chogo-Ri with Eckenstein.

Before leaving Mexico, however, he had learned, as a result of his meditations and work with some of the basic Golden Dawn documents how to discard all ceremonial, reducing this one Neophyte ritual to a series of mental gestures or operations. I can best describe this simply by stating that a G.D. document named Z-2 broke the Neophyte Ritual down into discrete parts or gestures. On the basis of this formula-tabulation, several quite different types of ceremonies could be developed under the headings of the letters in the name of God, as the means of classification. The Tetragrammaton, as the four-lettered name of God YHVH is called, becomes the Pentagrammaton when Shin is added. Shin represents the descent of the Holy Ghost, splitting open and thus consecrating the elemental God, transforming it into YHSHVH, Yeheshuah or Jesus. This formula of the Holy Spirit, was then sub-divided into three more sections, based on certain complex Golden Dawn theorems and postulates. The third part of the formula was called the Shin-of-Shin operation, and it comprised, essentially, the invocation of the Higher Self in the form of a ceremony. I have given an example of this towards the end of *The Golden Dawn, Vol. III.*

Two years just prior to the Mexico period we are now considering, Crowley had written a lengthy poem, *The Invocation.* To all intents and purposes, it is a versified rendition of the Shin of Shin operation. Its opening lines are:

> O Self Divine! O Living Lord of me!
> Self-shining flame, begotten of Beyond!
> . . . . . Come forth, I say, to me,
> Initiate my quickened soul; draw near
> And let the glory of thy Godhead shine.
> . . . . O thou Starlight face . . . .
> Form in my spirit a more subtle fire
> Of God, that I may comprehend the more
> The sacred purity of thy divine
> Essence . . . .

Other of its lines that may throw some light on the entire theme are:

> For I invoke thee by the sacred rites
> And secret words of everlasting power

> By the swift symbol of the Golden Dawn
> And all its promise, by the Cross of Fire
> And by the Gleaming Symbol; by the Rose
> And Cross of Light and Life; the Holy Ankh
> The Rose of Ruby and the Cross of Gold.

It is this poem *The Invocation* which includes those meaningful lines to which earlier I had called attention:

> I am the Heart of Jesus girt about
> With the Swift Serpent . . . .

In another of the Order documents, Mathers I believe had described clairvoyantly what occurred to the Candidate during the Neophyte initiatory ceremony. One of these clairvoyant pictures represents the Candidate standing between the two pillars as enclosed in a force-field, an aura or Akasic egg of varying colors, above which a White Light descended. Crowley appropriated this description and added it to the above Shin-of-Shin operation, and through meditation developed a technique that eliminated all ritual. The following is his simple description of his newly developed technique:

> 1. Ray of Divine White Brilliance descending on the Akasic Egg set between the two pillars.
> 2. Aspire by the Serpent, and concentrate on Flashing Sword. Imagine the stroke of the Sword upon the *Daath* junction (nape of the neck).
> 3. Make the Egg grow gray, by a three fold spiral of light.
> 4. Make the Egg grow nearly white. (Repeat spiral formula.)
> 5. Repeat 2. Above head. Triangle of Fire (red).
> 6. Invoke Light. Withdraw. See Golden Dawn symbol.
> 7. Let all things vanish in the illimitable Light.

I first became familiar with this abbreviation of Shin-of-Shin very many years ago. It must be admitted that it did not mean much to me then, any more I suppose than it can mean much to the ordinary reader now. But I can honestly say that as I write these words now, I develop an even more profound appreciation for Crowley's genius. It implies that he was not only willing to follow Order teaching, but over and beyond this, he was able to pierce through the outer form to the heart and core of the practice, which he then proceeded to simplify. After he had worked through the mental operations of the Shin operation, he was able to re-write it in dramatic and symbolic form years afterwards, when the task fell upon him to provide the Official Instructions for the Order that he and Jones founded. Even if the above description may not mean much, and the following section from Liber HHH may not convey much more, nonetheless for completeness' sake, I am giving it since it meant a great deal to me.

0. Be seated in thine Asana, wearing the robe of a Neophyte, the hood drawn.

1. It is night, heavy and hot, there are no stars. Not one breath of wind stirs the surface of the sea, that is thou. No fish play in thy depths.

2. Let a Breath rise and ruffle the waters. This also thou shalt feel playing upon thy skin. It will disturb thy meditation twice or thrice, after which thou shouldst have conquered this distraction. But unless thou first feel it, that Breath hath not arisen.

3. Next, the night is riven by the lightning flash. This also shalt thou feel in thy body, which shall shiver and leap with the shock, and that also must both be suffered and overcome.

4. After the lightning flash, resteth in the zenith a minute point of light. And that light shall radiate until a right cone be established upon the sea, and it is day.

With this thy body shall be rigid, automatically; and this shalt thou let endure, withdrawing thyself into thine heart in the form of an upright Egg of blackness; and therein shalt thou abide for a space.

5. When all this is perfectly and easily performed at will, let the aspirant figure to himself a struggle with the whole force of the Universe. In this he is only saved by his minuteness. But in the end he is overcome by Death, who covers him with a black cross.

Let his body fall supine with arms outstretched.

6. So lying, let him aspire fervently unto the Holy Guardian Angel.

7. Now let him resume his former posture.

Two and twenty times shall he figure to himself that he is bitten by a serpent, feeling even in his body the poison thereof. And let each bite be healed by an eagle or hawk, spreading its wings over his head, and dropping thereon a healing dew. But let the last bite be so terrible a pang at the nape of the neck that he seemeth to die, and let the healing dew be of such virtue that he leapeth to his feet.

8. Let there be now placed within his egg a red cross, then a green cross, then a golden cross, then a silver cross; or those things which these shadow forth. Herein is silence; for he that hath rightly performed the meditation will understand the inner meaning hereof, and it shall serve as a test of himself and his fellows.

9. Let him now remain in the Pyramid or Cone of Light, as an Egg, but no more of blackness.

10. Then let his body be in the position of the Hanged Man, and let him aspire with all his force unto the Holy Guardian Angel.

11. The grace having been granted unto him, let him partake mystically of the Eucharist of the Five Elements, and let him proclaim Light in Extension; yea, let him proclaim Light in Extension.

This beautifully written instruction, however obscure and symbolic it may seem, is none other than the original Shin-of-Shin ceremony, with every trace of ritual eliminated. It incorporates the basic mental elements as visualized by Crowley in Mexico in 1901, plus Yoga breathing and its sequel of hyperventilation-tetany about which he learned more later in Ceylon. He has combined these with the meditation skills that started with Oscar Eckenstein, and the result is the above. It is a marriage of different systems. And it is an example of what Crowley did to the bare-bones of the different systems with which he became acquainted. Each one became transformed, beautified by his prose, and integrated into a larger whole.

Before he left Mexico, with many pangs of regret, he wrote:

> I strolled across to Juarez to kiss my girl good-bye. O Mexico, my heart still throbs and burns whenever memory brings you to my mind! For many other countries I have more admiration and respect, but none of them rivals your fascination. Your climate, your customs, your people, your strange landscapes of dreamlike enchantment rekindle my boyhood.

Then he was off. A few days in the Chinese quarter of San Francisco; then on the 3rd of May 1901, he embarked on a Japanese vessel bound for Hawaii, the first stage of his voyage to Ceylon. While ship-life conduces ordinarily to relaxation and sheer laziness, this was not to be the case with Crowley. His record begins the very next day with practices, concentration and magical exercises, without cessation. Every day, his devotion to the Great Work kept him busy with something—astral projection, assumption of God-forms, the mental gestures of the Shin of Shin, or a simple concentration exercise. He did not know laziness—or else he was driven; driven either by his aspiration or his neurosis! Regardless of what it was that motivated him there is no doubt that he worked hard to attain his goals.

For example, on May 6th, there is the entry that he concentrated on the symbol, the Egg between the two white pillars. Total time was 32 minutes. There were ten breaks, which is not really bad, all things considered, but he noted that it was better towards the end; best after the tenth break. Concentration must have then lasted six or seven minutes. This was considerable improvement. But just so as to ensure that he could develop no intellectual pride in his accomplishment the next day's entry was different. Same subject as before, but the time was only six minutes. There were three breaks; "I seemed to collapse suddenly." But later that evening, he must have recovered somewhat. There was no despair; no desperate repudiation of the entire venture, for he meditated anew, this time on the Golden Dawn symbol, a white triangle surmounted by a red cross for some fourteen minutes, in which there were only three breaks. This was infinitely better!

The schedule that he had previously embarked on in Mexico apparently still held good on board the ship for Japan; for there are several entries describing practical work with each one of the many items scheduled. The stateroom he occupied could not have been large, but in it he performed several ceremonies. He practiced the rituals of the Pentagram and Hexagram, attempted to acquire skill with the Enochian calls or invocations which proved infinitely valuable eight years later, and invoked Thoth by the use of Liber Israfel. This latter consisted of a rendition of versicles from the Egyptian *Book of the Dead,* which he inherited from Allan and which he improved upon so far as literary style is concerned. It became a work of art in his hands, encouraging me to reprint most of it in the anthology *The Best of Crowley.*

In the middle of the month, there is recorded the fact that he experimented with God-forms. This consists in imagining the classical image of the Egyptian God-form as enveloping and enclosing oneself. It requires a vivid imagination and a great deal of concentration. "Assumption of the God-form of Harpocrates; it lasted nine minutes; the result was good, for I got a distinct aura around me." The next day he confined himself to just plain concentration exercises, using the Tattwa image previously mentioned. But day in, and day out, all across the ocean to Hawaii, this went on without pause. This surely is the purest form of persistence.

Symonds notes, in his account of Crowley's adventures, that "On Waikiki Beach he met an American woman of Scottish origin, ten years older than himself, married to a lawyer in the States, and mother of a teen-age boy. She had, Crowley said, come to Hawaii to escape hay fever. He fell in love with her, wrote a long poem, *Alice: an Adultery* under her inspiration, took her with him to Japan and left her there. He was very pleased with *Alice,* which contains fifty poems, one for each day of his passion." The sonnet for the first day is:

> The waving surf shone from the Peaceful Sea.
>> Young palms embowered the house where Beauty
>>> sate
>> Still but exultant, silent but elate
>> In its own happiness and majesty
> Of a mild soul unstirred by rivalry
>> Of any life beyond its own sweet state.
>> I looked around me, wondered whether Fate
>> Had found at last a woman's love for me.
>
> I had no hope; she was so grave and calm,
>> So shining with the dew-light of her soul,
>> So beautiful beyond a woman's share.
> Yet—here! Soft airs, and perfume through the palm,
>> And moonlight in the groves of spice, control
>> The life that would not love and yet be fair.

By the fourteenth day, they were passionately involved.

> All day we chose each moment possible
>> When to the other's face each face might cling,
>> Each kiss burn forth, a double fiery sting

Exulting us in joy foreseen to swell
A mighty exultation; it befell,
However, that I saw the shadowy thing
Lurk behind love, to flap a scornful wing,
Seeing our honour stood a citadel.

I saw the foolishness of love that saith:
"I am not exalted over shame and death,
But will not take my fill of death and shame."
For each kiss leaps, a more insistent breath,
And adds fresh fuel to the amorous flame,
Not quells it—Is not honour but a name?

And so on, day by day, he wrote a sonnet inspired by
Alice who had moved him to the core. It ended, as most such
affairs must end, with cynical relief "Thank God I've finished
with that foolishness!" to be followed in the final sonnet by
a more accurate evaluation:

Now, when the sun falls in the dismal sky
And no light leaps beneath the plunging prow,
I know the fullness of my sorrow now:—
That all my talk and laughter was a lie;
That as each hour widens the gulfs that sigh
Between us; the truth scores upon my brow
Sigils of silence, burns in me the vow
"I love you, and shall love you till I die."

Whether next year, as fondly as we made oath
Shall see us meet at last, whether as wife
I shall at last gather the whole vow's breath—
Not heaven nor hell shall break our solemn troth.
I love you, and shall love you all my life.
I love you, and shall love you after death.

The Symonds narrative concludes this episode with a
totally false and inaccurate evaluation, so typical of this
constantly sneering author who seized every opportunity to
denigrate Crowley whom he understood not at all. "Crowley

did not say what caused the break-up of their love, but whatever it was, it left him conscious of the sadness of life and of the mysterious demon who drove him darkly onwards. Alice was the first of a long line of women who taught him that he was not made for love."

This is *not* what this long line of women had taught him. He was capable of love, of a deep and passionate love; and he loved in his own way, whether Symonds approved of it or not. Many women loved him, and he them—devotedly. What is clearly evident here is not that he was incapable of love, but that he was incapable of a permanent interpersonal relationship or marriage. Love and an enduring marital relationship are two entirely different things. Ancient astrologers showed the fifth house of the horoscope to relate to love and pleasure, while the seventh house was allocated to marriage, contracts and partnerships. There was no necessary connection between them. For all of Symonds' mockery of Crowley and of mysticism and meditation, his insight is not adequate in the least to the task of evaluation. He has merely delineated his own limitations and his own psychological problems.

To conclude this chapter, I wish to include a few lines from a long poem of free verse that Crowley added as an epilogue to one of his early books. It opens with:

> When I think of the hundreds of women I have loved
>   from time to time,
> White throats and living bosoms where a kiss might
>   creep or climb,
> Smooth eyes and trembling fingers, faint lips or
>   murderous hair,
> All tunes of love's own music, most various and rare;
> When I look back on life, as a mariner on the deep
> Seas, tranced, the white wake foaming, fancies
>   nereids weep;
> As on a mountain summit in the thunders and the
>   snow,

I look to the shimmering valley and weep: I loved
     you so!
          . . . .

Your bodies had wearied me, but your passion was
     ever fresh;
You were many indeed, but your love for me was
     one.
Then I perceived the stars to reflect a single sun—
Not burning suns themselves, in furious regular race,
But mirrors of midnight, lit to remind us of His face,
Thus I beheld the truth; ye are stars that gave me
     light;
          . . . .

You have taught me in perfection to be satisfied;
You have taught me midnight vigils, when you smiled
     in amorous sleep;
You have even taught a man the women's way to
     weep.
So, even as you helped me, blindly, against your will,
So shall the angel faces watch for your own souls still.
A little pain and pleasure, a little touch of time,
And you shall blindly reach to the subtle and
     sublime;
You shall gather up your girdles to make ready for
     the way,
And by the Cross of Suffering climb seeing to the
     Day.
Then we shall meet again in the Presence of the
     Throne,
Not knowing; yet in Him! O Thou! knowing as we are
     known.

NOTES

[1] *Magick,* The Master Therion, Paris, 1929, p. 203. This book has been recently reprinted as *Magick in Theory and Practice* by Aleister Crowley, Castle Books, New York, no date.

[2] "This passage must not be understood as asserting that the Universe is purely subjective. On the contrary, the Magical Theory accepts the absolute reality of all things in the most objective sence. But all perceptions are neither the observer nor the observed; they are representations of the relation between them. We cannot affirm any quality in an object as being independent of our sensorium, or as being in itself that which it seems to us. Nor can we assume that what we cognize is more than a partial phantom of its cause. We cannot even determine the meaning of such ideas as motion, or distinguish between time and space, except in relation to some particular observer. For example, if I fire a cannon twice at an interval of 3 hours, an observer on the Sun would note a difference of some 200,000 miles in space between the shots, while to me they seem "in the same place." Moreover, I am incapable of perceiving any phenomenon except by means of the arbitrary instruments of my senses; it is thus correct to say that the Universe as I know it is subjective, without denying its objectivity." (A.C.)

[3] *The Golden Dawn,* Israel Regardie (Llewellyn Publications, St. Paul, Minn., 1969).

CHAPTER NINE

Ceylon

The trip from Japan continued, with Ceylon as its goal. Crowley was anxious to see Allan once again. With some relief, he had left Alice in Yokohama to return to her husband. It had freed a certain amount of time and energy for renewed devotion to his spiritual exercises. The diaries continued in exactly the same way as before. There were exercises in one special magical area in the morning; in the afternoon, well before dinner, another set; and late in the evening, a final set of practices.

His diaries are fascinating at this stage. Inner growth is depicted. For one thing they reveal his utter lack of knowledge at that time about Vedanta and Buddhism. There are some revealingly inaccurate entries such as "Meditation upon Nirvana" and "invoked Angel of Nirvana as Harpocrates sitting on the Lotus." So far as the former is concerned, he had no notion what Nirvana was, and secondly he had confused it with some previous material he had read and poorly digested. This deficiency in his knowledge of comparative religions was not remedied until he had been in Ceylon for some time and studied with Allan, who was about to become the Bhikkhu Ananda Metteya. From that time on, Crowley was second to none in his essential grasp of these two Oriental religious systems.

Not yet had he been introduced to the Yoga theories of breathing. On his own initiative, he had begun some experiments with respiration, even while continuing to practice concentration. On one occasion, he took a "hundred indrawn breaths in reclining position with belt on. 7 minutes 50 seconds. (4.7 seconds per breath)." Later on in that day, he experienced still further: "Ten indrawn breaths as slow as possible. 7 minutes 26 seconds. (44.6 seconds per breath)." About all he noticed was some heightening of the sense of relaxation, but nothing more. He had not discovered that breathing in certain prescribed ways could lead to hyperventilation of the brain, from which event certain psycho-physiological phenomena proceeded. This was yet to be discovered and explored.

Sometime during July, there is a simple entry: "Somewhere on this journey *became* the GREAT PEACE." That is all. No other comment; no excitement, no fanfare. The entries before and after this particular one still record daily exercises, meditating on different objects, attempting an astral projection, assuming a God-form. The cumulative result of all these exercises must have begun to slow down the incessant motion of his ever active mind, giving him access to hitherto inaccessible psychic material. It facilitated thinking and feeling in unfamiliar ways, allowing a perception of himself and the world around him in a totally new manner. This he experienced as a heightening of consciousness, which he considered the Great Peace.

Three weeks later, following a meditation lasting 28 minutes on selfishness, magical power, and Nirvana, he wrote: "After this meditation I arrived at the following decision: I must not cling to the Peace. It certainly has become real to me, but if I make a God of it, it will become but an illusion. I am ready to receive the Magical Power as I should not abuse it. I must needs accomplish the Finished Work." This speaks for itself. Even the meagre results he was obtaining and which he dearly needed, he was quite willing to renounce if they got in his way to reach to the very heights.

With all his literary skill, he could only say that he simply *became* the great peace. It is almost as if he were baffled at the possibilities of description of the spiritual state that had descended on him. Baffled? This is quite understandable.

In a lesser way, I once experienced a state of peace, quiet, serenity, stillness, blissfulness. It stayed with me for a long time, though the length of the experience was never more than an hour at most. I came to understand then something Crowley had written long years ago:

How shall I indite songs unto Thee, when even the memory of the shadow of Thy glory is a thing beyond all music of speech or of silence.

For a long time, I tried to work out some kind of verbal or literary description of this quiet, this stillness. But everything about it was paradoxical. There was serenity and there was ecstasy. But the stillness was a vital, dynamic and energetic quiet. It was not static, not still, not dead. It was almost an alive silence. Even now, as I sit at my typewriter thinking on these transcendental things, the joy-song mounts within, as tears well up within the eyes, but it is no more possible now to describe that state of inner peace which at the same time was high excitement, than it was then. It was this impossibility which enables me to appreciate Crowley's simplicity, when in spite of everything, he could not dilate on the phrase "became the Great Peace."

It must have had a considerable psychological effect, for the diary entry of the next day reads: "Meditation on Buddha. 33 minutes. The best meditation I have so far done. I regard this as a *real* meditation; for 13 minutes quite forgot time."

On August 6th, he finally arrived at his Eastern destination, and on the very next day, hastened to visit his old friend, Allan Bennett. Though Allan's intention was to become a Buddhist monk, for the time being he was studying Yoga and Hinduism with a Tamil guru who was none other than the Solicitor General of Ceylon, who upon retirement became Shri Parananda. Crowley in effect had two gurus at this time, Allan and Parananda. Actually, however, Allan was his guru or teacher, any problems arising were taken to Parananda for final counsel.

Forthwith Allan and Crowley began working together once more. There was no delay. A program of intellectual study was inaugurated so that Crowley might become familiar with the fundamental propositions of both Vedanta and Buddhism. At the same time a program of practical work was also instituted. This was conducted along purely classical lines of Yoga in all its manifold branches.

What is Yoga? I will let Crowley provide the answers in passages taken from various of his writings, prose and poetry, both serious and humorous, but all explanatory and illuminating. He had a fine talent for exposition, second to none where he was writing about his own experiences and the deductions to be made from them.

There are many expositions of Yoga amongst his various writings. *Part I of Book IV* is a little book written around 1912-13, consisting of a fine detailed analysis and simple explanation of the various steps of Yoga. A few years before he died, he gave lectures on the subject, which subsequently were printed and entitled *Eight Lectures on Yoga.* In it, he provided a short, snappy, and succinct definition:

> Sit still!
> Stop thinking!
> Shut up!
> Get out!

Shortly after the Ceylon episode that we are dealing with, he provided some notes, caustic, informative and amusing, to *The Sword of Song.* This latter consists of two long poems, *Ascension Day* and *Pentecost,* both written in Browningesque style in reply to some of Browning's work.

"I must apologize," he explained in the Introduction, "for the new note of frivolity in my work; due doubtless to the frivolity of my subject; these poems being written when I was an Advaitist and could not see why—everything being an illusion—there should be any particular object in doing or thinking anything . . . . I must indeed apologize to the illustrious Shade of Robert Browning for my audacious parody in title, style and matter of his "Christmas Eve and Easter Day."

Among these notes is to be found a jingle describing the purpose of Yoga. It becomes intelligible if the reader recollects that one of the tenets of Buddhism which he was just studying is *Sabbé Pi Dukkham*, "All is Sorrow."

> First, "Here's a johnny with a cancer;
> An operation may be useless,
> May even harm his constitution,
> Or even cause his instant dissolution:
> Let the worm die, 'tis but a goose less!"
> Not you! You up and take by storm him.
> You tie him down and chloroform him,
> You do not pray to Thoth or Horus
> But make one dash for his pylorus;—
> And if ten years elapse, and he
> Complains. "O doctor, pity me!
> Your cruel 'ands, for goodness sakes
> Gave me such 'orrid stomach-aches."
> An order for some soda-mint.
> So Yoga. Life's a carcinoma,
> Its cause uncertain, not to check.
> In vain you cry to Isis: "O Ma!
> I've got it fairly in the neck."
> The Surgeon Crowley, with his trocar
> Says you a poor but silly bloke are,
> Advises concentration's knife,
> Quick to the horny growth called life.
> "Yoga? There's danger in the biz!
> But, it's the only chance there is!"
> (For life, if left alone, is sorrow,

And only fools hope God's to-morrow.)

By far, however, the best poetic description of Yoga that
he wrote is to be found in *Aha!* which is a very long poem
detailing all his syncretistic ideas about magic, yoga,
mysticism, and his own particular message of *The Book of
the Law.* I quote the section dealing with Yoga:

> There are seven keys to the great gate,
> Being eight in one and one in eight.
> First, let the body of thee be still,
> Bound by the cerements of will,
> Corpse-rigid; thus thou mayst abort
> The fidget-babes that tease the thought.
> Next, let the breath-rhythm be low,
> Easy, regular, and slow;
> So that thy being be in tune
> With the great sea's Pacific swoon.
> Third, let thy life be pure and calm,
> Swayed softly as a windless palm.
> Fourth, let the will-to-live be bound
> To the one love of the profound.
> Fifth, let the thought, divinely free
> From sense, observe its entity.
> Watch every thought that springs; enhance
> Hour after hour thy vigilance!
> Intense and keen, turned inward, miss
> No atom of analysis!
> Sixth, on one thought securely pinned
> Still every whisper of the wind!
> So, like a flame straight and unstirred
> Burn up thy being in one word!
> Next, still that ecstasy, prolong
> Thy meditation steep and strong,
> Slaying even God, should he distract
> Thy attention from the chosen act!
> Last, all these things in one o'erpowered
> Time that the midnight blossom flowered!
> The oneness is. Yet even in this,
> My son, thou shalt not do amiss

If thou restrain the expression. Shoot
Thy glance to rapture's darkling root,
Discarding name, form, sight, and stress
Even of this high consciousness;
Pierce to the heart! I leave thee here:
Thou art the Master. I revere
Thy radiance that rolls afar,
O Brother of the Silver Star!

This is the system then in which he was being
indoctrinated by Allan in Colombo.

Within a few days, Crowley found Colombo
unsatisfactory; it was a sea-port and there was too much
hustle and bustle to suit him. He wanted a quiet spot where
he could make a complete retirement, to devote himself
exclusively to the practice of Yoga. Therefore on the 17th of
August, they both left for Kandy, where they rented a
furnished bungalow on the hills overlooking the lake. Here,
the previous training afforded him by Eckenstein was utilized
fully. It had been a real advantage. The area of concentration
and meditation was no longer a closed field, or a mysterious
subject. Allan quickly broke him in to the principles of Yoga
practice over and beyond what Eckenstein had taught him.
Crowley experimented with Yoga postures and position, with
Mantras designed to empty the mind wholly of all other
thoughts and thus facilitate concentration, and with the Yoga
methods of breathing. This latter is called Pranayama, the
control of Prana which is defined as the universal life energy
concentrated within the organism by means of specific
exercises. One of the early results of these recorded by
Crowley is that the Nadi (the invisible Yoga nerve plexuses
and channels) become purified. According to the ancient
texts the signs are: a clear complexion, a sweet voice, a calm
appearance, bright eyes, hearing constantly the Nada. These
are sounds heard within the mind when concentration
becomes intense or when Pranayama concentrates a sufficient

quantity of energy within certain areas.

By the 29th of August, things began to occur. His diary reads:

> Began mental muttering of 'Aum Mani Padme Hum' while meditating on Buddha. This developed into Pratyaharic Dharana; loss of Ego and a vision of mysterious power; loss of all objects mental and physical. I do not know how long this lasted. I woke meditating on Anahata. The voice of Nada was like a far-off solemn song; it became Aum only, dropping 'Mani Padme Hum' and then was more like thunder without harmonics.

In other words, he had begun to use the mantram by means of which, through constant and interminable repetition, his mind would be forced into concentration. It did develop into a species of introspection and concentration, with a withdrawal of energy from external objects. Anahata is the name of the hypothetical nerve center in the heart region, from which the mystical sounds are said to emanate. He went at this business of Yoga practice with determination and vigor, and nothing was going to stop him. Nothing *could* stop him, now that he had some real guidance which he had not had since Allan had left England long before.

In *The Book of Lies* where Crowley has described some of his most transcendental insights and experiences in paradox and seeming cynicism, there is one descriptive little chapter entitled *King's College Chapel:*

> For mind and body alike there is no purgative like Pranayama, no purgative like Pranayama.
> For mind, for body, for mind and body alike, alike! there is, there is, there is no purgative, no purgative like Pranayama—Pranayama!—Pranayama! yea, for mind and body alike there is no purgative, no purgative, no purgative (for mind and body alike!) no purgative, purgative, purgative like Pranayama, no purgative for

mind and body alike, like Pranayama, like Pranayama,
like Prana — Prana — Pranayama! — Pranayama —
Pranayama! Amen.

Continuing with the practices prescribed by his teacher, he
soon experienced further results that were confirmed by the
ancient writings. For example on one occasion he reported:
"I felt a spiral force whirring around the top of my spine.
This signifies an induction current of Prana." "At one point
there were two or three distinct sharp throbs in the third
eye." "Concentration on Anahata gives sleepiness at once. I
felt the pump action of the blood very plainly and also
experienced Sukshma-Kumbhaka, the subtle involuntary
Kumbhaka."

Sukshma-Kumbhaka is the technical term for the
automatic and involuntary holding of the breath as the
muscles suddenly go rigid altogether independently of the
will. It is said to represent a definite mark of progress. All of
these phenomena are explained traditionally in terms of the
concentration of Prana or life-force in the subtle body. A
number of these phenomena have been noted by present-day
physiologists and psychologists as a result of experimental
work in the field of aviation. Following hard upon this, the
entire subject of hyperventilation of the brain has been
studied intensively, with the gradual development of a
comprehensive literature.

In Crowley's day there was no literature at all on this
subject. Several years ago, K. T. Behanan, Ph.D., wrote a
book on the subject of Yoga from a rationalistic, occidental
point of view, without one word being mentioned concerning
hyperventilation. It was still a relatively unknown subject.

As a result of some clinical work in which I was engaged
some time back, I made an experimental study of
hyperventilation to write a book on some aspects of Reichian
psychotherapy in which these effects and phenomena were

listed. I therefore extrapolate from that book *New Wings for Daedalus*.

First however I must note that changes in breathing alter the chemistry of the bloodstream. If the breathing is forced, much carbonic acid is blown off, the blood stream becoming therefore more alkaline. This changes the internal environment of the organism as a whole, and of the brain in particular. Most authorities believe that hyperventilation induces a condition of hypocapnia (reduced carbon dioxide) resembling intoxication. A partial loss of control, a depressing of some of the inhibitory centers, and less critical evaluation of affective behavior, are some of the simpler signs and symptoms of cerebral intoxication. From this intoxication of the cerebral cortex with oxygen, a pseudo-pathological condition follows that in many ways resembles a mild delirium. Delirium means literally "out of the groove." When hyperventilated, one is out of the common groove of restrained responses, and behaves characteristically in a less critical, less controlled and less inhibited manner than he otherwise would.

The so-called 'hyperventilation syndrome' reported by neurophysiologists describes in great detail the symptoms that develop as a result of overbreathing. They conclude that while the etiology is not always psychogenic, emotional manifestations are almost always evident as a result of it. The physiological symptoms are classified under several headings—central neurovascular, muscular, respiratory, cardiac, gastro-intestinal, psychic and general. These are attributed to the resultant hypocapnia and alkalosis which alters the internal environment of the brain. In hyperventilation induced spontaneously among anxiety neurotics, the "shakes" and the "trembles" comprise outstanding symptoms responsible for alarm. Many a physician has been telephoned out of bed in the small hours of the morning to treat such reactions—most of the time with sedation of one kind or another.

According to the oldest Yoga texts, the four characteristic results of Pranayama are: (1) profuse perspiration; (2) rigidity of the body as a whole; (3) jumping about like a frog; (4) levitation. Crowley has recorded in his diary that he had experienced the first three results, but the last one never. However, he has written about the observation he once made when he went into Allan's cabin one day, after no one had managed to get any response for some time. And lo! and behold! there was Allan in Padmasana (the lotus posture), tilted to one side. Crowley reasoned that once in Padmasana you cannot fall over on your side; the very position of the locked legs militates against this. Therefore he concluded that Allan, while in Samadhi, had levitated above the level of the floor, but had descended on his side instead of down into the previous position. From this has developed the legend that he had seen Allan levitated.

Now let us compare these Yoga results with those that occur with hyperventilation. I should mention here that I use hyperventilation daily in conjunction with my psychotherapeutic work along Reichian lines. This has enabled me over a period of some years to classify the results as they occur in most patients during several sessions.

1. As the patient proceeds with the forced respiration aided by the therapist, there soon occurs a considerable flushing of the face with a feeling of warmth suffusing the body as a whole. There may be an increase in perspiration all over. More or less quickly, this is followed by a sense of light-headedness accompanied by a well-defined dizziness. Some relaxation usually occurs at this point.

2. Pallor and blanching of the skin follow next. More often than not, the feet begin to feel very cold. If not, the hands, chin or some other area of the body begins to cool.

3. As the patient becomes aware of the impending chill, some fear and anxiety may arise. There often occurs, at this

stage of the work, a little trembling. It may be light, but as the breathing continues, it may develop into a vigorous quivering—first in the lips, then on the chin, the shoulders or the pectoral muscles. Then the trembling tends to spread, from the abdomen to the knees and thighs, from there becoming generalized through the body.

4. Deep yawns may develop next, indicative of an increasing degree of relaxation. Little tics may appear here and there, muscular twitchings on the eyes, neck or abdomen. If they are tolerated by the patient, they soon disappear to be replaced by sensations of energy streamings. These sensations were once interpreted as an influx of Prana.

5. The tics may be followed by clonisms, heavy jerks and muscular spasms. Some patients respond actively to these, and spontaneously rock on the couch, quite involuntarily, rather like a jumping frog. The motor activity often resembles a running motion.

6. Other patients experience some very profound body feelings and emotions, including anxiety and anger. But these are invariably accompanied by other autonomic manifestations.

7. Still another group of patients experience tetany. This is a rigidity which begins almost imperceptibly, as the patient breathes. It may be confined to a limb or an extremity only. It may spread to the whole body. Sometimes it is painful too, in which case some effort has to be made to relax the painfully rigid areas. When eventually, a relaxation from this rigidity is engineered, it is eminently pleasurable and satisfying.

8. During the relaxation period, tingling or buzzing sensations develop. Some more discerning patients have described these sensations as if they were connected to an instrument delivering a strong galvanic current. These sensations are described in terms similar to those produced by Yoga practices.

9. Sometimes the tingling spontaneously disappears, to be
replaced by a deep inner vibration, or a well-defined
streaming or energy pulsation. It is invariably described as
relaxing and ecstatic—some more sensitive and perceptive
patients using such words as *melting, sweet,* and *yielding.*

It has proved illuminating to me to make comparisons
between the hyperventilation symptoms and the results
produced by Pranayama. There does seem to be a well
defined relationship. In other words, Crowley's contention
seems to be confirmed. One's original philosophical theories
or religious attitudes do not matter a bit. The only thing that
counts is getting down to work, away from arguing and
thinking; just working, just practising. Results follow from
that—not from your intellectual orientation, which does not
matter in the least. You can be a highly religious person or an
atheist. It does not interfere with the practice of Yoga.

To this extent, Magic is a good deal different from its
Eastern analogue. Magic does require faith in some religious
hierarchy. These concepts may be modified or extended as
you begin to obtain results, but at the beginning faith may be
required. It is difficult to intone and vibrate invocations or
prayers when you know you are a thoroughgoing hypocrite
to address these invocations to someone or something whose
very being you deny. For the beginning student therefore
whose faith long since vanished, Yoga makes the best
introduction to the Great Work.

This is a theme running like a golden thread through all of
Crowley's philosophical and mystical writing. But it is
perhaps stated more clearly and strongly in his *Confessions:*

> Any religion must rest on revelation, and cannot be
> proved by reason or experience. It is at once necessary
> and impudent to claim the exercise of faith. From this it
> follows that religion must always be repugnant to
> reason, and its upholders must be prepared to be called
> charlatans.

There is, however, one issue from this dilemma. It is possible to base a religion, not on theory and results, but on practice and methods. It is honest and hopeful to progress on admitted principles towards the development of each individual mind, and thus to advance towards the Absolute by means of the consciously willed evolution of the faculty of apprehension. Such is in fact the idea underlying initiation. It constitutes the absolute justification of the Path of the Wise, as indicated by the Adepts, whether of the Magical or Mystical schools. For Yoga offers humanity an organ of intelligence superior to intellect, yet co-ordinate with it, and Magic serves to arouse spiritual energies which, while confirming those of the mind, bring them to their culmination.

All through the rest of August and September, Crowley worked hard, fabulously hard at his Yoga. His schedule included four or five different working periods of varying lengths. Each one was devoted to posture, to pranayama, to maintaining and continuing the mantram, and to concentration. He found one very curious result which is often mentioned throughout most of his later writings. That is, if you meditate on any part of your body for any length of time, awareness of that part is at first heightened, then is expunged completely.

For example, as he meditated late on the night of 6th of September he experienced this specific effect of meditation and recorded clearly the event in his diary: "Dharana on tip of nose. I obtained a clear understanding of the unreality of that nose. This persists. An hour later whilst breathing on my arm as I was asleep, I said to myself: "What is this hot breath from?" I was forced to *think* before I could answer "my nose." Then I pinched myself and remembered at once; but again breathing the same thing happened again. Therefore the "Dharanation" of my nose dividualizes Me and My Nose, affects my nose, disproves my nose, abolishes, annihilates and expunges my nose."

He attempted something similar a few days later which carried forward the entire project. "Dharana on nose 9 minutes 50 seconds. I actually lost the nose on one occasion, and could not think what I wished to find or where to find it; my mind having become a perfect blank." Allan interpreted this as a very good result; it meant that "neighborhood concentration" was being approached.

He attempted the same concentration exercise the next day. "I did Dharana as before on my nose. I understand one Buddhist conception now, for: I was (a) conscious of external things seen behind, after my nose had vanished, *i.e.* altar, etc; and (b) that I was *not* conscious of these things. These two consciousnesses being simultaneous. This seems absurd and inexplicable, it is noted in Buddhist psychology, *yet I know it*."

This may seem inconsequential at first sight, but it is a conclusion fraught with profound mystical consequences. What is true of the nose becomes equally true of any part of the body—in fact it may become true of the ego itself. It too is eventually destroyed under the impact of concentration and meditation. At times, the meditating student may feel lost, as though he were not all here, when he is approaching this particular phase of the work. It may provoke panic if he is not under guidance. That is, until a new center is established, and ego perception is submerged into or exchanged for the Self.

Crowley wrote one instruction that was based essentially on the Ceylon experience, which he repeated again and again. It provided the base for the meditation exercise, which he describes in *Liber Yod:*

> 1. Let the Hermit be seated in his Asana, robed, and let him meditate in turn upon every several part of his body until that part is so unreal to him that he no longer includes it in his comprehension of himself. For

example if it be his right foot, let him touch that foot, and be alarmed, thinking, "A foot! . . . . foot! What is this foot? Surely I am not alone in this Hermitage!"

And this practice should be carried out not only at the time of meditation, but during the day's work.

2. This meditation is to be assisted by reasoning; as, "This foot is not I. If I should lose my foot, I should still be I. This foot is a mass of changing and decaying flesh, bone, skin, blood, lymph, etc., while I am the Unchanging and Immortal Spirit, uniform, not made, unbegotten, formless, self-luminous," etc.

3. This practice being perfect for each part of the body, let him combine his workings until the whole body is thus understood as the Non-Ego and as illusion.

4. Let then the Hermit, seated in his Asana, meditate upon the Muladhara Cakkra and its correspondence as a power of the mind, then destroy it in the same manner as aforesaid. Also by reasoning: "This emotion (memory, imagination, intellect, will, as it may be) is not I. This emotion is transient; I am immovable. This emotion is passion. I am peace," and so on.

Let the other Cakkras in their turn be thus destroyed, each one with its mental or moral attribute.

5. In this let him be aided by his own psychological analysis, so that no part of his conscious being be thus left undestroyed. And on his thoroughness in this matter may turn his success.

6. Lastly, having drawn all his being into the highest Sahasrara Cakkra, let him remain eternally fixed in meditation thereon.

7. AUM.

By the middle of the month, the prolonged discipline which was totally unlike anything he had ever undertaken began to tell on him. In England, when he had practised magic in its various forms, he had not really made many changes in the details of his everyday living. In Mexico, when Oscar had made suggestions as to elementary methods of achieving concentration, he had been actively engaged simultaneously in climbing mountains and exploring the country roundabout. There was not a forced seclusion, an isolation from external stimuli, from contact with other people, and certainly no real abstention from sex. Around the 12th of September he threw the whole bag of Yoga tricks in the air, going off to Colombo for a week or ten days. His activities there can only be guessed. But we would not be far afield if we assumed that he found himself a willing native girl, and spent the remainder of the week in bed. He spent himself completely in sexual activity, and was then ready to go back to work, to lead the ascetic life.

Many, many years after the Ceylon retirement, he had to write a letter to a disciple defining asceticism. This is what he had to say about it, since it bears upon the above incident.

Asceticism is all right when it is the proper means of attaining some special end. It is when it produces eructations of spiritual pride and satisfied vanity, that it is poisonous. The Greek word means an athlete; and the training of an athlete is not mortification of the body. Nor is there any rule which covers all circumstances. When men go 'stale' a few days before the race, they are 'taken off training' and fed with champagne. But that is *part* of the training. Observe, too, that all men go 'stale' sooner or later; training is abnormal, and must be stopped as soon as its object is attained. Even so, it too often strains vital organs, especially the heart and lungs, so that few rowing "Blues" live to be 50. But worst of all is the effect on the temper!

When it is permanent, and mistaken for a 'virtue', it poisons the very soil of the soul. The vilest weeds spring up; cruelty, narrowmindedness, arrogance—everything mean and horrible flowers in those who 'mortify the flesh'. Incidentally such ideas spawn the "Black Brother." The complete lack of humour, the egomaniac conceit, self-satisfaction, absence of all sympathy for others, the craving to pass their miseries on to more sensible people by persecuting them; these traits are symptomatic.

These latter symptoms are those that Wilhelm Reich has also described as the Emotional Plague. He considered it the major disease that burdens our modern society.

Back to work went Crowley. The emphasis was on concentration and pranayama. I wonder whether the average man and woman can really appreciate the awful drudgery involved in these exercises, and how absolutely motivated one must be in order to persist. Pranayama especially is the height of boredom, particularly when sitting in an excruciatingly painful Asana, or Yoga posture. One almost craves for some interference with the routine. Every nerve cell and fibre is straining to reach out for something, anything at all, that will serve as a decent excuse to terminate the session. It requires a vast exercise of will-power to continue in this tedium that is beyond all other tediums.

Tedium? There is no question about this. Altogether apart from the lofty results that later occurred, on the basis of this particular discipline he was able to write instruction manuals of great lucidity. *Liber E vel Exercitiorum* is a fundamental treatise dealing with all phases of preliminary mental discipline and training, in simple and yet strictly scientific language. The following consists of quotations taken at random from various sections.

> It is not necessary at this stage for us to declare fully the ultimate end of our researches; nor indeed would it be understood by those who have not become proficient in these elementary courses.
>
> The experimenter is encouraged to use his own intelligence, and not to rely upon any other person or persons, however distinguished, even among ourselves.
>
> The written record should be intelligently prepared so that others may benefit from its study . . . . The more scientific the record is, the better. Yet the emotions should be noted, as being some of the conditions . . . .
>
> You must learn to sit perfectly still with every muscle tense for long periods . . . . When you have progressed

up to the point that a saucer filled to the brim with water and poised upon the head does not spill one drop during a whole hour, and when you can no longer perceive the slightest tremor in any muscle; when, in short, you are perfectly steady and easy, you will be admitted for examination . . . .

Constrain the mind to concentrate itself upon a single simple object imagined . . . . Note carefully the duration of the experiments, the number and nature of the intruding thoughts, the tendency of the object itself to depart from the course laid out for it, and any other phenomena which may present themselves. Avoid overstrain; this is very important . . . . Endeavour finally to shut out all objects of any of the senses, and prevent all thoughts arising in your mind. When you feel you have attained some success in these practices, apply for examination, and should you pass, more complex and difficult practices will be prescribed for you.

Liber Ru vel Spiritus is another official instruction predicated on all the work he did with Eastern breathing techniques. In it, he differed from most of the traditional authorities--no wild claims are made that pranayama will cure dandruff or athlete's foot, or result in the achievement of longevity! It is structured on the simple thesis that certain results follow from certain procedures. Investigate! This is where Crowley shines.

Let the Zelator attach no credit to any statements that may have been made throughout the course of this instruction, and reflect that even the counsel which we have given as suitable to the average case may be entirely unsuitable to his own.

Another month went by, with this same patient, persistent adherence to the schedule laid down. A period of dryness intervened, a dryness in which nothing seemed to be happening. The tedium mounted, and an urge developed, as though sent by the devil incarnate, to stop work. "Another month of this great work commences, and though the toil has not been wasted the reward seems still far off."

Yet the reward was really in the offing, for a few days later, he wrote "at last the Golden Dawn. This, as my intuition had already taught me, had the effect of slowing the Dhyana and also keeping me fixed therein. Yet, I fear, of partially destroying its perfection—He knows."

The next day: "After some eight hours' discipline by Parnayama arose 'The Golden Dawn'." Again, I repeat this is the most gruesome kind of hard work. Discipline is the right word indeed.

> While meditating, suddenly I became conscious of a shoreless space of darkness and a glow of crimson athwart it. Deepening and brightening, scarred by dull bars of slate-blue cloud arose the Dawn of Dawns. In splendour not of earth and its mean sun, blood-red, rayless, adamant, it rose, it rose! Carried out of myself, I asked not 'Who is the Witness,' absorbed utterly in contemplation of so stupendous and so marvellous a fact. For here was no doubt, no change, no wavering; infinitely more real than aught 'physical' is the Golden Dawn of this Eternal Sun! But ere the Orb of Glory rose clear of its banks of blackness—alas my soul!—that Light Ineffable was withdrawn beneath the falling veil of darkness, and in purples and greys glorious beyond imagining, sad beyond conceiving, faded the superb Herald of the Day. But mine eyes have seen it! . . . .

And the next day:

> Again, by the Grace Ineffable of Bhavani to the meanest of Her devotees, arose the Splendour of the Inner Sun. As bidden by my Guru, I saluted the Dawn with Pranava. This, as I foresaw, retained the Dhyanic Consciousness. The Disc grew golden: rose clear of all its clouds. flinging great fleecy cumuli of rose and gold, firey with light, into the aethyr of space. Hollow it

seemed and rayless as the Sun in Sagittarius, yet
incomparably brighter: but rising clear of cloud, it
began to revolve, to corruscate, to throw off streamers
of jetted fire! . . . .

For days he remained in silence, communing with this new
Glory that had dawned upon him after months of the most
arduous of all work, the control of his own mind. It was the
most important spiritual result that he had achieved thus far,
the beginning of a new life-cycle, of a new approach to life
itself.

Its effect on him is best described in an essay *Science and
Buddhism* that he wrote shortly thereafter. It is based on
studies he made in Ceylon to become familiar with Vedanta
and Buddhism. The essay, as some Buddhist missionaries have
told me, is a very fine introduction to and survey of the
fundamental tenets of Buddhism, and as far as I am
concerned one of the best of his earlier writings. In it, he
wrote:

Suppose, however, a dream so vivid that the whole
waking man is abased before its memory, that his
consciousness of it appears a thousand times more real
than that of the things about him; suppose that his
whole life is moulded to fit the new facts thus revealed
to him; that he would cheerfully renounce years of
normal life to obtain minutes of that dream life; that his
time sense is uprooted as never before, and that these
influences are permanent. Then, you will say, delirium
tremens (and the intoxication of hashish, in respect
more particularly of the time sense) afford us a parallel.
But the phenomena of delirium tremens do not occur in
the healthy. As for the suggestion of autohypnosis, the
memory of the "dream" is a sufficient reply. However
this may be, the simple fact of the superior apparent
reality—a conviction unshakable, *inépuisable* (for the
English has no word) is a sufficient test. And if we
condescend to argue, it is for pleasure, and aside from

the vital fact; a skirmish, and not a pitched battle.

Crowley's little book on Yoga, *Part I of Book IV,* also sets out to explain, among other things, the nature of this Dhyana which he had experienced. He wrote that it is to be understood that Dharana (concentration), Dhyana and Samadhi form a continuous process, and exactly when the crisis comes does not matter. But the crisis is a matter of direct experience, and a very striking one.

> In the course of our concentration we noticed that the contents of the mind at any moment consists of two things, and no more: the Object, variable, and the Subject, invariable, or apparently so. By success in Dharana the object has been made as invariable as the subject. Now the result of this is that the two become one. This phenomenon usually comes as a tremendous shock . . . . All the poetic faculties and all the emotional faculties are thrown into a sort of an ecstasy by an occurrence which overthrows the mind, and makes the rest of life seem absolutely worthless in comparison . . . . One of the simplest forms of Dhyana may be called "the Sun." The sun is seen (as it were) by itself, not by an observer; and although the physical eye cannot behold the sun, one is compelled to make the statement that this "Sun" is far more brilliant than the sun of nature . . . . The conditions of thought, time and space are abolished . . . . A further development is the appearance of the Form which has been universally described as human; although the persons describing it proceed to add a greater number of details which are not human at all. This particular appearance is usually assumed to be "God" . . . . The Samadhi par excellence, however, is Atmadarshana, which for some, and those not the least instructed, is the first real Samadhi, for even the visions of "God" and of the "Self" are tainted by form. In Atmadarshana the All is manifested as the One; it is the Universe freed from its conditions. Not only are all forms and ideas destroyed, but also those conceptions which are implicit in our ideas of those

ideas. Each part of the Universe has become the whole, and phenomena and noumena are no longer opposed . . . . There is, however, a very much higher state called Shivadarshana, of which it is only necessary to say that it is the destruction of the previous state, its annihilation; and to understand this blotting out, one must not imagine "Nothingness" (The only name for it) as negative, but as positive . . . .

For the next few months after the Dhyana, paradoxically enough, he gave up Yoga practices almost entirely. But as respite from the daily hard grind of meditation exercises and the intellectual study of Oriental religions, he did attempt the writing of some poetry. Several of these poems are included in *The Collected Works*; "The Dance of Shiva," "Sonnet for a Picture," "The House," "Anima Lunae," "Sabbe Pi Dukkham," but above all some versifications of the Dhammapada, the noblest of the Buddhist scriptures. He did not get very far with this latter task. It palled on him. After only a few verses were rendered, he gave it up as a bad job. Here is a sampling of the effort:

> All that we are from mind results, on mind is
>   founded, built of mind.
> Who acts or speaks with evil thought, him doth pain
>   follow sure and blind;
> So the ox plants his foot and so the car-wheel follows
>   hard behind.

> All that we are from mind results, on mind is
>   founded, built of mind.
> Who acts or speaks with righteous thought, him
>   happiness doth surely find.
> So failing not, the shadow falls for ever in its place
>   assigned . . . .

> They who see falsehood in the Truth, imagine Truth
>   to lurk in lies,
> Never arrive to know the Truth, but follow eager
>   vanities.

> To whom in Truth the Truth is known,
>   Falsehood in falsehood doth appear,
> To them the Path of truth is shown; right aspirations
>   are their sphere . . . .
>
> The Bhikku who in earnestness delights, who fears
>   dispersions dire,
> His fetters all, both great and small, burning he moves
>   about the fire.
>
> The Bhikku who in Earnest delights,
>   Dispersion sees with fear,
> He goes not to Destruction; he unto Nibbana
>   draweth near . . . .

He traveled the length and breadth of Ceylon, studying the people and their ancient customs, and gathering information and knowledge. November ended, he traveled to Madura, thence to Calcutta. For the whole month that he was there he was sick with malaria and fever. With the turn of the year, he made up his mind to go to Burma.

After the Ceylon experience, when he had begun to travel and go big-game hunting and lusting after the joys of the flesh and of the world, Allan had finally become a Buddhist monk. Having done so, he went to a monastery in Burma, and with the turn of the year this is where Crowley decided to go also. For a whole month he journeyed around Rangoon, visiting many of the shrines, monasteries and so-called holy men.

Symonds' brief account is worth quoting here. "He sailed for Rangoon, and from there proceeded up the River Irrawaddy. He decided to cut across country from Midon but before the wild Arakan hills his coolies refused to go on, so Crowley and his companion (a man called Edward Thornton whom he had met in Calcutta) decided to turn back. They hired a thirty-five foot long, dug-out type of boat with an awning in the middle, just broad enough for two men to pass,

and started downstream. Although ill with malaria,
Perdurabo sat at the stern with a rifle across his knees,
potting at every animal that came in sight."

Dhyana had done little to assuage the deep hostility
within. It emerged periodically in shooting and big-game
hunting. In his human relationships it also emerged, for apart
from Allan and Oscar, there was absolutely no one whose
friendship persisted for any length of time. In the form of
arrogance and sarcasm, his hostility always intervened.

One more technical point needs mentioning. On the basis
of his magical work in England, Scotland and Mexico, he laid
claim (again on what authorization I know not) to the grade
of 6=5 Adeptus Major, taking the magical motto of O.S.V.
He was following protocol, I suppose, having assumed that in
having completed the prescribed work for the 5=6, and
knowing that he was competent in that work, he was entitled
to the next higher grade. After the Ceylon discipline, with
the arising of Dhyana, he promoted himself from 6=5 to the
grade of 7=4 Adeptus Exemptus, with the name O.M. There
is absolutely no clue in any of his writings as to authorization
for these promotions, save for his own realization that he had
satisfactorily completed the work prescribed for that grade.

When referring to the mystical state of Dhyana that
Crowley had attained in Ceylon, Symonds commented:
"Combining certain ideas from Western magic with Eastern
yoga, he developed a technique whereby he could make even
the dullest person into a genius. When Crowley became a
Master himself, this was one of his abilities which attracted
the backward, but ambitious, pupil."

What Crowley discovered was the secret that long had been
known by the masters of Yoga and Tantra. Hundreds of years
before, a little boy in Tibet was, in effect, adopted by a
tantric Guru named Marpa, who in turn, had received his
initiation at the hands of another Kargyupta guru before him.
Marpa employed a traditional combination of lamaistic

magic, Buddhistic tantra, and concentration exercises. The result was that his young pupil, who like Crowley must have been endowed with the patience and perseverance of the devil himself, climbed up the rungs of this noble ladder of attainment. He became the sainted yogi Milarepa of whose fame and sanctity songs are sung in Tibet even to this day.

So there was nothing outrageous about this combination of magic and yoga that Crowley employed as a means to the attainment of genius. The Golden Dawn had used the word Genius as depicting the higher creative Self of each individual. Were one opened by discipline and contemplation to that Self, certainly one would have arrived at the status of genius.

It was the intent of all spiritual techniques, be they yoga or magic or mystical prayer, to produce nothing else but spiritual genius. I would say that the great mystics the Roman Catholic Church and the Eastern Orthodox Church have produced are geniuses of the religious life. Whether we regard them as natural mystics by right of birth or divine Grace, or as mystics who achieved their heights through the specific training proferred by the monastic Orders within the body of the Church, there really is no difference. All climbed higher and ever higher towards their Goal through training, discipline, and hard work. The world is the richer because of them.

It is no discredit to Crowley to have supposed that the use of his twin technique of Magic and Yoga predisposed towards the development of genius. The more credit to him! These methods required hard work. Few are they who are willing or capable of devoting their full time and energies to the Great Work.

I will be foolhardy enough now to acknowledge that I myself was attracted initially to the Great Work by the promise implicit in Crowley's writing. I was and still am one of the "ambitious but backward pupils." That I never achieved genius or a higher degree of creativity is no discredit to Crowley. It is a blot against my own escutcheon that I did not have the patience and persistence required to work more devotedly on the practices laid down by Crowley. That is my own sad lot. The lack of sought-for achievement is due solely to my slothfulness, not to Crowley's high promise.

Having mentioned Milarepa, it has often occurred to me that some scholar should attempt a comparison of classical Tibetan Tantric texts with some of Crowley's so-called official instructions. Crowley had never reached Tibet in any of his travels. Nepal and Sikkhim were the nearest he got. But it was close enough. Some of the religious customs and magical practices of Tibet have overflowed into the surrounding countries where he could have picked up a great deal of information.

Aside from that, at the present day there are such classical texts as Dr. Evans Wentz's translations and commentaries, which are encyclopedic. He has accomplished a sorely needed task in making these texts available in English. Then there are the several Tantra texts of Sir John Woodroffe. By comparison, Crowley's writings on Yoga and Tantra are far clearer, to say nothing of the fact that Crowley's literary style is infinitely superior to that of the modern translators of the older Tibetan and Hindu writers. There is no phase of Tantra that he has not practised and covered in his writings.

By the same token, Yoga is a generic term covering at least five different groupings of disciplines. There is Hatha Yoga, Raja Yoga, Bhakta Yoga, Gnana Yoga and Karma Yoga. Each one of these major disciplines has been worked upon by Crowley at some time or other in his life, enabling him to distil from his wide experience the clearest essence for incorporation into the official instructions of his Order. No phase was ever neglected. The student who has obtained a birds-eye view of Crowley's writing has, in effect, an encyclopedia of *all* the Yogas and all the Tantras.

For example, Bhakta Yoga is the devotional method of achieving union with God. Some of Swami Vivekananda's writing on this phase of yoga is as sensitively done as anything yet in print. But in Crowley's hands, this superb accomplishment was excelled. *Liber Astarte vel Berylli* is defined as "The Book of Uniting Himself to a particular Deity by Devotion." It describes a number of considerations such as technique, meditations and ceremonies, concerning which he came to note:

> Now learn that thy methods are dry, one and all. Intellectual exercises, moral exercises, they are not Love. Yet as a man, rubbing two dry sticks together for long, suddenly found a spark, so also from time to time will true Love leap unasked into thy meditation. Yet this shall die and be reborn again and again. It may be that thou hast no tinder near.
>
> In the end shall come suddenly a great flame and devouring, and burn thee utterly.
>
> Now of these sparks, and of these splutterings of flame, and of these beginnings of the Infinite Fire, thou shall be thus aware. For the sparks thy heart shall leap up, and thy ceremony or meditation or toil shall seem of a sudden to go of its own will; and for the little flames this shall be increased in volume and intensity; and for the beginnings of the Infinite Fire thy ceremony shall be caught up into ravishing song, and thy meditation shall be ecstasy, and thy toil shall be a delight exceeding all pleasure thou hast ever known.
>
> And for the Great Flame that answereth thee it may not be spoken; for therein is the End of this Magick Art of Devotion.

In the face of all possible criticism, I declare that there has been no contemporary capable of writing on this topic with such simplicity, directness and clarity. He goes straight to the heart of the matter, for example, in his *Eight Lectures on*

Yoga, as no one else has. He debunks ruthlessly, is intolerant of mystification, and expounds superbly. There is no attempt to mislead, to introduce extraneous crackpot theories, to complicate the practice with religious or metaphysical beliefs—and this is rare.

His colossal ego and his ebullient sense of humor become apparent right from the start, as, for instance, in his choice of nom-de-plume—Mahatma Guru Shri Paramahamsa Shivaji. The entire series of lectures is permeated with trenchant sarcasm—as in the very sub-titles, *Yoga for Yahoos* and *Yoga for Yellowbellies*—bitter irony as well as the keenest and most profound philosophical insights conceivable. There is no other scholar who is capable of so doing, because there is no one who, having had the practical Yoga experience, is yet capable of bringing lucid scholarship and impeccable logic to bear on what is palpably a most difficult subject to elucidate.

For example, his comments on Yama and Niyama, the preliminary conditions to be met, or the rules to be complied with:

> There are all sorts of good rules which have never occurred to a teacher of Yoga: because those teachers never conceived of the condition in which many people live to-day. It never occurred to the Buddha or Patanjali or Mansur-el-Hallaj to advise his pupils not to practise in a flat with a wireless next door . . . . I wish to thunder forth once more that no questions of right or wrong enter into our problems. But in the stratosphere it is "right" for a man to be shut up in a pressure-resisting suit electrically heated, with an oxygen supply, whereas it would be "wrong" for him to wear it if he were running the three miles in the summer sports in the Tanezrouft . . . . You will find that you cannot conquer the obstacle of Yama, and dismiss it from your mind once and for all. Conditions favourable for the beginner may become an intolerance nuisance to the adept, while, on the other hand, things which matter very little in the beginning become most serious obstacles later on.

He cuts through all the traditional rules, treating them as mythologies, insisting only that the rule of life, while practicing Yoga, be one which will facilitate compliance with the accepted goal—to be able to concentrate the mind at will.

The following is characteristic of his attitude and his capacity to adjust to difficult situations:

> I may go so far as to say that just before I began Yoga seriously, I had almost invented a Yogic method of practicing Magick in the stress of circumstances. I had been accustomed to work with full magical apparatus in an admirably devised temple of my own. Now I found myself on ship board, or in some obscure bedroom of Mexico City, or camped beside my horse among the sugar canes in lonely tropical valleys, or couched with my rucksack for all pillow on bare volcanic heights. I had to replace my magical apparatus. I would take the table to be my bed, or stones roughly piled, for my altar. My candle or my Alpine lantern was my light. My ice-axe for the wand, my drinking flask for the chalice, my machete for the sword, and a chapati or a sachet of salt for the pentacle of art! Habit soon familiarised these rough and ready succedanea. But I suspect that it may have been the isolation and the physical hardship itself that helped, that more and more my magical operation become implicit in my body and mind, where a few months later I found myself performing *in full* operations involving the Formula of the Neophyte (for which see my treatise on *Magick*) without any external apparatus at all.

Apart from one series of entries relating to dreams and their classification, of no special interest to us here, Crowley kept no record of meditations or magical work for the first three months of 1902. It seems as though he were played out by the tremendous achievement of Dhyana. There was no further incentive—except to live the life of a man of the world as he knew it.

On the 23rd of March he joined his old mountain-climbing friend Oscar Eckenstein in Delhi. From Rawal Pindi, together with their companions they set out together for the long-planned assault on Chogo Ri. The *Equinox* account, presumably written by Fuller, has it that:

"For a space of nearly six months P. and D. A. journeyed amongst the vast mountains beyond Cashmir, and though during this period no record of his meditations has been preserved, time was not idled away and exercises in meditation of a more exalted kind, on the vastness of Nature and the ungraspable might of God, were his daily joy and consolation."

The expedition against this mountain resulted in failure. But it was a heroic failure. They were camped on the Baltoro Glacier for some sixty-three long bitter days, in the worst kind of weather conceivable, and for that time held the world's record.

"The Abramelin demons that Crowley had invoked at Boleskine" romanticizes Charles Cammell, "would seem to have formed a secret alliance with their cousins of the Himalayan heights. The expedition encountered climatic conditions of the most formidable hostility. The health of these strong men was shattered by the prolonged violence of the blinding blizzards, by the intensity of the cold, by the enforced delays, due to the appalling weather, at altitudes where the lack of oxygen destroys vitality. The elements and last camp in that heroic onslaught on the giant mountain was pitched on the great glacier at a height of 20,000 feet. There exhaustion and disease held the explorers in a deadly grip. Crowley, though ravaged by fever and attacks of snow-blindness, reconnoitered alone to an altitude of about 22,000 feet. The weather and consequent illness defeated the party at last. Chogo Ri remained, and to this day remains, unconquered. The celebrated Italian explorer, the Duke of the Abruzzi, considered Chogo Ri to be "unclimbable", quite apart from "the effects of the high altitude." Crowley declared that only the weather prevented him from climbing it."

Late in the Fall of 1902, he left India. During his travels in Ceylon, Burma and India, he always studied the local religions and beliefs, and so had gathered a vast store of out-of-the-way practices and customs which became a permanent part of his intellectual equipment. The following anecdote from the *Confessions* is a good example of his attitude in this respect:

> The rock temples of Madura are probably the finest in India, perhaps in the world. There seems no limit. Corridor after corridor extends its majestic sculptures, carved monoliths, with august austerity. They are the most impressive evidence that the faith which created them is as vital to-day, as when India was at the height of its political power. My experiences of Yoga stood me in good stead. I knew, of course, that the average European would not be permitted to visit the most interesting parts of the Temple, and I thought I would see what I could do to take a leaf out of Burton's book. So I disposed of my European belongings, and took up my position outside a village nearby, with a loincloth and a begging bowl. The villagers knew, of course, that I was an Englishman, and watched me suspiciously for some time from the edge of the jungle. But as soon as they found that I was really expert in Yoga, they lost no time in making friends. One man in particular spoke English well and was himself a great authority on Yoga. He introduced me to the writings of Sabapati Swami, whose instructions are clear and excellent, and his method eminently practical. My friend introduced me to the authorities at the big Temple at Madura, and I was allowed to enter some of the secret shrines, in one of which I sacrificed a goat to Bhavani.

He stayed in Egypt this time for only a few days. His heart

was elsewhere. After the defeat by Chogo Ri, there was a restlessness in him, so without any further inner leads there was no motivation to study. Off then to Europe he went, arriving in Paris in November, to stay there until April of the next year, 1903.

Here in Paris, he was joined by his old friend Gerald Kelly the painter, and together they proceeded to paint the town red. Naturally, he had to re-visit his old superior and chief in the Order, MacGregor Mathers. But whatever the tie was that once had bound them together, Crowley found this time it had dissipated. Very quickly they drifted apart. Crowley made some nasty allegations concerning Mathers and his wife which were typical of Crowley at his worst. The attainment of Dhyana had done nothing to transform his character. His vices remained the same. His neurotic character-structure remained unaltered. His spiritual attainments are unequivocal, but they did nothing for the rest of him.

Kelly introduced Crowley to a clairvoyante in Paris. Let her be called Sybil only, for the sake of the record. Under Crowley's direction, she "traveled to" or "perceived" that Mathers and his wife were obsessed. This word was used not in the modern psychiatric sense, but in an occult sense. Their own "selves" had been forced out of their bodies which were now occupied, of all things, by Mr. and Mrs. Horos, whose bodies at that very moment were incarcerated in an English prison. It is an unlikely story, but this is the one that Crowley professed to believe. It is evident that he needed some pretext of this kind in order to have an incentive for demoting Mathers from his Chieftainship of the Order. Now he had no further loyalty to Mathers. There was nothing to stop him from laying claim to the leadership of the Order whenever he felt ready to step into those shoes. The way had been cleared. Only time was required for him to take the next step, and the occasion appeared during the year 1909.

Having gotten rid of Mathers, there was nothing once more

to keep him in Paris. So he returned to England, and by May had gone north to his house at Boleskine in Scotland, again intending to complete the magical retirement he had started when the Revolt broke out years before. He had developed a thoroughly sceptical outlook so far as philosophy was concerned. He admitted that certain phenomena did accompany the use of certain ceremonial work; all he denied was their usefulness to the "white adept." Yoga methods of concentration he considered useful to the beginner, and for this reason would not consider their rejection at once. The Von Eckhartshausen theme of a hidden Sanctuary of Saints

> I leave for ever, and appear in the character of an inquirer on strictly scientific lines. This is unhappily calculated to damp enthusiasm; but as I so carefully of old, for the magical path, excluded from my life all other interests, that life has now no particular meaning, and the Path of Research, on the only lines I can now approve of, remains the one Path possible for me to tread.

In a rather desultory mood, he began some practices once more, some Pranayama, some concentration, and some work on the Buddhist meditation called Mahasatipatthana. This is a meditation designed to eradicate the ego point of view, being essentially an observation practice predicated on the basis of the question "What is it that is really observed?"

This retirement culminated in no particular illumination. It was just drudgery. For the time being there was a hiatus in his life, and he did not know what else to do. He kept up this program without much enthusiasm for about a month or so, only dropping it when events produced something far more exciting and fulfilling.

Meantime, I should call attention to the fact that in his essay *Science and Buddhism,* he has described this Buddhist meditation at some length: "The purpose of this essay" he wrote, and it is dated sometime in 1903, about the time he returned to Boleskine, "is to draw a strict comparison between the modern scientific conceptions of Phenomena and their explanation, when such exists, and the ancient ideas of the Buddhists; to show that Buddhism, alike in theory and practice, is a scientific religion; a logical superstructure on a basis of experimentally verifiable truth; and that its method is identical with science."

The essay is split up into various sections. One deals with the so-called Four Noble Truths, another with the Noble Eightfold Path, and still a third with the Three Characteristics. The section on the *Mahasatipatthana* carries the description forward after raising the above noted question:

> The Ego-idea is resolutely excluded from the start .... The breathing, motions of walking, etc. are merely observed and recorded; for instance, one may sit down quietly and say: 'There is an indrawing of the breath.' 'There is an expiration', etc. Or, walking, 'There is a raising of the right foot', and so on, just as it happens. The thought is of course not quick enough to note all the movements or their subtle causes. For example, we cannot describe the complicated muscular contractions, etc.; but this is not necessary ....
>
> When this through habit becomes intuitive ... one may begin to analyze, as explained above, and the second stage is "There is a sensation (Vedana) of a raising, etc." Sensations are further classed as pleasant or unpleasant.
>
> When this is the true intuitive instantaneous testimony of consciousness .... we proceed to Sanna, perception. "There is a perception of a (pleasant or unpleasant) sensation of a raising, etc."
>
> When this has become intuitive—why! here's a strange result! The emotions of pain and pleasure have vanished. They are subincluded in the lesser skandha of Vedana and Sanna is free from them .... The two further stages

Sankhara and Vinnanam pursue the analysis to its ultimation. "There is a consciousness of a tendency to perceive the (pleasant or unpleasant) sensation of a raising of a right foot" being the final form. And I suppose no psychologist of any standing will quarrel with this . . . .

I have called this meditation the most famous of the Buddhist meditations, because it is stated by the Buddha himself that if one practice it honestly and intelligently a result is certain. And he says this of no other . . . .

What will occur when one reaches the final state of Vinnanam, and finds no Atman behind it? Surely the Vinnanam stage will soon seem as unreal as the former have become. It is idle to speculate; but if I may escape the imputation of explaining the obscure by the more obscure, I may hint that such a person must be very near the state called Nirvana, whatever may be meant by this term . . . .

So ends the description of the section on this particular meditation. The conclusion of the essay gives a rapid resumé of "what we have gone through":

(a) We have stripped Science and Buddhism of their accidental garments, and administered a rebuke to those who so swathe them.

(b) We have shown the identity of Science and Buddhism in respect of:
(1) Their fact.
(2) Their theory.
(3) Their method.
(4) Their enemies.

(c) While thus admitting Buddhism to be merely a branch of Science, we have shown it to be a most important branch, since its promise is to break down the wall at which all Science stops. Buddhism is a logical development of observed facts; whoso is with me so far is *Sammaditthi*, and has taken the first step on the Noble Eightfold Path.

Let him aspire to knowledge, and the Second step is under his feet.

The rest lies with Research.

Aum! I take my refuge holy in the Light and Peace of Buddha.

Aum! I take my refuge, slowly working out His Law of Good.

Aum! I take my refuge lowly in His Pitying Brotherhood.

CHAPTER TEN

China

The biographers have recorded a large cluster of events occurring within a matter of four or five years. Of themselves, they are not particularly pertinent to my narrative. Both Cammell and Symonds in their accounts, as well as Crowley in his own autobiography, have dealt with these well enough. They warrant only slight mention here to keep the narrative straight, as well as to provide some kind of psychological or spiritual referent to what was happening.

For example there is the Gerald Kelly matter mentioned towards the close of the last chapter. Kelly and Crowley had met during the latter's last term at Cambridge, as a result of Crowley's publication of *Aceldama,* his first book of verse. Apparently what intrigued Kelly was Crowley's quotation from Swinburne!

> I contemplate myself in that dim sphere
> Whose hollow center I am standing at
> With burning eyes intent to penetrate
> The black circumference, and find out God.

The publisher brought these two young men together, a warm friendship soon developed, to last over many long and happy years. At that time Kelly was an aspiring young painter, who had not yet been knighted, nor elected President of the Royal Academy. While Crowley had been climbing in the Himalayas, Kelly had been serving his artist's

267

apprenticeship in the city of artists, Paris. It was there that Crowley met him again, and because of a clairvoyant contact of his, severed his connections with Mathers forever.

It was in the year 1903, perhaps in July, that Kelly introduced his sister Rose to Crowley. No great infatuation occurred right away, but through a series of fortuitous events coupled with Crowley's unequivocal romanticism he and Rose got married. There was no courting, no engagement, no waiting. Impulsively they just decided to get married. The original intent of the marriage was solely to assist Rose to evade some other marriage repugnant to her. Crowley merely offered, in effect, to let her use his name—and call it quits. Once, however, she was married to Crowley, she made up her mind it was to be a marriage in fact, not merely in name.

With the occurrence of this marriage, for a second time the proposed Abramelin operation never had a chance to get more than started. The first time was towards the close of the century, just before he had taken his Adeptus Minor degree in Paris. He had offered his fortune and services to Mathers at the time of the Revolt. At that time too, the operation was premature.

His account of the marriage indicated that it was an unblemished and prolonged sexual debauch. It afforded him almost complete happiness. His poetry reached some of its greatest and most sustained lyrical heights at that time. There are several lengthy poems dedicated and devoted to Rose. *Rosa Mundi, Rosa Coeli,* and *Rosa Inferni*—all being paeans of joy and ecstasy married to her.

> O Rose all roses far above
> In the garden of God's roses,
> Sorrowless, thornless, passionate Rose, that lies
> Full in the flood of its own sympathies
> And makes my life one tune that curls and closes
> On its own self delight;
> A circle, never a line! Safe from all wind,

Secure in its own pleasure-house confined,
Mistress of all its moods,
Matchless, serene, in sacred amplitudes
Of its own royal rapture, deaf and blind
To aught but its own mastery of song
And light, shown ever as silence and deep night
Secret as death and final. Let me long
Never again for naught! This great delight
Involves me, weaves me in its pattern of bliss,
Seals me with its own kiss,
Draws me to thee with every dream that glows,
Poet, each word! Maiden, each burden of snows
Extending beyond sunset, beyond dawn!
O Rose, inviolate, utterly withdrawn
In the truth:—for this is truth! Love known!
Ah! Rose of the World! Rose! Rose!

One of the funniest things I have read for a long time is the letter he wrote to his mother advising her of his marriage. I doubt if it was the "need to communicate something of the unusual and significant event of his marriage" as Symonds has seen it. In spite of himself, he was torn, I fancy, by a sense of obligation to let his mother know, and the conflicting contempt he felt for anything to do with her. The result is a classical psychoanalytical compromise, which turns out to be a glorious piece of leg-pulling.

I was sorry you would not come to the wedding—it was a very grand affair, plumed hearse and all, and the mutes recalled the delicious mutes of thirty years ago. The Rev. F. F. Kelly, the bride's father, preached such a beautiful sermon over the open grave. His text was from the 44th verse of the 44th chapter of Isaiah—"And the Lord said unto Moses, and he arose and smote him." Thirty six pipers played "the voice that breathed o'er Eden"—some reference to Whistler whom her brother so much admires, I suppose—and as the earth was shovelled reverently by 12 stalwart professors of Esperanto, taxidermists, and assorted Mormon Missionaries (with

such dear destroying angels) ovei the last mortal
remains, a heartfelt sob of relief burst from the
assembled multitudes, and tears of bitter joy streamed
down in such profusion as to enable us to carry out our
nearly abandoned project of beginning the honeymoon
in a canoe. This we did and shot Barnes Bridge in the
astonishing time of 2 h. 43 m. 2½ s. Thence to seas of
molten glory in the glowing west where we still are

c/o God

Heaven

will always find us.

There were some shenanigans attending the whole business
of this sudden wedding, because they embarked upon the
project in such a hurry. As a result of this, Gerald, the bride's
brother, became angry, and a fight with Crowley almost
started. It brought about a temporary break in the friendship
of these two men, the poet and the painter. Time healed the
wound quickly, however, making the friendship fast and
secure again. And so it remained, until many years later when
it finally fell apart, never to be resumed again.

The occasion I presume was the break-up of the marriage.
After some years of marriage to Crowley, Rose apparently
became a dipsomaniac and had to be committed. There was a
divorce. We can only surmise that Sir Gerald Kelly was not at
all happy about the way his sister had fared in her marriage
to his best friend. So the friendship suffered.

Crowley's reply to the disruption of this friendship was
typical. It expresses completely the extraordinary set of
paradoxes that this man was capable of. Throughout the
three volumes of his *Collected Works* there is reference after
reference to Gerald, indicating how fondly Crowley regarded
him, and in what high esteem he held him. In *Equinox IX*
published around 1913, however, Crowley tears into Kelly
with a vicious diatribe entitled *A Quack Painter.* It opens
with:

"Algernon Agrippa Dooley was the Only-begotten Son of the Reverend Archibald Agrippa Dooley." Crowley follows this immediately with:

> Algernon gave no early sign of his eventual P.R.A.; he passed scatheless through dame's school and Harrow. It was the talk made in undergraduate circles by the decadents that caught his puberty, and thrust it in that direction. And of original genius or capacity he had none. Of all essentials he had none. But, on the other hand, of inessentials, of all superficial qualities, he had all. His mimetic faculty was fine, almost incredibly fine. Fortunately for my credit, my collection comprises not only borders and initials of which probably no expert would care to swear that they were not the work of William Morris, but pencil sketches of Rosetti girls and Burne-Jones girls done with equal excellence and Beardsleyesque drawings imitating even the miraculous fineness of that great draughtsman's execution. Some one had said to him that Beardsley's line showed no rough edge under a glass. He satisfied himself of the fact, and in a few weeks came near to rival the master . . . .
>
> Another evil influence was a very old friend, a surgeon whose sole claim to distinction was his beautiful bedside manner, and his deference to the heads of his profession. I remember Dooley criticizing him one night at Lavenne's for this fault. "When you see him with the big man," he said, "it's—damn it, it's almost like this." With his perfect art of mimicry, he gave the smile and the hand-rub of the shop-walker. In twelve months he was doing the same thing himself.

Finally, at the close of the essay Crowley wrote: "Such degradation can hardly go further; it only remains to set the seal upon it. As valour is not increased, but only recognized, by the Victoria Cross, so nothing can be done for Dooley but to make him A.R.A."

Kelly was not only made A.R.A. but later he was knighted

and became the President of the Royal Academy, a most distinguished honor. This must have galled Crowley no end—awakening in him a kind of jealousy which he could neither accept nor handle.

As an aside, it is interesting to note relative to this essay about Gerald Kelly, that there is a paragraph dealing indirectly with the late Somerset Maugham. He is not specifically mentioned by name, but in the rather accurate description of the man, one comes face to face with Crowley's contempt for him also. No clue exists anywhere, as far as I know, for the origins of this attitude, save in the *Confessions* only just recently published by Cape in England and Hill & Wang Inc. in New York. Certainly the novel *The Magician*, which is an overt attack on Crowley, cannot be held responsible for this contempt. Crowley rather enjoyed the book, believing that despite Maugham's criticisms the novel nonetheless managed to convey something of the power and superior ability of the Magus. Again, Crowley felt that since every knock was a boost, as it were, any mention of him, no matter in what vein, was an explicit advertisement of his identification with the Great Work—an acknowledgement of the existence of the Great Work, and so might be successful in bringing some aspirant into active participation in his Order.

The section of the essay in question deals with some of the people who had an effect on Kelly, who here is called Dooley. It says:

> Yet a third; a medical failure who fancied himself as a playwright, and by adapting 15 year old Palais Royal farces captured the English stage. He also had the impudence to publish novels page after page of which was stolen almost verbatim from various other books. His only other qualification was his stutter, and his incapacity to conceive of greatness of any kind. That Dooley should have taken this creature seriously, even thought him an artist, exhibits the melancholy ruin into which his critical faculty had followed his aspirations.

Crowley was ambitious. Despite denials, he had always wanted to be accepted, and when he was not he felt overwhelming frustration, attacking the general public as too bourgeois to realize how great his genius was. He wanted his friends and colleagues to join in this attack on the staid bulwarks of conventionality and society. When however one of them "made it" Crowley turned his attack and venom on the friend, believing himself to be betrayed and outraged. This is the other determinant in his attack upon his brother-in-law.

Rose was no intellectual giant. But apparently Crowley was content with that. Using her as an excuse—though actually he needed none—he wrote some pornographic jingles and skits for her, to placate her during pregnancy. I have never seen a copy of this *Snowdrops from a Curate's Garden,* but I am told that some of the verse is quite brilliant. A very small edition was printed but never put on sale to the general public. Years later, together with a collection of some other materials. these books were held by the Customs authorities and destroyed.

"Crowley" comments Symonds, "always did everything to excess. He married to help a poor girl out of a jam; within twenty four hours he felt himself slipping into love with her. A few days later he was being consumed by wild passion. During the three weeks that followed their runaway wedding he was in an ecstasy of love and only once turned Rose up and walloped her. He explained that her love for him—she apparently started all this love business—began to evoke his love for her; and that, to begin with at least, he was carried away on the wings of her rapture. As he was a man whom only the best could satisfy, he soon discovered that he was married to 'one of the most beautiful and fascinating women in the world.' Toward the end of the summer he carried her off to Paris, the first stage of a honeymoon that they had planned for themselves in the East."

From Marseilles they took a boat to Cairo. About the only meaningful incident in this trip to Egypt was showing his young wife the Great Pyramid at Gizeh. In order to show off to her, and to help her realize what a great magician she was married to, they stayed overnight in the King's Chamber of the Pyramid, where he invoked some elementals by means of the "Preliminary Invocation of the Goetia." His own account reads:

> We reached the King's Chamber after dismissing the servants at the foot of the Grand Gallery. By the light of a single candle placed on the edge of the coffer I began to read the invocation. But as I went on I noticed that I was no longer stooping to hold the page near the light. I was standing erect. Yet the manuscript was not less but more legible. Looking about me, I saw that the King's Chamber was glowing with a soft light which I immediately recognized as the astral light . . . . The King's Chamber was aglow as if with the brightest tropical moonlight. The pitiful dirty yellow flame of the candle was like a blasphemy, and I put it out. The astral light remained during the whole of the invocation and for some time afterwards, though it lessened in intensity as we composed ourselves to sleep.

Beyond this there was nothing to keep them in Egypt. It was his original intention to visit China with Rose, but he had first to make a stop at Ceylon. However Allan was no longer there. He had not only terminated his relationship with his Tamil guru, the Solicitor-General of Ceylon, but as stated above he had adopted the yellow robe to become a Buddhist monk. From Ceylon, he had gone to a Burmese monastery for further study. Crowley was determined to visit him in Burma a bit later on, enroute to China. Meanwhile, here he was in Ceylon. And so far was Magic and meditation out of his mind that he went big-game hunting.

This is another seemingly contradictory aspect of Crowley.

Mystic, mage, mountaineer, poet, lover, and hunter. Big-game hunting appealed to him, and his life-history contains many instances where he went off on safari somewhere, shooting and killing. It gave him a great deal of pleasure. "There was more than one Crowley," asserted Symonds, "for in him existed a number of different and conflicting personalities. There was Crowley the god, Crowley the clown, and Crowley the English gentleman of Trinity College, Cambridge, whose occupations, so far, had been that of mountaineering, exploring and poetizing. The role of Crowley the English gentleman was in opposition to Crowley in either of the other two roles; for there is nothing gentlemanly about a demoniac genius."

From one point of view, one would be justified in assuming then that this man was not a rigid, unyielding personality tightly encased in an imprisoning armor. He could change his behavior when the occasion warranted, and assume a different mask. It is not an altogether unflattering picture.

But this criticism forces me to wonder whether Symonds had this ability, this flexibility? Or is it possible that Symonds is a stiff, tight, armored person who while envying anyone who is otherwise, vents his venom on that person at the same time? It may interrupt the continuity of this narrative to speak of Symonds thus, but I feel it is imperative to do so since his book *The Great Beast* has had a pernicious effect on many otherwise uninformed people.

Crowley was so far removed from the structure and behavior of the ordinary person that his multiple personalities glowered overtly at the biographers. He *was* far removed, it is true. But his different egos merely accentuate what is actually operative in the "ordinary man" whom Reich contemptuously calls *homo normalis.* The latter usually is so innocuous and dull that his different egos remain in a state of latency only. It would be up to initiation or psychotherapy to awaken them from their dormant state. Madame Blavatsky is another similar case in point.

When he wrote his commentaries to *The Book of the Law* in the latter part of the Cefalu period Crowley quite honestly and overtly confessed to a considerable amount of pleasure in hunting and killing. It was his idea of virility, of manliness. It would have been his contention that underneath all our life is a not-so-concealed current of hostility. It comes out in overt violence every so often in social and international affairs. These disasters cannot disappear from our lives so long as the violence is present in the Unconscious. How to get rid of it? I am not sure he would condone the idea at all. Violence and killing brings out the best, he claimed, following Nietzsche, the virility in any human race.

THE SMOKING DOG

Each act of man is the twist and double of an hare.
Love and Death are the greyhounds that course him.
God bred the hounds and taketh His pleasure in the sport.
This is the Comedy of Pan, that man should think he hunteth, while those hounds hunt him.
This is the Tragedy of Man when facing Love and Death he turns to bay. He is no more hare, but boar.
There are no other comedies or tragedies.
Cease then to be the mockery of God; in savagery of love and death live thou and die!
Thus shall his laughter be thrilled through with Ecstasy.

This was his answer to the pacifists, and to the kind-hearted liberals, the "sweet light" ones whose violence is just not there. In them, the psychosomatic symptoms that eternally plague them are the equivalents for the energy of life they have lost. They are the "mockery of God" to whom he addressed in vain this injunction in *The Smoking Dog*, to live and die in the savagery of love and death.

As an aside, it is interesting to note that long prior to
Freud's formulation of his instinctual theory of Eros and
Thanatos, Crowley as a poet and mystic had written of Love
and Death as the greyhounds that pursue man. There are
profound depths of insight and understanding in his writing.

Of these two greyhounds he had ample first-hand
experience. His whole life was "like the twist and double of
an hare." The North Africa experience with *The Vision and
The Voice* brought him very close to the understanding of
the death that ever lurked within him. He was never quite
able to unite orgastically with it to transmute and transform
it into Eros—even though he has written often and eloquently
of the specific formula by means of which this is
accomplished.

This manliness theme of his, I should add, was one of the
several provocative reasons for his sincere expressions not
merely of respect but of love for the Arabs and the North
African continent. Apparently, his homosexual component
came to full flower whenever he was in Arab countries. It was
the spontaneous recognition of his own homosexuality that
made him acceptable, without any questions, to the Arabs
whenever he wandered amongst them—which was as often as
he could get there. Deep in him surged an undying love of the
sand and the desert—and of the homosexual Arabs. "I, too,
am the Soul of the Desert. Thou shall seek me yet again in
that wilderness of sand."

The homosexuality of the Arabs has been noted before by
many writers, but I became even more sharply aware of its
existence when recently reading Jung's post-humous
biographical book *Memories, Dreams, Reflections:*

> In the comparative coolness of this green shade
> strolled figures clad in white, among them a great
> number of affectionate couples holding one another in
> close embrace—obviously homosexual friendships. I felt

suddenly transported to the times of classical Greece, where this inclination formed the cement of a society of men and of the *polis* based on that society. It was clear that men spoke to men and women to women here. Only a few of the latter were to be seen, nun-like, heavily veiled figures. I saw a few without veils. These, my dragoman explained, were prostitutes and children.

But killing and hunting, as well as mountain-climbing and exploring, stood out vividly for him as the hallmarks, as the main credentials of masculinity.

Crowley's biography indicates that as a boy he was rather sick and puny, certainly not given to athletics of any kind. In fact, one of the several causes for his turning bitterly and violently from the religion of his family, was the tortures and continuous bullying to which he was subjected at the Plymouth Brethren school. As reported earlier, it had the effect of precipitating a kidney disease with severe albuminuria, for which he had to be taken out of school for a couple of years. He didn't fight back until the Malvern period, just preceding his being sent to Cambridge.

There is also the childhood story he tells with some relish to prove that he had had a great deal of scientific curiosity and that he did not take things on hearsay. He once heard that a cat had nine lives. So with almost mechanical precision, in order to verify this hearsay, he proceeded to kill a cat in nine separate ways. I would not doubt that he did this. I merely question the too obvious motivation for embarking upon this youthful sadism, for that is exactly what it was—scientific interest notwithstanding.

Were we to employ the psychoanalytic method more vigorously we would have to enquire into the effect that his whole sad childhood had on his developing character structure. There are, first of all, the bullying episodes at school, which must have gone on for a considerable length of time. There was also a great deal of abuse from the uncle—if not physical, then psychological and emotional. In this connection, I feel compelled to repeat the story about his Uncle trying to indoctrinate him with a feeling of sin and guilt.   Bishop dramatized this by giving certain vices the rulership of a king. Thus two vices which were to be scrupulously avoided were Smo-King and Drin-King. We can imagine the uncle's consternation when Crowley reminded him that there was a third King, whose name began with F.

The sexual inhibition foisted on him at an early age in that fanatical religious home—whether he recalled it or not—must have set up a variety of inner defense-mechanisms of varying magnitude. For instance, in the *Confessions* he substantiates this attitude by stating, relative to masturbation, that he "frequented the boys whose reputation for wickedness was best established, and was further directed in my enquiry by an intuitive sense of magnetism or appreciation of physiognomy. But the reign of terror was so firmly established in the school that nobody dared tell me outright the nature of this sin, even when the knowledge of it was admitted. Mysterious hints were given; and at last a boy named Gibson told me what action to make, but he did not tell me to what object to apply the process. It seems extraordinary that nature should have afforded me no indication. I nowise connected the organ of reproduction with any voluntary act. I made conjectures dictated by purely intellectual considerations, and carried out experiments based on their results; but they were absolutely ill-directed. I never guessed what organ was in question. The discovery was delayed for years."

Nature afforded many indications, as she always does. Crowley here is actually complaining about the enormity of the psychic defense-mechanisms he had had to forge. They produced a full-fledged scotoma which continued to function even while he was writing his own biography long years afterwards. He always did things to excess. Even his defense-mechanisms were so sturdily constructed that, in spite of his own very full adult sex life, they prevented him from perceiving the facts.

As a result of this, some of the primary instinctual drives which were blocked off and repressed became transformed, as Wilhelm Reich has so eloquently demonstrated, into secondary urges of aggressiveness and sadism and homosexuality. These are indicated quite clearly in the cat incident mentioned above, and secondly in the big-game hunting, and finally in his pre-potency, as it were, to break with the dearest of his male friends. His relationship with women was also marred by the presence of sadistic impulses. There is thus far more to this business of big-game hunting than first meets the eye.

While in Ceylon, he was also moved to write lyrical poetry. Rose still moved him passionately—and *Rosa Mundi* was the outcropping. There we read:

> I am dumb with the rapture of thy loveliness.
> All metres match and mingle; all words tire;
> All lights, all sounds, all perfumes, all gold stress
> Of the honey-palate, all soft strokes expire
> In abject agony of broken sense
> To hymn the emotion tense
> Of somewhat higher—O! how highest! than all
> Their mystery; fall, O fall,
> Ye unavailing eagle flights of song!
> O wife! these do thee wrong.

It was while they were in Ceylon that he discovered Rose was pregnant. Thus the trip to China was put off, and they went back to Europe. They stopped off in Cairo again, and in March 1904 took a flat near the Cairo Museum. He had adopted the quiet pseudonym of Prince Chioa Khan, apparently on the presumption that the bourgeoisie, being snobs, cater more obsequiously to those with titles. It also demonstrates what an egotist he was, to say nothing of a snob. And yet, he was always condemning the landed gentry and the titled aristocracy—no doubt eaten up with jealousy, wishing that his family had belonged in that category instead of merely to the upper middle class, a family which had made its money out of beer.

It was during this Egyptian stay that Rose in some curious way became involved in a set of psychic stimuli which resulted in his writing down *The Book of the Law.* It was strange because he had, at least consciously and on the surface, relinquished most, if not all, of his magical interests, living altogether the life of a young man about town, a man of the world. This document was repugnant to him then, so he proceeded to ignore it for a long time. But many years later, he came to the realization that this was the most important event of his entire life. In fact, he saw that it was the central pivot around which all his activities, conscious or unconscious, revolved. This may or may not be so. But since this matter needs to be dwelt on at some length, it will be postponed to a later chapter.

In April of that year of 1904, they returned to Paris. He was writing furiously. It was a period of enormous creativity. None of it concerned the mystical experience or that way of life to which he had been so dedicated previously, and a rationalism, akin to Buddhism, had taken its place in his writing. But he was no Buddhist now. He had already worked his way through that phase. It had given him what he wanted; now he could discard it. He wrote some trenchant analyses of Pansil, the five obligatory denials necessary to the monk, and the Four Noble Truths, the backbone of classical Buddhism, which are altogether devastating.

It was in a book review in *Equinox III* that there first appeared his criticism of Pansil. These precepts or moral commands are for the monk only. He must not kill, steal, commit adultery, lie, or drink intoxicating liquors. With a show of fine humor as well as of incisive analysis, Crowley tears each one apart, point by point. He wrote, that though forced to admit the general excellence of Buddhism, nonetheless the five precepts are nonsense, philosophically. They must either be rejected or re-interpreted. He contends that they are meant to be sarcastic and biting criticisms on existence.

Briefly, I have abstracted the following from his brilliant commentary to each of the precepts:

First. The fact that the Buddha who had spoken this command was not the same as the Buddha before he had spoken it, provides the proof that by speaking this command he had at the same time violated it. More, not only did he slay himself, he breathed in millions of living organisms and destroyed them. He could neither eat nor drink, or even breathe without murder implicit in each act. For example, by taking quinine, the monk does so with the deliberate intention of destroying innumerable living beings. Whether this is done by stimulating the phagocytes, or directly, is morally indifferent.

Crowley took this occasion to make a sly dig at his old friend and guru by stating: "How such a fiend incarnate, my dear brother Ananda Metteya, can call him 'cruel and cowardly' who only kills a tiger, is a study in the philosophy of the mote and the beam!" The footnote attached to this dig reads "The argument that 'the animals are our brothers' is merely intended to mislead one who has never been in a Buddhist country. The average Buddhist would, of course, kill his brother for five rupees or less."

Second. The discussion is opened up by insinuating that by commanding others not to do something, the Buddha deprives them of the right to follow their own wills. All voluntary action limits in some degree, however minute, the volition of others. If I breathe, I diminish the stock of oxygen available on the planet. In some far distant time, when the Earth shall be as dead as the moon is to-day, my breathing now will have robbed some being then living of the dearest necessity of life. That this theft is miniscule is no answer to the moralist, to whom degree is not known. Nor to the man of science, who sees the chain of nature missing no link. All theft is temporary, since even a millionaire must die. Also it is universal, since even a Buddha must breathe.

Third. A jibe at British morality starts off this discussion. Since the public has a dirty mind, Crowley stated that it should find the subject of adultery an opportunity for its favorite game of slander. "I would premise in the first place that to commit adultery in the Divorce Court sense is not here in question. It assumes too much proprietary right of a man over a woman. We may more readily suppose that the Buddha was condemning incontinence."

Fourth. His criticism here is very fine and subtle, on purely philosophical grounds. It too is a strong *reductio ad absurdum.* He concludes the discussion by stating "If personality be delusion, a lie is involved in the command of one to another. In short, we all lie all the time. We are compelled to it by the nature of things themselves—paradoxical as that seems—and the Buddha knew it!"

Fifth. What Buddha really commands, with that grim humor of his, is—avoid intoxication! But then Crowley asks, what is intoxication, unless it be the loss of power to use perfectly a truth-telling set of faculties. A doctor might tell you that all food intoxicates. All—here as in every part of the universe, of every subject and in every predicate—is a matter of degree! Our faculties never report the truth. Our eyes say flat when our fingers say round. The tongue sends a set of impressions to the brain which our hearing declares to be nonexistent—and so on!

"What is this delusion of personality but a profound and centrally-seated intoxication of the consciousness? I am intoxicated as I address these words; you are drunk—beastly drunk!—as you read them; Buddha was as drunk as a voter at election time when he uttered his besotted command.

"Buddha was not a fool, asking men to do the impossible or unwise. Easy rules, easily interpreted, cannot avail against the sorrow of existence. A sorrow by the inherent necessity of the way it is made; sorrow not by volition, not by malice, not by carelessness, but by nature, by ineradicable tendency, by the incurable disease of Desire, its Creator, is it so, and the way to destroy it is by the uprooting of desire, and this is accomplished by the severe roads of austere self-mastery and of arduous scientific research."

And that was that! In similar ways, he explored all of the tenets of Buddhism, took what he wanted, and rejected the rest. It had affected him profoundly, however. Its residuum is to be perceived in many parts of his philosophy, the philosophy that he created on the basis of his own vast spiritual and intellectual experience.

To Scotland they returned. He needed to find a new outlet for the several books he had printed and published himself. With tongue in cheek, and yet serious at the same time, he registered the new name of his outlet—The Society for the Propagation of Religious Truth, Boleskine, Foyers, Inverness. It was to publish some of his new writing, as well as the *Collected Works*. However much of a gag it was intended, or was interpreted, there was a great deal of religious or mystical material in those three volumes of the collected works.

In the early summer of 1904, well after they had returned from Egypt, he was visited in Boleskine by Jacot Guillarmod who bore with him a copy of the book he had written about the unsuccessful expedition a couple of years earlier to K-2, *Six Mois dans l'Himalaya*. Guillarmod was a medical doctor. At one time Crowley thought that his medicine was like his mountaineering, pretty awful. But it is fairly evident that this opinion had its origins after the Kangchenjunga expedition.

Most of that year was spent in Scotland—again without reference to magic and the Great Work. That winter, he and Rose went to St. Moritz, for skating and skiing. It was the usual life of the average upper middle class family in England. Very prosaic! The winter over, in the spring of 1905 they returned to Scotland. Once again, he wrote furiously and intensely—and published equally furiously. Book after book appeared, beautifully printed and bound. *The God-Eater, The Star and the Garter, The Argonauts, The Sword of Song, Rosa Inferni, Orpheus* and *Gargoyles.* There was an edition of *The Goetia* or *The Lesser Key of King Solomon,* a book on magic for which he had commissioned Mathers years earlier to make an English translation. It included the Preliminary Invocation or the Bornless Ritual, as well as an introduction of considerable interest. It explained magic on purely rationalistic lines, without any reference to the traditional hierarchical concept. It gives us an idea of how he felt at that time.

Guillarmod had come to talk to Crowley late in 1904 about another Himalayan expedition. He had become obsessed by the great peaks in the North of India, and because of the failure to scale K-2 successfully, proposed another chance at one of those great giants. Kangchenjunga was his choice. Mount Everest was said to be the highest peak of the Himalayan range, K-2 had been considered the third, with Kangchenjunga the second, with a height estimated to be at 28,225 feet above sea level. It has been called the showpiece of the Himalayas for it is not hidden, like K-2, by satellite peaks, but can be readily and clearly seen on a bright day from the mountain stopping place Darjeeling. It lies on the border between Sikkim and Nepal, fourteen miles from Tibet.

If Guillarmod offered this peak as bait, Crowley swallowed it without blinking. There and then they worked out plans to materialize almost a year away, in the Spring and

Summer of 1905. Though Oscar Eckenstein was invited, he was unable to accept. In his own inimitable way, Symonds deduces from this that since Crowley was to be the leader of the expedition, Eckenstein declined feeling that Crowley's judgment and leadership were not to be trusted. There is no evidence to warrant this assumption. The contract that was drawn up expressly agreed that "Aleister Crowley shall be sole and supreme judge of all matters respecting mountain craft, and the others will obey his instructions."

The next year, in May 1905, he left for the East, with Rose and the baby remaining at Boleskine. A desultory week was spent in Cairo, Crowley hoping that there might be a recrudescence of the strange inspiration of the preceding year. Since nothing much happened, he went to Bombay, arriving on the 9th of June. He then took a train to Calcutta and called on Edward Thornton, who had accompanied him into the interior of Burma four years previously. I would suggest that he consulted Thornton, amongst other things, for advice concerning Allan Bennett who was now the Bhikkhu Ananda Metteya, studying in the monastery at Rangoon. Crowley wanted to see Allan. There had been too long a hiatus in their relationship.

The expedition began, as always, from Darjeeling. And off they went. The assault on Kangchenjunga has been fully described by Crowley in his *Confessions,* by Guillarmod in the slender book he wrote about the climb, as well as by Symonds in his attempt to summarize both writers. There is nothing I can add to these accounts either factually or by contribution of psychological insights, so the matter can be left there. As far as I know, there were no specific meditation or occult practices recorded during those two summer months of July and August, 1905 though I fancy it was never really far from his mind.

The climb against the great god of the mountain failed. Tragedy was in the air. Men died, a mutiny occurred, and nobody's reputation was enhanced.

Crowley came down from the mountain, disappointed, dispirited, and, so Symonds says, infected with the Kangchenjunga phobia. He received an invitation to go big-game hunting, which he accepted with alacrity. He needed something to kill, some outlet for the frustration and the hostility which had been engendered on the mountain. Some of it erupted and was discharged in the hunt.

For the rest, it came out in a moody letter he wrote to Gerald Kelly, in which he confessed:

> After five years of folly and weakness, miscalled politeness, tact, discretion, care for the feeling of others, I am weary of it. I say today: to hell with Christianity, Rationalism, Buddhism, all the lumber of the centuries. I bring you a positive and primaeval fact, Magic by name; and with this I will build me a new Heaven and a new Earth. I want none of your faint approval or faint dispraise; I want blasphemy, murder, rape, revolution, anything, bad or good, but strong.

His confession of weakness and folly was, after all, meant only for a friend. We would do well to remember that. And it would be wise to remember too that his concept of weakness might be a great deal different from ours. The last several years had seen him work diligently through so many of the systems which had previously meant much to him. Yoga for him now was merely a system of mental calisthenics and athletics—useful certainly, but that is all. The hierarchy of Magic was discarded. Angels and demons were merely component parts of the brain; we would now use the word "unconscious." Buddhism had failed him. It was subject to all the criticism that he had learned to level against everything else. All his "absolutes" were dissolving in thin air. And he was sick of them.

Though he had rejected, or better still *ignored, The Book of the Law,* dictated to him in 1904, this note to Gerald

Kelly is practically a re-statement of some of the contents of that strange Book. It was a harbinger of what was to come. A total conversion to or acceptance of that dynamic call to blasphemy and revolution—and strong! It shows above all what was stirring in the unconscious depths of his psyche. Stirring—and gathering strength for a subsequent emergence.

While in Calcutta, an alarming incident occurred—which bore every mark of destiny. He was wandering in the streets of Calcutta one night, making for a place called Culinga Bazaar, a real den of iniquity. It was a feast night, Durga Puga, and there were hordes of people about, singing, shouting, dancing. As he walked along, he felt he was being followed. He was now in a narrow labyrinth of tiny alley-like streets. Suddenly he found himself pinioned against the wall. Almost without thinking, he clutched the automatic in his pocket, and once, twice, it went off. Two men fell on the street, two others vanished. He too fled, after first having gone through the motions magically of rendering himself invisible by clothing himself imaginatively with the god-form of Harpocrates. Whether this last exercise of invisibility was successful or not we do not know, and it does not matter. But the next morning the newspapers were full of an account of two native ruffians having been killed while attempting to waylay and rob a European. The Commissioner of Police offered a reward for the apprehension of the unknown European.

No doubt Crowley became alarmed by this publicity, and while he had not yet been apprehended as the one who had shot and killed a couple of natives, he felt the time had come to get out. In the meantime, Rose and his daughter had arrived from England. He told her they had to get out quickly; the choice of destination was hers. One place or another made little difference. But she had remembered that on the trip a couple of years earlier they had intended to go to China. So China it was!

There is a little back-tracking to do. Much of the narrative described above is a narrative of externals only. As such it is part of the truth, but part only. There is a paragraph or two in the spiritual biography in *Equinox VIII* which should be added to the above, when immediately the subsequent chain of events is transformed into a meaningful experience.

After the newspapers had publicized the killing of the two natives, Crowley went to see Edward Thornton again with an attorney friend. Both of them counselled him to lie low, Br'er Rabbit-like, or get out as quickly as possible. That was that; and certainly there was no quibble about it.

While driving through Calcutta with Thornton, they discussed some abstruse philosophical topics. This would imply that while up in the mountains and hunting, Crowley's mind was not altogether devoid of preoccupation with the deeper issues of his spiritual life. True, he might have been attempting to avoid them deliberately; suppressing them in fact, so as to free himself to cope with the more pressing problems of the immediate present. But every now and again, this preoccupation would force an emergence from the deeper levels of his mind, demanding attention. It was this emergence that he discussed with Thornton, for Crowley was complaining that the analysis of sense impressions showed no causal connection between them. There was no coherence in the world of things, in the universe. It was simply a discontinuous sequence of events, of things, without any necessary connecting link.

This is the old absolute idealistic position. This philosophy attempts to prove intellectually that because there is no coherence or reality in the phenomenal world, the only reality is in the world of mind, the noumenon, which in effect was the Mind and Body of Godhead.

Traditionally, this Berkeleyan position had been attacked by Douglas Hume, who applied the same critical technique to the ego itself. He concluded that just as there was no connection between time-space events in the phenomenal world, so similarly impressions, sensations, and perceptions—the material of the psyche itself, were also disconnected. There was no causal link, and certainly no integrating ego, or noumenon, behind it. The universe, within and without, was simply a sequential flow of sensations and impressions.

Crowley had been familiar *intellectually* with all of this. He had not studied philosophy for nothing. In fact, with his superb mental equipment, this was duck's soup for him. But now, after the isolation and tragedy of the mountains where quite evidently he had been doing some serious introspection, the world had fallen apart. And now he complained that the universe was not causally connected, just a disconnected set of phenomena that he perceived. It was shattering to him, and apparently quite unexpected, when Thornton reminded him that the same criticism applied to the Ego as well. It fell on him with the force of a thunderbolt, and literally threw him for a loop. He had known it intellectually for a long while. Now it stabbed him to the heart, and threw him into a real impasse. The time was ripe.

So long as one is merely *speculating* about philosophical ideas, and arrives at certain conclusions, there is no mischief done. All right, you have propounded a set of very interesting ideas. But this is not what Crowley was involved in. He had been through that phase six or seven years previously when studying the history and principles of philosophy. His broad reading had made him familiar with every branch of philosophical endeavour, from Plato to Aristotle to Kant and Hegel. He had saturated himself in the Advaita philosophy of the Indian Peninsula, as well as with Gautama's destructive counter to that. This was intellectual exercise, sharpening the mental wits. It gave one some idea of what different people thought about the universe in which we live. But with his inner quest, to find "the hub of the wheel", what had it to do with him?

Because of the use of the mind as a tool, when one attempts to transcend that operational tool to reach a higher level of spiritual perception and experience, a serious impasse is reached. It produces a species of insanity. Symonds, lacking philosophical understanding of what was involved, and deliberately using misplaced bits of Crowley's own language as another whip to beat him with, wrote that "He admitted, and in print, that for a time he was not in his right mind. Whether this was due to the practise of a form of magical invocation which he called Augoeides—shouted out amid the deserts and hills of this part of Western China—or to a fall of forty feet over a cliff (when his pony backed and threw him), is not clear."

It is not clear to Symonds only because he is determined to show his contempt and derision for Crowley, that he was altogether unable to perceive what Crowley was stating with a great deal of vigorous clarity. It is not easy to understand such transcendental matters, admittedly. But with a little sympathy, it is easy to feel the enormous anguish and mental torture that Crowley was experiencing as he struggled inwardly with these tremendous conclusions. Conclusions? They were less conclusions, intellectually obtained, than spiritual and cataclysmic events functionally experienced. He tried afterwards to express this in two different documents.

I will quote the first one, *Liber Os Abysmi*—The Book of the Entry to the Abyss—because it accurately indicates in simple intellectual terms what happened to him on his way from Calcutta to Rangoon.

> 1. This book is the Gate of the Secret of the Universe.
> 2. Let the Exempt Adept procure the Prolegomena of Kant, and study it, paying special attention to the Antinomies.
> 3. Also Hume's doctrine of Causality in his

"Enquiry."

4. Also Herbert Spencer's discussion of the three theories of the Universe in his "First Principles", Part I.

5. Also Huxley's Essays on Hume and Berkeley.

. . . .

11. Let him subtly and exactly demonstrate the fallacies of every known solution, and let him seek a true solution by his right Ingenium.

12. In all this let him be guided only by clear reason, and let him forcibly suppress all other qualities such as Intuition, Aspiration, Emotion and the like.

13. During these practices all forms of Magick Art and Meditation are forbidden to him. It is forbidden to him to seek any refuge from his intellect.

14. Let then his reason hurl itself again and again against the blank wall of mystery which will confront him.

15. Thus also following is it said, and we deny it not.

At last automatically his reason will take up the practice, *sua sponte,* and he shall have no rest therefrom.

16. Then will all phenomena which present themselves to him appear meaningless, and disconnected, and his own Ego will break up into a series of impressions having no relation with one another, or with any other thing.

17. Let this state become so acute that it is in truth Insanity, and let this continue until exhaustion.

18. According to a certain deeper tendency of the individual will be the duration of this state.

19. It may end in real insanity, which concludes the activities of the adept during this present life, or by his rebirth into his own body and mind with the simplicity of a little child . . . .

So he was, in truth, insane. The whole world, within and without, had fallen like a pack of cards. And there was nothing, absolutely nothing, to cling to. If this happened to any one of us, we too might feel we had become insane.

Insanity, we must remember, under ordinary circumstances has absolutely nothing to do with what we are now discussing. It has, under ordinary circumstances, everything to do with a need to escape from some life situation which is felt to be too difficult to face. The result of this escape within is to be overwhelmed by the repressed contents of one's own psyche, never previously realized. They can either be, as in the Freudian sense, infantile affects and fantasies, or in the Jungian sense, eruptions from the archaic and primitive levels of the collective Unconscious. Nothing here has application to this ordeal embraced by Crowley.

It was an insanity that was deliberately induced. It had a deliberate process of induction. It was for deliberate and foreseeable ends. This was not going "out of one's mind" in the vernacular of the ordinary man. Symonds does not know how to make it clear to himself or the reader that we are dealing with a very extraordinary man, going through a most extraordinary initiatory process. Initiatory in the sense of provoking and promoting an especial kind of inner movement and growth.

To me, this experience of crossing the Abyss bears a great resemblance to Zen Buddhism. Not beatnik Zen or book Zen, but Zen understood as a meditative process, as a spiritual technique. For months or years, the candidate has been learning to concentrate his mind and to meditate. He has explored by this method the depths of his inner being. Its connections with his past and present and with the outside world in which he lives are probed and analyzed, by the meditative process which is at once corrosive and destructive, until the reality of the world and of the Ego is perceived to be most tenuous. He is then given by his Roshi, his teacher, certain types of *koans* or phrases or sentences which make no sense at all or are not soluble by intellectual means. They pose problems. Since, by this time, he is an adept with the meditative device, he learns to focus all his attention on this *koan* until, as Crowley asserts, the mind takes it up *sua sponte*. In other words, the Ego becomes wholly obsessed by this insoluble intellectual problem. Then indeed is the student insane. He is altogether *obsessed* and can find no rest or peace or gratification in any insane activity in the insane world in which he insanely lives. Then—he must either remain stark raving mad, or something else happens—a transcendental process comes into operation. He is flung over the mental conflict which he has deliberately induced, thrown through the Abyss into a transcendental spiritual noumenal State where the intellect and the phenomenal world are perceived in their right places. It is a spiritual rebirth—the crossing over into ineffable radiance and Light.

> Blind horror catches at my breath.
> The path of the Abyss runs through
> Things darker, dismaller than death!
> Courage and will! What boots their force!
> The mind rears like a frightened horse.
> There is no memory possible
> Of that unfathomable hell.
> Even the shadows that arise
> Are things too dreadful to recount!
> There's no such doom in Destiny's
> Harvest of horror. The white fount
> Of Speech is stifled at its source.
> Know, the sane spirit keeps its course
> By this, that everything it thinks
> Hath causal or contingent links.
> Destroy them, and destroy the mind!
> O bestial, bottomless, and blind
> Black pit of all insanity!
> The adept must make his way to thee!
> This is the end of all our pain,
> The dissolution of the brain!
> For lo! in this no mortar sticks;
> Down comes the house—a hail of bricks!
> The sense of all I hear is drowned;
> Tap, tap, tap, and nothing matters!

Senseless hallucinations roll
Across the curtain of the soul.
Each ripple on the river seems
The madness of a maniac's dreams!
So in the self no memory-chain
Or causal wisp to bind the straws!
The Self disrupted! Blank, insane,
Both of existence and of laws,
The Ego and the Universe
Fall to one black chaotic curse.

. . . .

Black snare that I was taken in!
How one may pass I hardly know.
Maybe time never blots the track.
Black, black, intolerably black!
Go, spectre of the ages, go!
Suffice it that I passed beyond.
I found the secret of the bond
Of thought to thought through countless years,
Through many lives, in many spheres,
Brought to a point the dark design
Of this existence that is mine.
I knew my secret. *All I was*
I brought into the burning-glass,
And all its focused light and heat
Charred *all I am*. The rune's complete
When *all I shall be* flashes by
Like a shadow on the sky.

Then I dropped my reasoning.
Vacant and accursèd thing!
By my Will I swept away
The web of metaphysic, smiled
At the blind labyrinth, where the grey
Old snake of madness wove his wild
Curse! As I trod the trackless way
Through sunless gorges of Cathay,
I became a little child . . . .

This lengthy extrapolation from *AHA!* shows what was happening. He was driving through the streets of Calcutta with Edward Thornton who, inadvertently, acted as an initiator to Crowley spurring him on to the next step on the path.

Crowley had laid claim to the grade of 7=4 Adeptus Exemptus with the pseudonym of O.M. as a result of his work in Yoga, with the attainment of Dhyana. How he claimed it, and who conferred it, we shall never know. We must not fall into the pitfall however that confronted Symonds, and assume that because Crowley *was* an egotist, everything that happened to him related only to this trait. This would be to simplify entirely too much. There is infinitely more to the Path and to Crowley than this. It is quite possible that he was both an egotist and an exhibitionist, but at the same time a sincere initiate of high calibre working his way to noble ends.

As I see it, it is too bad that, apart from people like Allan Bennett and George Cecil Jones, and an accidental catalyst like Eckenstein or Thornton, there was no one available to act as his teacher and pinpoint the defects and flaws in his character structure. This is the role of the guru, as it is of the good psychotherapist. He had neither.

We cannot understand how or why he claimed the Adeptus Exemptus grade. Nor on the other hand can we brush off this attainment with a smart reference to his egotism.

The ultimate task of the Adeptus Exemptus is indeed to give up his adeptship. It is really to renounce everything that he is, and everything that he had gained on the Path through the Great Work, and throw himself into the Abyss. This symbolic language means ultimately that he is to destroy the Ego. Yet it is not the ego itself, but his *identification* with it, so that thereafter it is perceived and known to be a tool, as one psychological tool amongst many, to be used by whatever the ultimate Reality is. We can give It any name we

like—but whatever It is, it is thereafter regarded as the Self.
Tat tvam asi. It sounds remarkably simple, and in many ways
it must be. At the same time it carries with it the implication
of destroying oneself, or what one considers oneself all one's
life. "He that loses his life shall find it." Yet none of us can
look forward with alacrity to self-destruction!

So with this metaphysical jolt administered by Thornton,
he started out for Rangoon, early in November, 1905. With
him were Rose and their child, the child's nurse, and Salama,
the faithful Kashmiri who had accompanied Crowley on
previous expeditions. It was a weird assortment of five
human beings that sailed for Rangoon. Crowley was the most
impatient of the lot. Not merely because he had to get out of
India in a hurry, but because he was anxious to get to the
Choung, the monastery where he would find Allan. He had
great need of Allan at this moment.

On the way there, he wrote in his diary:

> I realize in myself the perfect impossibility of reason,
> suffering great misery. I am as one who should have
> plumed himself for years upon the speed and strength of
> a favourite horse, only to find not only that its speed
> and strength were illusory, but that it was not a real
> horse at all, but a clothes-horse. There being no way—no
> conceivable way—out of this awful trouble gives that
> hideous despair which is only tolerable because in the
> past it has ever been the Darkness of the Threshold. But
> this is far worse than ever before; for it is not a despair
> of the Substance, but of the Form. I wish to go from A
> to B; and I am not only a cripple, but there is no such
> thing as space. I have to keep an appointment at
> midnight; and not only is my watch stopped, but there
> is no such thing as time. I wish to make a cannon; and
> not only have I no cue, but there is no such thing as
> causality.

So he wound up in Rangoon. One of the first things he did
was to consult hurriedly his former guru, Allan, seeking aid

and counsel, which he desperately needed. For three days only—this was the maximum period permitted to the non-resident monk—he stayed at the monastery, attempting to follow Allan's recommendations. This was to institute the *Sammasati* meditation.

Allan had written a fine essay describing this meditation published by Crowley many years later in one of the *Equinoxes*. This was when Crowley had already broken through his obstacles, and perceived the validity of the recommendation. The *Sammasati* meditation consists essentially of training the mind to think backwards so that, in effect, one has acquired the ability to break through the barriers of death and its forgetfulness, to become conscious of the underlying purpose running through one's life. It is a method of becoming aware of what Crowley subsequently was to call the True Will. But the three days in the monastery were in no way adequate to accomplish this tremendous task. It did start him off, and that was the important issue.

The company of five sailed up the Irriwaddy River in Burma to Bhamo which is near the Chinese border. From there they travelled into China proper, on pony back. In his *Confessions,* Crowley called this experience a walk across China. Crowley really walked across the lower or Southern borders of China, just north of what was then known as French Indo-China. It was still quite a wild experience for a European with a wife, child, nurse and a Kashmiri servant, to make a trip of this kind. It is still relatively rough and hazardous country.

While travelling across this lower portion of China, on pony back, he was concentrating on the philosophical problem which harrassed his very being. He was occasionally sick—for later when he returned to England surgical intervention was needed on his eye, his throat, and heaven alone knows what else. Abstracted as he was a great deal of the time, preoccupied with his inner strivings, he must have been thrown over a cliff when his pony missed its footing. It was a miracle indeed that he was not killed or even badly injured. It served only to deepen his meditation, his search for some purpose or meaning in his life, beside writing poetry and climbing mountains and performing Yoga and Magic. There had to be something he *had* to do. He had not survived this accident and so many other near-misses in his adventurous life for some trivial end. What was he here for? What meaning had he?

The answers to these questions were not immediately to be found. Some time had to elapse before he was able to discover the meaning of it all. That he did ultimately discover answers to these personal questions seems evident from the narrative that follows.

Meanwhile, it must be stated that it was this unusual set of experiences that provided him with the basic material from which he wrote, during the vital *Equinox* period, an important instruction for his Order called *Liber Thisarb*. *Thisarb* is the reverse spelling of the word *Berashith*, the first word opening the Hebrew version of Genesis. It means "In the beginning . . ." *Thisarb* therefore depicts a method or technique of thinking backwards, in order to seek out the origins of the events in the Adept's life. Its purpose is thereby to gain insight into the meaning of those events. In this respect, it borrows heavily from an essay entitled "The Training of the Mind" by Ananda Metteya, printed in *Equinox V*.

The instruction that Crowley wrote opens with: "This book is not intended to lead to the supreme attainment. On the contrary, its results define the separate being of the Exempt Adept from the rest of the Universe, and discover his relation to the Universe. It is of such importance to the Exempt Adept that we cannot over-rate it. Let him in no wise adventure the plunge into the Abyss until he has accomplished this to his most perfect satisfaction." To this statement, he appended a footnote: "One must destroy one's false notions about who and what one is before one can find the truth of the matter. One must therefore understand these false notions before giving them up. Unless this be done perfectly, one will get the True mixed up with the remains of the False."

Though *Liber Thisarb* was not written until well after 1909, it does serve to give more than an inkling of what Crowley was doing in his meditation in China. These efforts of his cannot be dismissed facetiously or casually. The man was seriously embarked upon the most serious work of his life-time.

In the instruction, Crowley proceeded to state that "Memory is essential to the individual consciousness; otherwise the mind were but a blank sheet on which shadows are cast." The whole of the adept's past is thus subjected to the most incisive scrutiny. Every minute vestige of memory trace has to be excited, examined and exhausted. "The stimulation of memory useful in both practices is also achieved by simple meditation, in a certain stage of which old memories arise unbidden. The adept may then practice this, stopping at this stage, and encouraging instead of suppressing the flashes of memory." The most important result as regards the adventure into the Abyss "is the freedom from all desire or clinging to anything which it gives."

Continuing the instruction, therefore, and pointing to his own experience on this particular occasion, Crowley wrote: "Now that he is on the point of plunging into the Abyss a giant Why? confronts him with uplifted club . . . ."

He describes the type of analysis of the ego, its experience, its environment, and its significance in these words: "There is no minutest atom of his composition which can be withdrawn without making him some other than he is; no useless moment in his past. Then what is his future? . . . ."

Finally, in a footnote to this passage, Crowley wrote: "A

brother known to me was repeatedly baffled in this meditation. But one day being thrown with his horse over a sheer cliff of forty feet, and escaping without a scratch or a bruise, he was reminded of his many narrow escapes from death. These proved to be the last factors in his problem, which thus completed, solved itself in a moment."

CHAPTER ELEVEN

Augoeides

Had McGregor Mathers accomplished nothing more for students of the Golden Dawn than the translation from the French of *The Book of the Sacred Magic of Abramelin the Mage* he would still deserve our gratitude. His translation is an excellent one, coherent, and expressing most sympathetically the thought of the medieval writer, whoever he may have been.

The author is supposed to have been one Abraham who, in describing and bequeathing the system to his son Lamech, acknowledges its receipt from an Egyptian named Abramelin. There is undoubtedly mythology here, but that is altogether unimportant. Regardless of its origin, its date, and its authorship, all of which are periodically challenged and criticized, this work was found to be of value to the sincere student. Abraham makes no impossible demands such as are found in the fraudulent grimoires concerning the blood of bats caught at midnight, or the fourth feather from the left wing of a completely black cock, or the stuffed eye of a virgin basilisk, and so on. Though perhaps some of the requirements set down by Abraham are difficult to follow, there is always an excellent reason for their statement. They are not intended to be subtle tests of the skill of the operator.

Written in an exalted style, there is nothing in this book to insult the intelligence of the reader. On the contrary, the

303

operation proposed is the apotheosis of simplicity, and the method itself is in entire accordance. There are, naturally, certain preliminary prescriptions and injunctions to be observed, but these really amount to little more than common sense counsel, to observe decency in the performance of so august an operation. One must, for example, possess a house where proper precautions against disturbance and interference can be taken. This having been arranged, there remains little else to do but to aspire with increasing concentration and ardour for six months towards—as it is called—the Knowledge and Conversation of the Holy Guardian Angel.

One of the most important requirements is good physical health. That absent, the body "is subject to divers infirmities, whence at length result in impatience and want of power to operate and pursue the Operation; and a sick man can neither be clean and pure, nor enjoy solitude; and in such a case it is better to cease."

The time required to bring the Operation to a successful conclusion is six lunar months, so that if commenced in March it should end about the middle of September. The whole period of six months is divided into three definite periods of two months each, each period being characterized by the increasing severity of the self-denials, but mainly by the addition of further invocations, thus heightening the concentration.

While on this topic of the Abramelin method, I must mention that throughout the years many students have reported to me some of their efforts and experiments in this direction. All, without exception, have failed, their sincerity notwithstanding. Some few then turned their backs on the whole subject of the Great Work, and spewed their frustration and sense of futility on all who came within their sphere. A few others, on the basis of this failure, began to ask "Why?"

There is no easy answer to this question. So many factors have to be considered. Yet, when all is said and done, there is one requirement which only a handful seem to perceive. That is, the need for a prolonged period of inner discipline of one kind or another. It is this arduous training which then comes to the aid of the aspirant during the six month term of his retirement, making possible or feasible the ultimate attainment.

Discipline is not welcome as a rule among occult students, which was why Crowley insisted so emphatically upon its necessity, and why he tended to be rude and contemptuous when students sought the highest goals without proper preparation. It seems to me, then, that when aspirants seek to perform the Abramelin operation in the six months mentioned, and reject any kind of preparatory mental or magical discipline, their aspiration needs to be held in question. I rather fancy many of them are neurotic escapists who cannot tolerate themselves and their emotional difficulties. They hope and fantasy that the Abramelin operation will "cure" them of their problems, which will thus not have to be faced. Escape is no part of the Great Work—failure can only ensue. Discipline and training, the traditional requirements in magic as well as elsewhere, are the only factors that can bring the student through. There is no other way.

In the book there is some preliminary discussion as to the nature of the scene of the Operation. Solitude is one of the major considerations. Mention is made of the type of house required if the work is to be performed in a town or village. Emphasis is laid on the construction of the Oratory so-called, which is to serve as the Temple. From this Oratory, a window is to open out onto an open balcony or a Terrace, the floor of which is to be covered with a layer of fine river sand. In *AHA!* Crowley made a rendition of possible variants of the scene of the Operation:

. . . . Choose tenderly
A place for thine academy.
Let there be an holy wood
Of embowered solitude
By the still, the rainless river,
Underneath the tangled roots
Of majestic trees that quiver
In the quiet airs; where shoots
Of the kindly grass are green
Moss and ferns asleep between,
Lilies in the water lapped,
Sunbeams in the branches trapped
—Windless and eternal even!
Silenced all the birds of heaven
By the low insistent call
Of the constant water fall.
There, to such a setting be
Its carven gem of deity,
A central flawless fire, enthralled
Like Truth within an emerald.

In China, Crowley had to compromise a very great deal. The classical conditions as laid down in the text were impossible to fulfill. He lacked many things. But what was lacking in fact, was made up by his powerful imaginative faculty, as I hope to show.

From a book I wrote in the early thirties, *The Tree of Life,* where some of this Abramelin Operation was described at some length, the following is extrapolated:

"Before commencing the Operation, it would be well for the Magician to formulate an oath that he will perform this sacred Magic, and to put it clearly in writing. The will and the determination to succeed must be expressed in words, and these words by deeds. For, during the dark night of the soul, when the spiritual eye is closed and all insight has departed, when the acolyte is weakened by temptation and distress of mind, it is only by adhering to the letter of the oath that the Magician may hope to bring this operation to a satisfactory climax. The direct expression of Will, in any event, is speech, and the recording of a willed determination in a written oath is in accord with the fundamentals of the magical philosophy."

It is certain, wrote Cammell in his book about Crowley, that Crowley entered upon this Operation in a spirit of the most exalted enthusiasm. But then Cammell proceeds to that kind of moralizing which utterly negates all his previously fine writing, reducing him to the level of an ordinary prig. "Whatever may have been Crowley's acts during his attempt to operate Abramelin, we may be certain that his mind, so passionately and often rabidly sensual, could not have attained the purity which is a condition of success in this, and in all theurgical operations. How far his sense of Prayer was developed and in what direction we cannot—so contradictory and unstable was his mind—fairly conjecture. His failure to accomplish the Operation at the appointed time or place is significant; that he should fail to derive from it the desired profits spiritual or material, was to my mind a foregone conclusion."

Crowley's failure to accomplish the Operation in Boleskine in 1899 has already been simply explained. If it is significant in some other way to Mr. Cammell, I do not see it, and can only assume that our good Mr. Cammell is examining a situation blinded by his own moral scotoma. Crowley gave up the Operation when he learned that Mathers was in trouble. Whatever may or may not have been Crowley's ideas of loyalty he generously offered both his services and his fortune to Mathers when the revolt broke out. And that is all there is to it.

The second renunciation of the Operation was on an even simpler basis than the first. He met Rose Kelly, and impulsively married her. His preoccupation with his new wife was so complete that naturally there was neither the time nor interest in anything else. That the operation *failed* is simply

Mr. Cammell's own conclusion which in no way whatsoever is substantiated by the diaries nor by any of the available records. The fact is, it barely got started!

This is the formal oath that Crowley took in Scotland when originally he intended to perform the Abramelin operation:

> *The Obligation of the Operation.*
> I, Perdurabo, in the Presence of the Lord of the Universe, and of all Powers Divine and Angelic, do spiritually bind myself, even as I am now physically bound unto the Cross of Suffering.
>
> 1. To unite my consciousness with the divine, as I may be permitted and aided by the Gods Who Live for ever, the Aeons of Infinite years, that, being lost in the Limitless Light, it may find Itself: to the Regeneration of the Race, either of man or as the Will of God shall be. And I submit myself utterly to the Will Divine.
>
> 2. To follow out with courage, modesty, loving kindness, and perseverance, the course prescribed by Abramelin the Mage; as far as in me lies, unto the attainment of this end.
>
> 3. To despise utterly the things and the opinions of this world lest they hinder me in doing this.
>
> 4. To use my powers only to the Spiritual well-being of all with whom I may be brought in contact.
>
> 5. To give no place to Evil; and to make eternal war against the Forces of Evil: until even they be redeemed unto the Light.
>
> 6. To harmonise my own spirit so that Equilibrium may lead me to the East; and that my Human Consciousness shall allow no usurpation of its rule by the Automatic.
>
> 7. To conquer temptations.
>
> 8. To banish the illusions.
>
> 9. To put my whole trust in the Only and Omnipotent Lord God; as it is written, 'Blessed are they that put their trust in him.'
>
> 10. To uplift the Cross of Sacrifice and Suffering; and to cause my light so to shine before men that they must

glorify my Father which is in Heaven.

The oath of course is predicated on the philosophic content of the Golden Dawn. It is predicated on the structure of the Adeptus Minor obligation which is attributed, clause by clause, to the ten Sephiroth of the Qabalistic Tree, representing his aspirations as they existed at the outset of his Order career.

But then Cammell makes further comments that render me wholly indignant. He wrote:

"I believe firmly that Crowley's rapid fall from the ideals to which he aspired, and in which he so ardently believed, when he made this fatal oath—a fall that entailed the violation of his oath—exposed him to spiritual reprisals of a formidable kind. That violation brought upon him inexorably the malediction, pronounced by himself upon the violator. Who shall say how far the Abramelin oath reacted upon the life and character of the young adventurer (he had not yet completed his twenty-fourth year) who so confidently, rashly, unwisely, uttered it?"

I will agree with Cammell to the extent that Crowley was rash, over confident, young, and would certainly have rushed in where angels feared to go. Apart from that—nonsense! The facts are that in the episode of his life that we are about to discuss he did embark upon the Abramelin operation under the most disadvantageous conditions conceivable. There was no Temple in the classical sense of the word. Solitude was marred by his having to be the responsible head of a small expeditionary force travelling across the southern margins of the Chinese border. His physical health was disturbed by malaria and a variety of bodily problems, and his intellectual stability was shaken—not by the kind of insanity that both Symonds and Cammell might have gloated over—but by the meditative dissolution of the "girders of the soul."

This man Crowley travelling day after day for four solid

months on a back of a pony persevering in his magical work within the confines of his own mind is not my idea of one who has sadly fallen from spiritual heights. It is more a heroic picture of true dedication.

If Symonds claims he was bellowing out the magical and barbarous words of evocation in the Chinese solitude, with his family and servants around him, then I say Symonds has read him wrong. He was misinterpreting Crowley because he knows nothing of Magic. I will affirm vigorously that it is possible to perform this and similar magical work without anyone knowing in the least what is going on.

At the time I was developing *The Art of True Healing* from the rudimentary schema provided by the Golden Dawn, I was walking daily in the area of the Crystal Palace in London building up the Middle Pillar of the Tree of Life in my imagination, and vibrating sub-vocally the magical names appropriate thereto. I am certain that no-one in London at that time had the foggiest idea of what I was doing. This being true of myself with regard to a very simple technique, I am sure of my ground when I assert that Crowley could do his ceremony on the back of a pony without anyone having the slightest notion of his inner activity.

But let me return to the resumé of the Abramelin operation. The first two month period is to be directed towards building up the requisite concentration and tranquillity of mind and emotion necessary for illumination. This calmness and serenity acquired, the magician should supplicate the Lord of the Universe "that in time to come He may be willing and pleased to regard you with pity and grant you His grace and goodness to send unto you His Holy Angel, who shall serve unto you as a guide."

One of the injunctions in the book that left an indelible impression on Crowley, so that it runs through all his later writings like a colored thread is that "it serveth nothing to speak without devotion . . . . Inflame yourself with praying."

During the advent of the second period, much the same procedure is followed except that the Operator is exhorted to cause his invocations to be more intense and fiery and "Ye shall lengthen your prayers to the utmost of your ability." As the second period draws to a close, and with it the fourth month of continuous invocation, the mind of the Operator should be gradually drawing to a single point by virtue of the tranquility and calmness he has been cultivating.

Finally with the advent of the third period, most of the ordinary preoccupation and activities of life are to be discarded, and the invocations are to become more and more frequent. There are hosts of other relatively insignificant rules laid down. But if all goes well, the six month period of aspiration and invocation should have resulted in the achievement of a higher form of consciousness which Abramelin has summarized under the heading of the Knowledge and Conversation of the Holy Guardian Angel.

Now it is quite evident that, in the walk across China, a number of modifications would have to be worked out. Crowley eliminated everything but two most important ideas. One was "Invoke often." The other "Inflame thyself in praying." No matter what occurred, he persistently went ahead with the prayers or invocations. He discarded all the traditional prayers and invocations which he had learned in the last several years—all of them, in favor of one. This was the Bornless Ritual, or the Preliminary Invocation of the Goetia. He knew this by heart, having memorized it years earlier when working with Allan. It stood him in good stead. And as a result of daily working with it he found he was able to improvise some very important elaborations on it, including a rubric for its use.

In order to clarify the point of view that must be expounded at this juncture, I would like to remind the reader of the previous anecdote relative to Crowley's being a good chess player. He liked the game, studied it assiduously and practised it when he could. In blindfold chess or multiple games, he was equally adept, as I have attempted to show.

The above is within the area of my personal experience, and I can vouch for its veracity. Another variation of the above, however, is pure hearsay, and while I cannot vouch for it in the same way as I can my own experience, there is a ring of truth to it which I would not question. The apocryphal story is that he would be in one room with his lady love, making passionate love to her, while in the room adjoining, the door being open, sat one of his friends or disciples confronting a chess board. He would make a move, call it out to Crowley who, while continuing his love-play, would respond with his move. And so on to the end of the game. I am told he invariably won—that is the chess game—and I can well believe it. It gives one some idea of Crowley's ability to concentrate on the one hand, and to visualize or imagine vividly with the mind's eye, on the other. This is the vital issue I emphasize here. It must not be lost sight of.

I wish to convey this picture of his prowess in this regard, not because chess or love-making is important to this narrative. It is to preface the events in China, when he performed the Abramelin operation. As I have described this operation above, it calls for working within the confines of a Temple of some kind. Abramelin describes a simple kind of place. But anyone who had passed through the Golden Dawn would be more prone to interpret the word Temple, in terms of his own Order experience.

There is a specific Golden Dawn document describing the inner Temple that the Adept should construct imaginatively while participating in the initiatory rituals. This must have influenced Crowley to a very great extent.

This is, in point of fact, what he actually did. While riding on his pony every day, he would construct in his imagination a Temple. Because of the keenness of his imaginative faculty, plus the hard-earned ability to concentrate that his Yoga practices in Ceylon had given him, we may be assured that it was a clear picture in every detail. This ability to play blindfold chess, as I have described it above, would more or less confirm my proposition that he had skill to do so.

While holding firmly in mind this imaginative Temple, in which he would be able to function with as much facility as if it were a physical one, he would recite sub-vocally the Preliminary Invocation from the Goetia, his favourite invocation. He had elaborated it, from the simple form in which it had first been given to him by Allan Bennett, to include a complicated series of Golden Dawn concepts.

I have stressed earlier that the five initiatory ceremonies after the Neophyte or 0=0 Ritual were devoted to invoking the elements. The intent was that they—both the ritual and the elementals invoked—would stir up and awaken within the Candidate the corresponding depths of his structure. They were the fundamental basis of his total organismic operation. So in this Goetia invocation containing the peroration, "I am He the Bornless Spirit," etc., Crowley's rendition was so arranged that it conformed in all details to the Golden Dawn system. This was one of my several motives for having given so much detail of those grades earlier.

The first statement of the ritual was—"Thee I invoke, the Bornless One." It would be followed by several sections devoted to invoking in the four cardinal quarters the elements of Earth, Air, Water and Fire, culminating in the invocation of Akasa or Ether, the quintessential element. Finally, there is the ecstatic section culminating in the attainment of or identification with the Higher Self, the Augoeides. It requires some strenuous magical work, in the sense of the need to concentrate and the trained magical ability to let the ritual exalt the consciousness until it overleaps all barriers to induce Samadhi.

"To let himself go," wrote Symonds in his book, "to hurl himself over the brink of consciousness, was an urge by which Crowley was constantly possessed. It arose out of a state of tension which he normally relieved by sexual intercourse. It is the key to his personality and his philosophy."

It is the key to much modern thinking too. For example, Wilhelm Reich's concept of the orgasm reflex is similar in some ways to Crowley's. It is a natural organismic discharge of tension in a series of body clonisms that arise during coitus, and which eclipse consciousness. It is a natural means of discharging tension—and this is the context of his book *The Function of the Orgasm.*

Crowley and Reich were dedicated to gaining access to a different level of psychic functioning; Reich through his vegeto- and orgone-therapy which levelled its attacks on the neurotic armoring which bar the individual from participating more intimately in the whole Life process, Crowley through the yoga and magical processes which he acquired in the various phases of his quest.

The Augoeides invocation was accomplished by means of the Preliminary Invocation of the Goetia. I am reproducing the major portions of it, deleting only the long lists of barbarous names of evocation which would be wholly meaningless to the general reader. These barbarous names are words capable of exegesis by Qabalistic and other magical techniques. Some understanding of their latent symbolism may be obtained in this way. However, from another point of view this is hardly necessary. The method of employment depends on permitting them, in their mystery and unintelligibility, to exalt consciousness, to awaken awe and excitement which, upon reaching a certain peak, induce the psychological spasm during which the mystical experience may occur.

Crowley's childhood reading of the Bible predisposed him

to his attraction to and fascination with such barbarous names of evocation. When a youngster, about the only literature to which he was exposed was the Bible. So, like any child, when barred from pleasure in one direction, he would seek it in another. He would wade through Genesis, and other books of the Bible, delighting in the long lists of strange Hebraic names which followed each other in wild profusion. The "begats", although meaningless to a child, aroused long and wonderful streams of fantasy which transported him far away from the restrictive family prison where he was confined. Apparently, this conditioned him forever. When he came to the Golden Dawn, to be introduced to the archaic literature of prayers and invocations, he immediately found himself at home. The strange and barbarous names of the Bornless Ritual were almost like old friends with whom he could consort and communicate.

Following is the basic form of this invocation, minus all addenda which are predicated on the application of Golden Dawn formulae:

> 1. Thee, I invoke, the Bornless One.
> Thee, that didst create the Earth and the Heavens.
> Thee, that didst create the Night and the Day.
> Thee, that didst create the darkness and the Light.
> Thou art Asar Un-Nefer ("Myself made perfect") Whom no Man hath seen at any time.
> Thou art Ia-Besz.
> Thou art Ia-apophrasz.
> Thou has distinguished between the Just and the Unjust.
> Thou didst make the Female and the Male.
> Thou didst produce the Seed and the Fruit.
> Thou didst form Men to love one another, and to hate one another.
> I am Ankh-f-n-khonsu, thy Prophet, unto whom thou didst commit thy mysteries, the Ceremonies of Khem.
> Thou didst produce the moist and the dry, and that which nourisheth all created Life.

2. Hear Thou me, for I am the Angel of Ptah-Apo-Phrasz-Ra; this is Thy true name, handed down to the Prophets of Khem.

(Here follow the first list of barbarous names.) Hear me, and make all spirits subject unto me, so that every spirit of the firmament and of the ether, upon the earth and under the earth, on dry land and in the water; of Whirling air and of Rushing Fire; and every Spell and Scourge of God the Vast One may be made obedient unto me. (This section is attributed to Air.)

3. I invoke Thee, the Terrible and Invisible God; Who Dwellest in the Void Place of the Spirit. (The second list of barbarous names follows here.) The Bornless One.

Hear me and make all spirits, etc. (This section is attributed to Fire.)

4. Hear me! (Here follows the third list of barbarous names.) Mighty and Bornless One!

Hear me, etc. (This section is attributed to Water.)

5. I invoke Thee: (Here follows the fourth list of names). Hear me, etc. (This section is attributed to Earth.)

6. Hear me (Then follows the fifth list of names.)

This is the Lord of the Gods.

This is the Lord of the Universe.

This is He whom the Winds fear.

This is He, Who having made Voice by His commandment is Lord of all Things; King, Ruler and Helper. Hear me, etc. (This section is attributed to Akasa.)

7. Hear me (Then follows the final list of names.)

I am He! The Bornless Spirit! having sight in the feet; Strong, and the Immortal Fire!

I am He! the Truth!

I am He! Who hate that evil should be wrought in the World!

I am He, that lighteneth and thundereth!

I am He, from whom is the Shower of the Life of Earth!

I am He whose mouth ever flameth!

I am He, the Begetter and Manifester unto the Light!

I am He, the Grace of the World!

"The Heart Girt with a Serpent" is my Name!
Come thou forth and follow me, and make all spirits, etc.
IAO. SABAO. Such are the words!

This, then, was the Augoeides invocation which he used daily during this walk across the lower boundaries of China. It was the old Preliminary Invocation modified and expanded by the addition of the basic Golden Dawn formulae, which were embedded so deeply in the warp and woof of his intellectual equipment that nothing that Crowley did can be understood without them. None of his biographers have fully appreciated this one fact; therefore, all their biographical narratives are stigmatized in one way or another by inadequacy.

It was on the 15th of November 1905, that he and his little group sailed for Bhamo, up the Irrawaddy. The daily Augoeides invocations had not yet commenced; he was still involved in this process of working through his spiritual conflicts on the intellectual level. Phenomena were consecutive—nothing but a sequence of impressions—but not causally connected. The misery attending these realizations was agonizing. The "insanity" persisted through the travels, only beginning to break around the middle of February 1906.

The *Equinox* account is illuminating on this episode. It asked the question—"How did this come about?" This resolution of his philosophical problem? Not from the meditations on the intellectual level at all. He learned from this that the problem of reason is not soluble on its own plane unless transcended in some manner. Unless reason is used to destroy itself in this conflict, no solution is probable or possible.

The cortex, or intellect, was evolved for the express purpose of dealing realistically and immediately with problems relating to survival. It is a good instrument for commerce, for business, for the language of daily activity. There is not a better one. But its nature does not fit it to be a tool for coping with higher philosophical or spiritual matters. So it must be transcended. The difficulty is that our culture:

1. Has not taught us to use other tools.
2. Has forced identification with it.

To transcend it, one must leave it for use in practical mundane matters only. It must seem like suicide or insanity to attempt to drop it without having forged another set of tools.

It would seem that the opposing intellectual viewpoints of Hume and Berkeley are both valid, but are dependent on the *kind* of person using them. It is probably confirmatory of the attitude of Jung, who dealt with this problem in another way in *Psychological Types,* but above all in that beautiful piece of reasoning, *Two Essays on Analytical Psychology.* There he showed at some length that both the Freudian and the Adlerian viewpoints are equally valid. It is simply that the psychological structures of Freud and Adler were different. And these differing viewpoints were predicated on opposing character-structures. In much the same way, we can assume that those who assume the Berkeleyan philosophical attitude are as intellectually valid as those who assume the Hume point of view. Their major difference is that their inner psychological needs are poles apart, based on different structures.

But both views—whether represented by different character types or not—are reconcilable only by reference to a higher and transcendental unitary process. So long as the thinking process stays on the level of ratiocination, each one will retain his own separate point of view. Or, if he has reached the stage of growth where he is capable of manipulating one attitude against the other, he will produce the kind of mental tension that inevitably results in the

temporary insanity we are considering in Crowley. Crowley
ended his conflict by returning to the *Sammasati* meditation
that he had begun in the Rangoon monastery at the
suggestion of Allan. He had pursued it for only three days at
that time. But something new had happened, altogether apart
from the mental confusion, that prompted him to return to
it.

Some weeks earlier, a few days before Christmas 1905, he
attempted to jump on to his Burmese pony a few yards after
fording the stream which marks the Chinese frontier. The
animal, however, backed before he was in the saddle. Both
the pony and Crowley fell over a cliff some forty feet in
height. Neither of them was hurt, miraculously enough. Later
on, another incident happened; he was kicked on the thigh
by a mule.

Both these events, plus the private insanity, produced in
him a very considerable pause. It was this that in February
1906 provided the stimulus for the *Sammasati* meditation.
There is yet another factor here, however, demanding
attention, as it throws a light on the vital process that was
going on inside.

We have already determined that he was a 7=4. Whether he
laid claim to this grade on his own volition, or it was
bestowed on him by another, is no concern of mine at this
juncture. We have to assume in view of all the hard work that
he had been doing that, in a sense, he was entitled to that
grade. He knew enough, without knowing much more, that
one of the functions of this grade was to prepare to give up
one's Adeptship, that is, to relinquish everything one had
gained preparatory to the next step. What this next step on
the Path might be, he had only the foggiest notion. He knew
it had something to do with the achievement of Samadhi,
with the destruction of the Ego, with the jumping through
the Abyss. We can define the Abyss, in philosophical terms,
as that real or imaginary gulf existing between the noumenal

and phenomenal world. That is all he knew.

He was now right *in* this Abyss—and he suffered. Something had to have meaning. But what meaning? Where was he to find meaning? Nothing meant anything to him in this world where no one thing was connected causally with anything else. He was a psychological cripple in a no-man's-land. To clutch at a straw would be natural under the circumstances.

He had no guru to guide him at this stage of the game. Hence the two miraculous escapes from death must have had considerable meaning for him. He was on his way to the obligation of the initiate of the next higher grade, the 8=3, who is sworn to regard every phenomenon, no matter how trivial or profound, as a particular dealing of God with his soul—regardless of how he interpreted God or the soul. It is reminiscent of the old cynical prayer "O God, if there be a God, save my soul, if I have a soul!" But for Crowley at this juncture, there was no cynicism here. He was deadly serious once more; this was a matter of life and death.

Without wanting to enlarge too much on the sequel to this *Sammasati*, he concluded that he was kept alive for a particular purpose. And that purpose, simply, was to teach! Teach what? The next step for all mankind—the knowledge and conversation of the Holy Guardian Angel. This was his life mission. In this formidable phrase, we have already seen that there is implied only the mystical experience. And if we want to express this in the language of his father, who was an itinerant Plymouth Brother preaching the gospel of Jesus wherever he went, it was to bring everybody to God. The language differs; the goal is the same. The method differs; the goal is the same. The people are different; the goal remains ever the same. He was his father's son!

Beginning around the 12th of February 1906, while walking through China, he began to work on his Augoeides ritual, as I have described it above, sometimes twice or more a day. He was proving to himself beyond doubt that these goals were possible, no matter where or who one was. He was occasionally sick, disturbed by all sorts of inconveniences—but he persisted with his Bornless Ritual. Is this courage? Is it schizophrenia?

His diaries from this date until the end of the year—almost eleven months—are relatively simple, dull in one sense, because they give merely a sentence or two for each day, and are monotonous. A typical entry is the following:

Feb. 22. A∴ in p.m. poor (sleepy)

     23. A∴ in a.m. poor.

          A∴ in p.m. rather good.

A∴ is his abbreviation for the Preliminary Invocation of Augoeides, his higher Self. As is evident his diary evaluates each effort in terms of poor or otherwise. There is no attempt to pull the wool· over his eyes, to over-evaluate it, to congratulate himself. He was attempting to be as objective and as systematic with this kind of astral working as he had been with his Yoga practices in Ceylon. There he had used a stopwatch to time the meditation and to record the number and type of breaks from the concentration on a single object, whatever it may have been. His mind was well trained now, so that he could evaluate with some degree of fairness whatever he was doing where his self-disciplines were concerned.

On they rode; and he invoked. In the process there was the incessant business of the camp to attend to, accidents always occurring. On one occasion they had to cope with slippery wet sand and cobblestones. Another entry recorded rain, wind, horse trouble, mud and more cobbles. In the middle of March he was nearly drowned when his dug-out twice hit rocks on the dangerous rapids of the Red River. A few days later he confessed to some sea-sickness when on a tramp steamer packed three-deep with pigs. But the diary continues with the daily inscription: "A∴ in a.m. A∴ in p.m., good, fair," or whatever it was!

In April he became aware that Easter was in the offing. Classically this was the time to start the Abramelin operation. His diary reads: "The Operation of Abramelin being due to commence on Easter Sunday, me thinks it would be well to make a certain profound conjuration of Augoeides on that day with a view to acquiring a proper knowledge of the Method of the Great Retirement. The Augoeides should be definitely invoked for this purpose with all possible ceremony. Is it not written: "Unto whosoever shall draw nigh unto Me will I draw nigh"? And, as I have proved, the help of Augoeides is already given as if the Operation were successfully brought to an end. Only can this right be forfeited by slackness toward the obligation? From this, then, O Holy Exalted One, preserve me!"

And so he continued. Day after day, there was the Augoeides invocation—with its tremendous strain on all his imaginative and other spiritual resources. There was a vision on the 24th, to which on the 25th he comments:

"Yesterday's vision a real illumination, since it showed me an obvious mistake which I had utterly failed to see. The word in my Kamma-Work (in Burma) was *Augoeides*, and the method Invoking Often. Therefore a self-glittering One, whether my conscience approves or not, whether my desires fit or not, is to be my guide. I am to *invoke often,* not to criticize."

A couple of weeks later, still pursuing the Great Work, he entered in his record: "This work of Augoeides requires the Adept to assume the woman's part: to long for the bridegroom, maybe, and to be ever ready to receive his kiss; but not to pursue openly and to use force."

What he learned from this particular experience became incorporated into his whole frame of spiritual reference. A year or so later, when he began work on his inspirational books, he wrote a small section in *The Book of the Heart*

Girt with a Serpent, or Liber LXV, which reads:

> Awake Thou! Wait no more!
> Nay, Lord! But I am come to Thee. It is I that wait at last.
> The prophet cried against the mountain: come thou hither, that I may speak with thee!
> The mountain stirred not. Therefore went the prophet unto the mountain, and spake unto it. But the feet of the prophet were weary, and the mountain heard not his voice.
> But I have called unto Thee, and I have journeyed unto Thee, and it availed me not.
> I waited patiently, and Thou wast with me from the beginning.
> This now I know, O my beloved, and we are stretched at our ease among the vines.
> But these thy prophets; they must cry aloud and scourge themselves; they must cross trackless wastes and unfathomed oceans; to await Thee is the end, not the beginning.

This narrative of the diary should note that the trip through China was terminated early in March. They sailed down the Red River to Tong King in North Vietnam. On the 20th of March, 1906, they arrived at Hai Phong. From there, Crowley went to Hong Kong on his way to Shanghai in order to see a former Soror of the Golden Dawn with whom he stayed for twelve days. Meantime Rose was sent back to England. From Shanghai he sailed for the United States on the Empress of India, arriving in New York on May 16th. Let it be noted that there was absolutely no let-up in the daily work of invoking and praying. The message he had received earlier said "Invoke Often", and he was being wholly faithful to it. A few days later, he sailed for Liverpool.

Finally he was rewarded. Some mystical results began to break through. Even in his current diaries, he is not very communicative, and does not elaborate very much on the nature of the illumination that occurred.

For example, on May 30th, the diary reads: "Augoeides, very good indeed. Renewed the terrible vows of this initiation, and was rewarded by the Divine Kiss. O Self-glittering one, be ever with me! Amen."

"May 31. Augoeides better than ever yet. Vision quite perfect; I tasted the sweet kiss and gazed in the clear eyes of that Radiant One. My own face became luminous."

I notice that Symonds, in writing of the China incident, says: "About this time he achieved his ambition of completing the Operation of Abra-Melin, i.e. the bringing forth of his Holy Guardian Angel, Aiwass. *The Magical Record,* or diary, however, contains but scant reference to this great event."

It seems to me that Symonds was either in a hurry to complete his pot-boiler, or was not able to read or understand the entries in the Diary. It is very clear from my study of this record, as indicated above, that Crowley persevered faithfully and devotedly until he was able to invoke his higher Self. There are several brief references to the ecstasy of Samadhi, with its mystical language of the Kiss, etc. He reached some height of mystical experience on his way back to England from China, the long bout of so-called private insanity notwithstanding.

I must call attention, briefly, to a personal tragedy that overtook him. Symonds remarks that Crowley's attitude "towards Rose was, at best, ambivalent, alternating between love and hate. He'd left her in Tong-King and raced after his demon, but somewhere between China and New York a longing for her arose, and he wrote *Rosa Coeli.*"

I resent Symonds' implication that Crowley must have been some kind of monster in being ambivalent toward Rose. It is basic to psychoanalytic thinking that most people to-day are ambivalent to their love-objects. Is not Symonds ambivalent towards his own wife? Are not most men ambivalent toward their wives? And wives, of course, toward their husbands? Having engaged in the practice of various forms of psychotherapy for nearly thirty years, it seems to me that most people are decidedly ambivalent. Many do not know it. Or, if they are aware of it, have no knowledge of how to handle it.

To this extent, Crowley was not very different from most people of his generation, or of ours. But Symonds seems determined to show Crowley as an unnatural or demoniacal character, seizing upon every conflictual event in Crowley's life to make it bear witness to what Symonds chooses to diagnose as Crowley's schizophrenia. Perhaps the only difference between Crowley and most other people was this—he did not and could not keep his attitudes a secret. Whether this was because he chose to be an open and transparent person, or evidence of his confirmed attack upon Mrs. Grundy, is altogether irrelevant.

"When he arrived at Liverpool on the 2nd of June 1906," continues Symonds in his book, "he was sent reeling at the news that his little girl had died in Rangoon. He blamed Rose: 'She had neglected to cleanse the nipple of the feeding bottle, and thereby exposed the child to the germs of typhoid.' He experienced no remorse at having left her and Rose in Tong-King."

Crowley's diary for this first week of June is sparsely entered, but eloquent withal. "June 9: Still breaking down at intervals and staggering from nervous weakness. Dropping off to sleep at odd times and places. Augoeides practically nil."

The emotional reaction to the death of his child—however little remorse he may have had about leaving his wife and child in Siam—continued, though he was struggling against giving in to his feelings. The ordeal was complicated by the debilitating physical sequelae to malaria while in China, by almost continual headaches, and by some throat pathology.

Early in July he was ordered by his physician to undergo surgery for the latter—at first sight it seemed a toss-up between cancer or a tubercular throat. The surgery was a success, neither of the pathological alternatives being present. Several days relaxing in bed soon cleared up the headaches.

Surely the mood he was experiencing was the one he recaptured the following year when, in *LXV*, he wrote:

> Weary, weary! saith the scribe, who shall lead me to the sight of the Rapture of my master?
> The body is weary and the soul is sore weary and sleep weighs down their eyelids; yet ever abides the sure consciousness of ecstasy, unknown, yet known in that its being is certain. O Lord, be my helper, and bring me to the bliss of the Beloved!

Persistency must have been his second name, for all through this he continued with his invocations, even noting that the first twenty-two weeks were over. This number—that of the number of letters in the Hebrew alphabet, and so of Qabalistic significance—came within the especial purview of his oath to regard all things as a dealing of God with his soul, that is of having specific meaning for him.

While still convalescing in the nursing home, he consulted once more with his old mentor, George Cecil Jones. What actually transpired between the two men is not really clear. But without question there was an analysis of the methods that Crowley was using, and the results that had so far been obtained. The impression given was that Jones suggested the continuation of the magical method being used. It was a word of encouragement from an old and trusted friend and guide. Perhaps, with Allan far away, Crowley felt the need to regard Jones as his superior in the Order, as his teacher. This is not clear.

However, toward the end of July, he left the nursing home, and went down to Basingstoke to stay with Jones for a

while. There is an extraordinary entry in the record at this
time:

> Fra. P. was crucified by Fra. D.D.S., and on that cross
> made to repeat this oath: "I, P . . . ., a member of the
> Body of Christ, do hereby solemnly obligate myself, etc.
> to lead a pure and unselfish life, and will entirely devote
> myself so to raise, etc. myself to the knowledge of my
> higher and Divine Genius that I shall be He."
> In witness of which I invoke the Great Angel Hua to
> give me a proof of his existence.

No one should write this off as being fanciful, or implying
a species of egotism. On the contrary, the formula is
recommended on the highest authority. For example, in
some papers relative to clairvoyance which thirty years ago I
synthesized and re-wrote for the fourth volume of *The
Golden Dawn,* there is a passage, unquestionably written by
McGregor Mathers, that may throw some further light on the
experience under consideration.

As prelude to a direct quotation from Mathers, I wrote this
couple of sentences. "Developing still further from this, there
is another practice which passes beyond mere clairvoyance,
though making use of it. This is called Rising on the Planes,
and is a spiritual process after spiritual conceptions and
higher aims." Then follows the paragraph written by Mathers.
"By concentration and contemplation of the divine, you
formulate a Tree of Life passing from you to the spiritual
realms above and beyond yourself. Picture to yourself that
you stand in Malkuth, then by the use of the Divine Names
and aspiration, you strive upwards by the Path of Tau
towards Yesod, neglecting the crossing rays which attract you
as you pass up. Look upwards to the Divine Light shining
downward from Kether upon you. From Yesod, leads
upward the Path of Samekh, Temperance; the Arrow,
cleaving upwards, leads the way to Tiphareth, the great
central Sun."

D.D.C.F. also suggests that, having risen to Tiphareth, the Adept skryer should formulate to himself that he is bound to a Cross, exactly as occurred in the Adeptus Minor Ceremony, and by invoking the Great Angel HUA beseech help and guidance in the pathway of Light. By this method, he may more easily ascend the planes which lead to the glory of the Crown.

Both Jones and Crowley were Golden Dawn adepts who, during the 5=6 initiation, had been bound on a Cross where they were obligated, amongst other things, to perform the Great Work. This was specifically interpreted then to mean achieving some higher relationship with the higher and Divine Genius and so, God willing, becoming more than human.

The inference of this entry then is that following Mathers' suggestion, some semblance of the 5=6 ceremony was performed at Jones' home with Crowley as candidate, in which he was re-confirmed in both his aspirations and ideals. There would be one major difference between this new experience and that earlier one in Paris, when Mathers had initiated him. Crowley had gone a very long way since then, spiritually. Moreover, his China experience had taught him to function easily in the astral or imaginative Temple. Hence in this Ceremony initiated by Jones, his technical training would enable him to pass through it rapidly and beyond to the heights to which he was aspiring. He would be able to embrace the Light here and now as he had been unable to do then.

While, therefore, being obligated anew on the Cross of Suffering, as an Adept, he was magically working in the inner Temple, striving to reach higher and higher. One result of this was a visionary experience: " . . . . The Pylon of the Camel open, and a ray therein: withal a certain vision of A∴ remembered only as a glory now attainable."

This entry is in the Qabalistic language, which needs translation, and I shall try to do this as simply as possible.

Connecting the various centres on the Tree of Life in the
Qabalah are a number of Pathways. To each one of these is
attributed a Hebrew letter, together with a vast number of
other ideas, symbols, attributions. The pathway which goes
from the mind (the Ruach, as it is called) to Kether and
Yechidah, the Holy Guardian Angel, is attributed to the
letter G or Gimel. This is the third letter of the Hebrew
Alphabet, any letter of which may be spelled in full, as in the
Greek alphabet (Alpha, Beta, Gamma). When spelled out as
Gimel it means a Camel, in Moslem mythology a symbol of
Death. This path of the Camel crosses the Abyss, that
imaginary gulf existent between the ideal and the real,
between the noumenal and phenomenal worlds, between
time and Eternity.

Hence the inference of the cryptic entry is that this
Pathway was opened to him and he was able to ascend,
though the full memory of such divine ascent was gone,
leaving only the enchanted memory of the ineffable glory
that he attained.

Crowley liked this symbolism of the Camel. He came to
call the Abyss a desert, a desert of impressions, barren and
worthless. For the grade of 8=3 which he achieved through
the crossing of the Abyss, and overcoming the temporary
insanity that harrassed him in China, he chose the name *Vi
Veri Universum Vivus Vici,* abbreviated as V.V.V.V.V., which
initials he poetically described as the five footprints of a
camel. When some years later he came to write *The Book of
Lies.* his little book of Zen-like paradoxes, he wrote one
chapter called *Dust-Devils:*

> In the Wind of the mind arises the turbulence called I.
> It breaks; down shower the barren thoughts.
> All life is choked.
> This desert is the Abyss wherein is the Universe. The
> Stars are but thistles in that waste.
> Yet this desert is but one spot accursed in a world of

bliss.

Now and again, Travellers cross the desert; they come from the Great Sea, and to the Great Sea they go.

As they go they spill water; one day they will irrigate the desert, till it flower.

See! five footprints of a Camel! V.V.V.V.V.

One of the Supernals above the Abyss, one of the aspects of the higher consciousness, can have attributed to it a variety of concepts. One is Saturn, with its meaning of Death, the Great Reaper, Black in color. Another is the Great Mother, the Light Mother, Aditi of the Indian philosophy. As such she is Shakti, energy—pure energy from which the Universe is structured. Also, the Qabalistic symbolism portrays her as the Great Sea, from which all has issued and to which all must in due time return. The symbolism of Light, energy, and Sea are not conflicting, merely fulfilling. Each helps to give a degree of comprehension to that which cannot be intellectually grasped.

The travellers of course are the Adepts whose goal is to reach beyond phenomena and illusion to the heart of Reality. The whole section reminds me vividly of that final verse in the classic of Mahayana Buddhism—the Mahaprajna Paramita, which reads:

> Therefore one ought to know the great verse of the Prajna-paramita, the verse of the great wisdom, the unsurpassed verse, the peerless verse, which appeases all pain—it is truth, because it is not false—the verse proclaimed in the Prajna-paramita: "O Wisdom, gone, gone, gone to the other shore, landed at the other shore. Svaha!
>
> Thus ends the heart of the prajna paramita sutra.

So, Crowley continued working, after this session with Jones. I would say that there were many sessions if he stayed in the Jones' Basingstoke house for a while. It gave them many opportunities for communication of ideas and experience.

His health was still only fair. All that summer he had some neuralgia and an obstruction of an eye duct which required several surgical interventions. But through all of this sickness, there were the daily invocations. Whatever results were achieved are recorded with scant detail; they are just barely mentioned. For once he was struck literally speechless. So that we might be misled if we glossed over the records of this period because they do not contain the verbal fullness of his earlier ones. Thus the weeks and the months went by, never ceasing his daily devotions, until the whole of the summer had passed. The records following are so full of blinds and hieroglyphic entries that it is nearly impossible to decipher them. The only one of that period that does make sense is:

> Oct. 9, Tested new ritual and behold it was very good! Thanked gods and sacrificed for—
> In the 'thanksgiving and sacrifice . . .' I *did* get rid of everything but the Holy Exalted One, and must have held Him for a minute or two. I did. I am sure I did.

It is followed by:

> Oct. 10. I am still drunk with Samadhi all day.

Whatever this attainment was, its effect continued for a couple of weeks—a lifetime in itself. Towards the end of the month, still devoted steadfastly to the curriculum he had laid out for himself, he made some very interesting entries.

> Once again I nearly got there—all went brilliance—but not quite.

> . . . . But there is always the consciousness behind thoughts. Thus, when the consciousness realizes that "I am apart from my thoughts", that thought itself is pictorially shown as a thought.

It seems to mean that he again experienced a kind of Samadhi known as Atmadarshana, but his complaint momentarily was the inability to pass beyond.

His literary abilities were taxed years afterwards when he made the attempts to analyze and describe the mystical experience labelled Samadhi. There is a chapter in a little book on Yoga, that he called *Part I of Book IV,* a masterpiece of clarity and straightforward elucidation, where he struggles to describe both Dhyana (first experienced in Ceylon) and Samadhi:

> All the poetic faculties and all the emotional faculties are thrown into a sort of ecstasy by an occurrence which overthrows the mind, and makes the rest of life seem absolutely worthless in comparison .... But even when one has become accustomed to Dhyana by constant repetition, no words seem adequate .... The conditions of thought, time and space are abolished. It is impossible to explain what this really means; only experience can furnish you with apprehension .... A further development is the appearance of the Form which has been universally described as human; although the persons describing it proceed to add a great number of details which are not human at all. This particular appearance is usually assumed to be "God" ....
>
> The Samadhi *par excellence,* however, is Atmadarshana, which for some, and those not the least instructed, is the first real Samadhi; for even the visions of "God" and of the "Self" are tainted by form. In Atmadarshana the All is manifested as the One; it is the Universe freed from its conditions. Not only are all forms and ideas destroyed, but also those conceptions which are implicit in our ideas of those ideas. Each part of the Universe has become the whole, and phenomena and noumena are no longer opposed.

In November, some of the ecstasy and glory had naturally diminished, with a psychological reaction setting in. Demons of the most profound doubt obsessed him. He doubted he had achieved anything, doubted he was anybody, and wondered if all his striving and effort had been for nothing. It was temporary however, and soon vanished, for in December Samadhi again recurred—and he knew!

The realization also dawned upon him that his colleague and friend George Cecil Jones had achieved a similar state. Strange that he had not suspected this before! When he got back to Boleskine in the middle of December, he received a long letter from Jones. We shall never know what the contents of that letter were, save for one quotation: "How long have you been in the Great Order, and why did I not know? Is the invisibility of the A.A. to lower grades so complete?" I do not wholly understand this.

Months and years of hard, persistent work came to a climax here. The lure of the far horizons which had seemed in 1898 so very far, was no longer a lure. It was attainment. What this meant to him was something he could not and would not accept for some time. A full discussion of its meaning will have to be postponed for the chapter on North Africa, where he again experienced Samadhi and a second crossing of the Abyss, which made him fully aware of his destiny.

His discovery, however, that Jones had also attained and had been a member of the Great Order forces me to think back to the letter of dedication for the essay *Eleusis* in Volume III of the *Collected Works* that Crowley wrote. It must have been penned just about this time; it is dated November 18, 1906. The letter addressed him as "My Dear Ion" and reminds Jones that it was he who acted as Kerux when Crowley was first initiated.

> Eight years ago this day you, Hermes, led me blindfold to awake a chosen runner of the course. "In all my wanderings in darkness your light shone before me though I knew it not." To-day (one may almost

hope, turning into the straight) you and I are alone.
Terrible and joyous! We shall find companions at the
End, at the banquet, lissome and cool and garlanded;
companions with a Silver Star or maybe a Jewelled Eye
mobile and uncertain—as if alive—on their foreheads. We
shall be bidden to sit, and they will wreathe us with
immortal flowers, and give us to drink of the seemly
wine of Iacchus—well! but until then, unless my heart
deceives me, no third shall appear to join us. Indeed,
may two attain? It seems a thing impossible in
nature . . . .

Some months after the above had been drafted, a current
of reflection arose on this obscure relationship of Jones with
Crowley. I wondered whether there might be other references
here and there that would clarify the situation. One day,
while glancing through *Equinox VI,* in search of other
pertinent material, I accidentally came across an essay by
Crowley entitled *The Electric Silence.* Suddenly, it came alive
and conveyed new meaning to me.

The short essay is, in effect, a spiritual biography in highly
symbolic terms. It mentions Crowley's two principal
mentors. For example:

And at that moment was there a glimmer just before
me of a white shining triangle, and what was most
strange, rather an impression than a vision of a man that
hung upon a gibbet by one heel. This, said the fair man,
is a most notable sign that we travel the right road.

Now by the light of the triangle I perceived another
wonder; for my friend was not swimming as I was in the
stream, but was borne by a boat, frail indeed, yet
sufficient. Within this shallop or cockleshell he pulled
me, and set me at the bench. Then (still by the light of
the triangle) I saw a dark man at the thwart, rowing a
strong stroke.

We pulled on almost in silence; for when I asked of
the fair man his name he answered me only "I wish to
know", and of the dark man "I wish it were light" . . . .

Quite evidently the "fair man" refers to *Volo Noscere,* which was the Golden Dawn motto of George Cecil Jones, and "the dark man" to *Yehi Aour,* Allan Bennett.

A few paragraphs later, the narrative declares that:

> there was given unto me by my fair brother (for so I may now call him) a little book, wherein it was written how a man might build himself a shallop, and have for steersman one appointed thereunto. This then I laboured to build, and the toil was great . . . . However, at last I had it perfect, and was about to set sail at dawn. But first the dark man my brother departed from us, and went his way.

This implies to me that it was Jones who introduced Crowley to the book of *The Sacred Magic of Abramelin the Mage,* and that Allan had left England for the Orient.

> Then came an earthquake as he (the old man of the tower) had foreseen; and he and the boats also were swallowed up. In the tidal wave of the earthquake I was borne far away, even from the fair man my brother; and in the darkness he was lost to me. I knew not even whether he had perished.

I imagine this to relate to the revolt within the Golden Dawn, and to Crowley's travels all over the world in quest of the secret wisdom.

> Now in this cataract I had most surely been wrecked but that I clung tightly to the boat. This indeed floated as serenely as if it had been upon the still waters of a lake; and when I had plucked up courage, I saw sitting at the helm him that is appointed to steer; I saw him face to face.

The symbolic narrative proceeds with the account of his illumination in the East, and with the passage across the Abyss in China, and the rebirth as a Babe of the Abyss as a result of the Augoeides invocations.

> This then endured for a space; and with his aid I began ship-building. "For" (said he) "there are many that swim, and find no boats. Be it thy task to aid them."

I surmise this to relate to the motivation leading to the formulation of the order of the A.A., and the writing of the official instructions of that Order.

> Of my journey to the House he spake nothing. But in the shipbuilding came the fair man my brother to my help; and one evening as we sate at meal he said: May it please you to enter the House; for there is prepared for you a goodly bed-chamber. But I would not at that time; for I was ashamed, being unclothed; not understanding that in the House robes are provided by him that is appointed to provide them.

Quite evidently this passage refers to Jones assisting him in the formulation of the Order, and perhaps confirming him in the attainment of the grade of Magister Templi, 8=3, which Crowley rejected or could not accept during that year of fulfillment, 1907. Crowley's account had it that this grade was not accepted until after the Enochian adventure in the desert towards the end of 1909. Anyway, this is the last reference to Jones in this symbolic story of his pilgrimage.

Before I leave this topic, I feel constrained to quote two more sections from *The Electric Silence*. They are eloquent in what they imply about Crowley. Since so much has been said that is derogatory about him, these two must redress the balance. Someone must speak for him, since so many have spoken against him.

> Upon the breast of the river came a wild swan, singing, and for a moment rested upon mine image reflected in the water. And I said: "Come up hither."

And the wild swan said: "How shall I come up thither?"

I: I will guide thee.

The Swan: Who art thou?

I: My Father is the keeper of the King's Cup: I have prepared a little ship wherein I may go on my journeys upon the great river.

Who will draw it?

The Swan: I will draw it.

So we set forth together .... And the end shall be as is appointed by the master of the House; but this I know, that this ship is the King's ship. And in my bosom are the champak-blossom, and the mustard seed, and the oak-leaf, more lovely than before.

And upon us watcheth ever he that is appointed to watch.

And the wild swan sings ever; and my heart sings ever.

Whatever else may be said of Crowley—whether of blame or praise, stressing his errors and peccadilloes or pointing to his writing and life-work—this little parable says more about him than anything or anybody else. For the swan is the spirit of ecstasy, and the swan is the eternal Self which is beyond all opposites and logical contradictions and all human thought. And it is this swan which Crowley suffered to lead him all his life. So that in all his ways, stupid and foolish as some may appear, he yet was divinely guided.

The Electric Silence closes with the following:

Now then I had laid aside the pen, and a voice cried: Write!

Fear not!

Turn not aside!

Is it not written that Sorrow may endure for a night, but joy cometh in the morning?

Sleep therefore in peace and in faith: shall he not watch whose eye hath no eyelid, who to this end is appointed?

And my heart answered: Amen!

. . . .

The Magician
Crowley stands at the altar in his robe and Uraeus serpent
crown, armed with wand, cup, sword, bell, phial of holy oil,
The Book of the Law, and the Stele of Revealing.

Aleister Crowley
around time of writing *Konx Om Pax*.

CHAPTER TWELVE

Five Vees

I await Thee in sleeping, in waking. I invoke Thee no
more, for Thou art in me, O Thou who hast made me a
beautiful instrument tuned to Thy rapture.
Yet art Thou ever apart, even as I.

These few lines from *The Book of Lapis Lazuli* indicate
what a profoundly changed person Crowley was after the
events described in the previous chapter. Evidently this
metamorphosis in attitude occurred in late 1906. It was a
basic one without parallel in Crowley's life. Whatever
happened—Samadhi or a lesser spiritual state—towards the
close of that fateful year, it resulted in the reaping of a
bountiful and glorious harvest. The published diaries are not
very informative concerning the year 1907, the year of
fulfillment. We learn but little from them. We know merely
that a great deal of fine writing was accomplished that year,
but it was an entirely different type of writing than he had
ever done before.

Moreover—and this too is symptomatic—his attitude
towards it was different. Previously, he would have been
quite willing to brag about any poem or lyric in an overly
egotistical manner. Quite easily it could have been the best
thing written since Shakespeare. Regarding the so-called holy
books which came to be written at this time, he was
relatively silent. It was as though he were awed by the

sublimity and ineffability of the devotion that had come through him.

The same kind of wonderment, if not modesty, characterized Crowley in other of his activities during this period. Undoubtedly, it too stemmed from the attainment of the high rapture of the preceding winter.

For example—regardless of all possible considerations as to who conferred it, he laid claim to the grade of 8=3, the grade of Magister Templi. By virtue of his inner experiences and the actual work performed, he was entitled to that exalted grade. Yet, curiously enough, he refused to acknowledge overtly the attainment for a good couple of years. He had to wait, he forced himself to wait for the repetition of the initiatory experience through other technical means before he could bring himself to claim the attainment. It is almost as if the years before 1907 were the years of incubation, a gestation period, in which a higher consciousness were coming slowly to birth, the emergence of Self-realization.

With this grade of Magister Templi, he adopted the motto of *Vi Verum Universum Vivus Vici*—or five Vees, as I abbreviate it for my own convenience. In the selection of this motto, paradoxically there is no trace of modesty. Yet, for him, there was no exaggeration either. These five Latin words can be translated: "In my lifetime I have conquered the Universe by the force of Truth."

In less than ten years, he had literally scaled the heights from a Neophyte of the Golden Dawn to—the very heights themselves. It was less than a lifetime. And his own determination and dogged persistence, plus whatever genius he had brought with him into birth, had enabled him to conquer his own universe, himself, and bring himself to the other shore!

He took the view that Aleister Crowley who had adopted in 1898 the magical pseudonym of Frater Perdurabo was, and simultaneously was not, five Vees. Nor was five Vees considered to be his Holy Guardian Angel, but a full-blown Master of the Temple, 8=3. The evidence appears to be that he split himself up into at least four component parts, each one functioning on its own level or plane without reference to or interference from any one of the other components.

In one of the koan-like paradoxes of *The Book of Lies,* he himself asked facetiously: "Who knows which is Frater P. or the imp Crowley?" That question has been seriously asked many times since by many different people. The answer is not at all easy.

There was Aleister Crowley, the man of the world who was a poet, mountaineer, and a perfect bounder at the same time. It is easy to perceive that Frater Perdurabo, who was sworn to the accomplishment of the Great Work, is an idealization of Crowley's aspirations and holiest desires. Somehow Frater "The Heart of Jesus girt about with the Swift Serpent" got lost in the shuffle of magical personalities, and perhaps because he is Christian he does not enter. Beyond these there was five Vees, the Master of the Temple. In effect then he is a personification of the Atman, the universal Self, the Life principle of the entire Cosmos that pulses in every atom. The empirical ego has been abnegated or destroyed in the sense that no longer can it rule the roost. It has been forced to take its rightful place with the rest of the constituents of the organism as one more operational tool of the psyche, and nothing else. It does not usurp the place of the other and higher faculties. The experience of crossing the Abyss extinguishes the ego; it thus becomes equivalent to the Buddhist concept of Nirvana. The self has been blown out like a candle, but "there is that which remains."

Adonai, the holy Guardian Angel, is an individualized center of the Universal living Spirit. It is not personal in any sense; it is the Atman, the Self, of whom Shankara once said: "Brahm is true, the world is false, the Soul is Brahm, and nothing else!"

Even better stated than this, however, is Crowley's own hymn to the Self, originally composed for a play called *The Ship,* and then extracted and made a part of *The Gnostic Mass.* Its first few lines are:

> Thou, who art I, beyond all I am,
> Who hast no nature and no name,
> Who art, when all but Thou art gone.
> Thou, centre and secret of the Sun,
> Thou, hidden spring of all things known
> And unknown, Thou aloof, alone,
> Thou, the true fire within the reed
> Brooding and breeding, source and seed
> Of life, love, liberty and light.
> Thou beyond speech and beyond sight,
> Thee I invoke . . . .

Yet all of these are hierarchical levels of whatever Aleister Crowley may or may not be. There is a faint reminiscence here of the modern interpretation of the central nervous system as a hierarchy of neurological functions, beginning with the lowest simple reflex of the spinal cord, and culminating in the highest functions situate in the neocortex.

There was another signature often used by Crowley. It could be appended to any one of the above hierarchical names. It was simply *666.* Sometimes it was the *Beast,* or the *Beast 666;* more often than not just plain 666.

When a child is "naughty", very often a parent will rail against it, calling it "bad", "wicked", "a devil", etc. Depending on how much affect is loaded onto the phrase, just so is the effect it will have upon the child. In a religious household, more often than not a Biblical phrase or word of admonishment will be used to strengthen parental authority. Sometimes the effect of this may persist throughout the lifetime.

For example, I recall a patient some years ago, who remembered having called her sister a fool in a moment of anger. Her mother, a daughter of a minister, immediately lectured the child, quoting a verse from the Bible to the effect that whosoever calls another a fool will be damned for ever. It would be altogether impossible to describe the emotional abreaction that resulted when this patient brought her Bible to the office for a momentous session. After reading this verse originally quoted by her mother, she immediately fell upon the Bible, screaming and crying, tearing every page of the book into minute shreds with calculated, methodical thoroughness, motivated by pure hatred. My office looked as though a snowstorm and a tornado had hit simultaneously.

When Crowley was a small boy, his mother, in moments of exasperation no doubt, would call him "a beast." With his knowledge of the Bible, as I have indicated before, it did not take too long for him to find out about the Beast of *Revelation*, the Beast who was anti-Christ. He identified himself with that Beast.

The upshot was that when he revolted and turned against Christianity, there could be no alternative but that he had to ally himself with those forces that ran counter to the religion of his parents. He *became* the Beast. Since *Revelation* counted the number of the Beast and found it to be 666, the number of a Man, he turned all his Qabalistic skill of later years to finding this number in any word or motto that came his way. He found the number in all sorts of places and situations and people. And whenever he did, he concluded that it had profound significance for him, as in the case of the preliminary events attending the dictation of *The Book of the Law* in 1904.

His last magical motto *To Mega Therion* adds to 666 when its Greek letters are computed. The three words mean not merely the Master Therion, but the Great Wild Beast. This served his Dionysiac purpose very well, for he opposed his exotic, exuberant and erotic Dionysian concept of life to the austere, chilled and non-affective Apollonian style of life which characterizes the Western Christian world.

In one of the footnotes which serve as the commentary to *The Vision and The Voice,* Crowley himself confirms this view of mine. He wrote: "So the Master Therion is of the root Aleister Crowley, instead of being a Magus *de novo.*"

Though not directly pertinent here, one other item should be mentioned at least casually. Married or no, mystic or no, there was a steady parade of mistresses and lovers in and out of his life. His devotion to the Great Work did not modify or eliminate his powerful sexual drives, any more than it changed his gourmet inclinations. If he cared for oysters and chateaubriand before his Samadhi, the same liking persisted afterwards.

It would also be safe to assume that his homosexual tendencies were not diminished either. The *Holy Books* give ample evidence of the intrusion of such homo-erotic attitudes into his mysticism. He begins to appear far more androgynous than merely homosexual.

In one chapter of his book, Symonds comments—again with the intent to deride—that Crowley appeared to regard *all* sexual acts—be they hetero-, homo-, or auto-erotic—as religious acts, as magical acts, as equally divine. His derision of Crowley is evident through the entire book.

I make no plea here for homosexuality or masturbation or for any other kind of sexual practice. This is not the issue. What is at stake here is *attitude.* I put it to you to decide which is the more noble, and which the more corrupt. The view that sex is a dirty business, pleasurable certainly, but somehow not quite proper or clean; that it is to be indulged in secretly and passionately, but to be hurried through and gotten over quickly. Any reference thereafter to it is either in cold, highly intellectual terms as in a pseudo-scientific study, or pornographically with jokes and snickers. Compare this with the utter simplicity of the attitude that Crowley believed. Sexual ecstasy, thought Crowley, is akin to divine ecstasy. Both are there for us to take as we will.

Crowley accepted the one simple fact that sex—sex in any shape or form, the emergence of instinctual, that is, divine tendencies—is not to be thwarted or warped. So long as no one is hurt or injured, it is a private matter between any two people as to what form or practice of sexuality they wish to indulge in.

His interpretation of sex is then clear. You have the right, the divine right in his opinion, to express sexuality in your own particular way. "Take thy fill of love where, when, and with whom thou wilt—but always in the love of Me!" Or again, "Veil not your vices in virtuous words!" He certainly did not, at least not in that area.

In the terminal essay of *Konx Om Pax,* an essay entitled *The Stone of the Philosophers* comprising different types of poetry and some philosophical meanderings on the part of five characters, Crowley manages to get this point across:

> On the question of motive, though, said the Doctor, I like your theory of Messalina as an ascetic. Since the divine consciousness only appears as the negation of the human, and is only to be attained by wearing out all the sensation-points, till no response occurs to any stimulus—
>
> Nonsense! interjected the big man, one can control them, not destroy them. Only morbid "Union with God" is attained by fast, vigil, scourging, and the like.
>
> Morbid or no, continued the doctor, most saints have used this method. What I was about to say was that since we wish to overcome the body by fatigue, we shall do just as wisely to seek Union with God in excessive debauch. If done with the same purpose, and sleep successfully banished, the same result will occur. If your Messalina failed—well, what does the poet say; Try, try, try again! . . . .
>
> You may be right, said Basil, in thinking as you evidently do that much of the ceremonial debauchery of

the Pagan worshippers was a true mystical process. Indeed, at this day there are many cults in India (also, I believe, in the South Seas) of what is called Vamacharya. Religious frenzy is invoked by the aid of the Erotic and Bacchic frenzies mingled with that of the muse of the Tom-Tom, Soma, bhang, arraq, and the Uniting of the Lingam and the Yoni! All, mind you, by a most elaborate ritual.

But, on the other hand, there is perfect purity of thought in much of the avowedly Phallic symbolism of the world. For just as the sexual pleasure is entirely in a class by itself among (or rather, above) physical pleasures; so is Samadhi—union with God—in a class by itself among (or rather, above) mental pleasure. Who, therefore, would make a hieroglyph of the latter formless ecstasy can do no better by drawing a picture of the former, under the image of its physical instruments.

Much of the foregoing discussion of *Konx Om Pax* which comprise essential parts of his sexual philosophy, came to be expanded later and incorporated in the so-called Official Instructions. Among these, I would mention *Liber A'ash vel Capricorni* as well as *Liber Cheth vel Abiegni*, both of which I have reproduced almost *in toto* in *The Best of Crowley*. Mention should also be made of a brilliant essay entitled *Energized Enthusiasm* in *Equinox IX*, which deals at some length with Vamacharya.

A few quotations at random from this latter essay would not be amiss here. For example:

The Greeks say that there are three methods of discharging the Leyden Jar of Genius. These three methods they assign to three Gods.

Now it would be a great mistake to imagine that the Greeks were recommending a visit to a brothel. As well condemn the High Mass at St. Peter's on the strength of having witnessed a Protestant revival meeting. Disorder is always a parody of order . . . . Some writers suppose that in the ancient rites of Eleusis the High Priest publicly copulated with the High Priestess. Were this so, it would be no more "indecent" than it is "Blasphemous" for the priest to make bread and wine into the body and blood of God . . . .

Agree then that it does not follow from the fact that wine, woman and song make the sailor's tavern that those ingredients must necessarily concoct a hell-broth.

There are some people so simple as to think that, when they have proved the religious instinct to be a mere efflorescence of the sex-instinct, they have destroyed religion.

We should rather consider that the sailor's tavern gives him his only glimpse of heaven, just as the destructive criticism of the phallicists has only proved sex to be a sacrament. Consciousness, says the materialist, axe in hand, is a function of the brain. He has only re-formulated the old saying, "Your bodies are temples of the Holy Ghost." . . . . The spiritual flower of this process is that at the moment of discharge a physical ecstasy occurs, a spasm analogous to the mental spasm which meditation gives. And further, in the sacramental and ceremonial use of the sexual act, the divine consciousness may be attained.

The sexual act being then a sacrament, it remains to consider in what respect this limits the employment of the organs . . . . Admit its religious function, and one may at once lay down that the act must not be profaned. It must not be undertaken lightly and foolishly without excuse . . . . If the fact in itself is to be the sacrament in a religious ceremony, this act must be accomplished solely for the love of God. All personal considerations must be banished utterly. Just as any priest can perform the miracle of transubstantiation, so can any man, possessing the necessary qualifications, perform this other miracle, whose nature must form the subject of a subsequent discussion . . . .

Physical strength and beauty are necessary and desirable for aesthetic reasons, the attention of the worshippers being liable to distraction if the celebrants are ugly, deformed, or incompetent. I need hardly emphasize the necessity for the strictest self-control and concentration on their part. As it would be blasphemy to enjoy the gross taste of the wine of the sacrament, so must the celebrant suppress even the minutest manifestation of animal pleasure . . . .

So who really is dirty? Crowley with his frank and unashamed adoration of the sexual drive as God? Or Symonds with his insidious ridicule and contempt of sex?

With this interpretation of sex, it is no wonder that in one form or another it makes entry into every phase of Crowley's life and into every type of writing. It was supremely important to him.

Sometimes he used anagrams and ciphers in his writing to reveal and simultaneously to conceal the name of the sexual partner who inspired his rapture, thus opening the doors and pathways to higher mystical states. Many of these anagrams were in reality private dedications when no open one could be permitted. A little alertness is all that is required to perceive these ciphers. For example, in *Liber LXV*, the reader could find an anagram in a verse towards the end, reading: "Adonai, divine Adonai . . . . !" Ada!

There is another one that only recently, while preparing the anthology *The Best of Crowley*, did I discover in *The Book of Lies:*

Love Alway Yieldeth; Love Alway Hardeneth . . .
. . . May be; I write it but to write Her name.

The anagram spells Laylah. This was his Qabalistic rendition of the first name of an Australian violinist, Leila Waddell. Just before World War I, he was desperately in love with her, a fact which produced some of his finest poetry.

The so-called holy books—this is his term for a small handful of writings like *LXV* and *The Book of Lapis Lazuli*, and others—include dialogues between the component parts of the personality of this extraordinary man, as suggested above.

For example:

> Further Adonai spake unto V.V.V.V.V. and said:
> Let us take our delight in the multitude of men!
> Let us shape unto ourselves a boat of mother-of-pearl from them, that we may ride upon the river of Amrit!
> Thou seest yon petal of amaranth, blown by the wind from the low sweet brows of Hathor?
> (The Magister saw it and rejoiced in the beauty of it.) . . . .

And again:

> And Adonai said: The strong brown reaper swept his swathe and rejoiced. The wise man counted his muscles, and pondered, and understood not, and was sad.
> Reap thou, and rejoice!
> Then was the Adept glad, and lifted him arm . . . .

There is a further instance of the ordinary Frater P. speaking and the answers that were given him:

> Weary, weary! saith the scribe, who shall lead me to the sight of the Rapture of my master? . . . . O Lord, be my helper, and bring me to the bliss of the Beloved! . . . .
> Thou dost faint, thou dost fail, thou scribe, cried the desolate Voice; but I have filled thee with a wine whose savour thou knowest not . . . . O my darling, I also wait for the brilliance of the hour ineffable, when the universe shall be like a girdle for the midst of the ray of our love, extending beyond the permitted end of the endless one.
> Then, O thou heart, will I the serpent eat thee wholly up; yea, I will eat thee wholly up.

Here is another example of this inner dialogue that I have mentioned above:

> (The scribe was wroth thereat. He spake:
> O Adonai and my master, I have borne the inkhorn

and the pen without pay, in order that I might search this river of Amrit, and sail thereon as one of ye. This I demand for my fee, that I partake of the echo of your kisses.)

(And immediately it was granted unto him.)

A few verses later on, there is another dialogue:

Adonai spake yet again with V.V.V.V.V. and said:
The earth is ripe for vintage; let us eat of her grapes, and be drunken thereon.
And V.V.V.V.V. answered and said: O my Lord, my dove, my excellent one, how shall this word seem unto the children of men?

A chapter or so later on, we read:

Then the adept was rapt away in bliss, and the beyond of bliss, and exceeded the excess of excess.
Also his body shook and staggered with the burden of that bliss and that excess and that ultimate nameless.

Again, and the emphasis on the separate actors is even more distinct here:

Thus spake the Magister V.V.V.V.V. unto Adonai his God, as they played together in the starlight over against the deep black pool that is in the Holy Place of the Holy House beneath the Altar of the Holiest One.
But Adonai laughed, and played more languidly.
Then the scribe took note, and was glad. But Adonai had no fear of the Magician and his play.
For it was Adonai who had taught all his tricks to the Magician.
And the Magister entered the play of the Magician. When the Magician laughed he laughed; all as a man should do.
And Adonai said: Thou art enmeshed in the web of the Magician. This he said subtly, to try him.
But the Magister gave the sign of the Magistry, and laughed back on Him: O Lord, O beloved, did these fingers relax on Thy curls, or these eyes turn away from

Thine eyes?
And Adonai delighted in him exceedingly.

There are many, many others which point in the same direction, indicating an inner dialogue between the hierarchical aspects of the man Crowley.

Finally, there is the following, fraught with enormous significance for Crowley. In one way or another, this occurs throughout all his magical writings. And it can be cited as either the cause of his megalomania, or the source of it:

> But thou shalt heed none of this. Thou shalt be ever the heart, and I the serpent will coil close about thee. My coils shall never relax throughout the aeons. Neither change nor sorrow nor unsubstantiality shall have thee; for thou art passed beyond all these.
> Even as the diamond shall glow red for the rose, and green for the rose-leaf; so shalt thou abide apart from the Impressions.
> I am thou, and the Pillar is established in the void.

All of these quotations are from one of the books which is called *The Book of the Heart Girt with the Serpent,* or Liber LXV.

It needs to be re-emphasized again how all of this sentiment is rooted in the Golden Dawn and its magico-mystical formulae. First of all the title of the book comprises a line from the Bornless Ritual which was appropriated by some members of the Golden Dawn, and then was passed on to Crowley. Second, the number LXV consists of a *double entendre*. It is first of all a play on LVX, the Light, which is the central thesis of both the Neophyte and the Adeptus Minor Rituals. Especially in the latter, the notion of LVX is stressed in a wide variety of ways, all of which duly impressed themselves on the consciousness of Crowley. Also, its enumeration, 65, (or gematria as it is known technically) is the number of *Adonai,* a Hebrew word for Lord which Crowley employed as a synonym for the

Higher Genius, the term used by the Golden Dawn, and for the Holy Guardian Angel, the phrase employed by Abramelin. All of these ideas are descriptive of the nature and content of the sublime writing itself, and at the same time exhibit their historical descent from the Golden Dawn.

There are several books of this type that were written in this period of exaltation. In addition, there is *Liber Liberi vel Lapidis Lazuli,* or *Liber VII,* from which I shall quote a number of the more exuberant and devotional passages. There is also *Liber Ararita* or *Liber 813,* focalized about a number of different interpretations of the Qabalistic Tree and *Liber Tregrammaton* or *Liber 27,* which does not yet mean very much to me. But the height of the mystical exaltation is contained essentially in *LXV* and *VII,* for both of these are, quite patently, literally inspired.

Both of these books—in fact, most of the writing of Crowley, whether prose, poetry, or inspired prose-poems—are marred periodically by the intrusion of gross imagery. It is the sort of thing that many commentators have labelled blasphemy or demonic. I cannot take this stand. Mine is much more simple, though perhaps not so eloquent or inspired. If we take one of his later formulations that poetry is the geyser of the Unconscious—which is a competent and valid interpretation—then whatever inspiration may or may not be, if it enters through the Unconscious, it must push up with it some of the hidden contents of the personal Unconscious. And it has long been established that this level of the psyche contains repressed material of sexuality, hostility, masochism, exhibitionism, and polymorphous perversion. Some of it may not appear attractive to us at all. It strikes one as odd, at first, that some of this quite unattractive material should appear side by side with the most sublime aspirations. It would seem that there is no necessary connection between them at all, but every now and again, some of this quite odd material slips through. And while Crowley apparently tried to justify it in his commentaries, I must be hidebound enough, or armored psychically, so that I cannot appreciate it as he has.

But first of all I would like to give examples of some of the lovely devotional yearning that appears in *Liber VII*.

The following are some quotations that through the years have been especially meaningful to me.

> I pluck Thee, O my God, like a purple plum upon a sunny tree. How Thou dost melt in my mouth, Thou consecrated sugar of the Stars!

This mysticism has a personal intimacy. It is sensuous and sensual and Dionysian; there is no nirvanic aloofness here. It is as though he has managed to bring the two worlds together in the realization that appearance is reality, and vice versa.

> The world is all grey before mine eyes; it is like an old worn wine-skin. All the wine of it is on these lips . . . .
> O God of mine. Thou art like a little white goat with lightning in his horns!
> I love Thee, I love Thee.
> Every breath, every word, every thought, every deed is an act of love with Thee.
> The beat of my heart is the pendulum of love.
> The songs of me are the soft sighs.
> And my deeds are the myriads of Thy children, the stars and the atoms . . . .

A few lines further on, there occurs:

> Bury me unto Thy Glory, O beloved, O princely lover of this harlot maiden, within the Secretest Chamber of the Palace!
> It is done quickly; yea, the seal is set upon the vault. There is one that shall avail to open it.
> Nor by memory, nor by imagination, nor by prayer, nor by fasting, nor by scourging, nor by drugs, nor by ritual, nor by meditation; only by passive love shall he

avail.

He shall await the sword of the Beloved and bare his throat for the stroke.

Then shall his blood leap out and write me runes in the sky; yea, write me runes in the sky.

And here the mystical experience particularly points out a meaning:

There are deep secrets in these songs. It is not enough to hear the bird; to enjoy song he must be the bird.

I am the bird, and Thou art my song, O my glorious galloping God!

Then there is another:

By Silence and by speech do I worship Thee.

But all is in vain.

Only Thy silence and Thy speech that worship me avail . . . .

O dear my God! what a feast Thou has provided.

Behold the lights and the flowers and the maidens!

Taste of the wines and the cakes and the splendid meats!

Breathe in the perfumes and the clouds of little gods, like wood-nymphs that inhabit the nostrils!

Feel with your whole body the glorious smoothness of the marble coolth and the generous warmth of the sun and the slaves!

And finally:

O my God, but the love in Me bursts over the bonds of Space and Time; my love is split among them that love not Love. My wine is poured out for them that never tasted wine.

Certainly in studying the records that Crowley made of all the occult practices that he engaged in since 1898, one is struck by the fact that he was doggedly persistent. And if ever he was impatient for results, it never showed in his diaries. So far as his patience is concerned, *LXV* describes it superbly in a parable:

> Let not the failure and the pain turn aside the worshippers. The foundations of the pyramid were hewn in the living rock ere sunset; did the king weep at dawn that the crown of the pyramid was yet unquarried in the distant land?

And where his dogged persistence and will-power are concerned, the same book has this to say in a rather longer parable:

> There was also an humming bird that spake unto the horned cerastes, and prayed him for poison. And the great snake of Khem the Holy One, the royal Uraeus serpent, answered him and said:
> I sailed over the sky of Nu in the car called Millions-Of-Years, and I saw not any creature upon Seb that was equal to me. The venom of my fang is the inheritance of my father, and of my father's father; and how shall I give it unto thee? Live thou and thy children as I and my fathers have lived, even unto an hundred millions of generations, and it may be that the mercy of the Mighty Ones may bestow upon thy children a drop of the poison of eld.
> Then the humming-bird was afflicted in his spirit, and he flew into the flowers, and it was as if naught had been spoken between them. Yet in a little while a serpent struck him that he died.
> But an Ibis that meditated upon the bank of the Nile, the beautiful god listened and heard. And he laid aside his Ibis ways, and became as a serpent, saying Peradventure in an hundred millions of millions of generations of my children, they shall attain to a drop of the poison of the fang of the Exalted One.
> And behold! Ere the moon waxed thrice he became an Uraeus serpent, and the poison of the fang was established in him and his seed even for ever and for ever.
> O thou serpent Apep, my Lord Adonai, it is a speck

of minutest time, this travelling through eternity, and in Thy sight the landmarks are of fair white marble untouched by the tool of the graver. Therefore Thou art mine, even now and for ever and for everlasting. Amen.

1907 was a magnificent year. Crowley's mysticism came to full flower. Though the published diary records are sparse, we can deduce that there were many conferences with Jones. Between them they must have decided finally to formulate in the near future a new Order that would eliminate the gross faults of the old Golden Dawn and point the way to a new approach. I quote here from *Liber LXI,* which is the history lection. It gives us some clues as to what was occurring in this year of inspiration as well as in the year that followed:

22. Therefore by order of D.D.S. did P. prepare all things by his arcane science and wisdom, choosing only those symbols which were common to all systems, and rigorously rejecting all names and words which might be supposed to imply a religious or metaphysical theory . . . .

23. Deliberately, therefore, did he take refuge in vagueness. Not to veil the truth to the Neophyte, but to warn him against valuing non-essentials . . . .

25. Now when P. had thus with bitter toil prepared all things under the guidance of D.D.S. (even as the hand writes, while the conscious brain, though ignorant of the detailed movements, applauds or disapproves the finished work) there was a certain time of repose, as the earth lieth fallow . . . .

29. Also one V.V.V.V.V. arose, an exalted adept of the rank of Master of the Temple (or this much He disclosed to the Exempt Adepts) and His utterance is enshrined in the Sacred Writings.

30. Such are Liber Legis, Liber Cordis Cincti Serpente, Liber Liberi vel Lapidis Lazuli and such others whose existence may one day be divulged unto you. Beware lest you interpret them either in the Light or in the darkness, for only in L.V.X. may they be

understood.

31. Also he conferred upon D.D.S., O.M., and another, the authority of the Triad, who in turn have delegated it unto others, and they yet again, so that the Body of Initiates may be perfect, even from the Crown unto the Kingdom and beyond.

The organization that Crowley and Jones founded in the year 1909 was called the A∴A∴. Symonds reads the name as *Astrum Argentinum,* the Silver Star. I fancy he is far nearer the truth this time than most of the other weird interpretations that would have elicited groans of horror from Crowley.

The name of the Third Order of the Golden Dawn was never given, so far as I am aware. The only possible reference in the Order literature, to explain Crowley's choice of A∴A∴, is in the name of one of the Tarot Trumps. This is the "High Priestess", referred to the path Gimel (meaning a Camel) on the Middle Pillar of the Qabalistic Tree of Life. Her full title is "The Priestess of the Silver Star", and usually refers to the initiated intuition or spiritual perception.

This Order had three sections: The Order of the Silver Star, which is the highest, corresponding to the Secret Chiefs of the old days. The second order of the Rose Cross, and the outer Order of the Golden Dawn. Each order is attributed to a different level or triad on the Qabalistic Tree, as in the old Golden Dawn. "The general characteristics and attributions of these Grades are indicated by their correspondences on the Tree of Life . . . ."

One new grade was added, that of Probationer 0=0; the Neophyte was now called 1=10, and the Theoricus grade was eliminated. The tasks of each grade were far different from those in the Order Mathers had instituted. Ceremonial initiations were eliminated. All the emphasis was now on practical personal work. This at least had the effect of modifying or reducing the sin of vanity where grades were concerned. The only way to promotion to a specific grade was through the accomplishment of a certain kind of work, either Yoga or Magick, or one of the combinations of both. For each of these grades, Crowley wrote what have come to be known as the Official Instructions which describe in detail, and with clarity and beauty, the specific nature of the work to be done.

The Probationer grade was of great importance in this Order. Here the aspirant was permitted to do any practices he wanted to do, but was directed to become familiar with *all* the official instructions and to experiment with all phases of the work, and where his own practical work was concerned to keep a diary detailing his activity. All of this has been adequately described by Crowley in Liber 185, and with more detail in an essay *One Star in Sight*. Of Liber 185, Crowley wrote in addition that it "is needful only to say that the Aspirant is trained systematically and comprehensively in the various technical practices which form the basis of Our Work. One may become expert in all of these without necessarily making any real progress, just as a man might be first-rate at grammar, syntax, and prosody without being able to write a single line of good poetry, although the greatest poet in soul is unable to express himself without the aid of those three elements of literary composition."

Crowley had developed some interesting theories which he put into effect in dealing with this task of the Probationer. First of all, as I have stated, the aspirant was left entirely to his own devices to select just those magical or meditative practices that he wished. True, he was advised to familiarize himself with *all* of them. But in that first year of Probationership, there was just so much work that the candidate could really perform. The intent of this was to determine the natural bent of the aspirant. The unconscious factors in the selection of a certain type or number of practices would provide the teacher with ample clues to character structure. Both his characterological strengths and weaknesses would be indicated, giving his teacher a chance to point them out so that the student could take the necessary steps to remedy the situation, or to heal the breach, and so round out his developing personality.

Secondly, Crowley insisted dogmatically that no Order superior should intrude on the freedom or the ingenium of the candidate, to tell him which practices he should or should not engage in. I fancy he severely reprimanded anybody who did just that. One of the several reasons why Crowley and Captain Fuller ultimately fell out and parted company was that the latter without authority made such recommendations to a certain Frater Achad. I am sure there were other far more personal factors promoting this split, but this could well have been one of them.

Thirdly, the Order system as he inaugurated it was based on what in the East is called the *Guru parampara* chain. In other words, the Probationer's teacher is really a Neophyte, one who holds the grade next above. A Zelator is the guru of the Neophyte. The Zelator has as his teacher a Practicus, and the Practicus has as his teacher a Philosophus, etc. By this device authority from the highest echelons could swiftly be passed down through the grades when indicated. The chain of authority would pass unbroken from the highest grade down to the lowest, to the humblest beginner on the Path. Responsibility to teach is thus delegated to each student as he begins his spiritual ascent, a responsibility for which he was held strictly accountable by his own superior.

In this way too, the teacher, of whatever grade he happened to hold, would always be able to impart the benefits of his own personal experience to his student of the grade below. Sometimes, too great a gulf can develop between teacher of exalted experience and student of none, so that communication is rendered very difficult, if not impossible. By this device of the *guru parampara* chain, this gulf of communication is bridged on the basis that there is not too much distance between the student and his immediate superior or teacher. If the latter runs into any pedagogical problems with his inferior, he can always appeal to his own teacher for help, and so on up the scale.

To do Crowley full justice regarding the structure, function and goals of his Order, the reader should consult the late essay of his entitled *One Star in Sight*. It is unfortunately too long to include here, and to give merely short excerpts from it would fail of effect.

The essay is a most important one. It describes the three sections of his Order, names and describes the ten grades, and above all specifies the detailed practical work that properly belongs to each one. It contains some of Crowley's most profound philosophical constructs, and serves moreover to outline his conceptions of the high goals of the mystic path. Again I must reiterate on the basis of this particular essay and other of his writings discussed here, anyone who derides Crowley and mocks him—thus selling him short—merely exposes his own ignorance and blindness.

Apart from the instructions concerning meditation and magical practice, this year also saw the writing down of Liber 777, an elaborate Qabalistic table of correspondences, and a delightful book entitled *Konx Om Pax*. These three words are right out of the Golden Dawn's Neophyte ritual and are part of a mystical declaration: "Khabs Am Pekht. Konx Om Pax. Light in Extension." It asserts the wish, the hope that you too may receive the Light.

Actually, I would say that this was his first serious book about magical philosophy. It served as a more complete statement of his own personal rebellion against Mathers and the Golden Dawn, as well as a public declaration of his spiritual attainment. The book includes satire, fantasy, a delicate whimsey, cruel humor, lovely lyrics, philosophy of a sublime and profound nature comparable only to the highest flights of Mahayana Buddhism, and evidence of his intimate relationship with George Cecil Jones.

The book has four sections, each fascinating in its own individual way. Each is a thoroughgoing refutation of complaints made both by some Golden Dawn zealots and some of his own equally fanatical admirers, that the Golden Dawn played only an insignificant role in his later thinking. Actually, *Konx Om Pax* is Golden Dawn from beginning to end, with of course the Crowley genius running through every chapter not merely like a pale silver thread, but more like a vast intricate network of golden cords.

The first section is called *The Wake World*. It appears at first sight to be a lovely fairy story describing the Qabalistic Tree of Life and the Golden Dawn system of grades. The whole concept of illumination is described as a waking-up process. It is altogether reminiscent of the Zen notion that, essentially, everyone is a Buddha or has a Buddha-consciousness, and is fully illuminated here and now, but he does not know this. He is asleep, as it were, or deluded. The entire scheme of self-discipline and meditative training is to facilitate the waking process.

The human ego is called Lola "because I am the Key of Delights, and the other children in my dream call me Lola Daydreams." The Fairy Prince whom she seeks "is a dark boy, very comely; I think everyone must love him, and yet every one is afraid. He looks through one just as if one had no clothes on in the Garden of God, and he had made one, and one could do nothing except in the mirror of his mind. He never laughs or frowns or smiles; because whatever he sees, he sees what is beyond as well, and so nothing ever happens. His mouth is redder than any roses you ever saw. I wake up quite when we kiss each other, and there is no dream any more." This Fairy Prince is none other than V.V.V.V.V. The story describes in detail on the basis of personal realization each Sephirah and each Grade and each connecting pathway. It is a lovely provocative attempt to deal with a profoundly difficult subject.

The second essay *Ali Sloper or the Forty Liars* is mainly a satire on the Golden Dawn. He throws barbs at its membership, and its teaching. There is absolutely no way of appreciating this essay or understanding it in any way unless this one fact be realized. The remaining part of *An Essay on Truth* focuses around a metaphysical dialogue between Bones and Bowley—none other, of course, than George Cecil Jones and Crowley himself. It describes with considerable humor his efforts to prepare amongst other matters the tables that ultimately would comprise 777.

The *Dramatis Personae* at the opening of the essay is to me one of the funniest things in the world. Most of its humor has gone unappreciated for the most part because it is so essentially esoteric in the sense that it relates to the Golden Dawn. Unless one has some knowledge of the society, and can recognize the names of some of its members, and understand some of the obscure Qabalistic references, the whole thing is likely to go over one's head. And this, I think, is a great pity. For example, the following basically ridicules those parts of the Old Testament employed by the Golden Dawn in some of the elemental grade rituals.

GRAND PATRIOTIC SPECTACLE.

Warlike Preparations—General Eloah arrives from Temain of Edom—Colonel Holium summoned from Mount Paran—The Wilderness of Seir—The Tents of Cushan—A Dervish stronghold—General Tetragrammaton's flying column—City of Meroz I.V. desert in a body—A traitor in the camp?—Melchizedek Pasha's cunning move—The river Kishon sweeps away the Moabites (by Mr. Frank Parker)—Battle at last—Desperate stand of the Kings of Edom—Marshall Jah's flank attack—Everlasting Mountains scattered—Perpetual Hills bowed (by Mr. Frank Parker)—Charge of the gallant Karnaim—Rout of the Edomites—The Dukes in full flight—And Grand Finale "Blowing up of the Tower of Babel" (by Mr. Frank

Parker).

GOD SAVE THE KING.

An Essay on Truth which follows this spectacle is a dialogue, combining transcendental thinking with humor. For example:

> Now it hath occurred that some of the younger Adepts, the light-hearted and foolish of the Great White Brotherhood, those who slip back oftenest to normal consciousness of the Universe, so that even their pure wings are soiled in the mire of sense-perception, reason, and their foul kind, some of those boys, I say, forget the Writing on the outer Veil of the Indicible Arcanum, that rune which is written "No separate existence!" in golden letters on the silver of the veil (just as within is written "No existence!" in silver letters upon the golden veil).
>
> (Bones *smiles, seeing the way to destroy the argument of the Paper.*)
>
> That rune these boys forgot, miserable ones!
> Therefore, lost in the unthinkable depths of their depravity, do they dream evil dreams called "Others," "Fellow-men" and the like (Fellow-men is really a nightmare so appalling that only the "passmen" of the G.W.B. ever dream it, since it implies the ghastly and horrible phantasm of "mankind").
> Now in their better selves is a certain force whose troubled reflection is called "Love". This tinctures the dream, and they instantly feel compassion for the "Others"—who, being merely unpurified parts of their consciousness, simply need annihilating—and set to work (if you please!) to redeem these "Others," to initiate these "fellow-men", to emancipate these "separate beings."

The humor as well as the transcendental philosophical attitude displayed in this kind of thinking calls to mind the response made by Henrich Zimmer, the orientalist, when he was dealing with *prajnaparamita* in his book *Philosophies of*

India. He wrote what is so applicable to this particular case:

> The Illumined Ones behave in a way that should be rather shocking and confusing to any sound thinker, who, from habit and firm determination, is resolved to keep his feet on the ground. In a sort of mocking conversation, these Buddhas and Bodhisattvas entertain themselves with enigmatical statements of unstatable truths. They delight in declaring, time and again, that there is no such thing as Buddhism, no such thing as Enlightenment, nothing remotely resembling the extinction of Nirvana, setting traps for each other and trying to trick each other into assertions that might imply—even remotely—the reality of such conceptions. Then, most artfully, they always elude the cleverly placed hazards and hidden pitfalls—and engage in a glorious trans-Olympian laugh; for the merest hint of a notion of Nirvana would have betrayed a trace of the vestige of the opposite attitude, samsara, and the clinging to individual existence.[1]

Many of the paradoxes that I have called koan-like in *The Book of Lies* (falsely so-called) incorporate exactly this kind of trans-Olympian humor coupled with the transcendental insight (*prajna*) which denies that reality is apart from appearance. Only awakening from the foul grasp of delusion will enable one to realize the ecstasy and divinity of That which is simultaneously both appearance and reality. It seems to me that Crowley's insights were far ahead of his time, when little of the Mahayana and Zen literature had appeared in English.

The third section of *Konx Om Pax* is called *The Synagogue of Satan.* A consideration of this section forces me to assert dogmatically that anyone who says Crowley was a Satanist and a devil-worshipper should have his head examined. There may be an occasional reference to, or even a sardonic admission of this throughout different of his writings. But they are primarily due to the fact that he was being defiant in his own inimitable manner, or trying to shock a segment of his reading audience, or pulling someone's leg, or just being sarcastic. He actually had adopted Blavatsky's point of view that Lucifer was really the Light-bringer—altogether apart from his profound need to demonstrate that if the God described by the Plymouth Brethren of his childhood were responsible for the infamies of the Plymouth Brethren, then he far preferred the Devil of whom they were so mortally frightened.

Indeed, he makes this splendidly clear during a discussion of what is perceived in so-called astral vision, or skrying in the spirit vision, as it is called in the Golden Dawn teaching. In *Magick*, he wrote:

> On the higher planes, the diversity of form, due to grossness, tends to disappear. Thus the Astral Vision of "Isis" is utterly unlike that of "Kali". The one is of Motherhood and Wisdom, ineffably candid, clear, and loving; the other of Murder and madness, blood-intoxicated, lust-befogged, and cruel. The sole link is the Woman-symbol. But whoso makes Samadhi on Kali obtains the self-same Illumination as if it had been Isis; for in both cases he attains identity with the Quintessence of the Woman-Idea, untrammelled by the qualities with which the dwellers by the Nile and the Ganges respectively disguised it.
>
> Thus, in low grades of initiation, dogmatic quarrels are inflamed by astral experience; as when Saint John distinguishes between the Whore BABALON and the Woman clothed with the Sun, between the Lamb that was slain and the Beast 666 whose deadly wound was healed; nor understands that Satan, the Old Serpent, in the Abyss, the Lake of Fire and Sulphur, is the Sun-Father, the vibration of Life, Lord of Infinite Space that flames with His Consuming Energy, and it is also that throned Light whose Spirit is suffused throughout the City of Jewels.[2]

Somewhere in the writings of Swami Vivekananda, a beautiful anecdote is told about his own teacher Shri

Ramakrishna, who had been accused of insanity. So far from defending himself against this slur, he agreed, adding however: "Of course I am insane. So are you! and everybody else! The only difference between our insanities is that I am mad about God. It is the only thing I care about. You are mad about money, sex, possessions, prestige, etc. Mine is a divine insanity. What is yours? And which of the two do you really believe is best?"

Crowley was really God-intoxicated. All the writings that I have marshalled in *The Best of Crowley* and in this present biographical study indicate exactly this. One must consider all his exercises and practices in Yoga and Magic, the official instructions he wrote for his own reformulation of the Golden Dawn, the divine intoxication of *Liber LXV* and *Liber VIII* and the very many poems which I have quoted here and there—to realize one thing, and one thing only. He was actually God-intoxicated.

If Symonds, Mannix and other critics wish me to consider his drug addiction, his irresponsibility, his apparent abuse of women as evidenced by the shortness of their stay with him, I would only answer in terms of that delightful story given in Madame Alexandra David Neel's book about Tibet:

> He (Tsang Yang Gyatso) would seem to have been initiated into certain methods which permit—or perhaps even encourage—what appears to be debauchery, and would indeed be so in the case of any other than an "initiate" into that singular training of which it is difficult to speak outside of a medical treatise.
>
> What leads one to suspect that Tsang Yang Gyatso was an adept in these practices is, among other indications, an evidently fantastic story, though one whose symbolism is perfectly clear to anyone acquainted with the training in question. Here is the story:
>
> Tsang Yang Gyatso happened to be on the upper terrace of his palace at the Potala, accompanied by those who were scandalized by his licentious conduct.

"Yes, I have mistresses," he said in answer to their reproaches, "and you who blame me also have them, but do you think that the possession of a woman is the same thing for you as it is for me?"

He then approached the edge of the terrace and made water over the balustrade. The liquid flow descended to the base of the Potala and then "ascended" to the higher terrace and returned into the Grand Lama along the same channel by which it had gone forth.

The Grand Lama now addressed those around Him:

"You do the same," he said, "and, if you cannot, understand that my relations with women are different from yours."[3]

When Crowley's critics can duplicate the holy books and his illuminations as recorded in the published diaries, then I will be more prone to examine their criticisms and give them validity. In the meantime, I can only tell these critics my feelings in terms of a quotation from Captain Fuller's writing in *Equinox IV*.

Similarly the Yogi says: I have arrived at a state of Superconsciousness (Samadhi) and you, my friend, are not only blind, deaf and dumb, but the son of a pig into the bargain. You are totally immersed in Darkness (Tamas); a child of ignorance (Avidya) and the offspring of illusion (Maya); as mad, insane and idiotic as those unfortunates you lock up in your asylums to convince you, as one of you yourselves has very justly remarked, that you are not all raving mad. For you consider not only one thing, which you insult by calling God, but all things to be real; and anything which has the slightest odour of reality about it you pronounce an illusion.

To read Crowley's essay *The Synagogue of Satan* is to become aware of the Golden Dawn's concept of the spiritual dialectic as I have called it, as a medium to express the complexities of the philosophy that he had developed in the several years since he had first been initiated.

He spoke of the pairs of opposites in the moral and

intellectual life and the contradictions, together with the social ills, naive perhaps in the social and political sense, but certainly valid in the broader philosophical and spiritual sense.

For example, I quote the following section that in *The Best of Crowley* I called "The Manifesting of Simplicity", because more than anything else I know, it represents just what Crowley stood for in those days.

> The laws of the physical world are precisely paralleled by those of the moral and intellectual sphere. To the prostitute I prescribe a course of training by which she shall comprehend the holiness of sex. Chastity forms part of that training, and I should hope to see her one day a happy wife and mother. To the prude equally I shall prescribe a course of training by which she shall comprehend the holiness of sex. Unchastity forms part of that training, and I should hope to see her one day a happy wife and mother.
>
> To the bigot I commend a course of Thomas Henry Huxley; to the infidel a practical study of ceremonial magic. Then, when the bigot has knowledge and the infidel faith, each may follow without prejudice his natural inclination; for he will no longer plunge into his former excesses . . . .
>
> I have been taxed with assaulting what is commonly known as virtue. True; I hate it, but only in the same degree as I hate what is commonly known as vice.
>
> So it must be acknowledged that one who is but slightly unbalanced needs a milder correction than whoso is obsessed by prejudice. There are men who make a fetish of cleanliness; they shall work in a fitter's shop, and learn that dirt is the mark of honourable toil. There are those whose lives are rendered wretched by the fear of infection: they see bacteria of the deadliest sort in all things but the actual solutions of carbolic acid and mercuric chloride with which they hysterically combat their invisible foemen: such would I send to live in the bazaar at Delhi, where they shall haply learn that dirt makes little difference after all.

There are slow men who need a few months' experience of the hustle of the stockyards: there are business men in a hurry, and they shall travel in Central Asia to acquire the art of repose.

So much for the equilibrium, and for every month in every year each member of your governing classes shall undergo this training under skilled advice.

But what of the Great Tao? For one month in every year each of these men shall seek desperately for the Stone of the Philosophers. By solitude and fasting for the social and luxurious, by drunkenness and debauch for the austere, by scourging for those who are afraid of physical pain, by repose for the restless, and toil for the idle, by bull-fights for the humanitarian, and the care of little children for the callous, by rituals for the rational, and by philosophy for the credulous, shall these men, while yet unbalanced, seek to attain unity with the great Tao. But for those whose intellect is purified and co-ordinated, for those whose bodies are in health, and whose passions are at once eager and controlled, it shall be lawful to choose their own way to the One Goal; *vide licet* identity with that great Tao which is far above the antithesis of Yang and Yin.

Many people would hesitate reading the essay merely on the basis of the title. *The Synagogue of Satan*? Why bother? I assume he still retained some naiveté in supposing that the public would take the time and trouble to investigate whether he was a demonolatrist or merely pulling one's legs. There really is not that much time or energy available in this strange world of ours to devote to this sort of thing. He was naive, too, in not realizing that the world is full of sick, vicious people, those whom Wilhelm Reich had called sick with the Plague, the Emotional Plague. This so-called Plague is a composite of paranoid trends with psychopathic tendencies, overlaid with suspicion and jealousy and pure hatred, rooted in the involuntary employment of such psychodynamics as repression, projection and massive reaction-formation. It is the disease of mass movements, providing the bitter opposition to any forward progress on the part of mankind. In the individual case, Freud has called it resistance; where the mass is concerned Reich has called it the Plague. It was this that Crowley had not taken into consideration, until too late.

In other words, however funny such a title as *The Synagogue of Satan* may have struck him, and regardless of how actually serious he may have been in presenting his view of moral solutions to social and political problems, he placed himself unequivocally in the position of asking for trouble. In that title he challenged the morals and prejudices of his culture—and he got hurt!

Other times, he has mentioned that he employed bloody sacrifices. Well, I am sure that on occasion he did, as when he walked through the Sahara Desert with Victor Neuburg towards the close of 1909. For one specific purpose, it is clear that he used the blood of some pigeons; that is admitted as a fact unmodified by symbolism or humor.

But when he wrote in *Magick* that in a single year he performed the bloody sacrifice about 150 times, the very language should have made the casual reader give pause. He was stating that he had performed sexual intercourse 150 times that year, as his diary indicated. Moreover, when he claimed that the victim should be male, pure, and of the highest intelligence, one has to understand some of the gyrations of Crowley's mind.

In the Commentary to *The Book of the Law*, he wrote:

> I take it as certain that every offering of this talisman infallibly begets children on one plane or another of this our cosmos, whose matter is so varied in kind. Such a child must partake of its father's nature; and its character will be determined, partly by the environment in which it is bred to manifestation, lives and ultimately changes in what we call death, and partly by the inmost

will of the father, perhaps modified to some extent by his conscious will at the time of his slipping the leash.

So that just as the father—whose name is Aleister Crowley—was pure and of the highest intelligence, in his estimation, so also the lion serpent, as he called the spermatazoon, the magical son or talisman, which has to be offered up magically, partakes of the nature of the father. There are so many references and cross-references to what he believed, that it is altogether beyond me that anyone could have seriously believed that he sacrificed 150 male children in one year.

The truth of the matter is that despite all his masculine adventuring around the world, despite all his big-game hunting and his verbal glorification of killing, he was a rather squeamish kind of person. Even if the Betty Loveday testimony were wholly true about the attempted sacrifice of the black cat in Cefalu, it should still be clear that if this were a man used to doing idiotic things of this kind, he was remarkably inept on that particular occasion. And this does not ring true. He *was* inept on that occasion, and did a pretty clumsy job because of the obvious fact—he was not accustomed to cutting the throats of small animals. If so, why he resorted to it in Cefalu is something else. I cannot say that I have all the answers here; nor do I admire this sort of conduct.

Anyway, back to the *Synagogue of Satan.* In every one of his dialectical attempts to provide answers to some of the most stubborn problems that have long assailed humanity, his imp-like humor intrudes. It tends to take the edge off the over-seriousness of the problems, and his solutions. The humor bubbles. Whenever I read *Konx Om Pax* and *The Book of Lies*, contemplating his rich though esoteric humor, I often find my mind flitting to the contemplation of Zen masters, and the wide range of interpretation used by modern writers. Some dismiss the entire subject as idiocy and nonsense; others are philosophical, seeking to describe or explain the way in which these Zen masters point directly to the truth. But there is a midpoint between these two extremes which incorporates both attitudes, and quite clearly this is where Crowley and his humor comes in.

I occasionally think that the traditional Zen master, in a mood perhaps of exasperation, engendered sometimes by the exigencies of everyday practice, must have got awfully fed up from time to time with the constant stream of visitors or students who would come to see him, demanding words of wisdom from his lips. Most of the time, I am sure, he would be in a calm and tranquil mood, respecting their sincerity and their aims. But surely, there must have been occasions when, no matter how completely he was identified with the Transcendental Wisdom, he must have been thoroughly exasperated.

It is quite possible that he would like to have shouted, or done something ridiculous, or to have kicked one of these young monks in the gluteals out of sheer pique or boredom, if nothing else. It is conceivable that if one of such monks had asked seriously "What is the essence of mind which is intrinsically pure", he might have replied, with a wise twinkle in his eye, with some obvious triviality, a coarse obscenity, or thwacked the poor monk on the head with his walking-stick.

Now it is also possible that were the student otherwise prepared, by long training, by meditation, by life itself, the impact of such an idiotic answer or the sharp blow on the shaven head, could provide the necessary shock to shatter his psychological defense mechanisms, and permit illumination. Let us not lose sight of the fact that the motive or intention of the Master may have been quite prosaic. He was just fed up, annoyed, irritated. It was just one of those days! He had had it! If another stupid student posed another stupid question—well . . . .!

Let us give credit to these wise men for having some kind

of humor. They were not serious *all* the time. Probably they exploded into peals of laughter on occasion. It did the student a lot of good. Obviously, such spontaneous behavior did the Master a lot of good too. Both could howl hysterically with laughter over the entire incident.

During the lengthy process of psychoanalysis, the analyst's sense of humor comes to his rescue in similar situations. It might enable him to make, for instance, some ridiculous dream interpretation that conceivably might shock and irritate the patient. This could have a koan-like effect, to provide the patient with some real insight. It would also serve as a spontaneous outlet for whatever was bothering the analyst on that particular occasion.

I sometimes think along this track too when contemplating the life of one of the great saints of the Church—like St. John of the Cross or St. Theresa of Avila. Perhaps more the latter than the thin, tubercular St. John. Part of their duties, from time to time, was to receive confessions from the nuns in the Retreat. I am sure that the larger part of the time their duties were performed conscientiously and effectively. Altogether apart from their mystical experiences and their high office in the Church, surely as human beings they lapsed into an occasional low mood. Perhaps the night before, insomnia had troubled them? A cough had made their bronchi and sinuses raw? Or the chronic arthritis annoyed St. Theresa? Is it not possible that when confronted by one of the young fluttery females in the Order, she took a dim view of the whole thing?

This is of course pure speculation. But I am certain these people were human beings, and pretty complete human beings at that. Under certain circumstances, they may have felt like this. Perhaps most of the time they managed to keep these feelings to themselves, though we are told that on occasion, the arthritic St. Theresa did get highly irritated. I would not doubt it for one moment. Irritability and sanctity often go together!

Now in Crowley's case, this did happen. I am sure this is one of the several reasons why he was such a prankster. He was a prankster with an alive sense of humor which overflowed when confronted by such ridiculous situations. He did not contain himself. The essays in *Konx Om Pax* are everlasting testimonies to the richness of his brilliant humor. Of this there is no doubt at all!

Yet—there is a paradoxical question to all of this that he himself has raised in *Haggai-Howlings* from the *Book of Lies*:

> Haggard am I, an hyaena, I hunger and howl. Men think it laughter—ha! ha! ha!
>
> There is nothing movable or immovable under the firmament of heaven on which I may write the symbols of the secret of my soul.
>
> Yea, though I were lowered by ropes into the utmost Caverns and Vaults of Eternity, there is no word to express even the first whisper of the Initiator in mine ear: yea, I abhor birth, ululating lamentations of Night!
>
> Agony! Agony! The Light within me *breeds* veils; the song within me dumbness.
>
> God! in what prism may any man analyze my Light?
>
> Immortal are the adepts; and yet they die—They die of SHAME unspeakable; They die as the Gods die, for SORROW.
>
> Wilt Thou endure unto The End, O Frater Perdurabo, O Lamp in the Abyss? Thou hast the Keystone of the Royal Arch; yet the Apprentices, instead of making bricks, put the straws in their hair, and think they are Jesus Christ!
>
> O sublime tragedy and comedy of THE GREAT WORK!

Then there is another in the same book called *Onion Peelings*:

> The Universe is the Practical Joke of the General at the Expense of the Particular, quoth Frater Perdurabo, and laughed.

But those disciples nearest to him wept, seeing the Universal Sorrow.

Those next to them laughed, seeing the Universal Joke.

Below these certain disciples wept.

Then certain others laughed.

Others next wept.

Others next laughed.

Next others wept.

Next others laughed.

Last came those that wept because they could not see the Joke, and those that laughed lest they should be thought not to see the Joke, and thought it safe to act like Frater Perdurabo.

But though Frater Perdurabo laughed openly, He also at the same time wept secretly; and in Himself He neither laughed nor wept.

Nor did He mean what He said.

NOTES

[1] Heinrich Zimmer, *op. cit.*, p. 483.

[2] The Master Therion, *op. cit.*, p. 250.

[3] *Initiations and Initiates in Tibet*, A. David-Neel, Rider & Co., London, 1931, p. 141.

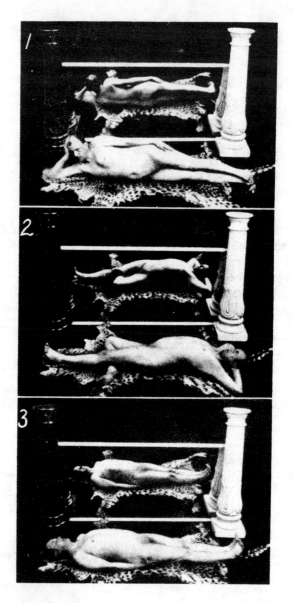

1. The Dying Buddha.
2. The Hanged Man.
3. The Corpse.

These three recumbent positions are more suitable for repose after meditation than for meditation itself.

CHAPTER THIRTEEN

North Africa

The initiatory experience that occurred late in 1909 on the African continent where Crowley had gone with Victor Neuburg, is very difficult to describe. Perhaps this is why Symonds burlesqued the entire episode in one diminutive chapter of *The Great Beast,* Chapter X, "The Ordeal of Brother Perdurabo." Perhaps this is also why the ordinarily sympathetic Cammell has got so many of his facts altogether topsy-turvy. Neither evidently felt equal to the task, nor understood what really transpired. I too feel far from equal to this prodigious undertaking, and my insights into *The Vision and the Voice,* a colossal apocalyptic series of visions, are still only fragmentary.

The A∴A∴ as instituted by Crowley, was functioning after a manner around the time of this North African experience. There were a few students, a small handful, who had pledged themselves to perform the Great Work, having begun the various practices of Yoga and Magic laid down in the official instructions. One of these probationers was a young man by the name of Victor Neuburg who had just graduated from Cambridge. He was a highly sensitive youth, and a fine poet according to Cammell. After having read Neuburg's *Rosa Ignota,* I can well believe it. Of course the Crowley influence is apparent, but the poem shows great promise independently of his mentor's magical touch. Of Jewish stock, he came from a good family that had both wealth and breeding. What the innermost problems were that hurled him towards the great Quest, I do not know. But he found his way to Crowley, with whom he experienced the heights and the depths. Cammell who also knew Neuburg presents a remarkable description and has some interesting things to say about him.

"Neuburg's appearance was certainly a surprise to me," avers Cammell when first meeting him in London, in 1930, after corresponding with him for some time. "I had thought the woodcut portrait, drawn by himself for frontispiece to his book *Larkspur,* was a fantasy; but as far as the figure was concerned it was true to life; the head, of course, was a caricature. Neuburg was small, dishevelled and gnome-like. I believe he was one of those faery-people imprisoned in a human body whom Maurice Hewlett wrote about in that wonderful book *Lore of Proserpine.* His head and face were powerful and impressive, with strongly marked Jewish features; his genius was manifest . . . .

"It was Captain Fuller who introduced Neuburg to Crowley. Neuburg was then at Trinity, Cambridge, about to take an Honours degree in languages Medieval and Modern. He was, too, a brilliant classical scholar . . . . The impression he had made on Crowley at first acquaintance was very curious. Through arrogant, already over-sophisticated eyes, Crowley saw Neuburg as a naive, callow youth, innocent and ignorant of his (Crowley's) vaunted Knowledge of Good and Evil. At the same time he recognized, by that gift of intuition on which he so much prided himself, and which was not infrequently inaccurate, that this youth possessed genius, and twofold genius—a genius for poetry and a genius for magic."

Cammell then describes how Neuburg, after his graduation from Cambridge, went off to Paris with Crowley and there was deliberately debauched, disillusioned of his brightest dreams, had his highest ideals destroyed, and robbed of any real happiness or self-respect for the rest of his life. All this

Crowley did "while assuring himself and others with that unparalleled sophistry which was his peculiar weapon, that he did it for Neuburg's good, and that by vitiating him he was fortifying his soul. To my mind this was one of the worst actions of Crowley's life."

Cammell makes me think of the prig, of the Victorian moralist, the superior snob who passes judgement when he is incapable of perceiving the motivating facts. I will not question any or all of Cammell's allegations. Yet, it must be obvious that it takes two to make and perpetuate a homosexual relationship.

"How or why Neuburg endured Crowley is to me a mystery; but Neuburg's courage was not in tune with his genius, and neither his physical nor his moral strength commensurate with his intellectual power."

Neuburg endured Crowley because he *needed* Crowley. It was as simple as that. It has absolutely nothing whatsoever to do with cowardice. In a symbiotic relationship, one partner contributes something, and the other takes. And this relationship is never static; it is always reciprocal. Masochist has need of the sadist, and the sadist needs the masochist. Unconscious emotional factors, whatever they were, forced Neuburg into the maintenance of the relationship. And this is not to condemn him, by any manner or means. I personally can honestly and sincerely say—there but for the grace of God! Few of us really know what we are like in the depths. Sometimes it takes a shattering experience for us to become aware of the monsters that lurk within—demons or gods, as the case may be.

Neuburg's contact with Crowley was shattering, I am sure, and on this basis alone I can deeply sympathize with him. I know what it was like to be in the atmosphere of this man. But in this instance the fault is not wholly Crowley's. In some measure Neuburg had to be a willing partner in whatever occurred between them, sexually, socially and spiritually.

Many of the "facts" used in Cammell's book are erroneous. Crowley's preparation relative to the Enochian system started ten years earlier in 1899, because it was an intrinsic part of the Adeptus Minor curriculum of the Golden Dawn. There were several documents describing in great detail the Enochian Tablets, the attributions of the Qabalah and the Tarot to each square of the Tablets, and the complex methods by means of which each minute attribution was engineered. The Tablets are mentioned, but nothing more, in each one of the Grade Rituals. The perceptive student would have been able to see the Tablets on the wall when he was in the Temple. As part of the Adeptus Minor curriculum, Crowley had studied them intensively with Allan Bennett—at least intellectually. He had acquired a solid grasp of the principles of the Enochian scheme long before he left for Mexico.

It has already been laid down in an earlier chapter that while in Mexico in 1900 he attempted to obtain a series of visions based on the Enochian formulae, but was thwarted in that endeavor for one reason or another. His own explanation was that he had not yet acquired the necessary grade of magical maturity or spiritual growth to enter such exalted levels of consciousness represented by the Thirty Aethyrs. Only two visions were obtained, pretty obscure and inconsequential at that, and then he went off to other things. He used some of the Enochian formulae in other of his ceremonies from time to time, but never attempted to complete the Thirty Aethyr project until he went to Algiers with Victor in that year, 1909. But the Enochian system was an intrinsic part of his make-up long before then.

The Golden Dawn left its marks indelibly on his poetry. A number of these poems, dealing quite openly with magical themes, were written during his close association with Allan. A couple included renditions of some of the Enochian calls or invocations into verse. For example, one of these is to be

found in "The Temple of the Holy Ghost" in Volume One of
the *Collected Works*; it is entitled "The Athanor". In Volume
Two, "Invocation", to which I have already made several
references, contains several lines in the Enochian tongue.
Immediately prior to it in the book called "Oracles" is
another poem entitled "Call of the Sylphs". This is a
rendering from the archaic English translation by Dr. John
Dee from the original Enochian:

> Behold, I am; a circle on whose hands
> The twelvefold Kingdom of my Godhead stands.
> Six are the mighty seats of living breath,
> The rest sharp sickles, or the horns of death,
> Which are, and are not, save in mine own power.
> Sleep they? They rise at mine appointed hour.
> I make ye stewards in the primal day.
> And set your thrones in my celestial way.
> I gave ye power above the moving time
> That all your vessels to my crown might climb.
> From all your corners of your fortress caves
> Ye might invoke me, and your wise conclaves
> Should pour the fires of increase, life and birth,
> Continual dewfall to the thirsty earth.
> Thus are ye made of Justice and of Truth,
> The sound of Fury, and the Lords of Ruth.
> In His great Name, your God's, I say, arise!
> Behold! His mercies murmur in the skies.
> His Name is mighty in us to the end.
> In Him we cry: Move, answer, and descend!
> Apply yourselves to us; arise! For why?
> We are the Wisdom of your God most high!

This rendition of one of the Calls was written long prior to
the African expedition, perhaps in the neighborhood of
1901-1902. Quite clearly, then, this disposes of the notion
that he first began to study the Enochian system in North
Africa. At the time of his trip there with Neuburg, he was
already an old hand at the game.

"The history of the book" wrote Cammell of Meric Casaubon's volume *A True and Faithful Relation of What passed for many Years Between Dr. John Dee and Some Spirits, etc.*, "and of its authors is curious, and considering the effect of its relevations on Crowley, peculiarly interesting. Henceforth, not only Crowley's Magic, but his entire Philosophy, was coloured and largely transformed by his study of Dee."

This again is only partly true. It is largely untrue insofar as Cammell and other similar biographers have not realized that the John Dee-Edward Kelly system was incorporated into the Golden Dawn system by Mathers, or whoever it was that inspired Mathers to write the original documents for that Order. Whoever is unfamiliar with the Golden Dawn system simply cannot realize that the Dee-Kelly system, otherwise known as the Enochian system, was the crown and glory of the Golden Dawn. It served as the medium of synthesis for every little bit of teaching of any kind that the Order possessed. Everything was attributed to the Enochian Tablets. And when I say everything, I mean that literally.

Regardless of what phase of the Golden Dawn teaching was available, it was synthesized into the Enochian system with a fine touch so that it took its own place as an integral part of a colossal structure. As expanded by the genius of the Golden Dawn, the original simple Dee-Kelly system was soon lost amidst a host of comparative occult materials that neither of these two people knew anything about. They would never have recognized their petty system, as they had obtained it during the Elizabethan days, in the extraordinary structure that was erected on it by the Golden Dawn.

The following data is taken from an essay I wrote some thirty years ago to serve as an Introduction to the Enochian System that was published in Volume IV of *The Golden Dawn.* I am reproducing much of it here in this place because it will help to render intelligible much of the discussion that follows:

There was a considerable mass of detailed and highly complex instruction on this subject, contained in a number of documents. There are in my possession manuscripts totalling at least 70,000 words, besides some large charts, diagrams and coloured boards . . . . Because it is a synthetic amalgamation of all the Order Work, the student will find it necessary and imperative to have made himself thoroughly familiar with all the other items of knowledge taught by the Golden Dawn. He must know his Tarot and Geomantic attributions so well that the names, symbols and ideas are all at his finger tips—this, naturally, in addition to the basic knowledge items of the Hebrew Alphabet, Tree of Life, and the Qabalah generally. The formulae of practical Magic derived from the Z documents, dealing with the symbolism of the Candidate, the Temple, and the Ceremony of the Neophyte Grade, will require to be not only memorized and known, but understood. The student will need to be perfectly acquainted with the Pentagram and Hexagram Rituals, the formulae of the Consecration Ceremonies, the general art of invocation and formulating Telesmatic Images, and drawing Sigils . . . .

Very little is known about the origin of these Tablets and the invocations that accompany their use. Practically nothing was said in the Order which explained this matter, though in the Adeptus Minor Ritual it is said that Christian Rosenkreutz and his immediate colleagues, whose supposed date is *circa* 1400 A.D., transcribed some "of the magical language, which is that of the Elemental Tablets." So far as we are able to make out, however, the System originated by means of the ceremonial skrying of Dr. John Dee and Sir Edward Kelly towards the close of the 16th century. The original diaries of Dr. John Dee, recording the development of the system, may be found in Sloane Mss. 3189-3191 in the British Museum. But this stands out very clearly, that in these diaries is a rudimentary scheme which bears only the most distant relation to

the extraordinarily developed system in use by the
Order. Whoever was responsible for the Order scheme of
the Angelic Tablets—whether it was Mathers and
Westcott or the German Rosecrucian Adepts from
whom the former are supposed to have obtained their
knowledge—was possessed of an ingenuity and an
understanding of Magic such as never was in the
possession either of Dee or Kelly.

Some of the Order clairvoyants have claimed that Dee
and Kelly in some way obtained access to the
construction of the Enochian system whilst they were in
Central Europe. It is claimed that numerous Rosicrucian
centres existed in Germany, Austria, and Bohemia, and
both Dee and Kelly were received therein. Whilst this
may be a plausible theory, there is not the least vestige
of objective evidence for this assumption. Still others
have believed that it represents a revival of certain
species of Atlantean Magic, though those who press this
theory do not explain the Dee diaries, nor his account
of the method he and Edward Kelly employed to
acquire the roots of this system.

Roughly, the facts which are concerned with the
origins of the system are these. Over one hundred large
squares filled with letters were obtained by Dee and
Kelly in a manner which we cannot quite determine.
*(Cammell suggests that altogether apart from Kelly's
clairvoyance and use of the Crystal, there was "Direct
Voice" communication. This may have been altogether
possible.*—I.R.) When working, Dee, for example, would
have before him on a writing table one or more of these
Tables, as a rule 49" x 49", some full while others were
lettered only on alternate squares. Then Sir Edward
Kelly would sit down at what they called the Holy
Table on which were various magical pentacles, and
which also rested on wax seals. On this Table was a large
Crystal or Shewstone, in which, after a while, he
reported to see an Angel who would point with a wand
to letters on certain charts in succession. Kelly would
thereupon report to Dee that the Angel pointed, for
example, to column 4, rank 29, of one of the many
charts, and so on, apparently not mentioning the letter,

which Dee would then find on the table before him, and
write it down. When the Angel had finished his
instructions, the message—when it concerned certain of
the major invocations or Calls—was rewritten
backwards. It had been dictated in reverse by the Angel
since it was considered too dangerous to communicate
in a straightforward manner, each word being so
powerful a conjuration that its direct pronunciation or
dictation would have evoked powers and forces not
desired at that moment . . . .

The Outer Order rituals state, when the Tablets are
pointed out in the Temple to the Candidate, that they
are written in "what our Tradition calls the Angelic
Secret Language." . . . . This Angelic Secret Language,
whatever its origin, is a true language. It has, quite
clearly, a syntax and grammar of its own, and the
invocations in that language are not mere strings of
words, but sentences which can be translated, not
simply transliterated into English . . . .

D.D.C.F. says in his *Notanda* to *The Book of the
Concourse of the Forces,* that "the Tablets of Enoch
require in truth many years of study, and will repay
such an expenditure of time and energy. The knowledge
embodied in this manuscript is very superficial and
elementary, and entirely fails to do justice to the
Enochian scheme. You must take it as only a feeble
attempt to provide what is seen at first glance, by the
intellect, and as having no relation to the world of
Spiritual Truth which the Tablets enshrine and which a
high adept can make them give out."

Again, I assert, this elaborate Golden Dawn system became
part of Crowley's own inner world. It was an intrinsic part of
his psyche, bequeathed to him by both George Cecil Jones
and Allan Bennett. What he did with it, however, was
something else again. He carried it further than even the
Golden Dawn principals had envisaged. I know of nothing
within the Order documentary that even hints at the kind of
visionary and spiritual experience that Crowley managed to

get out of it.

It is not quite true therefore to say that Crowley's entire philosophy and magic was colored and transformed by Dr. John Dee. This is a superficial viewpoint—indeed it is only a half truth. More properly it could be said that Crowley's philosophy and Magic was essentially that of the Golden Dawn which, with his genius and adventuring spirit, he transformed creatively even as the Golden Dawn had transformed the original material of Dee and Kelly.

The Golden Dawn documents describe the invocations in the original Enochian tongue, give the English translation, and provide full instruction in their pronunciation. Basically, each letter of the Enochian alphabet was pronounced as if it were in Hebrew. Crowley's own document in *Equinox VII* merely repeats the Golden Dawn instructions.

Despite Cammell's statement that Crowley had discovered the true pronunciation of the Enochian language and that he (Cammell) had heard Crowley recite in that manner of solemn and sonorous intonation that he called "the Magical Voice", Crowley in reality possessed a thin, effeminate, rather squeaky voice. This was one of the most obvious areas where his homosexual components emerged. I would never have thought that his was a strong masculine voice, capable of booming out a sonorous invocation.

What was most important about Neuburg for Crowley was that the former apparently possessed some mediumistic ability. "Crowley had seen Neuburg from the first in the role of Sir Edward Kelly playing to his own role of Doctor Dee" surmises Cammell. This may well be.

> Let us endeavour to picture Crowley as he then was—this strange, dauntless, terrible man (sic!), turbaned and robed as the Moors are, thickly bearded, and sun-scorched to the hue of the desert-dwellers, striding forward, mile after mile, beneath the pitiless blaze of the African sun, over the eternal sand of the vast silent

> Sahara . . . . When travelling in the character of a
> wandering wizard, he actually disguised Neuburg as a
> familiar Djinn or Demon, shaving his head save for two
> tufts of hair which he twisted into horns, and leading
> him about on a chain. With his own formidable
> appearance in Eastern attire and a demon in leash, it is
> not surprising that the enchanter Crowley commanded
> the respect of the superstitious Arabs.

This does sound like Crowley, with the combination of his
sense of humor, exhibitionism, and sadism all rolled into one.
Neuburg as the victim put up with this nonsense mainly, I
could readily assume, because he was the devoted disciple
and Crowley the guru, and because he did not dare object too
strenuously by virtue of his great inner need for Crowley.
The paradoxical ingredient of Crowley's egocentric
exhibitionism lent a vivid hue to this scene, and must have
pleased Crowley enormously.

Whatever it was about this psychic ability possessed by
Neuburg, it must have stimulated Crowley's psychism
enormously. He was never particularly psychic; perhaps this
is why in later years he strained so much to train or develop
his women to be seers for him. But in North Africa, his vision
opened up fantastically. Whether this was due to the close
proximity of Neuburg, or the immediate result of all the hard
magical work he had only recently completed, is difficult to
say.

> As he advances, he recites in Arabic from the Koran
> to prepare his mind to receive the Vision. A thousand
> and one times each day during this march, Crowley
> recited the holy verses, and after every recitation he
> prostrated himself upon the burning sand.

It was only in the 9th Aethyr that he was specifically
instructed to do thus. There is no evidence that there was this
preparation for any of the preceding several Aires or Aethyrs.

It was Crowley's ability to play this role that led me to feel
some time ago that in this respect he had very much in

common with Shri Ramakrishna. He too was willing to experiment with every religious form, no matter what. Just as he had formerly experimented with Yoga and Western ritual Magic, and Buddhist meditation and Tantra, he now attempted to work with Mohammedan methods. It makes little difference basically whether he did this because he was commanded in the Vision to do so, or because he felt it would profoundly impress the superstitious Arabs about him and who would thus leave Victor and him severely alone. Either way, it was heroic behavior. Anyone who doubts it ought to try any one of these methods for a short period of time.

It is not at all clear what prompted him originally to resume work with this part of the Enochian system. His trip to Algiers with Victor was not at first, or at least not consciously, motivated by the desire to complete unfinished business. But at Aumale, as Crowley puts it dramatically, a Hand suddenly smote lightning into his heart, and he knew that now, that very day, he must take up the task where he had left it in Mexico in 1900. Parallel to this, it is also possible that he had in his ruck-sack one of his earliest notebooks where he had copied with infinite patience the Enochian calls or Keys that the Order had given him. This was part of an established set of habits with him.

It was then at Aumale, that he prepared to commence once more the investigations of these Aethyrs. Accordingly he bought a number of notebooks. The plan was simply that he would skry and Victor would record the dictation. After dinner, on the 23rd of November, 1909, he invoked the 28th Aethyr by means of the appropriate Call or invocation. When the result was compared with those of the 29th and 30th Aethyrs previously obtained, there were exhibited the same apocalyptic peculiarities of subject and style. This was true also of the succeeding ones. Yet there is a continuous advance towards coherence both in each Aethyr itself, and as regards its neighbor. The subject shows solemnity and sublimity as well as the tendency to fit in with those magnificent conceptions of the cosmos, those mystic laws of Nature and ideas of transcendental Truth which had already been foreshadowed in the more exalted trances Crowley had experienced prior to this date.

The method of obtaining *The Vision and The Voice* was as follows. Crowley had with him a large golden topaz (set in a Calvary Cross of six squares, made of wood, and painted vermilion) which was engraved with a Greek Cross of five squares charged with the Rose of 49 petals. Again, let me reiterate, this is all sound Golden Dawn procedure and symbolism; but he had made it all his very own. He held this Cross, as a rule, in his hand. After choosing a spot where he was not likely to be disturbed he would take this stone and recite the Enochian Call. When satisfied that the forces invoked were actually present, he made the topaz play a part not unlike that of the looking glass in the case of Alice. In short, it was a focus for concentration, and he used it like a crystal.

In the book *Magick* where he describes the technique of skrying or travelling in the Body of Light, he wrote pertinent to the above description: "With a little practise, especially if you have a good Guru, you ought to be able to slip in and out of your astral body as easily as you slip in and out of a dressing-gown. It will then no longer be so necessary for your astral body to be sent far off; without moving an inch you will be able to 'turn on' its eyes and ears—as simply as the man with the microscope can transfer his complete attention from one eye to the other."

He had long ago learned not to trouble himself to travel to any particular place in his Body of Light. He realized that Space was not a thing-in-itself, but merely a convenient category (one of many such) by reference to which we can distinguish objects from each other. Space and time are predicated on subjective factors.

Having done this, he would then describe audibly what he saw and repeat what he heard. Victor would write down his dictated words and incidentally observe any phenomena which struck him as peculiar. For instance, Crowley would at times pass into a deep silent trance so that many minutes might pass between two successive sentences, as indicated in the text.

So Crowley the Seer and Neuburg the Scribe walked steadily through the Sahara desert, invoking the Aethyrs, one by one, at convenient times and places, or when the Spirit moved them. As a rule, one Aethyr was obtained every day. By the time Bou-Saada was reached, and they had arrived at the 20th Aethyr, Crowley began to understand that these visions were, so to speak, cosmopolitan. They brought all systems of magical doctrine into harmonious relation. The rich symbolism of the Asiatic cults, the ideas of the Qabalah both Jewish and Greek; the arcana of the Gnostics and of ancient Khem, and so on. All systems of mysticism and religion including the code of the Book of the Law, fell into their proper place without the slightest tendency to quarrel. He was actually continuing along the line that was originally initiated by the Golden Dawn, a line he had intellectually pursued throughout the years, and which he independently recorded in the book 777. Now, the intellectual faculties were not involved. This was spiritual *experience.*

Apart from the first two minor visions obtained in Mexico, there were 28 more obtained in the Desert, making a total of thirty. Too much time would be consumed in analyzing or discussing each one; nor do I feel equal to this task. Crowley's own text and his Commentary, in the form of footnotes made years afterwards, need to be consulted. There are aspects of two or three of them, however, that should be mentioned as necessary sequels to the ordeals and attainment of three years earlier. At that time, in China, he had demonstrated to himself experientially the fatuity and futility of the intellect and its total inability to solve the great problems of existence. As a result of this he was plunged into the Abyss from which he was rescued by the Augoeides invocations pursued all through the year 1906, culminating in Samadhi. It was then that he laid claim to the grade of 8=3, though paradoxically refusing to accept it. Some of the events associated with certain of the Aethyrs resulted in a recapitulation of the transcendental experience of the crossing of the Abyss with its destruction of the character armor which distorted whatever the ego was, and his emergence as a full 8=3, a Magister Templi. It is with this phase of the visions that I propose to deal.

A few words of preliminary explanation, however, are required at this juncture. Since the Visions speak of Angels and other beings, I feel we ought to let Crowley's own writing explain what he means by these. In one essay, dealing with divination, he wrote: "We postulate the existence of intelligences, either within or without the diviner, of which he is not immediately conscious. (It does not matter to the theory whether the communicating spirit so-called is an objective entity or a concealed portion of the diviner's mind.)"

In his textbook *Magick,* he enlarged on this topic, in these words:

> We may consider all beings as parts of ourselves, but it is more convenient to regard them as independent. Maximum Convenience is our canon of "Truth". We must thus refer psychical phenomena to the intention of "Astral" Beings, without committing ourselves to any theory. Coherence is the sole quality demanded of us.
>
> Magic enables us to receive sensible impressions of worlds other than the "physical" universe (as generally understood by profane science). These worlds have their own laws; their inhabitants are often of quasi-human intelligence; there is a definite set of relations between

certain "ideas" of ours and their expressions, and certain types of phenomena. (Thus, symbols, the Qabalah, etc., enable us to communicate with whom we choose.)

"Astral" beings possess knowledge and power of a different kind from our own; their "universe" is presumably of a different kind from ours, in some respects. (Our idea "bone" is not the same as a dog's; a short-sighted man sees things differently to one of normal vision.) It is *more convenient* to assume the objective existence of an "Angel" who gives us new knowledge than to allege that our invocation has awakened a supernormal power in ourselves.[1]

In the 19th Aethyr, the emphasis is on death and destruction, presaging for him the crossing of the Abyss, and planting firmly in his spirit the true meaning of the word Nirvana as annihilation of the ego.

Now then at last cometh forth the Angel of the Aethyr, who is like the Angel of the fourteenth key of Rota, with beautiful blue wings, blue robes, the sun in her girdle like a brooch, and the two crescents of the moon shapen into sandals for her feet. Her hair is of flowing gold, each sparkle as a star. In her hands are the torch of Penelope and the cup of Circe.

She comes and kisses me on the mouth, and says: Blessed art thou who hast beheld Sebek my Lord in his glory. Many are the champions of life, but all are unhorsed by the lance of death. Many are the children of the light, but their eyes shall be put out by the Mother of Darkness. Many are the servants of love, but love (that is not quenched by aught but love) shall be put out, as the child taketh the wick of a taper between his thumb and finger, by the god that sitteth alone . . . . I am the Angel of the moon. I am the veiled one that sitteth between the pillars veiled with a shining veil, and on my lap is the open Book of the mysteries of the ineffable Light. I am the aspiration unto the higher; I am the love of the unknown; I am the blind ache

within the heart of man. I am the minister of the
sacrament of pain. I swing the censer of worship, and I
sprinkle the waters of purification. I am the daughter of
the house of the Invisible. I am the Priestess of the
Silver Star.

And she catches me up to her as a mother catches her
babe, and holds me up in her left arm, and sets my lips
to her breast. And upon her breast is written: *Rosa
Mundi est Lilium Coeli.*

We can, if we wish, see a glorified Oedipus complex in
operation here. The return of the repressed. His infantile
incestuous fantasies about mother, having been hidden away
under the weight of massive defenses of every kind, burst
through in full force. This is a valid line of interpretation, and
I see no objection to it. However, it explains but little. The
archetypal notion of Jung relative to the Great Mother and
the process of rebirth is a bit more explicit but still leaves
much to be desired.

I have grown greater, so that I am as great as the
Angel. And we are standing, as if crucified, face to face,
our hands and lips and breasts and knees and feet
together, and her eyes pierce into my eyes like whirling
shafts of steel, so that I fall backwards headlong through
the Aethyr—and there is a sudden and tremendous
shout absolutely stunning cold and brutal: Osiris was a
black god! And the Aethyr claps its hands, greater than
the peal of a thousand mighty thunders.

I am back.

We could pursue the oedipal interpretation, and give Osiris
the significance of the father, the father of Horus. He is
black, the color of death. Death is the sequel to all the
infantile fantasies of incest, and only repression can seal up
this dreadful knowledge of one's childhood. But repression or
no, death and violence haunted him for all of his life, from
the time of the childhood fantasy to the date of the vision. It

is significant of course, but hardly enough to warrant its climactic effect on him.

The footnote made by Crowley to the statement that Osiris was a black God is eloquent:

> This, to the Seer at that time, was revelation of the most appalling terror. The doctrine of the Third Order had not been promulgated. He expected to unite with the Great Mother in a Mode similar to that experienced in attaining to the Knowledge and Conversation of the Holy Guardian Angel. But the attainment of the Grade of Magister Templi involves the Annihilation of the aspirant. "Osiris was a black god"; i.e. of the nature of Binah—BLACK. The love of Binah is that of the Queen Scorpion who devours her mate. This revelation therefore, was much as if a romantic lover were suddenly made fully aware that the Maiden of his Dreams intended to conclude their first night of love by a Breakfast, of which he was to form the staple dish! The Doctrine implied is that one must not be the child, but the Mother.

Even Crowley's own interpretation stresses the overwhelmingly obvious fact that death awaited him. It was not an actual physical demise, but something which though more subtle was nonetheless real and overwhelming and perhaps even more devastating. It represents the annihilation of all that one is. It is a premonition of the passing of the ordeal of the Abyss, the extinction, like the blowing out of the candle, of the ego. It betokened the end of separate existence, the beginning of a Life that belonged to all. This is confirmed in the 14th Aethyr, where, after entering the vision, he perceived:

> Now the veil of darkness is formed of a very great number of exceedingly fine black veils, and one tears them off one at a time. And the voice says, There is no light or knowledge or beauty or stability in the

Kingdom of the Grave, whither thou goest. And the worm is crowned. All that thou wast hath he eaten up, and all that thou art is his pasture until tomorrow. And all that thou shall be is nothing. Thou who wouldst enter the domain of the Great One of the Night of Time, this burden must thou take up. Deepen not a superficies.

Here he is given further dramatic intimations of the goal he has all unconsciously been aiming at. From the beginning of his mystical career, he was striving for some more or less immortal medium of expression, something that would last beyond the mere span of years of a human lifetime. An achievement that future generations could point to, and say "this was the work of Aleister Crowley." The shock would be beyond description and verbalization to learn that though one aimed at the heights, the grave, literally, was the end.

There is an interesting philosophical footnote that he has provided to the angelic injunction not to deepen a superficies. He wrote: "It is useless to seek the soul of things beneath their surface; for their surface is their soul." This is the acme of the highest conceptualizations of Zen. Reality is appearance, and appearance is reality.

To end his struggles in this particular vision, he was warned to depart; this was in the mid-afternoon in the desert near Bou-Saada. He did not attempt to get back into the Aethyr until late that night. It must have shaken him to the core. And again, as premonitory of the fact that he was perceiving his own ego destruction, the Vision re-opens:

The blackness gathers about, so thick, so clinging, so penetrating, so oppressive, that all the other darkness that I have ever conceived would be like bright light beside it."

From here on out, all that was heard, perceived and sensed

in other ways was ominous, portentous, and prophetic. Every symbol and metaphoric phrase uttered by the Angel of the Aethyr foretells of doom, death and sorrow. These are all attributions of Saturn, of Binah, the dark night, of the Supernals that are above the Abyss, where no man can enter and yet emerge a man.

> Thou hast entered the night; dost thou yet lust for the day? Sorrow is my name and affliction. I am girt about with tribulation . . . . the light of the sun shall not shine upon thee, and the moon shall not lend thee of her lustre, and the stars shall be hidden, because thou art passed beyond these things, beyond the need of these things, beyond the desire of these things . . . .

Then followed what completely bowled him over, so completely unexpected was it in terms of his previous mystical frame of reference.

> What I thought were shapes of rocks, rather felt than seen, now appear to be veiled Masters, sitting absolutely still and silent. Nor can anyone be distinguished from the others.
>
> And the Angel sayeth: Behold where thine Angel hath led thee! Thou didst ask fame, power and pleasure, health and wealth and love, and strength and length of days. Thou didst hold life with eight tentacles, like an octopus. Thou didst seek the four powers and the seven delights and the twelve emancipations and the two and twenty Privileges and the nine and forty Manifestations, and lo! thou art become as one of These. Bowed are their backs, whereon resteth the Universe. Veiled are their faces, that have beheld the glory ineffable.
>
> These adepts seem like Pyramids—their hoods and robes are like Pyramids.
>
> And the Angel sayeth: Verily is the Pyramid a Temple of Initiation. Verily also is it a tomb. Thinkest thou that there is life within the Masters of the Temple, that sit hooded, encamped upon the Sea? Verily, there

is no life in them.

Again, there are some subtle Golden Dawn constituents here. In the Enochian system, each square of each elemental Tablet has a variety of attributions. To each is attributed a Tarot card, a Geomantic symbol, an element and an astrological quality. Thus there are four sides, making the four sides of a pyramid. But to complete the symbol, the apex of the pyramid is truncated to permit the attribution of the 5th element, Akasa, which was presaged in the grade of the Portal of the Vault of the Adepts.

In the Enochian documents later given to the Adeptus Minor, there is a comprehensive symbolism and practical magical system allocated to this pyramid. On the top of each pyramid is attributed an Egyptian God to represent the fifth element. The enterprising student was supposed to make little cardboard models of this scheme, in full color, so that before attempting to enter the pyramid by means of psychological identification and skrying in the spirit vision, he would be enabled to see it objectively before him. Within the pyramid, would be a Sphinx of elaborate symbolism.

But this Aethyr that Crowley was investigating now presented a novel but devastatingly new symbol. The pyramid was a tomb. His tomb!

I must again cast attention back to the theme of the beginning of Crowley's adventuring in the Golden Dawn system. Before he was admitted, he had written to Waite for counsel and advice. Waite, doing more than he himself bargained for, recommended the reading of Von Eckartshausen's *The Cloud Upon the Sanctuary*. It was in this text that Crowley was first introduced to the idea of a Secret School of Adepts, of holy Saints, of Secret Chiefs of the Order to which he aspired, guardians who watched over the destiny of mankind. It was his holiest aspiration to become one of their members, to be admitted to their sacred school. All through the Golden Dawn years, this had been the guiding star of his aspiration. As he became more sophisticated, the vision dimmed a little; eventually it was discarded, as we have already seen, as fanciful and unreal.

Here, in this Aethyr, he was suddenly confronted with the same idea, but with a somewhat different interpretation. These Chiefs were indeed part of a great School, but the students were those whose ego had been annihilated, and where the Teacher was Death itself. And now finally he had been admitted to this Assembly, where the credentials of admission were the evidence of his own decease. Nothing that he had experienced previously had prepared him for this. Not even his temporary insanity in China! Nor the passage through the Abyss by the Augoeides invocation that had followed hard upon this mind-shattering ordeal.

Time was given him to regain some composure. The following vision showed that he who had passed through the Abyss was given a new name, Nemo—no man! His spirit was mingled with the One Life; the dewdrop had slipped into the Shining Sea, or vice versa. Nemo had a specific work to do, of teaching, and preparing others for this ordeal also. This was described by the warden of the vision.

In the next Aethyr, an entirely new series of concepts appeared, revolving around the symbolism of the Beast and Babalon. The old Biblical spelling of Babylon was dropped; the newer spelling having a special numerical meaning for him. It revolved primarily around what is called in the Eastern Tantra system the Sakti-Shiva doctrine. That the goddess Sakti, universal energy from which the whole universe is evolved, is locked in a momentary but eternal sexual embrace with her consort Shiva, intelligence and spirit. It is a variation of the Sankhya dualism, of Prakriti and Purusha, matter-energy and Spirit. These are eternally conjoined. It is from their orgastic union that all things in the universe, on every plane, are formed. Momentary and eternal sexual embrace—for beyond the level of the Abyss in a time-transcending order, there is no time or space as we know them. The evolutionary process which has taken billions of years in our formal modes of intellection are but a fragment of time beyond. It is the ecstasy of union, which we in the realm of duality interpret as billions of years.

But Babalon as the personification of infinite energy, as Sakti, is pictured here for Crowley, who was born with and bred upon the Bible, as the Scarlet Woman.

> The voice continues: This is the Mystery of Babalon, the Mother of Abominations, and this is the mystery of her adulteries, for she hath yielded up herself to everything that liveth, and hath become a partaker in its mystery. And because she hath made herself the servant of each, therefore is she become the mistress of all. Not as yet canst thou comprehend her glory . . . . And the Angel sayeth: Blessed are the saints, that their blood is mingled in the cup, and can never be separate any more.

This intimation Crowley has always interpreted along purely Vedanta lines. The small human ego symbolized by the blood which is the life of the organism, is given up and mingled with the Universal Life, the Atman. *Separation is the heresy which has to be overcome.* Not by thinking, not by feeling, but by direct spiritual experience, the experience of psychically dying to be reborn. This Crowley had experienced in the China episode. Now he was to go through it again. He had been through it once, but he was to re-experience the challenge of the disintegration of the mind through the evocation of Choronzon, the demon of the Abyss, whose symbol is dispersion.

However, there are two important footnotes comprising the Crowley commentary that should be quoted here as explanatory of the experience of these Aethyrs:

> The Magister Templi is a little pyramid of dust in the

City of the Pyramids awaiting the Fire that shall burn him up to a white ash. But the original combination of Sankharas (tendencies—the elements of the character of the man) is void of the Ego. Ahamkara (the ego-making faculty) has been assimilated. The Sankharas are, however, still linked by the Karma of the Adept; for they had to be most strongly knit by him that he might be able to concentrate their whole Energies upon the Great Work of abandoning in a single gesture "all that he had and all that he is". They accordingly hold together; his Will has been accomplished, and he is free from them; but they depend upon the Elements which compose that true Will, which, *since he has succeeded,* can only be the Sublime Passion for Mankind to help it to "Conquer Space, and lastly climb the walls of Time, and by the Golden Path the great have trod, Reach up to God". A phenomenon of this nature thus appears "as a morning star, or as an evening star, to give light to them that sit in darkness and in the shadow of death." This is then the man himself, save that his separate individuality is no longer present; it is replaced by this single passion to rescue Mankind.

The second footnote was appended to the text where the Seer had mentioned an Angel, but had neglected to mention or describe the entry of the Angel into the Vision. There was also a long period of silence recorded by Neuburg, when quite evidently the Seer had a Samadhic experience.

In this preliminary and so to say, symbolic—crossing of the Abyss, His Holy Guardian Angel comes to the rescue of the Aspirant. Contrast the unspeakable Terror of the actual Crossing, when that Angel Himself abandons the Seer (see 11th Aire, the last paragraph.) Exactly how the Angel dealt with the Seer in this 20 minutes of earthly time is impossible to say; for he has no memory soever—nor had he even at the time—of what took place. We may, however, deduce from that fact that the Communion took place in a sphere beyond even Neschamah. It may well have been a Quintessence of Union sufficiently intimate to have identified the Seer with his Angel so perfectly as to have given him the right to make the passage fully, in every sense; and to have ensured his safety on the way. For the Angel cometh forth from above the Abyss, and dwelleth of right in the Bosom of the Great Mother. But the Angel deals not with the little pile of dust in the City of the Pyramids, (see 14th Aethyr) but with the Star that is cast forth to give light to the Earth.

It was on December 6, 1909, between 2 and 4:15 p.m. in a lonely valley of fine sand, in the desert near Bou-saada that Crowley made preparations then for a magical ceremony in which, in effect, he might pass through the Abyss. The preparations alone for conducting this ceremony must have taken some considerable length of time. A large Circle of rocks and stones had to be constructed in the desert sand, about which had to be traced some of the traditional names of God. Neuburg was seated in the centre of this Circle which was his sole protection against whatever demonic force might be invoked. Again, in traditional form, a relatively large Triangle was traced in the sand *outside* of the Circle, but quite near so that no effort would be needed to talk or hear, if anything or anyone should appear therein. Just as the role of the Circle was to protect the Scribe, so the role of the Triangle was to enclose but restrict the activity of the demonic personification of the Abyss. Around this Triangle, another set of divine names was inscribed.

The question arises as to the nature of the so-called demon Choronzon that is the personification of the Abyss. A footnote of Crowley's develops an interpretation and challenges it at the same time: "It is the personification of a moral idea in a much more far-fetched way than that in which we say 'Venus is the Lady of Love'. For one can imagine Venus as a living individual being, while Choronzon is essentially not any sort of person."

Another footnote provides the explanation that various elements within Crowley had been organized into a kind of bundle by the energy released by the invocation, and thus constituted a temporary being capable of momentary sensation and expression. The obsessing idea of any such being—aware that it is not a true integrated being but a pseudo-person threatened with immediate dissolution upon the completion of the operation—is of necessity fear and dread. From fear, pain and malice and envy are bred. These are the essential components of Choronzon. What further characterizes the latter are impotency in the sense of lack of control, and a tendency to dispersion. At the time, Crowley had no real idea of the psychological nature of the demon, but learned this from the experience itself.

It is the essence of the Abyss. And the essence of the Abyss is always disorganization and lack of coherency, as when the mind breaks down into its component parts later to be re-assembled on an entirely different basis after the Crossing. Choronzon is not a being *per se*.

It would be useful, it seems to me, to compare it with the figures seen in a dream interpreted by Jungian terms. As for example, when a dream depicts activities and characteristics which the analyst calls the Shadow. This is only the personification of the repressed components of the psyche. All the repressed fears and hostilities and fantastic elements that one consciously knows nothing about, that Freud had discovered through his investigation of the Unconscious facets of the psyche, these are the Shadow. If the Shadow is Choronzon, we are really confronted with the old theological idea of the Devil.

Now since Crowley had been brought up on the Bible and lived with it and breathed it for many long years, most of its elements must have persisted in one form or another in his Unconscious. We have already seen that he had long identified himself with the Beast of the Apocalypse. The Scarlet Woman-Babylon has become Babalon, the Sakti of

Hindu philosophy, the symbol of energy that constitutes the heart of all created things. The Beast thus becomes her consort Shiva, with whom she is eternally united in sexual congress. The only missing person is the Devil, who here has returned as the dweller of the Abyss, the symbol of all the fear, malice and destruction that lurked within. Therefore he had to be evoked and brought to visible appearance, since magically and traditionally, this was the means whereby the hidden denizens of the Unconscious could be made known and controlled and used.

Psychoanalysis has something to say about the Devil which may illustrate what Crowley was dealing with here. I am utterly fascinated by the revolutionary concepts enunciated and hinted at by Norman O. Brown in his critique of Freudian analysis *Life Against Death*. This book and Wilhelm Reich's *Function of the Orgasm*, more than any other works, and certainly more than any other specific writing on mysticism, are absolute requisites for any understanding of Crowley. Brown especially makes a considerable effort to bring psychoanalytic understanding to such obscure forces as The Devil, economic values, and to mysticism as well.

Martin Luther's concept of wealth and acquisitiveness as being evidence of bondage to the Devil becomes illuminating from Brown's most penetrating analysis. The mythical archetypes of the race, the Devil being one, say things which are not possible to say in any other way unless psychoanalysis has found a way. Through the archetype of the Devil man has said something about the psychological forces inside himself. These have everything to do with his whole life, his social structure in general, and his economic activity in particular. The Devil is the lineal descendant of the Trickster and the Culture-hero type in primitive mythologies. The Trickster is a projection of the psychological forces sustaining the economic activity of primitive peoples. Brown's evolutionarily tracing him to the Devil himself reveals that Luther's identification of the spirit of capitalism with the Devil draws on the tradition of the Devil as Trickster. For Luther, the Devil is the father of lies, of deceit, of trickery, a robber and thief. And usury is self-evidently, in Luther's eyes, trickery, robbery and theft also.

Freud too has demonstrated at great length that in the dreams of children, the Devil personifies a great many of their repressed fears and hostilities and power strivings relative to father. Just as an old aphorism says the Devil is the Reverse of God, so psychoanalytically we could say that the Devil is the "opposite" of the father whom one knows. The "opposite" contains those father elements that we do not wish to know, that we once repudiated and dissociated in order to survive as children. Though repudiated, these psychic elements persist in the Unconscious areas of the psyche, unknown and unsuspected, but influencing and directing our lives nonetheless.

What Crowley therefore was attempting to do was to evoke the Devil Choronzon, as the symbolic representation of the repressed father feelings of his childhood, into visible manifestation in order to control and thus to assimilate these hitherto non-assimilable elements of his own makeup. This done, no further need could possibly exist for the maintenance of the character-muscular armor, the entire system of psychic defense-mechanisms. Then the whole facade of neurotic character-structure would collapse, and the Self would be free. It would be free in a sense that is indescribable to ordinary common-sense, which is actually a symptom of the ego or character armor. This freedom could be called Dionysian. It would not be a dream but, to quote Norman Brown, "a drunkenness; not life kept at a distance and seen through a veil but life complete and immediate." Hence, says Nietzsche, "the entire symbolism of the body is called into play, not the mere symbolism of the lips, face, and speech, but the whole pantomime of dancing, forcing every member into rhythmic movement."

The human ego must face the Dionysian reality and therefore a great work of self-transformation lies ahead of it. The Apollonian preserves while the Dionysian destroys self-consciousness. The Dionysian ego would be freed from the limitations of genital organization, and so of the necessity of ridding the organism of generalized sexual cravings and concentrating them in the genital. The Apollonian ego is the ego of the sexual organs. The Dionysian ego would be once more a body-ego, not requiring dissolution in body-rapture. The relation of this notion to Crowley is obvious—but not to John Symonds.

The text of *The Vision and the Voice* is emphatic as to the position of Neuburg, but mysterious as to where Crowley was. All it says is that the Seer "shall retire to a secret place, where is neither sight nor hearing, and sit within his black robe, secretly invoking the Aethyr."

At first reading many years ago, it occurred to me that if Neuburg was employed as a medium, his position would be in the Triangle so that the demon could manifest through him. Crowley would have been in the Circle as the Magus governing the work of art. This had been my impression for many years, mistaken of course.

The question now is, where did Crowley hide himself? The footnote provided by Crowley does not clarify the issue. "The greatest precautions were taken at the time, and have since been yet further fortified, to keep silence concerning the rite of evocation. The Major Adept is warned most seriously against attempting to emulate this Operation, which is (in any case) improper for him to perform. To call forth Choronzon, unless one be wholly above the Abyss, is to ensure the most appalling and immediate catastrophe."

Cammell merely repeats the above without offering anything new when he says "Neuburg entered the circle. Crowley remained without, in a state of trance." Perhaps as we analyse this further we may be able to perceive in detail what really happened.

The text describes the instructions that Crowley gave to Neuburg to protect him from any possibility of disaster. "And let him beware lest he himself lean beyond the circle. And since he reverenceth the Person of the Seer as his Teacher, let the Seer bind him with a great Oath to do this." Neuburg did exactly this, climaxing his oath with: "And I summon mine Holy Guardian Angel to witness this mine oath, the which if I break, may I perish for sake of Him. Amen and Amen."

The Vision and the Voice provides us with the answer in spite of the great precautions which Crowley adopted to keep secret the exact details of the operation.

> Now, then, the Seer being entered within the triangle, let him take the Victims and cut their throats, pouring the blood within the Triangle, and being most heedful that not one drop fall without the Triangle; or else Choronzon should be able to manifest in the universe. And when the sand hath sucked up the blood of the victims, let him recite the call of the Aethyr apart secretly as aforesaid. Then will the Vision be revealed, and the Voice heard.

The victims are not other than three pigeons which they procured for this purpose, the consecration of the Triangle by blood. There is a psychic tradition that speaks of blood as being the perfect medium to facilitate astral materializations. The modern "psychical research" language might be that it releases ectoplasm and energy which the materializing entity can use.

Thus, with blood being available, and Neuburg as the Scribe and the Medium and the Magus who performs the banishing and other rituals, the only secret place where Crowley could be is in the Triangle itself. In other words, by meditating within the Triangle, his invocation would disengage this Devil in himself, which the mediumistic qualities of Neuburg could materialize. It put Crowley in a highly vulnerable position. Some have averred he never recovered.

And so Choronzon was evoked out of Crowley's psyche in the Triangle of the Art. The apparition took many shapes, both human and bestial; now as a fair woman, now as a monster, now with the voice of Crowley but never with his form. All with one end in view, to terrify poor Neuburg, and through him to destroy Crowley. Had the Scribe been unwise enough to pander to this appearance, he would have been torn apart. But this made him aware of the terror that had lurked unseen and unknown in Crowley's own heart, the terror which he had never before realized until now.

But what did really happen here? Was Victor the victim of hallucination? Or did he actually perceive phantoms that were evoked out of Crowley's psyche, and rendered objective or material by the use of blood and incense and ectoplasm? Or did Crowley, out of his mind temporarily, actually attack Neuburg?

The answer to this may never be known. Most critics of course assume that both men were hallucinated, and like any psychotic merely perceived projected psychic materials from the Unconscious levels of their respective psyches. It is a legitimate point of view. The study of any good textbook on psychopathology will provide much material to confirm it.

On the other hand, the study of the proceedings of the psychical research societies in England and in the United States might lend substance to the assumption that materializations do occasionally, if rarely, occur. Most of those duly recorded have occurred during dimly-lit seances, with the classical cabinet in the background. The incident we are considering employed none of the traditional accoutrements of the professional medium. The outdoors was the scene of the materialization. The only cabinet was the Triangle of Art. The substance for the materialization was supplied not by a medium aided by the sitters in the circle, but in this instance by the blood of three pigeons and the combined energies of Crowley and Neuburg.

I feel compelled to place myself on record with the statement that I incline to the latter belief.

In some strange way, Neuburg confessed afterwards, he felt himself protected during this weird rite, and this sense of security prevented his knowing fear. At that time he had not known that "he was wrong in holding much converse with the demon; for Choronzon, in the confusion and chaos of his thought, is much terrified by silence. And by silence can he be brought to obey. For cunningly doth he talk of many things, going from subject to subject, and thus he misleadeth the unwary into argument with him. And though Choronzon be easily beaten in argument, yet, by disturbing the attention of him who would command him, doth he gain the victory. For Choronzon feareth of all things concentration and silence; he therefore who would command him should will in silence; thus is he brought to obey."

After the conclusion of the ceremony, the Circle and Triangle were destroyed. The sand was scrupulously raked over to obliterate any trace of the proceedings, and a great fire was kindled to purify the place. And that was the end of the evocation of the demon of the Abyss.

But apparently poor Neuburg felt he had been taken down to the depths! It is said that he too bore the marks of this magical adventure to the grave. Whether he wrote of this experience or talked about it to his friends, I know not. However, I can well imagine that his equilibrium was brutally disturbed by what had occurred in this lonely stretch of the desert. This kind of experience, painful and disturbing that it was, is not given to any but a few. Whether they be chosen ones or the damned, is a choice that I do not have to make.

The Aethyrs that followed this monstrous Rite were lyrical paeans of joy and gladness. It was as if they commemorated the great victory that had been won in crossing the Abyss and by subduing its sole inhabitant, the Demon Choronzon. If we want to use psychoanalytic symbolism again, we would expect that with the vanquishing of the father, there would emerge, from beneath the now shattered defenses, feelings of joy and triumph to possess the pre-Oedipal Mother. She can now be wholly enjoyed without any fear of the spitefulness and revenge of the father, the monster in the way.

And so it is, for there is a song, repeated in joyful stanza and refrain again and again, welcoming the conquering Hero who has crossed through the dangerous pit. It is the archetypal representation of the theme of the ages, what Campbell has spoken of as the Hero with a Thousand Faces, the Masks of God. Jung has described the event a hundred times, and written of the primordial archetypal images that become awakened during the process of individuation. It is the birth of the Hero. So true is this of the process Crowley describes, that the Master of the Temple passing through the ordeal is called a Babe of the Abyss. And then he had the ecstatic and peaceful vision of the

> Daughter of the King. This is the Virgin of Eternity. This is she that the Holy One hath wrested from the Giant Time, and the prize of them that hath overcome Space. This is she that is set upon the Throne of Understanding. Holy, Holy, Holy is her name, not to be spoken among men. For Kore they have called her, and Malkah, and Betulah, and Persephone . . . .
> This is she that hath bedecked her hair with seven stars, the seven breaths of God that move and thrill its excellence. And she hath tied her hair with seven combs, whereupon are written the seven secret names of God that are not known even of the Angels, or of the Archangels, or of the Leader of the armies of the Lord.

It was in this Aethyr that he was commanded to affirm the unity of God in Mohammedan style, and to bow forehead to sand one thousand and one times to prepare himself for future inner experience. He did this, just as he was commanded.

Each of the remaining Aethyrs are important in themselves but to describe each one, even briefly, and comment on it would expand this book longer than my intention warrants. The text itself needs to be consulted and read; it would be a valuable and enlightening experience.

However, there is one of them that does warrant some attention, and this is the 5th Aethyr obtained near Tolga, in the desert, on December 12, 1909. The vision opens with a view of an avenue of pylons

> steep after steep, carved from solid rock of the mountain; and that rock is a substance harder than diamond, and brighter than light, and heavier than lead. In each pylon is seated a god. There seems an endless series of these pylons. And all the gods of all the nations of the earth are shown, for there are many avenues, all leading to the top of the mountain.

This is another variation of the old notion that all roads lead to Rome. But the important part of this Aethyr is the perception of an altar at the top of the mountain, surrounded by holy men forming a ring.

> I wish to see what is within their ring. One of them bends forward so that I may whisper the pass-word. The Angel prompts me to whisper: "There is no god." So they let me pass, and though there was indeed nothing visible therein, yet there was a very strange atmosphere, which I could not understand . . . .
> As I entered their ring, they bade me stand in their circle, and a weapon was given unto me. And the pass-word that I had given seems to have been whispered round from one to the other, for each one nods gravely as if in solemn acquiescence, until the last one whispers the same words in my ears. But they have a different

sense. I had taken them to be a denial of the existence of God, but the man who says them to me evidently means nothing of the sort. What he does mean I cannot tell at all. He slightly emphasized the word "there."

The following part of the vision is initiatory and ecstatic. In it he came to some understanding of the problem of motion, through the medium of an arrow. "I see that the crown of the Arrow is the Father of all Light, and the shaft of the Arrow is the Father of all Life, and the barb of the Arrow is the Father of all Love . . . . " There was something in this vision that made him shudder and tremble.

> And now there cometh a strange thought: this Arrow is the source of all motion; it is infinite motion, yet it moveth not, so that there *is* no motion. And therefore there is no matter. This Arrow is the glance of the Eye of Shiva. But because it moveth not, the universe is not destroyed. The universe is put forth and swallowed up in the quivering of the plumes of Maat, that are the plumes of the Arrow: but those plumes quiver not . . . .
> Thou canst not believe how marvellous is this vision of the Arrow. And it could never be shut out, except the Lords of Vision troubled the waters of the pool, the mind of the Seer. But they send forth a wind that is a cloud of Angels, and they beat the water with their feet, and little waves splash up—they are memories. For the Seer hath no head; it is expanded into the universe, a vast and silent sea, crowned with the stars of night . . . .

He was in Samadhi; the writing of the experience was left for the next day.

There is a footnote to one of the remaining visions, so apt that I must quote it in order to close this chapter. Crowley wrote: "The last three Aethyrs are so tremendously sublime that comment is only too likely to mar the effect upon the reader. They must be read as masterpieces of Art, and their full magical import apprehended as such. This remark, indeed, applies to the whole series, though not so formidably. The proper way is to study the book in detail, so as to assimilate perfectly its intellectual content, and then to read it (so to say) ceremonially."

Whatever the North African experience is finally reckoned to be, there is little doubt that it had a tremendous effect on the whole course of Crowley's subsequent life. One of the most immediate results was that he was able to lay claim firmly to the formerly achieved grade of 8=3, and soberly assume the responsibility relating to it. He came to accept the mission involved in *The Book of the Law* of disseminating a new moral code for mankind, and also became more willing to assume the role of teacher it had urged upon him.

There was also his Order to attend to, and the matter of his bi-annual publication the *Equinox*. These books were to be the official organ of his Order, to express whatever he had to say and teach. It was the beginning of a short but most important period—lasting through 1914—of high creativity, genuine accomplishment, as though he had finally come into his own.

NOTES

[1] The Master Therion, *op. cit.*, p. 246-47.

PART FOUR DESTINY

When you have proved that God is merely a name for the sex instinct, it appears to me not far to the perception that the sex instinct is God.

—Aleister Crowley

CHAPTER FOURTEEN

Attitudes

By the end of the *Equinox* period, the year 1914, Crowley was to all intents and purposes destitute. He had done an enormous amount of publishing, all in exquisite taste. The cost of printing the books had fallen mainly on his shoulders. Alone, he had borne all the expenses. The *Equinoxes*, one large volume issued twice every year for five years, printed in large type on good paper, must have cost a fortune. Some of his best writing appears in the different issues. Not enough copies were sold at that time however to bring in an adequate revenue. Today, there are still a few unused copies selling at two hundred dollars per set. But it is certain that Crowley obtained little ready money from those publishing ventures. Now all his money was gone. From this period on, he had to live by his wits, getting money where he could, from whom he could. In short, he was now a financial adventurer.

There was little he could do to earn a livelihood. As far as the practical work of this world was concerned he had received absolutely no training that could fit him in any of the worlds of finance, diplomacy, the professions, etc. He could write, of course, and he was a great writer, but nothing that he had ever written brought in any appreciable return. As to getting a job at anything, this was apparently altogether outside of the question. He was an unequivocal Tory. In his code, the English gentleman did not work.

Some of the more faithful disciples cannot believe that this was actually Crowley's attitude, and are indignant when I point out his written evidences. However, the following rationalization taken from a book written in the American episode, *The Gospel According to St. Bernard Shaw,* has this to say on the matter:

> I am bound to say that personally I regard a leisured class as the only possible field for the highest types of wheat to grow. The socialistic idea that everyone should work menially for an hour or so every day would check the entire race. Any mechanical labour degrades; it is necessary that it should be performed, and must therefore always produce a degraded class. To equalize men in this matter is to bring them all down to the level of the dock labourer . . . .
>
> Certainly I never could have arrived even at my present stage if I had to spend a couple of hours a day in cleaning out somebody's drains. For one thing, all the higher kinds of work require a fineness and delicacy both of manual and mental energy such that a life of leisure is absolutely necessary to their proper functioning.

Sometime during World War I, in New York, he did act as editor of the pro-German periodical *The International.* The salary derived from this, however, was negligible. A few dollars came along from disciples and devotees, from a member or two of the A∴A∴—and that was all.

He must have been truly devastated at first to realize that he was virtually penniless. True, there were prophecies in some of his more "inspired" writings relative to "a rich man from the West," but he really could not count on this, though a great deal of effort was expended in trying to fit one individual or another into the framework of this prophecy. He was stuck with a large stock of books, which sold in driblets only.

"That which he says of Mathers," wrote Cammell in his Crowley biography, "that 'he lost his integrity', is true of himself to my knowledge, and was largely the result of the shattering realization of this material ruin, with all the horrors which it entailed to a man of his free, proud, restless and imperious nature. If, as Crowley asserted, the translation and publication of the Abramelin magical treatise was the prime cause of Mathers' spiritual decline and fall, am I not right in believing that the same destroying potencies were at work on him also for having dared, with too much arrogance, too much confidence, over much of the world and the flesh in his thoughts, to perform that awful Operation?

"Whatever the causes of Crowley's financial ruin—and the materialist will sneer that the causes were his own folly, extravagance, and total incompetency in the management of his affairs—whatever the causes, the effect upon his life and character were disastrous in the extreme. The agonies of regret, of remorse, of self-reproach, of wounded pride and vanity, added to the incurable wound his heart had suffered by the fading of his Rose, brought forth in Crowley's scarred character all that was worst, all that was at once most pitiful, least scrupulous, most dangerous and malignant. Loyalties, friendships, the elementary moralities, one by one, went by the board. The daily vexations and humiliations which are the lot of all who, like himself, have descended in the social scale by loss of wealth, lashed him into a savage hatred and contempt of his tormentors—the base stinging insects who buzz around the misfortunes of their betters with intent to tease, mortify and madden—and this hatred and contempt extended to embrace the most of mankind."[1]

In such moralizing Cammell embodies all the class-segmented ideals which have resulted in the downfall of the British Empire—ideals which Crowley himself thoroughly despised, and of which, in spite of himself, he was the victim.

He gave himself a title, Sir Aleister Crowley; used among many others the pseudonym Count Vladimir Svareff; and in Cairo was the Prince Chiao Khan. If he had wanted to go somewhere incognito, it seldom occurred to him to use the name Joe Blow, or Bill Smith, or something of the kind. The sometimes corrupt English class-consciousness had contaminated him too.

Let me be the "materialist" that Cammell mentions above—though I can hardly say how silly such a statement is. I suggest, as I propose to show Crowley did himself, that Crowley lost his fortune because, as a result of inadequate training in the handling of money, he spent extravagantly and foolishly, was incompetent in the management of his estate, and had the delusion that there was an inexhaustible reservoir of money and that, no doubt, the powers-that-be would look after him. He published book after book on his own. And he did this, not economically, but in the most luxurious manner conceivable. All his books are superb examples of the art of fine and expensive book production. He neglected to set up a sensible organization for advertising and distribution. The result was that he was possesser of heaven-alone-knows how many volumes that were worth lots on paper, but nothing in cold cash.

Nor did he have the slightest appreciation of the value of money. He never acquired it, no matter how often he was beaten and outraged by ill-fortune.

Some people seem almost to be born with this sense of the value of money; others are not. Education will impart it to some people; even magnificent training will be altogether wasted on others.

Besides this, his fortune was never large anyway. Even if Crowley had inherited the Rockefeller or Carnegie fortune, with his opulent tastes, he would have been hard pressed to work his way through into poverty. But with his expensive ideas and basic financial irresponsibility, his small fortune was dissipated within a dozen years.

Crowley's own account of his early training, or rather, lack of it, where money is concerned, is to be found in *The*

Confessions. I quote the following, even though I find it most
unconvincing. People who have inherited far more money
than he ever had, and lost it due to one mishap or another,
have not considered it beneath their pride or dignity to learn
something new wherewith to recoup their fortunes. But one
phase of his ego was far too much in the way for him to
resort to so practical a measure.

But the one really disastrous feature was the attitude
which I was compelled to assume about money. I was
taught to expect every possible luxury. Nothing was too
good for me; and I had no idea of what anything cost. It
was all paid for behind my back. I was never taught that
effort on my part might be required to obtain anything
that I wanted; on the other hand I was kept criminally
short of pocket-money lest I should spend it in some
disgraceful way, such as buying books or tobacco, or
spending it on even worse abominations such as theatres
and women. (I was encouraged to keep a dog!) I had
therefore no sense of responsibility in the matter of
money. It never occurred to me that it was possible to
make it, and I was thus trained to be dependent to the
point of mendicancy. The effect was, of course,
disastrous. When I got to Cambridge, I still had
everything paid for me, and in addition I found myself
with unlimited credit which I could keep secret. When I
came into my fortune a year later, I was utterly
unprepared to use it with the most ordinary prudence,
and all the inherent vices of my training had a perfectly
free field for their development. Before, if I wanted to
give a dinner party every day of the week, I could do it,
but if I wanted a little cash my only alternative to the
card table was the pawnshop, till I came of age. After
that, it was simply a question of writing a cheque, which
gave me no idea of the nature of the transaction
involved. I doubt whether any one in history was ever
furnished with such a completely rotten preparation for
the management of practical affairs.

The evidence appears to be that even were Crowley left
with an adequate income for the rest of his life, and did not
descend in the social scale, his psychological problems would
not thereby have been ameliorated. His vanity, his pride and
colossal egotism would have persisted unabated and unaltered
by time; they could well have become more inflated than
they did. We could argue that poverty, or the life of being an
adventurer might have modified some of these non-survival
traits and given him a kind of acuity or stability that he could
never have developed otherwise. It has done this to many
other people. For example, Lewis Mumford in an article in
The New Yorker, reviewing Jung's posthumous biography,
wrote:

> The lives of Freud and Jung bear the same testimony.
> Each of them had a stable center of erotic interest and
> domestic responsibility, in a lifelong marriage that
> included the rearing of many children. The sexual
> discipline and order that family life imposes, with its
> integral gratifications, sacrifices, abstentions,
> sublimations, kept their libidos fastened to biological
> and social realities. However loose sexual ties may be in
> premarital relations among primitive peoples, every
> culture had recognized that erotic maturity involves a
> basic commitment to reproductive functions, in
> vicarious fatherhood and motherhood. Freud and Jung,
> fortunately, experienced both modes of commitment;
> not merely as family men but as teachers and
> physicians, they perfected themselves in the parental
> role . . . .
> As with primitive man, work for them was at once a
> personal function, an economic necessity, and a
> compulsive ritual whose daily repetition served, like the
> prayers of the faithful, to alleviate anxiety; above all,
> this life-nurturing routine was a means of keeping in
> check, for a large part of the day—in his prime Freud
> often received patients till nine in the evening—the
> inordinate, crazily destructive impulses that they might
> have found it impossible to control had they been

> "free"; that is, open to the demonic incursions of the
> unconscious. Through their devotion to reproduction
> and breadwinning, the nurturing parental functions,
> Jung and Freud kept their hold on reality . . . . Both the
> outer world and the inner world are real, but each needs
> the correction of the other, and if one is deformed or
> suppressed, the other loses an essential link with reality
> and to that extent becomes irrational and
> uncontrollable.

The question that should have been raised is not whether
he ever really recovered from the encounter with Choronzon
in the desert of North Africa, but whether he benefitted in
any way from that sinister experience. With some unerring
magical instinct, he had performed this ceremony entirely on
his own initiative. There is nothing anywhere in his writing,
no authorization recommending the evocation of the dread
demon of the Abyss. But he did do it spontaneously—and
came face to face with hate, fear, malice and chaos.

Apparently he was inclined at times to attribute these
psychological characteristics to the Abyss *per se*, as if the
latter had an actual reality. In one of his former essays, he
had defined all the magical hierarchies, divine as well as
infernal, as so many constituents of the total human
organism. Gods, angels and demons therefore were all
intrinsically parts of his own psyche. It should be evident
that Choronzon was no abstraction—no universal quality to
which he had merely given form. It was, above all else, the
dramatization of some of the more diabolical contents of his
own psyche.

Where Crowley failed, was not in the usual areas where
prejudicial critics have assailed him, that he performed the
Abramelin operation, or that he meddled with the Enochian
system, or that he was obsessed by Choronzon, or that he fell
because of the union of sex and magic.

The adventure with Choronzon in the desert was an ideal opportunity for him once and for all to confront himself or phases of himself that had hitherto escaped him. His own definition of certain phases of the Golden Dawn curriculum was that they were technical devices to facilitate self-awareness, in the broadest sense of the term. There was something about this particular episode however that escaped him. It would have been better for his entire future and welfare had he been able to realize, in all simplicity: "This is Aleister Crowley too! This is another phase of his personality. A phase I have not liked, and so repressed and ignored all these years. But this fear and hate and malice is my own!"

Had he been able to confront himself in this way, then he might have been able to embark on a new kind of moral adventure, and to achieve an integrity he never previously had.

Schizophrenic he was, but in a social sense quite other than that of which Symonds maliciously accuses him. Schizophrenic we *all* are. I am inclined to believe that schizophrenia is a mass disease of our western culture. We have split ourselves into manifold fragments, and there is no health in any of us. In fact, we are all sick unto death, as Kierkegaard has pointed out. Crowley had no direct awareness of hate and fear being those segments of his emotional life that he had first repressed and then dissociated from himself.

The result was that these negative emotions expressed themselves in his immediate environment all his life. A good example of this is to be found in the cruel and shabby way he once treated Norman Mudd. Mudd was a brilliant mathematician who became enamoured of Crowley's version of the Great Work. The price he paid for this interest was suicide—but in one sense he was murdered, no less than if Crowley had done it with his own hands. The entire incident is described in full by Symonds, not too inaccurately.

These emotions oozed unconsciously into his everyday dealings with people, as though issuing from a source other than himself. He projected the unconscious contents of his psyche, to use psychoanalytical language, and these personal projections fouled his whole life.

It was not the Choronzon incident *per se* that ruined him, causing a fall and degradation from a high spiritual state. Even with his fine gifts of insight and sharp perception, he never realized how strongly destructive his shadow side was. Owing to this unawareness, he was forced to rationalize it and apologize for it.

He often engaged in big-game hunting and shooting and killing, and thoroughly enjoyed it. He rationalized by believing that this sort of thing brought out the virility and best in the human race. He was able to buttress this belief by some rather unconvincing types of argument, but never once was he able to perceive the vision of fear and hate that lurked in his own unconscious depths. It remained wholly unconscious, but hardly inactive or static. As a set of dynamic repressions, it affected his behavior in a variety of ways—homosexuality, promiscuity, infidelity, sadism, big-game hunting, inability to employ his talents practically, and so on, without his ever suspecting that there was a demon within.

In North Africa, he had the supreme opportunity to exorcise this monster, and thus to assimilate it into his own consciousness, to make it a part of himself. It was here, I think, that he failed, so that in one way or another the monster as his own Shadow continued to persecute him throughout the rest of his career.

There was no real awareness of this part of his structure. This is substantiated by his attempt at self-characterization in *The Equinox of the Gods*,[2] from which the following excerpts are taken:

Morality—Sexually powerful and passionate. Strongly

male to women; free from any similar impulse toward my own sex. My passion for women very unselfish; the main motive to give them pleasure. Hence, intense ambition to understand the feminine nature; for this purpose, to identify myself with their feelings, and to use all means appropriate. Imaginative, subtle, insatiable; the whole business a merely clumsy attempt to quench the thirst of the soul. This thirst has indeed been my own paramount Lord, directing all my acts without allowing any other considerations soever to affect it in the least.

Strictly temperate as to drink, had never once been even near intoxication. Light wine my only form of alcohol.

General morality that of a normal aristocrat.

Sense of justice and equity so sensitive, well-balanced and compelling as to be almost an obsession.

Generous, unless suspicious that I was being fleeced; "penny wise and pound foolish." Spendthrift, careless, not a gambler because I valued winning at games of skill, which flattered my vanity.

Kind, gentle, affectionate, selfish, conceited, reckless and cautious by turns.

Incapable of bearing a grudge, even for the gravest insults and injuries; yet enjoying to inflict pain for its own sake. Can attack an unsuspecting stranger, and torture him cruelly for years, without feeling the slightest animosity toward him. Fond of animals and children, who return my love, almost always. Consider abortion the most shameful form of murder, and loathe the social codes which encourage it.

Hated and despised my mother and her family; loved and respected my father and his.

It is a superb though inaccurate account of his more noble, perhaps angelic side. But the dark representation of his Choronzon aspect is hardly mentioned. This is where he was blind; this his psychic scotoma. And because he was so unaware, he suffered abjectly all his life.

This self-descriptive account is worth balancing against

some of the telling evidences of the masochistic, even paranoid streak in his make-up. I doubt if he was fully aware of this either. It is rationalized in an elaborate framework of plausible near-facts, but the masochistic interpretation is clearly evident. I am positive that were another person to express these ideas, Crowley would have been the first to see the diagnosis.

The moral is that any one on the Path needs a guru—or a good psychotherapist. It seems altogether impossible that one can turn the searchlight of honesty and probity on all facets of oneself without the objective aid of a second person who is not emotionally involved in one's moral problems.

Frater Perdurabo specifically swore that He would renounce His personal possessions to the last penny; also that He would allow no human affection to hinder Him. These terms were accepted; He was granted infinitely more than He had imagined possible to any incarnated Man. On the other hand, the price offered by Him was exacted as strictly as if it had been stipulated by Shylock. Every treasure that he had on earth was taken away, and that, usually, in so brutal or cruel a manner as to make the loss itself the least part of the pang. Every human affection that He had in His heart—and that heart aches for Love as few hearts can ever conceive—was torn out and trampled with such infernal ingenuity in intensifying torture that His endurance is beyond belief. Inexplicable are the atrocities which accompanied every step in His Initiation! Death dragged away His children with slow savagery; the women He loved drank themselves into delirium and dementia before His eyes, or repaid His passionate devotion with toad-cold treachery at the moment when long years of loyalty had tempted Him to trust them. His friend, that bore the bag, stole that which was put therein, and betrayed his Master as thoroughly as he was able. At the first distant rumour that the Pharisees were out, his disciples "all forsook Him and fled." His mother nailed Him with her own hands to the cross, and reviled Him as nine years He hung thereupon.

This is as fine a classical Christian document as one could find anywhere. He struggled all his life to escape from his masochistic upbringing. Only the parts of language and names were changed—but the spirit remained. He was stuck with it, but never saw it.

This extraordinary passage is taken from a chapter in the book *Magick*[3] dealing with the significance of the magical Oath. He had sworn to give his all to the Great Work. In exchange, the powers-that-be, the Gods (whom he once said were the enemies of Man) or the Secret Chiefs of the Elect Community (of which he had become a member, he has told us) had exacted the full measure of value from his promise.

It never occurred to him that his own wilfulness and short-sightedness had anything to do with this; that in the dark depths of his own soul, Choronzon lurked, fear and hate and anger that operated completely outside of his conscious sphere of awareness. If his women drank themselves to death, it was never because he encouraged them to drink! Just because he could handle great quantities of alcohol without any too obvious signs of intoxication, he assumed that they could too. He always denied any complicity in whatever happened to him. It was always the other fellow. There is naturally some validity to this, but it was his own repressed psychic factors that delivered him bound and gagged to his enemies.

It is now also possible to gain some insight into the problem of his vast egotism. If an individual has suppressed and repressed vast quantities of emotion—and let us remember that powerful emotions like hate and malice when used can provide the motive power for enormous drive—it is equivalent to stating that he has lost a large part of himself. To the extent that this is true, the concept of inferiority would be a valid one. He would feel inferior, because in point of fact he *is*. There is functional inferiority because a considerable portion of the self has been repressed, and so prevented from developing and growing and being pressed into service on behalf of the organism as a whole. The inferiority is a factual feeling–predicated on the basis of partial loss of self.

For a person like Crowley, this would be altogether intolerable. He had great literary gifts, talent and genius. Inferiority feelings could never be tolerated. Thus compensatory trends would be instituted by one device or another. And so the ego that had been deprived of a large part of its armentarium became inflated by a fancied superiority, over and above the already existent and very real capabilities. These latter had become exaggerated and distorted and over-evaluated and so rendered virtually unproductive. It was this inflated sense of ego which dogged him most of his life. It was this hypertrophied ego, based on the loss of his power drives, which made it impossible for him to give up his life in Samadhi in order to find a larger one. It seems that regardless of his Samadhis and his trances and his mystical states, his ego cunningly played possum for a while and then emerged untouched and relatively unmodified.

One of the ideas that Crowley pushed persistently was "keep the planes separate." I suppose the general semanticists would now say "keep the levels of abstraction distinct and separate." One of the metaphorical ideas Crowley employed was that even if you were in Samadhi, and enjoying the knowledge and conversation of your Holy Guardian Angel, there would be no reason to comb your hair with a pitchfork. One does not employ a roadbuilding tractor in order to dig a hole for the planting of a rose bush.

Therefore it is my contention that neurotic problems must be dealt with on their own plane. Ecstasy and mystical experience do not dissolve them or eradicate them *per se*. Throughout the past three decades I have met people of authority in the metaphysical and occult movements of every kind. It once perplexed me that despite their illumination, genuine though it may have been, their psychoneurotic manifestations would be glaring. One man I knew, for whose spiritual attainment I still have great admiration, had bacteriophobia to a degree where he would almost avoid touching doorknobs until having polished them with his handkerchief. Another had an hypertrophied ego of gigantic proportions which was only a psychic compensation for his emotional insecurity and inferiority which Samadhi has not cured. Still another was characterized by rudeness and irrascibility in his everyday relations with his fellows. Another abused alcohol so that when dead drunk he was incontinent and micturated involuntarily. Others I have known were addicted to over-eating and became obese. Even Ramakrishna's intimacy with Mother Kali did not remove his several neurotic symptoms. It is as if these neurotic symptoms continued to exist unaltered, side by side with the illuminated spirit. But surely this is an indication that there is no integration, no fusing together of discrete elements, no essential wholeness.

It is just this wholeness that psychotherapy is intended to effect. Mysticism is not psychotherapy. There must be no confusion of the two. But it does seem to me that psychotherapy makes for an excellent preparation of the personality so that when illumination does eventually occur, there will be fewer distortions of the divine Light.

That Crowley was illuminated there can be no doubt whatsoever. The more significant doubt that has been brewing in my mind for over three decades is whether his spiritual experience could have resolved his large psychoneurotic problem. It is now my strongest contention that it could not. Crowley's autobiography, as well as the other critical biographies, infer unequivocally that it could not.

A few years ago, I had a pleasant dinner with Mrs. Ruth Fuller Sasaki and Dr. Henry Platov, both of whom are prominent in the Zen movement in this country, the latter being an authorized Roshi or teacher in this area. After a while the conversation turned to Zen and psychotherapy. Specifically I asked Mrs. Sasaki if the Zen disciplinary process (which is not merely a series of philosophical precepts) could cure a psychoneurosis. Emphatically she replied that Zen is not a psychotherapy. The inference is therefore that a frankly neurotic personality can co-exist with the highest illumination, the attainment of the Prajna Paramita.

On later occasions, discussing this problem with Dr. Platov, he took a somewhat different view that the different *satoris*, or illuminations, over a period of time may gradually heal the neurotic "lesion", if we may so call it, and tend to integrate the personality. In a Zen monastery, if a candidate presented a frank neurosis which markedly interfered with his acquiring the needed meditative skills, he would either be dismissed or asked to consult another Roshi, perhaps housed in the same monastery, for a species of psychotherapy; showing a clear realization that *Satori* however profound does nothing to the neurosis itself.

Some writers on modern Christian metaphysics, which is strongly tinged with a species of Mysticism, seem to feel that turning one's life over to Christ—done verbally and through the cultivation of the attitude of surrender—could result in the gradual transformation of the soul. The flaws in one's character would be transformed by the healing Presence. One would become in fact a Son of God, like Christ, perfect, divine, and free of all blemish. One of the better exponents of this New Thought school is the late Thomas Hamblin, whose ideas are constantly expressed in this form in the *Science of Thought Review*. It is much more overtly Christian in tone and more religious in attitude than is the corresponding American school called Science of Mind.

Perhaps The Unity School of Christianity is nearer the mystical attitude adopted by the British Hamblin school. I find myself much in sympathy with their outlook.

Surrender to God sounds simple—but it is not. It may require the most harrowing psychological disciplines to be able to achieve the simplicity of full surrender. "Thou strivest ever. Even in thy yielding, thou strivest to yield, and lo! thou yieldest not!" All the mystics of all time raise their voices to the need, as well as to the extreme difficulty, of this surrender. The metaphysical viewpoint, constantly borne in on me, is superficial to a degree. It does not take into account that the mysticism which scales the supreme heights is a laborious life-long discipline that encompasses more than the mere daily verbal affirmation that "I am a son of God", and that "Christ dwells in me." This is characteristic of the entire modern metaphysical field. There is a heavy miasma of superficiality and a contrived simplicity hanging over it which prevents any possibility of the development of a *bona fide* spiritual discipline.

What is enormously impressive about Aleister Crowley and his diaries is his uncompromising honesty with himself, which leads foolish biographers like Symonds altogether astray with rash assumptions. Never does Crowley make any attempt to minimize what most of us might label his worst traits in favor of the higher or more socially acceptable. It is here that is evident that magnificent difference which makes him altogether dissimilar to any other of the spiritual, metaphysical or philosophical instructors of our time. The average spiritual teacher is prone to advertise freely his possible illuminated state and the precise terms of his philosophy, yet remain wholly silent as to the contents of his private life. A dichotomy is set up. To the average disciple or student, it is as though the teacher had no private life, or if he did have one it differed in no way from his publicly discussed inner life.

Still other people will advertise the details of their so-called private lives, their sexual activities without giving any indication whatever of possible illumination. Clearly, no awakening has yet occurred. Crowley spoke overtly of both his inner and his outer or sexual activity. There was no separation into private and public, spiritual or sexual. He refused to institute the dichotomy that characterizes most of us. His personal honesty transcends all others.

Nor was there, in the scheme he enunciated at great length and with much diversity, any slick, oversimplified, or stereotyped formula. Though some other metaphysicians have asserted that all your wishes can be made to come true by affirmation or prayer, or "something bringing you the fulfillment of what you have hoped for," Crowley abhorred the superficiality and the utter inadequacy of such goals and methods.

His was one message only. It came to be couched in two entirely different ways—the Knowledge and Conversation of the Holy Guardian Angel, or the Discovery of the True Will. And though this was his basic message, he did not minimize the indubitable fact that self-discipline of the most far-reaching and adamant type was prerequisite.

To seduce the aspirant by the assumption that any idiot could attain was altogether beneath him. He preached an aristocracy of spirit, a brotherhood of illuminati—though he knew that were he to lower his sights by one iota, he could gather around himself a flock of adoring, but stupid, disciples. And while he did wish to have many disciples who would "give glory and worship to the Beast, the prophet of the lovely Star", he could never quite lower himself to so ignoble a set of tactics. An adventurer he might be—a dishonest teacher never.

I can only say, in all honesty and humility, that I have never seen an integrated and spiritually transformed person in or out of these popular movements. I have known many

members of such groups and a few of their leaders. Their
neuroses are blatant—though unrecognized. Most of them
would hardly know a neurosis if they saw one—certainly not
their own. Perhaps they have the weird, common, but
mistaken notion that a neurotic person is one who has those
all-too-obvious jerks of the head or mouth or eyebrows that
comedians love to simulate. Of the character neuroses they
appear to know nothing, despite the fact that several of their
more prominent members or leaders have been known to be
alcoholics or masochists or homosexuals or
megalomaniacs—and so on with the full list of distorted
character traits, all symptoms of the Emotional Plague. I say
this not in the spirit of carping criticism, but only to
elucidate my thesis, first stated in relation to Crowley, that
mystical experience is not curative of psychoneurosis.

"The term 'emotional plague' has no defamatory
connotation:" This is Wilhelm Reich's definition. It does not
refer to conscious malice, moral or biological degeneration,
immorality, etc., but a person who, from birth, is constantly
impeded in his natural way of living and so *develops
artificial forms of locomotion.* He limps or moves on
crutches, as it were. Similarly, an individual moves through
life by means of the emotional plague if, from birth, his
natural, self-regulatory instincts have been suppressed. The
individual afflicted with the emotional plague *limps,
characterologically speaking.* The emotional plague may be
considered a chronic biopathy of the organism. It is an
epidemic disease, like schizophrenia or cancer, manifesting
itself essentially in *Social living.* Schizophrenia and cancer are
biopathies resulting from the plague in social life, whose
effects are to be seen in the organism as in social living.
Periodically, like any other plague, it takes on the dimensions
of a pandemic, in the form of a gigantic break-through of
sadism and criminality, as for example in the Catholic
inquisition of the middle ages or the international fascism of

the present century.

In his *Confessions,* Crowley provided rather casually the anamnestic material explanatory of his neurosis without himself realizing its import. Though he regarded himself as a psychologist of sorts, little insight on his part was demonstrated where this matter was concerned. Yet the great classical themes of patricide and incest ran throughout all his writing, from beginning to end.

Years ago, I recall talking to him about some of his short stories entitled *Golden Twigs,* predicated on Frazer's *Golden Bough.* Chuckling quite happily, he told me:

"They are all about murder and incest!"

When I appeared unimpressed and unmoved, so vast was my naiveté in those days, he continued:

"The Editors of the *International,*" (this is the magazine where these stories were first published about 1917,) "had little notion of their contents."

"Didn't they read the stories?" I asked innocently.

"Yes. Of course they did. But the motif is not quite that on the surface."

He enjoyed this idea of having sneaked something past them. Little did he realize that he was considering his own history as well.

The facts are clearly indicated in his autobiography as well as by his life-history. For example, while his father Edward Crowley was alive, the boy Aleister was a model child. His behavior was exemplary. No sooner had father died when Crowley was about eight years of age, than the restraints were thrown off, and he got into mischief right away. "From the moment of the funeral the boy's life entered on an entirely new phase." This is Crowley writing about himself in the third person. "The change was radical. Within three weeks of his return to school he got into trouble for the first time. He does not remember for what offense, but only that his punishment was diminished on account of his bereavement. This was the first symptom of a complete reversal of his attitude to life in every respect. It seems obvious that his father's death must have been causally connected with it."

How? Though assuming there was a causal connection, he made no attempt in the autobiography to trace out or to analyze the subtle connection. It would seem that while father was alive, he did not *dare* misbehave. Despite speaking of his father as absolutely fair and honorable, it never consciously dawned on him that there was some fear connected with him. Father had humanity, was logical, and had some common-sense. His religious creed had convinced him that faith was more important to salvation than works. "With him, the reason for refraining from sin was simply that it showed ingratitude to the Saviour. In the case of the sinner, it was almost a hopeful sign that he should sin thoroughly. He was more likely to reach that conviction of sin which would show his need of salvation. The material punishment of sin (again) was likely to bring him to his knees."

This is the kind of father he had. His father was his hero and his friend, *"though for some reason or other, there was no real conscious intimacy or understanding. He* (Crowley) always disliked and despised his mother. There was a physical repulsion, and an intellectual and social scorn. He treated her always as a servant. It is perhaps on this account that he remembers practically nothing of her during this period. She always antagonized him."

The italics in the above passage are mine. There could be no real intimacy because some kind of contactlessness, as Reich would have put it, was necessary as a device to keep his hostility and death-wishes buried. The repression was complete, and with all his insights and meditative skills he was never able to excavate it.

There is a meaningful clue in another direction. Again

talking of himself in the third person Crowley wrote:

"When Alick was eight or thereabouts he was taken by his father to his first school. This was a private school at St. Leonards, kept by an old man named Habershon and his two sons, very strict Evangelicals . . . . In an examination paper, instead of answering some question or other, he pretended to misunderstand it, and wrote an answer worthy of James Joyce. Instead of selling a limited edition at an extravagant price, he was soundly birched. Entirely unrepentant, he began to will old Habershon's death. Strangely enough, this occurred within a few weeks, and he unhesitatingly took the credit to himself."

Like most children, he believed in the omnipotence of wishing. This is primitive thinking at its best. His desires would be realized, no matter what they were. In the case of old Habershon, who is clearly a father substitute, he did not mind taking upon himself the credit for the death. There was no such clear-cut honesty where father was concerned. He was far too afraid. With the religious training he received, there was a close association between God and father, and murderous fantasies were readily thought to be divinely perceived. Having been raised on the Bible, he knew it well; and as the *lex talionis* would be involved he could afford to take no chance. "Honor thy father and thy mother" advises the Commandment, because in effect if you do not you will get killed. "An eye for an eye . . . ."

Thus whatever hostile fantasy he indulged in would have to be repressed. His early training had resulted in the development of a severe conscience or superego, which enforced good behavior. But no sooner had father died than the barriers were slightly lowered—but not too much. Not enough for him to realize that he had been wishing for his father's death. His Christian conscience was too grim for that.

This patricidal theme is the most powerful one of his lifetime. His submission first to Mathers, the Chief of the

Order of the Golden Dawn, was succeeded by open hostility against him, with an undisguised gesture to replace him. This is one expression of the father theme.

Another is to be found in the story narrated by Symonds where Crowley and Thornton were sailing down the river Irrawady, right after the Chogo Ri expedition had resulted in failure. "Although ill with malaria, Perdurabo sat at the stern with a rifle across his knees, potting at every animal that came in sight." I will not exaggerate interpretation by defining *every* animal as a symbol of father, but there was plenty of murderous feeling being expressed on that and other similar occasions. He was frustrated because of the failure to reach the mountain peak, and murder was the answer.

The most blatant symbolic form of this patricidal theme however is to be found in the consideration of himself as the Logos of the Aeon, whose task was to utter a Word which would become the law of the New Age he was ushering in. In this dawning Aeon, Horus the Son was to be the presiding genius, Osiris the father having been deposed. In his new mythology, the past two thousand years of the dying patriarchal age were identified with Osiris, the father. It was Crowley's destined task to destroy this patriarchy, and to establish in its stead the Aeon of the crowned and conquering child Horus, who of course is no one else but Aleister Crowley. Even in these large terms of his own mythology, there is to be seen the symbolic return of the repressed patricidal impulse. His task was to kill father.

Regarding his mother he had very little to say, except that she was from a Devon and Somerset family, and because of her facies, her schoolmates called her the little Chinese girl. "She painted in water-colour with admirable taste destroyed by academic teaching, and that her powerful natural instincts were suppressed by religion to the point that she became, after her husband's death, a brainless bigot of the most narrow, logical and inhuman type. Yet there was always a struggle; she was really distressed almost daily at finding herself obliged by her religion to perform acts of the most senseless atrocity."

His memories, ample though they may have been in the supposed recollection of several previous incarnations, never were adequate to provide much material of his early life. There is very little he can say about his mother. This is very significant, and is the sign *par excellence* of repression.

I can only regard as evidences of defense his statements that he treated her as a servant, and that she was physically repulsive to him. Clinically, one could hardly develop a better or more effective armoring against incestuous feelings than to find the love-object repulsive. The very affirmation of the latter set of feelings can only indicate the opposite. With Crowley's fine appreciation for symbols and their opposites, as indicated in his Tarot book, he would have been the first to appreciate the validity of this line of interpretation.

In the process of breaking the moulds and shackles of parental sexual inhibition, Crowley loved to narrate his seduction of the family maid on his own mother's bed. This was his gesture of defiance, the hoisting of the emblem of revolt, the winning of his freedom. It was all of that—and something more. What is concealed in the details of the defiant act is the incestuous factor of his lifetime. Through the maid, he was not only defying his mother but in addition seducing her. So far as the unconscious elements of his psyche were concerned, this was incest pure and simple. He has confessed in his autobiography to treating his mother like a servant. One servant can therefore be substituted for another so far as the unconscious psyche is concerned; this is the meaning of symbolism.

This incestuous theme, as I have indicated, even runs through much of his mystical writing. Some of the magical instructions use the incestuous theme, even if it has to be

symbolically interpreted as he did. But regardless of symbols,
or shall we say because of the deliberate use of these symbols
it is evident that incestuous drives played a prominent part in
his emotional life.

On the other hand, his attitude towards women, which
surely must be the outcome of his earliest attitude toward his
mother, was not at all salutary. It was not even intelligent for
an extraordinary man like Crowley to have entertained. He
felt women were altogether beneath him. They existed for
nothing more than to satisfy his sexual feelings and drives.

"Morally and mentally, women were for me beneath
contempt" he wrote in the autobiography. "They had no
true moral ideals. They were bound up with their necessary
preoccupation, with the function of reproduction. Their
apparent aspirations were camouflage. Intellectually, of
course, they did not exist. Even the few whose minds were
not completely blank had them furnished with Wardour
Street Chippendale. Their attainments were those of the page
and the parrot. These facts did not deter me. On the
contrary, it was highly convenient that one's sexual relations
should be with an animal with no consciousness beyond sex."

So far as his sexual appetite is concerned, he required
coitus practically every other day, or so he averred in his
Confessions, and believed that a woman should be around for
that purpose rather like a milkman delivers milk at the back
door.

Other phases of his attitude toward women were quite
opposite and found idealization in his devotion to Nuit, the
Queen of Space, the Star whose prophet he announced
himself to be. This devotion had masochistic overtones to it
as: "I want to prostitute my manhood, to abase my Godhead
before my Lady. I want my crown crushed by Her feet; I
want my face fouled by Her feet; I want my heart torn by
Her boot-heel, my mind to be Her skirt-hem's rustle, my soul
to be Her privy."

Symonds expressed an opinion with exact precision when he said that Nuit who is the personification of Infinite Space, and her less abstract representative Babalon, who is the Sakti of Hindu philosophy, corresponds to the Virgin Mary of the Roman Catholic Church. Crowley was capable of expressing a sublime love and devotion to her that he was never able to do where a single terrestrial woman was concerned. And he expressed this in thoroughly sexual and incestuous terms.

Rather as Freud has indicated, Crowley split his mother-feelings into two well-defined parts. The pre-Oedipal mother who showered love upon him, pampering him and spoiling him, was sublimated into the ideal of Babalon years later. And with Babalon, as all his later writings show, he was involved metaphysically in a glorious incestuous affair. The post-Oedipal mother who had to discipline and train him for life and who so emotionally frustrated him that he was repulsed physically by her, was represented in his relations to the various women in his life. He loved them sexually for varying periods of time, used them as clairvoyantes where he could, but otherwise despised them, as he did his own mother. And not one of these relationships ever endured for any length of time. Several women were wholly faithful to him for many years, regardless of how cruel and faithless he was to them. They evidently had their own masochistic problems, which certainly were not helped by the relationship with him.

His homosexuality was self-admitted. He described his early affair with a friend of Aubrey Beardsley, an actor named Pollitt as "the ideal intimacy which the Greeks considered the greatest glory of manhood and the most precious prize of life. It says much for the moral state of England that such ideas are connected in the minds of practically everyone with physical passion." It is most rare for him to have said anything favorable about the moral state of England, which by and large he despised. While this homosexuality of his could in part have been rooted in some structural and hormonal defects connected with his slender, graceful thighs and his breasts "which are developed to a quite abnormal degree", on the other hand, there is ample clinical evidence to indicate a close relationship between this sexual trait and the psychological problems of mother-incest and patricide which we are discussing.

Earlier, it had been suggested that there was a father identification. Some of the evidence is suggested by the fact that both taught religion of one kind or another; both felt that works (that is, good deeds and high morality) were less essential to salvation than faith, and that their respective scriptures were absolutely immune to criticism and change. Such an identification of a man with his father before him is often unconsciously engineered on the basis of repressed hostility. The identification serves primarily as a barricade or a character-armor against the possible future eruption of the blocked-off affect.

It is worth reflecting on another passage that Crowley wrote in his book *Magick*. It has much significance for us in the present connection. "The aspirant on the threshold of initiation finds himself assailed by the complexes which have corrupted him, their externalization excruciating him and his agonized reluctance to their elimination plunging him into such ordeals that he seems (both to himself and to others) to have turned from a noble and upright man into an unutterable scoundrel."

In other words, initiation (no matter how defined) accomplishes the stimulation of all parts of the psyche. If then the latent contents of the Unconscious are awakened from their former seeming quiescence below the threshold, they need to be taken notice of and dealt with. They need to be assimilated into consciousness otherwise, having gained enormous charges of energy by the initiatory process, they may turn and rend their host.

I suspect that Crowley became subjected to this destructive process. The Oedipal dread and malice which had been concealed beneath his armor for years—expressing itself surreptitiously in hunting, hostility to former friends, arrogance and pomposity—had been brought into the light of day with the evocation of the demon of the Abyss. This is what he was in the depths of himself. But he protected himself against that realization by regarding the whole magical adventure on a metaphysical instead of on a personal psychological basis. And so the valuable opportunity for self-exorcism was wasted, to his life-long detriment.

His major years of productivity were gone within a few years of that ordeal in Algeria. It is my considered belief that he might just as well have died around 1914 and prepared for his next incarnation.[4] Sometimes we all live just a bit too long for our own good. To die early might be the better part of both valor and wisdom.

It is certain that almost all of Crowley's finest creative work was executed before the year 1914. From then on, with only a few minor exceptions, he marked time. Though he conferred higher grades upon himself, as all the texts and biographies indicate, his day was done. Thirty more years had to elapse before he was able to shuffle off this mortal coil, but in that period of time he did himself and his reputation incalculable harm. His reputation was not brightened one iota by his life after that date. It is largely for this reason, that I have not taken my story of his pilgrimage beyond the bright period of his highest creativity.

Having said this, something must be asserted to restore the balance. There is another brighter side of the picture. From his internal emotional conflicts, whatever they may have been, emerged, for one thing, a theory of sexuality which is remarkably modern. Symonds was absolutely right when he averred that Crowley hated the arbitrary division between religion and sexuality foisted upon our culture by the growth of Christianity when it sought to emerge victoriously from the antecedent pagan religions. Crowley abhorred this division, vowing to do all he could to unite them in a single rite.

"From out of the depths of Crowley's mind" wrote Symonds, "had come a very strange idea, one so old that men had forgotten about it. It told of the worship of the sun and of man's organ of creation, and of sexual union as the highest form of religious consecration."

Thus Symonds expressed Crowley's theme of a solar-phallic religion. The world has not yet seen this worship. But the day may indeed come when the names of Crowley, Freud, Reich and Lawrence are brought out from the darkness to be recognized as the prophets of a new age. In that age God might be worshipped not afar in distant space, nor artifically in a church built with hands, but interiorly in the vibrant coursing of life which flows between the sexes. Perhaps the worship of Sakti and Shiva may be given a new lease and a new vital interpretation. Not an endorsement of abstinence and continence which is so ruinous to body and mind, but in a living exchange of energy and body substance which the sexes will have to rediscover for themselves, and so vindicate the work of these rejected prophets of man's own creativity.

"The act of Love, to the bourgeois, is a physical relief like defecation," said Crowley in the unpublished commentaries to *The Book of the Law,* "and a moral relief from the strain of the drill of decency; a joyous relapse into the brute which he has to pretend he despises. It is a drunkenness which drugs his shame of himself, yet leaves him deeper in disgust. It is an unclean gesture, hideous and grotesque. It is not his own act, but forced on him by a giant who holds him helpless; he is half madman, half automaton when he performs it. It is a gawky stumbling across a black foul bog, oozing a thousand dangers. It threatens him with death, disease, disaster in all manner of forms. He pays the coward's price of fear and loathing when peddler Sex holds out his Rat-Poison in the lead-paper wrapping he takes for silver; he pays again with vomiting and with colic when he has gulped it in his greed.

"All this he knows, only too well; he is right, by his own lights, to loathe and fear the act, to hide it from his eyes, to swear he knows it not . . . ." This is Crowley's own declaration. It is not far from that of Reich who once wrote that of course it is true that sex is not everything in life. We could even add the additional fact that in healthy people sex is not a subject for constant discussion and not the prime center of thought.

It goes without saying that the integrity of electric wiring in a factory is the prerequisite of its functioning well, says Reich by way of illustration. Yet, those who work in the factory never give a thought to the wiring itself. They are completely concentrated on their work. The electricity and its wiring are, indeed, not 'everything.' There are other more important matters such as producing what the factory was set up to produce. But, for the sake of argument, let us assume that there is a short in the wiring, the flow of electricity is interfered with, the machines stop, and with that, the work.

Now, the workers' attention becomes centered exclusively on the wiring and the short, and how it can be fixed. But what if the foreman or the union representative were to argue that this silly electrical theory exaggerates the role of the wiring. It is true that the wiring is necessary, but that is not everything. We have other interests; there are other factors to be considered. In this case, argues Reich, the foreman *et al* would be laughed at, for one's first job would be to find and repair the short before one could 'think of other things.'

In such a situation, suggests Reich, is the sexual problem in our society. The flow of biological energy, of sexual energy, is disturbed in the vast majority of people. This is the reason why the bio-social mechanism of society does not function

well or at all. Thus our irrational politics, irresponsibility of
the masses of people, biopathies, murder and manslaughter,
in brief, the emotional plague. If everyone were able to fulfil
his natural sexual needs without disturbance, there would be
no talk about the sexual problem. Then one would be correct
in saying that there are other interests.

Many contemporary writers have written meaningfully
that the sexual revolution of our time has been almost
entirely abortive. Though society in the last score of years
has adopted a more tolerant view of such things as premarital
intercourse, sex techniques, homosexuality and obscenity, we
would be naive to assume that this constitutes anything more
than a superficial and mild liberal reform. In one way or
another, the basic diseased attitude about sexuality still
persists, evoking the diatribes of men like Reich who saw
how sick it was and voiced their protests in the forlorn hope
that Society might reap the harvest of their research. Despite
such diverse breakthroughs in the sexual area—like the
much-publicized Kinsey reports, novels with overlong
descriptions of all the details of the sexual act, and the
ballyhoo attending the discovery of the birth-control pills,
the moral authorities remain yet to be pulled off their
thrones. They remain for the simple reason that they have
now been internalized, not merely in the form of the
Freudian superego, but in the living tissue of our bodies, in
what Reich so eloquently came to call the muscular armor.
The manner in which they function is the emotional plague.

Again and again we are confronted by the superego. Our
narrow-minded grandparents with their moral prudery and
their Victorian puritanism are gone. But their blue-stocking
heritage to us persists as the internal arbiter of our morals, of
our sexual behavior, in a more damning form as the superego,
which is not quite so easy to get at and attack.

"The sexual act is a sacrament of Will." Thus stated
Crowley. "To profane it is the great offense. All true

expression of it is lawful; all suppression or distortion is contrary to the Law of Liberty. To use legal or financial constraint to compel either abstention or submission, is entirely horrible, unnatural and absurd."

Common to all current literary reactions about sex are the convictions that sexuality has an intrinsic validity of its own and "finally transcends the uses to which it is put." This is the expression of John C. Holmes in an article *Revolution Below the Belt.*[5] "That sex is not just a kind of visceral valentine you give your beloved, nor something as fleeting and emptily symbolic as a handshake. That it is not so much a specific emotion directed at a specific person, as it is an objectless, steadily coursing flow of energy out from the centers of the being which, like an underground stream, can course in an infinite variety of places, in an infinite number of ways. The homosexual pool is different from the heterosexual river only in that it has been dammed, but both rise from the same dark, subterranean watershed, ceaselessly flowing, seeping, searching its level." In all things living, Wilhelm Reich wrote, sexual vegetative energy is at work. Or, as D.H. Lawrence enjoined much earlier: "Accept sex in the consciousness and let the normal physical awareness come back, between you and other people. Be tacitly and simply aware of the sexual being in every man and woman, child and animal."

To the extent that Reich and Lawrence affirmed the important characteristics of sexual energy as primal creativity and undifferentiated flow, have they been unique harbingers of this sexual revolution that is quietly current.

There are a great many resemblances between the progressive sexual attitudes of Wilhelm Reich and those of Aleister Crowley. The several books of Reich very clearly provide lengthy expositions of what he stood for. Crowley's attitudes permeate practically every book he wrote, but they are scattered. It was not until he came to prepare the (as yet

unpublished) commentaries to *The Book of the Law* that he
clearly delineated what he believed and what he stood for
where the sexual problem was concerned.

In *Konx Om Pax,* the first truly mystical treatise he wrote,
there are some pregnant ideas that are wholly indicative of
the trend that he was embarking upon. *The Book of Lies*
contains several quite clearly stated paradoxical chapters
about sexual attitudes with a markedly mystical flavor that
are to be found nowhere else. For example, there is one that
Crowley called *Steeped Horse-hair:*

> Mind is a disease of semen.
> All that a man is or may be is hidden therein.
> Bodily functions are parts of the machine; silent,
> unless in dis-ease.
> But mind, never at ease, creaketh "I".
> This "I" persisteth not, posteth not through
> generations, changeth momentarily, finally is dead.
> Therefore is man only himself when lost to himself in
> the Charioting.

In *The Dewdrop,* another chapter of the same little book,
there is a further reference to the same profound sexual
philosophy, in these terms:

> Verily, love is death, and death is life to come.
> Man returneth not again; the stream floweth not
> uphill; the old life is no more; there is a new life that is
> not his.
> In the silence of a dewdrop is every tendency of his
> soul, and of his mind, and of his body; it is the
> Quintessence and the Elixir of his being. Therein are the
> forces that made him and his father and his father's
> father before him.
> This is the Dew of Immortality.
> Let this go free, even as It will; thou art not its
> master, but the vehicle of it.

His sexual philosophy is scattered throughout the so-called

official instructions of his Order. Even though a great deal of symbolism is deliberately employed, whatever time and effort may be expended to decipher the puzzle will be found infinitely worthwhile. There is an essay *Energized Enthusiasm* in the *Equinox IX* where a definite stand is taken on the marriage of religious ceremonial and sex, the worship of Dionysius, Aphrodite and Apollo—which he translated for us as the worship of wine, women and song! The unpublished commentaries to *The Book of the Law* contain page after page of patient, careful striving to explain what he felt so keenly about this.

But apart from this, some of his most passionate beliefs were incorporated in a book review here and there in the different numbers of the *Equinox*. For example, in *Equinox III*, which appeared early in 1910, while reviewing a book about Thomas Lake Harris, he wrote:

> So we need not be surprised if the Unity of Subject and Object in Consciousness which is Samadhi, the uniting of the Bride and the Lamb which is Heaven, the uniting of the Magus and the God which is Evocation, the uniting of the Man and his Holy Guardian Angel which is the seal upon the work of the Adeptus Minor, is symbolized by the geometrical unity of the circle and the square, the arithmetical unity of the 5 and the 6, and (for more universality of comprehension) the uniting of the Lingam and the Yoni, the Cross and the Rose. For as in earth-life the sexual ecstasy is the loss of self in the beloved, the creation of a third consciousness transcending its parents, which is again reflected into matter as a child; so, immeasurably higher, upon the Plane of Spirit, Subject and Object join to disappear, leaving a transcendent unity. This third is ecstasy and death; as above, so below.
>
> It is then with no uncleanness of mind that all races of men have adored an ithyphallic god; to those who can never lift their eyes above the basest plane the sacrament seems filth.

He had so much to say that is still valid. More than this, its depths remain yet to be explored, for ours is still a sex-negative culture, despite all that has been done by Freud and Reich and many others. For those who would deny that this culture of ours is sex-negative, a course of reading is prescribed in Albert Ellis' two books *The American Sexual Tragedy* and *The Folklore of Sex.*

"Therefore we hold Love holy, our heart's religion, our mind's science," wrote Aleister Crowley. "Shall He not have His ordered Rite, His priests and poets, His makers of beauty in colour and form to adorn Him, His makers of music to praise him? Shall not His theologians, divining His nature, declare Him? Shall not even those who but sweep the courts of His Temple, partake thereby of His person? And shall not our science lay hands on Him, measure Him, discover the depths, calculate the heights, and decipher the laws of His nature?"

It may well be that despite his pathologies which I have tried to illuminate here, Crowley was a far greater mystic and a wiser philosopher than either he or we could know. In spite of all his mistakes, and they were many, and all his excesses, it is possible that he was far nearer the truth of things than those of us who feel more restrained, less prone to excess and extravagance, and who are less overtly cruel and sadistic. Crowley's day may yet dawn. It may well be that he is really the prophet of the new Age, where life and sex and creativity will become intrinsic parts of our everyday lives, without hypocrisy and shame.

To stop here would be to do Crowley a great injustice. He was above all an apostle of a new kind of consciousness—the awareness that evidently belongs to a future time. There have been other writers and other teachers who have taken a similar stand. For example, there is Richard Bucke, the author of *Cosmic Consciousness.* In this book the author claims that just as ordinary self-consciousness differentiates man from the lower orders of animals and represents a great advance over their more simple kind of awareness, so Cosmic Consciousness is an advance over that of the average man today. This claim was illustrated by innumerable examples of men and women who had had flashes of the kind of awareness that is opened up by the mystical experience. This is one of the most favourable and useful aspects of the book.

The Aldous Huxley of his later years was another apostle more or less of the same type of consciousness. He brought to bear on this message a fine intellectual appreciation of mystical literature. His book *The Perennial Philosophy* must stand as testimony to his vast insight into and sympathy with these more advanced ideas. Gerald Heard is another modern writer among many others too numerous to mention who advocate the development of new standards and types of awareness.

Without any attempt at special pleading, I assert Aleister Crowley stands head and shoulders above any and all of these brilliant writers. Every bit of the material I have quoted here and in the anthology *The Best of Crowley* must stand as proof of this assertion. Where he differs from and transcends these other writers is that he had widely experimented with traditional mystical techniques of both the East and the West. I doubt if there was any method that he had not attempted to use. This made him an intrepid explorer in the world of mind and spirit, second to none.

In addition to this, as I have amply demonstrated, he achieved the mystical heights. Not only had he stated that the next step for man is the "knowledge and conversation of his Holy Guardian Angel", in a set of clichés deliberately chosen to express his concept of spiritual experience, his writings indicate that again and again he achieved this goal himself. It was that experience that in his later years he came to denominate as the discovery of the True Will.

This phraseology had its origins in his final identification with *The Book of the Law,* which he had fought for so many years. The "Holy Guardian Angel" language belongs to his earlier period when the Golden Dawn traces lingered on. Later he perceived that in the mystical experience, there might be ascertained the meaning and purpose to life—individual and unique for each person. No two people were alike, and no similar rules were applicable to all. The discovery of the True Will was the central task of every man. Until that were divined in experience, akin to awakening out of a long vivid dream, one was still asleep. This might help to explain in a small measure the shock tactics that he often employed, to the discomfiture of his pupils. It was to startle them, to awaken them to themselves. His first expression of this was in *Konx Om Pax,* in the fairy story entitled *The Wake World*, where, as in Zen, the mystical experience is likened to an awakening. An awakening to purpose and motive—an awakening to the meaning of the man of the future, to the man who does his will among the living.

Many have frequently wondered why Crowley bothered to use the Ordo Templi Orientis after he and Jones had so painstakingly formulated the A∴A∴ in 1909. The latter organization was a reformulation of the old Golden Dawn on the level of personal accomplishment and individual experimentation with classical mystical and occult techniques. Its goal was, in effect, that of the Golden Dawn too—the attainment of higher states of consciousness, the religious or mystical experience. The very heart of its program was predicated on the Tiphareth clause of the Adeptus Minor obligation:

> I further promise and swear that . . . I will, from this day forward, apply myself to the Great Work.

The Knowledge and Conversation of the Holy Guardian Angel was the language Crowley used, borrowed of course from *The Book of the Sacred Magic of Abramelin the Mage,* to describe the Great Work.

Crowley's order differed from the Golden Dawn in several major respects. It played down the grade system which was such a curse and *vanitas vanitatis* to the Adepti of the Golden Dawn, and it eliminated the ritual initiations. Further, it introduced as adjuncts definitively Hindu methods based on his own experimentation with Yoga training. His interpretation of the Great Work stressed above all other things a combination of Yoga and Ceremonial Magic as the operational tools by which the student could ascend to the very highest levels of spiritual attainment.

The O.T.O., on the other hand, while teaching a form of sex-magic, was perceived by Crowley as an ideal agent for promulgating the Law of Thelema—"Do what thou wilt!" Though the sex magic was kept a secret of the higher grades, the IX degree particularly, its secret was more a matter of personal accomplishment than a form of verbal initiation. It is really useless to describe the method, not because it is a secret, but only because its successful employment demands the ability to concentrate the mind and to visualize keenly, and these are faculties not commonly found. So he decided to subordinate the O.T.O. work to the more basic dissemination of the contents of *The Book of the Law.* Many of his later writings such as *The Equinox of the Gods, Liber Aleph,* and *The Tarot of the Egyptians* were published under the auspices of the O.T.O. rather than the A∴A∴. It almost seems as if he came to stress the universal importance of *The Book of the Law* as against the individual attainment of higher mystical states.

It may be that in this way he was really expressing his intense personal disappointment that out of the A∴A∴'s program of training in Yoga and Magic, there had been so few worthwhile results. Only Captain Fuller, Victor Neuburg, and later Charles Stansfeld Jones (Frater Achad) in America seemed to have gotten anywhere with these methods. And even these fell from grace, according to Crowley. He fell out with all of them. No one of any stature has emerged from the A∴A∴ and remained representative of the efficacy of the method. He was alone. So there must have been a profound sense of frustration and failure, which he but rarely expressed.

Because of this, he shifted his energies from the individual to large masses. He came to believe that the most important part of his life-work, his mission, was to convert people to the notion of fulfilling their destinies and finding their True Wills, as he expressed it, in compliance with the dictates of *The Book of the Law.*

The masthead of the *Equinox* bore the insignia—"the Aim of Religion, the Method of Science." Though this goal occasionally got lost, or shall I say partially submerged in a deluge of poems, plays, essays, stories, epigrams, and so forth, it was a worthy goal. The aim of religion always has been the induction of the mystical experience, superconsciousness as he occasionally called it, after the Yogis. By re-writing the traditional methods in a simple, direct way, eliminating the fantasy and superstitions and inessentials, and by insisting that every student keep a permanent record or diary of his daily devotions or exercises even as he had, he hoped to fulfil the second part of the mast-head, the Method of Science.

Even in his description of mystical states, more often than not he described a mysticism without God, and to this extent both his scientific training at Cambridge and his exposure to Buddhism with Allan were involved. For example, in his *Gospel According to St. Bernard Shaw*, he wrote:

> The mystic attainment may be defined as the Union of the Soul with God, or as the realization of itself, or—there are fifty phrases for the same experience. The same, for whether you are a Christian or a Buddhist, a

Theist or (as I am myself, thank God) an Atheist, the attainment of this one state is as open to you as is nightmare, or madness, or intoxication. Religious folk have buried this fact under mountains of dogma; but the study of comparative religion has made it clear. One has merely to print parallel passages from the mystics of all ages and all religions to see that they were talking of the same thing; one gets even verbal identities, such as the "That Tao which is Tao is not Tao" of the Chinese, the "Not That, not That" of the Hindu, the "Head which is above all Heads, the Head which is not a Head" of the Qabalists, the "God is Nothing" of the Christian, and "That which is not which is" of the modern atheistic or pantheistic mystic.

It was his contention that religious belief of any kind was not the necessary desideratum of mystical experience. By doing certain things, certain results followed; this is the scientific essence of his creed.

Let Symonds and the other mockers ridicule him if they wish, but future generations—if there are any that will survive the nuclear holocaust suggested by the verse in *The Book of the Law* "I am the Lord of the Forties; the Eighties cower before me, and are abased,"—may see him more clearly than we do now as an outstanding giant in an age of pygmies.

A friend of mine—a sincere and enthusiastic fan of Crowley's work—has said that regardless of his shortcomings and personal problems, Crowley had something which permitted his selection and use as a messenger. The Gods, whoever or whatever They may be, care nothing for human beings *per se*, save as they may be employed to further the work of the evolution of the human race. This business of evolution is never a smooth, forward-moving process. More likely it proceeds by sudden spurts and jolts, accompanied by social catastrophes and overwhelming cataclysms of nature which, somehow, promote the occurrence of mutations. It is the resulting mutant that is the evidence of evolution, as well as the promise of better things to come. He also suggested that Crowley may be one of these mutants, and that *The Book of the Law,* no matter how distasteful its violence and haughty disdain of our so-called civilized values may be to us, is the scripture as it were of violent change and evolutionary cataclysm from which mutants emerge.

There was no perfection about Crowley. None whatsoever. But he did possess several psychological characteristics which must have made him more useful as a mouthpiece, the Logos or Word of the new Aeon.

There is another piece of his writing which similarly has to be kept in mind, when discussing his character. His insights may have exceeded anything that any of us may have anticipated from him. For example, in the segment from *Magick* dealing with the Devil, which I used in an earlier chapter, he had this to say:

> He is Man made God, exalted, eager; he has come consciously to full stature, and so is ready to set out on his journey to redeem the world. *But he may not appear in this true form; the Vision of Pan would drive men mad with fear. He must conceal Himself in his original guise.*
>
> *He therefore becomes apparently the man that he was at the beginning; he lives the life of a man; indeed, he is wholly man.* But his initiation has made him master of the Event by giving him the understanding that whatever happens to him is the execution of his true will.

I have italicized the significant part of the passage. It reveals so much about him—and at the same time warns us not to be fooled and undervaluate him and whatever he stood for. Actually, he did herald the New Age, the future age where men will be self-determining, functioning in terms of the laws that Crowley came to state as Thelema.

Thou hast no right but to do thy will. Do that and no

other shall say thee nay.

This is what he stood for, and this is the way he lived.

And in all shalt thou create the Infinite Bliss and the next link of the Infinite Chain.

This chain reaches from Eternity to Eternity, ever in triangles—is not my symbol a triangle?—ever in circles—is not the symbol of the Beloved a circle? Therefore is all progress base illusion, for every circle is alike and every triangle alike!

But the progress is progress, and progress is rapture, constant, dazzling, showers of light, waves of dew, flames of the hair of the Great Goddess, flowers of the roses that are about her neck, Amen!

Therefore lift up thyself as I am lifted up.

Hold thyself in as I am master to accomplish. At the end, be the end far distant as the stars that lie in the navel of Nuit, do thou slay thyself as I at the end am slain, in the death that is life, in the peace that is mother of war, in the darkness that holds light in his hand, as an harlot that plucks a jewel from her nostrils.

So therefore the beginning is delight, and the end is delight, and delight is in the midst, even as the Indus is water in the cavern of the glacier, and water among the greater hills and the lesser hills and through the ramparts of the hills and through the plains, and water at the mouth thereof when it leaps forth into the mighty sea, yea, into the mighty sea.[6]

NOTES

[1] Charles R. Cammell, *op. cit.*, p. 89.

[2] *The Equinox of the Gods*, O.T.O., London, 1936, p. 110-111.

[3] *Magick*, The Master Therion, Paris, 1929, p. 127.

[4] I have reflected long on this early observation of mine, and have concluded that it should be modified. He did write *Liber Aleph* in that period, and the Tarot book, as well as some diary material which has never been, but should be published. It is possible that circumstances and my conscience may oblige me to write, later, another volume to this work dilating on his later experiences and literary as well as magical career.

[5] *Playboy*, July, 1964, p. 67.

[6] *Liber A'ash vel Capricorni.*

CHAPTER FIFTEEN

The Book of the Law

During their honeymoon in Ceylon in 1904, Crowley discovered that Rose was pregnant. All previous plans of going on to China were immediately scrapped, and after some big-game hunting in Hambantota county of Ceylon, they decided to go back home to Boleskine. However, on the way from the East it occurred to them to stop off in Cairo, renting a flat during the month of February—no doubt preferring to spend the winter in a warmer sunnier climate than Scotland, which could be dismally cold and grey during the winter months.

To have registered as Mr. and Mrs. Aleister Crowley would never have done; it sounded far too prosaic. So, "having to choose a Persian name," he wrote in his *Confessions*, "I made it Chioa Khan (pronounced Hiwa Kahn) being the Hebrew for the Beast. (Khan is one of the numerous honorifics common in Asia.) I had no conscious magical intention in doing so. (Let me here mention that I usually called my wife Ouarda, one of the many Arabic words for Rose.)

> I was not for a moment deceived by my own pretext that I wanted to study Mohammedanism, and in particular the mysticism of the Fakir, the Darwesh, and the Sufi, from within, when I proposed to pass myself off in Egypt for a Persian prince with a beautiful English wife. I wanted to swagger about in a turban with a diamond aigrette and sweeping silken robes or a coat of

cloth-of-gold, with a jewelled talwar by my side, and two gorgeous runners to clear the way for my carriage through the streets of Cairo . . . .

As to my study of Islam, I got a Sheikh to teach me Arabic and the practices of ablution, prayer and so on, so that at some future time I might pass for a Moslem among them. I had it in my mind to repeat Burton's journey to Mecca sooner or later. I learnt a number of chapters of the Qu'ran by heart. I never went to Mecca, it seemed rather *vieux jeu,* but my ability to fraternise fully with Mohammedans has proved of infinite use in many ways.

An incident occurred during this short stay in Cairo, in the early months of 1904, which Crowley averred continually for the rest of his earthly days was the most important single event of his entire lifetime. Everything prior was merely preparatory. Anything subsequent, he considered to be destiny and fulfillment. It dominated his every activity—after an initial five year period during which he was reluctant even to acknowledge it. But after this period of time, culminating in *The Vision and The Voice* experience of North Africa, he was identified with it, for good or for ill. Crowley and the document containing the phrase "Do what thou wilt" then became wholly inseparable.

What occurred in early April 1904 has been described by Crowley on several different occasions, and in several different books. It is a long, complex story, with subtle ramifications, but it can be reduced to the following simple account.

At one period in Cairo, after some intense magical working, his wife became restless and finally said to her husband, "They are waiting for you!" After many excursions, she finally persuaded him to conform to her "hunch"—and this I imagine was not easy. He sat alone daily in the living room of their Cairo apartment. For one full hour on each of three successive days, beginning on April 8, 1904, a Voice dictated to him what was called *The Book of the Law*. (It is sometimes written as Liber AL vel Legis.)[1]

This document of three short chapters purports to have been dictated by a praeter-human intelligence named Aiwass. For many long years Crowley claimed unequivocally that Aiwass was one of the Secret Chiefs of the Third Order of the Silver Star, an intelligence so far beyond Crowley's as his was superior to that of a bushman. Many years afterwards, he came to recognize and admit that Aiwass was none other than his Holy Guardian Angel. "I lay claim to be the sole authority competent to decide disputed points with regard to the Book of the Law, seeing that its Author, Aiwaz, is none other than mine own Holy Guardian Angel, to Whose Knowledge and Conversation I have attained, so that I have exclusive access to Him. I have duly referred every difficulty to Him directly, and received His answer; my award is therefore absolute without appeal."

If Aiwass was his own Higher Self,[2] then the inference is none other than that Aleister Crowley was the author of the Book, and that he was the external mask for a variety of different hierarchical personalities, as discussed earlier. Thus:

Frater Perdurabo 0=0 is Aleister Crowley
Frater "Heart of Jesus" etc. 5=6 is Aleister Crowley
Frater Ol Sonuf Vaorsagi 6=5 is Aleister Crowley
Frater Ou Mh 7=4 is Aleister Crowley
Frater V.V.V.V.V. 8=3 is Aleister Crowley
Frater To Mega Therion 9=2 is Aleister Crowley

The man Crowley was the lowest rung of the hierarchical ladder, the outer shell of a God, even as we all are, the persona of a Star. "Every man and every woman is a Star."

He is the author of *The Book of the Law* even as he is the author of the *Book of the Heart Girt with a Serpent* and *Liber Lapidis Lazuli,* and so forth. I have discussed earlier how these latter books reveal a dialogue between the component parts of Crowley. It seems to me that basically this *Liber Legis* is no different.

Crowley's attitude, however, is entirely different. He is willing to admit that, in a sublime sense, he was the author of *Liber LXV* and *Liber VII* mentioned above; but that in no similar manner was he the author of *The Book of the Law.* The latter, he claims, was dictated to him as objectively and as audibly as if I were dictating this material to my secretary.

He has, in part, anticipated this kind of argument. For example, in *The Equinox of the Gods,* he wrote:

"Of course I wrote them, ink on paper, in the material sense; but they are not My words, unless Aiwaz be taken to be no more than my subconscious self, or some part of it; in that case, my conscious self being ignorant of the Truth in the Book and hostile to most of the ethics and philosophy of the Book, Aiwaz is a severely suppressed part of me." Then he added a footnote to the above, reading: "Such a theory would further imply that I am, unknown to myself, possessed of all sorts of praeternatural knowledge and power. The law of Parsimony of Thought (Sir W. Hamilton) appears in rebuttal."

It can safely be said that current psychological theory would agree that any one person is possessed of all sorts of knowledge and power of which he is totally unconscious, Hamilton's law notwithstanding. Both Freudian and Jungian theory are on the side of such an assumption, though the complete spelling out of each theory in detail would present a different picture.

That Aiwass might, in truth, be a severely repressed or dissociated or hitherto unknown element of his psychic structure could be confirmed by the fact that even to his death in 1947 Crowley is said to have found some parts of the Book quite distasteful even to himself. Just what they were, I would not know. Some other verses of the Book relate quite clearly to material that he had once been consciously familiar with, but may have forgotten.

If a poem, or any work of art, is a geyser of the Unconscious, as Crowley wrote in the Preface to *The City of God*, then this *Liber Legis* must represent an upwelling of powerful images and affects from his Unconscious psyche. We have seen from the letter that he had written in 1905 to Gerald Kelly, after the failure of the Kangchenjunga expedition, that he was fed up to the gills with almost everything he had so far touched. As a result he now wanted something vehement and vigorous in his life, some murder or rape, or something equally dramatic and violent. Though written about a year *after* the dictation of *The Book of the Law* which he had by then repudiated, the letter gives us a sharp insight into what was troubling him. It depicts some of the raw conflicts and archetypal movements deep down in the unconscious levels of his psyche.

Though ostensibly he had repudiated the Book, there is a fascinating reference in his 1906 diaries, written right after the China episode, which indicates that it may have been very much on his mind after all. The 1905 letter to Gerald Kelly does not mention *The Book of the Law*, but on April 30, 1906, some days after he had left Shanghai, he wrote: "It has struck me—in connection with reading Blake—that Aiwass, etc. "Force and Fire" is the very thing I lack. My "conscience" is really an obstacle and a delusion, being a survival of heredity and education."

This is an illuminating admission. As a boy he was shy and bashful, regardless of how these neurotic characteristics came about. His early religious training would certainly have aided in the development of an extraordinarily rigid superego or conscience. In his subsequent revolt against Christianity, then, he must have yearned for qualities and characteristics diametrically opposed to his own. In *The Book of the Law* the wish is fulfilled. Simply stated, this emergence from his unconscious psyche represents, among other things, a colossal wish-fulfillment. Or, should we follow Jung, it represents an unconscious compensatory reaction to a top-heavy conscious attitude. Since it was unconscious, it was just as extreme as the conscious attitude was, and no equilibrium could have been reached unless and until each modified the other.

If he really wanted "blasphemy, murder, rape, revolution, anything, bad or good, but strong", as he averred in this significant letter to Kelly, then all I can say is that he got it. For the Book which he scribed contains all of this—and more!

Both the letter to Kelly and the Book express all the frustration and bitterness of his life, to which he was responding both consciously and unconsciously with all the violence, contempt and anger of which he was capable on the one hand; and with sublimity, majesty and delicacy on the other. The Book visibly embodies all the contradictions and internal conflicts of which he was capable and by which he was being torn. Though he categorically denies having any hand in its composition and creation—this may perhaps be literally true on the conscious level—if Aiwass is equated with his unconscious Self it is nonetheless his Book and his Law.

Sometime in 1907, when Crowley had reached the height of his writing about his mystical experiences, he wrote the book *Konx Om Pax*, in the third section of which he wrote:

> But let us consider the perfect man . . . . He lives (it is true) in Kether; but his mind and body, perfect though they are, work, as it were, automatically, on their own plane. At present I am quite unconscious of my heart beating; it is not even an illusion! Yet it maintains its just relation to the other illusory things. So, no doubt, an adept is quite unconscious of the acts and thoughts performed by him, acts and thoughts which seem to imply conscious volition.

The inference here may be that the Adept may do a large number of things without giving them due attention. He has a trained set of vehicles which continue functioning, each in its own way and each on its own plane, without needing conscious attention from him. In other words, the man Crowley may well have been only one of the more or less well-functioning vehicles of Aiwass the Holy Guardian Angel. The writing of *The Book of the Law* required merely some temporary attention from the scribe Aleister Crowley to align him with what Aiwass was doing on another psycho-spiritual level.

In discussing *The Book of the Law*, two main facts need to be remembered.

1. After the Ceylon illumination, Crowley more or less discontinued every type of occult practice.

From the moment of his marriage to Rose, or more accurately from the time of his Dhyana in Ceylon a couple of years earlier, he had tired of his mystical ambitions. "All that he had attained, he abandoned. The intuitions of the Qabalah were cast behind him with a smile at his youthful folly; magic, if true, led nowhere."[3] We must remember that this conclusion of his related to his concepts of magic prior to 1903. It had absolutely no reference to what he achieved three years later, in 1906, after the Augoeides invocations, nor to his Samadhi in 1909. "Yoga had become psychology. For the solution of his original problems of the universe he looked to metaphysics; he devoted his intellect to the cult of absolute reason." It took the experience of walking across the lower borders of China to remedy that situation, in the private insanity already referred to. There he was brought abjectly to his knees with the realization that reason *per se* is unable to solve the great problems of the universe. Below the Abyss, in the realm of the so-called practical, in the mundane areas of science, commerce and industry, it is a fine precision tool—but that is all.

He took up once more with Kant, Hume, Spencer, Huxley, Tyndall, Maudsley, Mansel, Fichte, Schelling,

Hegel, and many another; while as for his life, was he
not a man? He had a wife; he knew his duty to the race,
and to his own ancient graft thereof. He was a traveller
and a sportsman; very well, live it. So we find that from
November 1901, he did no practices of any kind until
the Spring Equinox of 1904, with the exception of a
casual week in the summer of 1903, and an exhibition
game of Magick in the King's Chamber of the Great
Pyramid in November 1903 . . . . We find him climbing
mountains, skating, fishing, hunting big-game, fulfilling
the duties of a husband; we find him with the antipathy
to all forms of spiritual thought and work which marks
disappointment.

Such was his point of view at the time.

2. His wife Rose was not the least bit interested in his
intellectual or spiritual pursuits.

However true these facts may be, one should keep in mind
that what was true many years afterwards may also have
obtained in 1904. Crowley felt constrained to use any device
to further or develop any latent clairvoyant ability in
whatever woman he lived with. His methods were none other
than the liberal use of alcoholic libations and sexual activity
pursued to the point of conscious exhaustion. Years later,
Rose became a dipsomanic, for which reason ostensibly
Crowley divorced her. I wonder whether some of this was not
brought about as a result of his tutelage?

He had yet to learn that the story of Balaam and his
prophetic ass might be literally true. For the great
Message that came to him came, not through the mouth
of any person with any pretensions to any knowledge of
this or any other sort, but through an empty-headed
woman of society.

Crowley has gone out of his way to tell us she was stupid. I presume he has done this, in part, to justify his writing some pornographic literature for her, but beyond this to render all the more impressive her bout of psychic perceptiveness in Cairo. Furthermore in one of the quotations I have given from the *Confessions*, it seems he regarded *all* women as his intellectual inferiors and therefore stupid. Perhaps then she really was not so dumb as he would have liked us to believe. This assumption however does not help very much where this Book is concerned.

When Rose began to say that "they are waiting for you" he may at first have attributed this kind of wild talking to a species of insanity he attributed to both menstruating and pregnant women. But when she began to use the cues in his own magical cipher, of which theoretically she could have known nothing, he had to sit up and take notice.

It was possible, of course, for Rose to have perused some of his notebooks where he was making tabulations and classifications of symbols and mythologies that one day would see the light as *Liber 777*. Like most married women, she had perhaps learned to sit quietly while her husband used her as a sounding board for his own reflections. It is conceivable she had heard him talk in the same way that he had written to her brother after the ill-fated K-2 venture. Crowley was never any good at keeping things to himself. When confronting Neuburg, even the demon Choronzon accused Crowley of talking too much. During their married years therefore, Rose must have heard him talk a great deal about his attitudes to life, magic, and everything else.

But this does not help us to understand why, during a trip to the Boulak Museum in Cairo, she led him to an exhibition case bearing the number 666, which was meaningful to him, or why she selected Horus of all the possible Egyptian Gods as the presiding genius of the events about to transpire. What is even more remarkable is that after the completion of the three days of dictation, it fell to Rose to fill in a couple of blank spaces for words that Crowley had not heard aright!

It would appear that she filled a temporary mediumistic role in these psychic episodes of 1904, and that Crowley heard "direct voice" communications together with other similar psychic phenomena. A large series of questions remain unanswered.

He did keep a diary during the opening phases of this cycle, but the entries are altogether obscure. His memory provided no clue as to the means of deciphering them. Even so, a couple of the entries are meaningful in one or more ways as we shall see. For example,

Feb.	7.	Suez.
Feb.	8.	Landed at Port Said.
Feb.	9.	To Cairo
	11.	Saw b. f. g.
		b. f. b.
Feb.	19.	To Helwan as Oriental Despot . . . .
Mar.	22.	X.P.B. احجا
		E.P.D. in 84 m.
	24.	Met احجا again.
	25.	823 Thus
		461 " " = p f l y 2 b z
		218

I have quoted thus far from the diary for two very important reasons. The symbols above are in Arabic script. Transliterated they spell AJIHA. An authority on Eastern languages at the University of California assures me that this word, *if* it is a word, is *not* Arabic. Under these circumstances, clearly in 1904 it must have had some private meaning for Crowley. The note in *Equinox VII* asks: "May this and the entry of March 24, refer to the brother of the A∴A∴ who found him?"

The entire entry therefore still remains an enigma. However, while referring since to *Equinox VII* and to its reproduction in *The Equinox of the Gods,* I came across another referent just prior to this script which may have some significance here. CHIOA is the Hebrew for Beast, and we have learned that in Cairo Crowley used this word with Khan, an Eastern honorific title. Moreover he transposed some of the letters of this word, to make it emerge as ACHIHA, which he says also means Beast. ACHIHA and AJIHA are not very far apart. Whatever difference exists between them may be laid at the door of someone anxious to transliterate letters of a meaningful word from one language to another, and therefore took liberties. We know Crowley got someone in Cairo to teach him Arabic. But when he came to write this section in the *Equinox* some years later, why did he not transliterate it as above? Had he forgotten his Arabic?

Yet to assume that these are equivalents, brings us no closer to a solution. For if Crowley wrote in his diary to the effect that he met the Beast, who is he referring to? Was he not the Beast himself? Or does it imply that he was the recipient of a vision or some other psychic experience in which he was confronted by his Angel to which he gave the name of the Beast 666? And also that Crowley himself was only the vehicle or agent of it?

To date there is no answer. The solution to this set of cryptic references is still due sometime in the future.

The second reason for quoting at length from the diary of 1904 is this. In *The Book of the Law,* one of the verses in the second chapter gives a whole string of letters and numbers that to date are wholly meaningless. Crowley himself had not the slightest idea to what they referred.

> Aye! listen to the numbers & the words: 4 6 3 8 A B K 2 4 A L G M O R 3 Y X 24 89 R P S T O V A L.

And it goes on to ask,

> What meaneth this, O prophet? Thou knowest not; nor shalt thou know ever. There cometh one to follow

472

thee; he shall expound it.

Crowley later was unable to decipher the letters and numbers he had written in his own 1904 diary. It is obvious that they had a meaning at the time, but that this had since been forgotten. No meditation or other form of psychic investigation ever enabled him to recall that significance, even after he had refused to rebel any further against the role he should play, as described in *The Book of the Law*. But that being the case, we should not expect a similar type of verse in *The Book of the Law* with their letters and numbers to be any more or less meaningful than his own diaries, which he himself could not later decipher. He was the author of both—both were mysterious to him.

On March 16th, apparently he used the old Bornless Invocation, dear to his heart as I have indicated many times before. The next day, the entry states that Thoth appeared.[4] This is difficult to grasp because there is no necessary connection between the Bornless ritual and the invocation of Thoth. Something may have slipped up. I will use Crowley's method of describing this slip-up. Suppose I make up my mind to go downtown to the Civic Center; that would be East of here. Later I find I have wound up at the beach, that is to the West. No matter how beautiful the surf and the sunset, it is not where I wanted to go. Something has gone wrong, and it will not mollify me to describe the scenic wonder of the beach. In the same way, no matter how wonderful Thoth was, he was not invoked. I am puzzled. Unless there was a Thoth invocation at the same time, and it was not mentioned.[5]

Be that as it may, on March 18th, he was told to invoke Hoori (that is Horus) in a new way.

It was probably on this day that P. cross-examined W. about Horus. Only the striking character of her

identification of the God, surely, would have made him
trouble to obey her. He remembers that he only agreed
to obey her in order to show her how silly she was, and
he taunted her that 'nothing could happen if you broke
all the rules.'

Here therefore we insert a short note by Fra. P. how
W. knew R.H.K. (Ra Hoor Khuit).

This segment is taken from *The Equinox of the Gods*, a fairly
late publication, though most of it is comprised of lengthy
excerpts from other of his writings.

1. Force and Fire (I asked her to describe his moral
qualities.)

2. Deep blue light. (I asked her to describe the
conditions caused by him. This light is quite
unmistakable and unique; but of course her words,
though a fair description of it, might equally apply to
some other.)

3. Horus. (I asked her to pick out his name from a
list of ten dashed off at haphazard.)

4. Recognized his figure when shown. (This refers to
the striking scene in the Boulak Museum, which will be
dealt with in detail.)

5. Knew my past relations with the God. (This
means, I think, that she knew I had taken his place in
temple, etc., and that I had never once invoked him.)

6. Knew his enemy. (I asked, "Who is his enemy?"
Reply, "Forces of the waters—of the Nile." W. knew no
Egyptology—or anything else.)

7. Knew his lineal figure and its colour. (A 1/84
chance.)

8. Knew his place in temple. (A 1/4 chance, at the
least.)

9. Knew his weapon (from a list of 6.)

10. Knew his planetary nature (from a list of 7
planets.)

11. Knew his number (from a list of 10 units.)

12. Picked him out of (a) Five (b) Three indifferent,

i.e. arbitrary symbols. (This means that I settled in my own mind that say D. of A, B, C, D, and E should represent him, and that she then said D.)

To apply test 4, Fra. P. took her to the museum at Boulak which they had not previously visited. She passed by (as P. noted with silent glee) several images of Horus. They went upstairs. A glass case stood in the distance, too far off for its contents to be recognized. But W. recognized it! "There," she cried, "There he is!"

Fra. P. advanced to the case. This was the image of Horus in the form of Ra Hoor Khuit painted upon a wooden stélé of the 26th dynasty—and the exhibit bore the number 666!

(And after that it was five years before Fra. P. was forced to obedience!)

This Stélé of Revealing, as he came to call it, has played a prominent role in the life of Crowley after the dictation of *The Book of the Law*. It had an important message for him. He had a copy made of the original in the Boulak Museum, and it accompanied him wherever he went. Some of his more enthusiastic disciples have either had copies similarly made, or else have had the colored reproductions in the *Equinox* mounted or framed. It is mentioned in *The Book of the Law*. Some of the versified translations of the Egyptian text of the Stélé were inserted into the body of *The Book of the Law*, as directed, apparently to save time. It was in this Stélé that the name Ankh-f-n-Khonsu, the priest of the Princes is mentioned. The case in which it was contained was numbered 666. Crowley came to believe that this was his name in a former incarnation.

He was prompted by Ouarda the Seer, or W. as he preferred to call Rose at that time, to perform a magical ceremony invoking Horus. As an affront to his knowledge and skill and to mortify his reason, he was to do it in a wholly unorthodox way, breaking all the technical rules that ordinarily would prevail. It was to be performed, said

Ouarda, "before a window open to the E. or N. without incense. The room to be filled with jewels, but only diamonds to be worn. A sword, unconsecrated, 44 pearl beads to be told. Stand. Bright daylight at 12:30 noon. Lock doors. White robes. Bare feet. Be very loud. Saturday. Use the Sign of Apophis and Typhon."

I want to quote a paragraph that Crowley or Fuller originally wrote as a preface to reprinting the Ritual to Horus. It is given here because, in spite of all protestations to the contrary, it does explain some of the idiosyncracies contained in *The Book of the Law*. "The MS. of this Ritual bears many internal marks of having been written at white heat and left unrevised, save perhaps for one glance. *There are mistakes in grammar and spelling unique in all MSS. of Fra. P.; the use of capitals is irregular, and the punctuation almost wanting.*" (The italics are mine.)

The Ritual referred to will not be given *in toto* here, but let me give a few curious mannerisms of phraseology to be found in it.

> My trust is in Thee; shall I be confounded? This Ritual of Art: this forty and Fourfold Invocation; this Sacrifice of Blood—these I do not comprehend . . . .
> For why? . . . .
> Enough! I turn toward Thy Promise . . . .
> Hail! Thou who bearest the Wand of Double Power! Thee, Thee I invoke! Thou about whose presence is shed the darkness of Blue Light . . . .

First of all, in connection with the above paragraph, beginning "The MS of this Ritual", let me give another paragraph written by Crowley in *The Equinox of the Gods:*

> Compare with this Book my "jokes," where I pretend to edit the MS. of another; "Alice," "Amphora," "Clouds without Water." Observe in each case the technical perfection of the "discovered" or "translated"

MS., smooth skilled elaborate art and craft of a Past Master Workman; observe the carefully detailed tone and style of the prefaces, and the sedulous creation of the personalities of the imaginary author and the imaginary editor.

These two paragraphs should be kept firmly in mind, so that in the further paragraph about to be quoted we will be able to feel our way around.

I may observe that I should not have left such obvious grounds for indictment as these had I prepared the Ms. to look pretty to a critical eye; nor should I have left such curious deformities of grammar and syntax, defects of rhythm, and awkwardness of phrase. I should not have printed passages, some rambling and unintelligible, some repugnant to reason by their absurdity, others again by their barbaric ferocity abhorrent to the heart.

This is not altogether the case. Some of the so-called holy books are characterized by just such passages, some rambling and unintelligible, some repugnant to reason by their absurdity, and their jarring goatish quality, as I have previously called it. For example, consider these verses from *Liber VII*:

12. I woo thee with a dagger drawn across my throat.
13. Let the spout of blood quench Thy blood-thirst, O my God!

Or a couple from the following chapter of the same book:

20. O all ye toads and cats, rejoice! Ye slimy things, come hither!
21. Dance, dance to the Lord our God!

And, once more:

51. They draw their shining God unto the land in

THE BOOK OF THE LAW 477

nets; they build a fire to the Lord of Fire, and cry
unhallowed words, even the dreadful curse Amri
maratza, maratza, atman deona lastadza maratza
maritza--maran!

52. Then do they cook the shining god, and gulp him
whole.

Then Crowley goes on to add:

> I should not have allowed such jumbles of matter,
> such abrupt jerks from subject to subject, disorder
> ravaging reason with disconnected sluttishness. I should
> not have tolerated the discords, jarred and jagged, of
> manner, as when a sublime panegyric of Death is
> followed first by a cipher and then by a prophecy,
> before, without taking breath, the author leaps to the
> utmost magnificence of thought both mystical and
> practical, in language so concise, simple and lyrical as to
> bemuse our very amazement. I should not have spelt
> 'Ay' 'Aye', or acquiesced in the horror 'abstruction'.

Be that as it may, and despite Crowley's emphatic
statement that "I am utterly incapable, even when most
inspired, of such English as I find in that Book again and
again", there are many points of resemblance to his other
inspired writing, and there are many places where Crowley's
own hand is to be detected, even though we were to admit he
were not conscious of doing so.

The Book orders dogmatically, "Change not so much as
the style of a letter." There are a few verses where ordinarily
one would feel most inclined to do a little editing. One feels
that, despite the inherent assumption that the Book was
dictated by a higher Agency, it is more than possible that
Crowley as the scribe accidentally wrote a semi-colon in the
wrong place—and so forth.

Vol. VII of the *Equinox* provides a startling confirmation
of my assumption. It gives a photographic reproduction of
the holographic record of *The Book of the Law.* It is

succeeded by Crowley's first attempt at a commentary on the Book, as he was advised to do. On page 397 of this particular volume of the *Equinox*, he wrote, as part of the Commentary, "the punctuation of the Book was done after its writing."

If so, his punctuation, which was added later, is no intrinsic part of the dictated contents of the Book. Therefore its command, "change not so much as the style of a letter" does not necessarily hold good for later alterations nor for the punctuation. There is also another verse (II, v. 54): "The stops as thou wilt; the letters? change them not in style or value!"

"I give unimaginable joys on earth: certainty, not faith, while in life, upon death; peace unutterable, rest, ecstasy; nor do I demand aught in sacrifice." It would seem most evident that the phrase "while in life" should be followed immediately by a semi-colon rather than by a comma. It would then read: "upon death, peace unutterable . . . . " etc. But Crowley did not dare change one for the other.

"I am the flame that burns in every heart of man" would seem to indicate that due to the speed of transcription the word "every" was mistakenly placed before "heart" instead of before "man".

"For why?" This is verse 13, of chapter II. As we have seen, Crowley used this curious phrasing in the Ritual, though it was originally used in one of the Enochian Calls. Elsewhere, in one of the commentaries, he admits to not liking the juxtaposition of such words. It bothered him. But he has used them.

"Ye, even ye, know not this meaning all." Is the word "all" transposed? Should it not be before "this"?

Verse 72 of Chapter III. There was a blank here. Apparently he did not hear the dictated words. It was filled in later by Rose. "I am the Lord of the Double Wand of Power; the wand of the Force of *Coph Nia*—." At first this looks as if it could have been the Hebrew word for *Ain Soph* the Infinite. Crowley of course would have known it. Its misplacement looks as if done by someone who did not know the direction of Hebrew letters, nor their meaning.

Crowley would have wholly disapproved of this discussion and analysis relative to *The Book of the Law.* He had laid down some strict rules shortly after the Cefalu period—which considered anyone who did discuss this Book as a center of pestilence. This may have been due to his disillusioning experiences with one Frater Achad in America, and Leah Hirzig and Norman Mudd having played around with and perverted the predictions implicit in this Book. They were flung into the outer darkness, as it were, for doing so. It was then that he uttered the dictum to regard anyone who discussed the Book as a center of pestilence, and thus to be avoided.

It has often occurred to me that, having been bred with the taste of the Bible in his mouth, the verse in *Liber Legis* "Change not so much as the style of a letter" must have its origins in the same book which gave him his honorific magical title, the Beast. And of course, there it is, in *The Book of Revelation,* 22, vv. 18-19. These verses forbid anyone from adding to or subtracting from the words of the book of prophecy under dire divine penalties. Having read these verses often as a child, they must have affected him deeply, leaving indelible traces which emerged when the Book itself percolated upwards from the depths.

On the other hand, the Book contains innumerable passages of superb beauty, nobility, and incomparable power and sublimity. The "transcendental point of view" is often depicted with clarity and precision.

Here is one of the longest verses in the Book:

But to love me is better than all things: if under the night-stars in the desert thou presently burnest mine incense before me, invoking me with a pure heart, and the Serpent flame therein, thou shalt come a little to lie in my bosom. For one kiss wilt thou then be willing to give all; but whoso gives one particle of dust shall lose all in that hour. Ye shall gather goods and store of women and spices; ye shall wear rich jewels; ye shall exceed the nations of the earth in splendour and pride; but always in the love of me, and so shall ye come to my joy. I charge you earnestly to come before me in a single robe, and covered with a rich head-dress. I love you! I yearn to you! Pale or purple, veiled or voluptuous, I who am all pleasure and purple, and drunkenness of the innermost sense, desire you. Put on the wings, and arouse the coiled splendour within you; come unto me!

Some of the others, scattered throughout the three chapters:

I am the Snake that giveth Knowledge & Delight and bright glory, and stir the hearts of men with drunkenness. To worship me take wine and strange drugs whereof I will tell my prophet, & be drunk thereof! They shall not harm ye at all. It is a lie, this folly against self. The exposure of innocence is a lie. Be strong, O man! lust, enjoy all things of sense and rapture: fear not that any God shall deny thee for this.
I am alone: there is no God where I am.
Behold! these be grave mysteries; for there are also of my friends who be hermits. Now think not to find them in the forest or on the mountain;

This part of the verse is worth comparing with the introduction to a long poem in free verse, *The Hermit's Hymn to Solitude*, that he dedicated to Bhikkhu Ananda Metteya, written about 1902, in which was asked whether he, Crowley, might not be more alone, more a hermit in the midst of civilization, than the Bhikkhu in retirement in his isolated Burmese monastery?
The verse continues:

but in beds of purple, caressed by magnificent beasts of women with large limbs, and fire and light in their eyes, and masses of flaming hair about them; there shall ye find them. Ye shall see them at rule, at victorious armies, at all the joy; and there shall be in them a joy a million times greater than this. Beware lest any force another, King against King! Love one another with burning hearts; on the low men trample in the fierce lust of your pride, in the day of your wrath.

The word of the Law is Thelema.

Yea! deem not of change: ye shall be as ye are, & not other. Therefore the kings of the earth shall be Kings forever: the slaves shall serve. There is none that shall be cast down or lifted up: all is ever as it was. Yet there are masked ones my servants: it may be that yonder beggar is a King. A King may choose his garment as he will: there is no certain test: but a beggar cannot hide his poverty.

O be thou proud and mighty among men!
Lift up thyself! for there is none like unto thee among men or among Gods! Lift up thyself, O my prophet, thy stature shall surpass the stars. They shall worship thy name, four-square, mystic, wonderful, the number of the man; and the name of thy house 418.

There are four gates to one palace; the floor of that palace is of silver and gold; lapis lazuli & jasper are there; and all rare scents; jasmine & rose, and the emblems of death. Let him stand on the floor of the palace. Will he not sink? Amn. Ho! warrior, if thy servant sink? But there are means and means. Be goodly therefore: dress ye all in fine apparel; eat rich foods and drink sweet wines and wines that foam! Also, take your fill and will of love as ye will, when, where and with whom ye will! But always unto me.

The ordeals thou shalt oversee thyself, save only the blind ones. Refuse none, but thou shalt know & destroy the traitors. I am Ra-Hoor-Khuit; and I am powerful to protect my servant. Success is thy proof: argue not; convert not; talk not overmuch! Them that seek to entrap thee, to overthrow thee, them attack without pity or quarter; & destroy them utterly. Swift as a trodden serpent turn and strike! Be thou yet deadlier than he! Drag down their souls to awful torment: laugh at their fear; spit upon them!

I am the warrior Lord of the Forties; the Eighties cower before me, & are abased. I will bring you to victory & joy: I will be at your arms in battle & ye shall delight to slay. Success is your proof; courage is your armour; go on, go on, in my strength; & ye shall turn not back for any!

This book shall be translated into all tongues: but always with the original in the writing of the Beast; for in the chance shape of the letters and their position to one another: in these are mysteries that no Beast shall divine. Let him not seek to try: but one cometh after him, whence I say not, who shall discover the Key of it all. Then this line drawn is a key: then this circle squared in its failure is a key also. And Abrahadabra. It shall be his child & that strangely. Let him not seek after this; for thereby alone can he fall from it.

There are many other passages in this Book that are savage, full of contempt, passionately angry, and altogether without mercy or compassion. I shall select a verse here and there to represent these moods.

These are fools that men adore: both their Gods & their men are fools.

For these fools of men and their woes care not thou at all! They feel little; what is, is balanced by weak joys; but ye are my chosen ones.

These are dead, these fellows; they feel not. We are

not for the poor and sad: the lords of the earth are our kinsfolk.

We have nothing with the outcast and the unfit: let them die in their misery. For they feel not. Compassion is the vice of kings: stamp down the wretched & the weak: this is the law of the strong: this is our law and the joy of the world.

In the *Confessions,* Crowley described an incident somewhere in the East of a native being beaten or tortured, I forget which. At first he was profoundly moved by the man's apparent quiet courage and stoicism. But he came afterwards to modify this viewpoint, believing that not all nervous systems are necessarily alike. There was no reason to suppose that this native's nervous system was as sensitive as, for example, his own. Or that the native felt pain as keenly as Crowley did. Only in this way, could he understand and appreciate the hardships and severe ordeals that some people undergo without wilting or shrinking. Their experience of pain and suffering is muted, whether by conditioning or structure made no difference. It was this realization that may have remained dormant, to be used in such passages in *The Book of the Law* as the above.

To continue with this theme:

There is great danger in me; for who doth not understand these runes shall make a great miss. He shall fall down into the pit called Because, and there shall he perish with the dogs of Reason.

Now a curse upon Because and his kin!

May Because be accursed forever!

If Will stops and cries Why, invoking Because, then Will stops and does naught.

If Power asks why, then is Power weakness.

Also reason is a lie; for there is a factor infinite & unknown; & all their words are skew-wise.

Enough of Because! Be he damned for a dog!

There is a veil: that veil is black. It is the veil of the modest woman; it is the veil of sorrow, & the pall of death: this is none of me. Tear down that lying spectre of the centuries: veil not your vices in virtuous words: these vices are my service; ye do well, & I will reward you here and hereafter.

Beware therefore! Love all, lest perchance is a King concealed! Say you so? Fool! If he be a King, thou canst not hurt him.
Therefore strike hard & low, and to hell with them, master!

Fear not at all; fear neither men nor Fates, nor gods, nor anything. Money fear not, nor laughter of the folk folly, nor any other power in heaven or upon the earth or under the earth. Nu is your refuge as Hadit your light; and I am the strength, force, vigour of your arms.
Mercy let be off: damn them who pity! Kill and torture; spare not; be upon them!

Let Mary inviolate be torn upon wheels: for her sake let all chaste women be utterly despised among you!
Also for beauty's sake and love's!

There are many traces of the Golden Dawn influence throughout the entire Book. Merely the replacement of Osiris by Horus has basic reference to the Ceremony of the Equinox, when one set of officers is installed to replace some other set. In the book are innumerable subtle references to Qabalah and Tarot—all contents of Crowley's mind, materials derived from the Order which shaped his life. It was also on the basis of one verse "Abrogate are all rituals, all ordeals, all words and signs.", that he wrote to McGregor Mathers informing him that the Secret Chiefs had appointed Crowley head of the Order.

"Ye are against the people."

This is one of the anti-democratic attitudes adopted by

The Book of the Law, calculated to be very disturbing to most of us indoctrinated with modern ideas of government and religion. This latter is slashed into ribbons by Aiwass. I suppose the justification for this is a simple one. The people, in the sense of the conservative masses, are against any real piece of scientific or social progress. They resist it ferociously.

The really great revolutionary advances in art, literature and science, incur only the hostility and resistance of the vast public. Were Christ to return, he could well be crucified once again. *The Book of the Law* then merely reverses this, arguing that this uncouth monster "the Common Man" is to be ignored—even put in his place. There is no room here for democracy, nor the respect for the ordinary man. There is only a haughty disdain for him.

There is a hint of this in *Konx Om Pax* written at a time when he lived and acted almost as though *Liber Legis* had never been dictated. He is discussing Samadhi, and refers to the delusion of other separate existences.

Regardless of how he operated consciously, it is evident that the contents of this book were part and parcel of Crowley's unconscious psyche. It makes little difference to this discussion whether it was dictated to him by a higher source, or whether it issued from his own creative depths. Once written, it had become a part of his total equipment, whether or not he was conscious of its existence at any particular moment of time.

For example, verse 34 of Chapter III reads:

> But your holy place shall be untouched throughout the centuries; though with fire and sword it be burnt down & shattered, yet an invisible house there standeth; and shall stand until the fall of the Great Equinox; when Hrumachis shall arise and the double-wanded one assume my throne and place. Another prophet shall arise, and bring fresh fever from the skies . . . .

In this eloquent passage there is a direct instruction

concerning the end of the Aeon—of that period of time with its philosophical outlook which both Crowley and Fuller had come to label as Crowleyanity. There was no need for him to be consciously aware of this verse from *The Book of the Law.*

(As a parenthetical comment to one observation of Symonds relative to Crowley's role as a teacher, let it be noted that in Crowley's mythology each Aeon lasts some two thousand years. Our current aeon, the age of the crowned and conquering child Horus—recognized in other mythologies as the Aquarian Age—was initiated in the year 1904. If Crowley did say once that a thousand years hence we would be bathing in the sunset of Crowleyanity, there is little mystery here. According to his schema, another Aeon, with another social formula and a different concept of law, will be ready to come into operation in a couple of thousand years hence.)

On a conscious level he had rejected the book itself for whatever reasons were valid to him at the time, but from the moment of its writing it had become a part of his make-up. Its persistence on an unconscious psychic level thus guaranteed, whenever the occasion arose it would percolate into consciousness to be used by him without the necessary conscious knowledge that this was in fact occurring.

Poor Charles R. Cammell was quite undone by *The Book of the Law.* Crowley at one time had given him a copy. Some passages disturbed Cammell so tremendously that he had to burn it. Here is what Cammell said about *The Book of the Law,* and how he came to reject it:[6]

> The Book of the Law is composed in that style of figurative eloquence characteristic of prophetic utterance. Its manner is that of the Hebrew Prophets, of the Koran, and of most other works of vaticination with which I am acquainted. Its matter, however, is distinct

and peculiar. This is no Book of Sacred Magic, like Abramelin's. A fierce and haughty disdain of humanity informs it; yet it embodies a savage and awe-inspiring justice. The mind behind the maxims is cold, cruel and relentless. Mercy there is none, nor consolation; nor hope save in the service of this dread messenger of the gods of Egypt. Such is *Liber Legis* in letter and spirit; and as such, and in consideration of its manner of reception, it is a document of curious interest. That it is in part (but in part only) an emanation from Crowley's unconscious mind I can believe; for it bears a likeness to his own Daemonic personality. With curiosity and interest I read it, on its appearance, till, reading it, I came upon a passage of enormous and atrocious blasphemy. No written or spoken words have ever angered or disgusted me as did these words. For publishing that phrase I have never forgiven Crowley. May God forgive him!

I have but the vaguest idea of the nature of this blasphemy that disturbed poor Cammell. *Liber Legis,* and indeed all of Crowley's writings contain blasphemies, if we wish to define blasphemies as passionate statements of revolt against and rejection of the household gods of every man, stated in unequivocal language. A great deal of it puzzles me, some disturbs me a little, but I cannot say that its blasphemies, so-called, would move me to any great heights of indignation. I am too familiar with blasphemies, and altogether inured to them to react in so emotional and infantile a manner.

After reviewing this topic, it is quite possible that the accused section from the Book which bothered Cammell so much might be the following:

> I am in a secret fourfold word, the blasphemy against all gods of men.
> Curse them! Curse them! Curse them!
> With my Hawk's head I peck at the eyes of Jesus as he hangs upon the cross.
> I flap my wings in the face of Mohammed & blind him.

With my claws I tear out the flesh of the Indian and
the Buddhist, Mongol and Din.
    Bahlasti! Ompehda! I spit on your crapulous creeds.

In one sense, Cammell's reaction is rather amusing—but
pitiful. He has permitted what appears on the surface to be
blasphemy to blind him to the perception of more adult
interpretations. In this case, he bears some resemblance to
Gilbert Highet who was able to see no sense in Crowley at all,
but did develop an occasional insight relative to Zen.

Yet Zen is loaded with palpable blasphemies. Perhaps these
have disturbed many seekers in years gone by. At the same
time they may have precipitated illuminations in a few others
who were not so readily fooled. Zen is a direct pointing to
the truth. It is not predicated on scriptures or authority of
any kind. Is not this also what Crowley was attempting both
to say and do?

I am reminded of some of the classical Zen Roshis who
attempted to convey the feeling of spiritual independence
and non-attachment to any authority, regardless of stature or
reverence. One of them said most irreverently that Buddha
was a great chatterbox! Another stated that if one truly
understood one would wash out his mouth for three days
after saying the word Buddha! A famous koan has a monk
asking the question "What is Buddha?" and receiving the
answer "Dried excrement."

The *piece de resistance*, however, is contained in the
injunction that nothing should be permitted to stand in the
way to the highest. If Buddha were to be found standing in
the way, then kill him!

Blasphemous? Sacrilegious? Of course these statements
are. All of them are blasphemies of the most outrageous type.
Crowley's blasphemies are no more and no less. They are
only blasphemies however to one who values forms above the
spiritual content. They are insults only to those who confuse

map with territory, symbol with reality, to take a leaf from
Korzybski.

Crowley and his Book were destroyers—but merely of the
illusions and dishonest deceptions that manacle man to what
appears to be the sorrowful world of which he is a part.

> Remember all ye that existence is pure joy: that all
> the sorrows are but shadows; they pass and are done;
> but there is that which remains.

> Obey my prophet! follow out the ordeals of my
> knowledge! seek me only! Then the joys of my love will
> redeem ye from all pain. This is so: I swear it by the
> vault of my body; by my sacred heart and tongue; by all
> I can give, by all I desire of ye all.

There are about three or four verses from this *Liber Legis*
which are, from Crowley's point of view, more important
pragmatically than the others. Whenever he would meet or
greet someone, his opening remark would be, "Do what thou
wilt shall be the whole of the Law." All his correspondence
opened in this way too! And his constant complaint about it
was that people were always misquoting it and otherwise
taking liberties with it, as in "Do as you will" etc.

Some of the other maxims are: "Love is the law, love
under will." This was the counter-reply to the first, so that if
greeted by the one, you replied with the other. It became a
kind of ritual amongst his disciples—about on the same
unthinking order as "How are you?" and "Thank you—fine!"

"Thou hast no right but to do thy will."

"The word of Sin is restriction."

"Every man and every woman is a Star."

"Enough of Because! Be he damned for a dog!"

"As brothers fight ye!"

The essence of these various maxims is essentially a simple
one, though all too many writers and commentators have
ridiculed it without attempting to understand either what the

Book has said or what Crowley has commented by way of explanation. All that those many phrases refer to is self-regulation. Every healthy living organism regulates its own activity on a homeostatic basis without reference to arbitrary man-made laws or codes. It rules itself, regulates itself, and does its own will. Every man and woman is thus autonomous. As soon as compulsory moral codes are adopted, and thrust on the natural growth and development of young children, autonomy goes out of the window. Instead, one perceives a conflict-ridden human being, subservient, diseased, and neurotic. All modern systems of psychotherapy are predicated on this one basis, that every human being has his own integrity, his own essential individuality, and that he must regulate his own behavior in order to remain healthy. Even that most passive of all current psychotherapeutic systems, non-directive counselling, is predicated on the basis of not attempting to interfere with the essential uniqueness of the counsellee by giving advice, counsel, or direction to his behavior. It seeks only to reflect the counsellee's behavior, verbally as well as physically and socially, so that he may perceive that he is not functioning in terms of his own inviolable integrity.

"Do what thou wilt" has no meaning other than this. It is entirely too bad that Crowley's own playfulness and energetic exuberance so darkened his reputation that practically no one took time out to try to grasp what he was talking about. It really was crystal clear all the time, and has been enunciated in other ways and in other terms by many people from time to time.

The physical organism functions on this basis. Homeostasis is the law which regulates its activities. No act of Congress or Parliament or any municipal government can enhance the manner in which it goes about its various functions. It has its own inherent laws by means of which it functions. Psychologically, the same is true. Man has always had thrust on him moral codes which seek to tell him how he should behave under this and that or the other circumstance, instead of helping the living person to function spontaneously. By so doing, one falls back instinctively on a non-verbal and non-rational code which has enabled the organism-as-a-whole to survive over millions of years and evolve into its present state. No arbitrary moral code was responsible for this. Survival is the integral property of the living person.

Reich was another advocate of the notion of the self-regulatory function of the human being. He claimed that if the infant were not basically interfered with biologically by having neurotic parental standards forcibly imposed on it, it would be able to be wholly self-determining throughout its entire lifetime. When first introduced to this idea, most people stand aghast at it—as if any individual would "go completely to hell" if permitted to express itself freely on an animal or biological level. I have heard parents say that if they let junior select his own foods, for example, they would consist solely of chocolate bars and pop. At first, this sounds *almost* as if it could be so—until one becomes familiar with some basic experimental work.

The most important of these experiments, which wholly corroborates the concepts of self-regulation and thus vindicates the spontaneity viewpoint, is cafeteria feeding. A group of several children was once selected, ranging from six months to two or three years of age. At feeding time, they were confronted by trays containing small portions of as many as twenty or thirty different foodstuffs. In the case of very young infants, when any one food was pointed to, the attendant spooned it out and helped the child eat. If it rejected the food by spitting it out, no attempt was made to force or cajole it into eating. Selection, apparently, was made on the basis of visual and olfactory interests. At the close of the experiments, after some months, it was determined that

the selection of the foods, so far as concerned basic food
elements such as minerals, vitamins, proteins, etc. would not
be other than would have been prescribed by a nutritional
expert. In other words, the infant selected—it was not
cajoled. There was no imposition of authoritarian
dictates—no matter how sound or reliable. The infant was
permitted to select on a spontaneous natural basis—and it
prospered.

This fact has long been known about animals and their
biological needs. It was always questioned, however, with
regard to human beings. But this question only indicates how
thoroughly it has been suspected that environmental
pressures of a neurotic culture invalidate the natural capacity
for self-regulation of any and all biological functions. What
has been discovered with regard to food, might be equally
true in most other areas. If biological urges are permitted to
operate without interference from compulsive moralities,
they tend to regulate themselves in a totally realistic manner.
Morality, as such, is not required. It is the result of
repression, which forces secondary and pathological or
substitutive drives into overt expression. These latter, once
developed, require regulation, discipline, and perhaps
compulsive suppression. The biological core of all living
things has functioned for aeons solely in terms of expression,
necessity and adjustment—survival being its keynote.
Morality, compulsive imposition of norms, and social
inhibition are creating pathological people whose resulting
sado-masochistic needs, if unchecked, may drive mankind
into total extinction.

This is the major implication of Crowley's "Do what thou
wilt shall be the whole of the Law." It means self-regulation
and autonomy on all levels. "Do that, and no other shall say
nay." "Also, take your fill and will of love as ye will, when,
where and with whom ye will! But always unto me."

He commented on this viewpoint in another way in another

place.

> Again "Do what thou Wilt", the most sublimely austere ethical precept ever uttered, despite its apparent license, is seen on analysis to be indeed "the whole of the Law", the sole and sufficient warrant for human action, the self-evident Code of Righteousness, the identification of Fate with Freewill, and the end of the Civil War in man's Nature by appointing the Canon of Truth, the conforming of things with themselves, to determine his every act. "Do what thou wilt" is to bid Stars to shine, Vines to bear grapes, Water to seek its level; man is the only being in Nature that has striven to set himself at odds with himself.

The formulation of this law in socio-psychological terms was similarly stated by Reich, whom I paraphrase:

We are dealing here with a decisive question of social culture formation. As the gratification of basic needs becomes underwritten by society and human structure changes accordingly, *moral* regulation of social life will become unnecessary. The final desideratum does not lie in the psychological but in the social realms. Every psychoanalysis which is successful automatically replaces moral regulation by a self-regulation based on a sound libido economy. When many psychoanalysts speak of the 'dissolution of the superego' through psychotherapy of any type, we realize that it is a matter of withdrawing energy from the inhibitions and their replacement by natural self-regulation.

Reich further added that the individual who is satisfied in his sexual and his primitive biological as well as cultural needs has no need of morality for self-control. On the other hand, the chronically unsatisfied person suffers from an increased inner excitation, seeking discharge in all kinds of anti-social and violent action unless his energies were blocked and absorbed by moral inhibitions.

One of the most glaring aspects of *The Book of the Law* is that its stand on almost every moral issue runs counter to the accepted social one of today. Certainly it is in direct opposition to our Judaeo-Christian mores. Up to the time of the dictation of *The Book of the Law,* Crowley's emotional momentum had led him to challenge and overthrow the basic moral attitudes of his parents, and the religion they and their representatives taught him. His life was an open revolt. There was no secret or mystery about this. It was stated a hundred times in one form or another in everything he wrote and everything he did.

Under these circumstances, it would be most surprising if this Book—whether dictated by a praeterhuman intelligence or composed by Crowley himself—did not take an identical stand. The miracle in his life would have been for this Book to have agreed with all that he had been fighting against. But this miracle did not occur. With considerable fervor, the Book echoes Crowley's underlying moral, social, and religious attitudes without equivocation or doubt. Dictated or created, it is his Book.

This rebelliousness, this overt need to shock Mrs. Grundy, was part of his make-up until the day he died. How early it began in his life is not made clear from his biography. But it is clearly evident, psychoanalytically, that this particular rebelliousness had its roots in early life, in anal hostility. Not too many overt references to this etiologic factor can be found in his history, but it is there by inference from the examination of everything he did. The unbroken record of quarrelling with all his friends and colleagues—with the exception of Bennett and Eckenstein; his homosexuality which is loaded with anal components; his self-admitted irrational spitefulness; and a reference here and there in his vast literary output. Psycho-analysis is more than useful here.

Regarding his anal homosexual components, some of his

jokes reveal the deepest unconscious trends of his psyche. One of his favorite jokes was that of an English aristocrat who was invited to a friend's house for dinner. As the butler wheeled in the trolley bearing a roast suckling-pig, the aristocrat was heard to mutter: "Poor little bugger. Poor little swine. Your arse is sewed up. And so is mine!"

Another gag is that pulled in *The Book of Lies*. Most of the material in this book is serious and profound, though paradoxical. For fun's sake, and to test out the reader, he has thrown in a few ribald entries. For example, toward the end of this particular book, he speaks of Chinese food and the wonderful sharksfin soup, etc., that he has eaten. But all of this is nothing compared to what Laylah left him when she went away. He reproduced a hieroglyph at this juncture to depict this present. It took me some years, so vast was my naivete, before I finally managed to decipher it. Deciphered it spells out a four lettered word for human excrement. In this way, he enjoyed his own joke, but poured out his own refuse on the reader.

His anal traits, however, left their psychological traces in a variety of mannerisms. His lack of sound judgment and foresight are merely two of them. But they are nowhere more dramatically spotlighted than in the selection of John Symonds as one of his three literary executors. This man's basic insincerity, demonstrated vividly in the first two or three chapters of the contemptuous treatment of *The Magick of Aleister Crowley* by John Symonds, seemed to have been wholly lost on Crowley. This book shows conclusively that the author's contact with Crowley was with tongue in cheek throughout, that he managed successfully to pull the wool over the dying man's eyes. For what motive? This has yet to be explicated.

One of the most paradoxical characteristics of Crowley is also shown here. Sooner or later he fell out with his most devoted friends and disciples on the most trivial of grounds, and then seemed to deliver himself, body and soul, to those miscreants who subsequently proved themselves as enemies of him personally as well as of his cause.

It cannot be said that the matter is of world-shaking importance. But I feel strongly about this, mostly because many of my friends and other students have been thoroughly put off from reading anything by Aleister Crowley after having seen Symonds' book *The Great Beast*. For these people, the book seemed to have borne the true stamp of authenticity, especially after having learned that Crowley had in fact named him as one of his literary executors. It is this reason largely, which serves as one of my motives for exposing Symonds, as well as to remove Crowley from the ridiculous pedestal on which some of his disciples have all too unthinkingly placed him.

Many of his jokes were interpolated in the most unexpected places. For example, in a footnote intended to be a serious exposition of Magick, there is a typical piece of ribaldry about the Papyrus of Ani otherwise known as the Egyptian *Book of the Dead*. Crowley commented that papyrus is the early origin of our word paper, and of course Ani relates to the anus. So *The Book of the Dead* can be translated as toilet paper!

There are many other footnotes in *Magick* which are nothing but cryptic references to homosexuality—brilliantly disguised by the reference to the Ordo Templi Orientis, but nonetheless clearly expressing his anality.

Some may fear that these were irreverent and obscene. Indeed they were. Some critics who, prior to publication, have read this section of my book have been horrified, fearing the general public will reject them as being plain dirt. Perhaps. To Crowley, apart from the unconscious factors, they merely prevented any subject from becoming intellectually burdensome and topheavy. Moreover, they served as a means to demonstrate the unity or identity of the highest and the lowest, the union of the opposites. From the vantage point of beyond the Abyss, there is nothing to choose between them.

His attitudes regarding money are further chaotic evidences of his anality. There was complete confusion in his life on this matter. Consciously, he was wholly unable to remedy the situation dictated by these infantile anal residues in the Unconscious.

The masochistic material quoted much earlier reveals still further his anality: "I want . . . . my soul to be Her privy." Most of his attitudes, however, are far more phallic than anal.

When the dictation of *The Book of the Law* was completed on that fateful day in April 1904, so was Crowley. There was much there he claimed that was repugnant to him, though what that could have been, I will never know. He put the manuscript aside, and to all intents and purposes lost it. But one coincidence after another occurred, until he could no longer believe they were mere coincidences. They were a string of events, apparently connected by some pre-arranged inevitability which *forced* him in line, to take up the burden of responsibility indicated in the Book. Crowley developed the theory that Aiwass—be he Angel or praeterhuman intelligence and a member of the Third Order or whatever—was able to influence the course of events in his life by subtle means, to bring him back to the way he must go.

Crowley was not merely a man of the world, nor yet a distinguished literary man nor a mystic of considerable attainment. Against his will, he had been transformed into a Man with a Message for the whole of mankind.

Though he claims to have wilfully rejected this Book, for which there is a good deal of evidence, there is a current of egotism and high ambition to teach men a new way of life in all he wrote and did. And yet this repudiated Book did at least two things. It flattered his already hypertrophied ego with such verses as "Worship and Glory to the Beast, the prophet of the lovely Star." It also told him specifically that he must fill the role of a teacher to men.

His account of the rejection seems a most unlikely story. What may perhaps explain more adequately his rejection of the Book are two distinct and clearly defined facts. First of all, the Book was dictated to him in terms of psychical phenomena, which he wholly distrusted. Second, and above all other things, he was *ordered* to do certain things.

It was this command which struck the rebellious note in him. Once his father died, the boy Crowley ceased to be docile and started to rebel in one way or another. Like a stubborn mule, he continued the process of rebellion all through his life, even when it was no longer useful or meaningful. It was his intrinsic rebelliousness that forced him to reject the Book.

The dictation of the Book was not a self-willed phenomenon. It was forced on him; he was merely a scribe, an instrument. I am sure this did not fit in with all he thought of himself.

These are the unvoiced arguments that I fancy forced him to reject the Book rather than its contents. I can see absolutely nothing in the Book which could possibly have offended his particular sensibilities at that time. Another person might have been offended by its lack of mercy and hope, by its no uncertain enslavement of all those who were not "kings", and its open invitation to war and bloodshed. But these things were not really abhorrent to Crowley, even at that time. The man who could climb high mountains, go big-game hunting, hate Christianity, despise the critics who would not acknowledge him as the greatest poet since Shakespeare, and deify sex in all forms and aspects, such a man could not possibly be outraged by any content of this Book. Rather, I would say that it blended in perfectly well with his own views, because in reality it was the direct expression of all he thought and felt.

Crowley seriously believed that the Wars of 1914 and 1939 were released as a direct result of the prior publication of *The Book of the Law*. For him these events were a fulfilment of its prophecies, that the planet had to be bathed in a baptism of blood before a new order of things could be developed.

Some of his disciples also call attention to the drastic way that the world has changed since the early days of the twentieth century. They seem to know little of literary, scientific, or social history which is prone to relate these vast changes to many other factors. Such as (a) Freud's discovery of the principles of psychoanalysis which opened the door to the dark and repressed denizens of the Unconscious. From then on, no one could be deluded by the fantasy that we were civilized human beings, when monsters of horror lurked beneath the surface ready to perpetrate every conceivable kind of crime and beastliness.

(b) The growing ferment of Karl Marx, who exposed the fantasies in the socio-economic sphere that are comparable to Freud's discovery in the psychological sphere.

(c) The scientific discovery of Einstein which led to the development of nuclear fission, with the result that all prior ideas about armaments were seen to be child's play. With this, and the development of jet-propelled air vehicles, the world indeed has shrunk to a tiny sphere. No one point is distant from any other point by more than a few hours by plane—and less by rocket.

Their reply to this statement is as might be anticipated. These are only the external signs of the advent of the New Aeon described by Aiwass, and written down by Crowley. Ra Hoor Khuit (a solar form of Horus) as the regent of this new age represents force and fire, and his advent can only bathe this planet in a baptism of fire.

However, in the year 1904 few could have predicted the rapid destruction of the political and economic world of the day, and its replacement by the system now temporarily in operation. *The Book of the Law* has correctly called the stops, and if it is to be believed, further drastic changes in the governance of this planet are in order. There can be little doubt of this proposition. "I am the Lord of the Forties: the Eighties cower before me, and are abased." Many voices are raised calling attention to the holocaust that seems to be in the offing, but none has a ready answer or solution to offer. I do not know if the advocates of *Liber Legis* proffer final solutions to lead us out of the present impasse. If "Do what thou wilt" is the answer it does give, then speculation as to how each government could interpret that command leads us no further out of the current debacle.

Relative to this timely topic, Crowley wrote and published under one of the countless pseudonyms he has employed a pamphlet purporting to be a scientific solution to the problems of government. In the opening pages of this broadside, several verses from the three chapters of *The Book of the Law* are given, followed by no more than a dozen terse, biting comments.

Outstanding among these is the flat statement that the average voter in a democracy is a moron. This is nothing new of course, it has been affirmed by hundreds of writers before. To Crowley, this moron displays more ignorance than the so-called illiterate peasant. He lives a life of purest fantasy in which prizes from this contest or the other will provide him with the magical means of fulfilling his frustrated desires and ambitions. But he has the vote! Though Thomas Jefferson emphasized that a well-informed citizenry is essential to the welfare of a democracy, he put the emphasis on being as intelligent and as well-informed as he was. The facts signify otherwise.

The average citizen has the vote—and so must be courted by the power-hungry politician. No longer can the demagogue appeal to the divine right of kings or some other archaic fiction to warrant the subjection or manipulation of the voter to his own schemes. The other court of appeal to-day is *science.* Things must be *scientific!* Even the cultists and faddists use this word and all it implies, as the final arbiter of judgment. And all the dictators of our time have courted science with veiled references to history and to "blood, race, and earth" and other pseudo-scientific fictions.

Hence, suggested Crowley, the problem of government is to find a scientific formula with an ethical implication. This formula is only to be found in Thelema, the law of "Do what thou wilt." It is, said he, infinitely elastic in that it does not specify what particular goals are desirable in any one particular instance, yet infinitely rigid in that it binds every man to pursue the function for which he is fitted by heredity, environment, experience, and self-development.

The catch here, however, is this. Were this formula to be accepted by every government, experts would immediately have to be appointed to clarify, when need arose, the details of the true will of every individual, and even that of every corporate body, whether social or commercial. A judiciary would have to be organized to determine the equity in the case of apparently conflicting claims. "The absolute rule of the state shall be a function of the absolute liberty of each individual will." And here, I think, we are back where we started!

There are several verses from *Liber AL vel Legis* which I should quote as pertaining to this problem—though I cannot in all honesty believe that the problem is thereby solved.

> Yea! deem not of change: ye shall be as ye are, & not other. Therefore the kings of the earth shall be kings for ever. The slaves shall serve.

> Stamp down the wretched & the weak: this is the law of the strong: this is our law and the joy of the world.

But the keen and the proud, the royal and the lofty:
ye are brothers!

As brothers fight ye!

Beware lest any force another, King against King.

Quotations could be multiplied *ad infinitum,* but I think
this will provide the basis for any consideration of the claims
of Crowley that a final solution to the problem of
government had been found by him—or, more accurately, by
The Book of the Law.

There is one other item, however, that may illuminate this
knotty problem somewhat. During the American phase,
sometime between 1914-19, he wrote a constitution for the
Ordo Templi Orienlis. Apart from an isolated student or two,
there was no Order, in any literal sense of the term, at that
time in the United States. Hence the constitution that he
wrote is either fanciful, or else preparatory for the day when
there would be retreats, endowments and profess-houses, etc.
It is an idealized statement of the policy and attitudes that
should prevail within and govern the Order. As such we might
deduce from this that some variation of this constitution,
predicated as it was even then on the Law of Thelema, would
be prescribed by him for use in larger national as well as
international bodies. It also serves to demonstrate many of
his serious ideals, as well as his concept of justice and
discipline.

In considering the contents of Chapter III of the Book,
where Aiwass expresses the martial viewpoint of Ra Hoor
Khuit, the presiding genius as it were of the new Aeon, one is
forcibly struck by certain similarities. First, the
bloodthirstiness of Horus is in many ways not unlike the
uncompromising attitudes of Jehovah in the Old Testament.
And it must not be forgotten that the Bible was to all intents
and purposes the only piece of literature to which Crowley

was exposed for many years as a boy. Consequently, his Unconscious psyche must have been simply saturated with the Jehovistic point of view. Moreover, just prior to the dictation of *The Book of the Law,* Crowley was immersing himself in the study of Islam. The characteristics of Horus as evidenced in the last Chapter of *The Book of the Law* bear many resemblances also to the Allah of the Moslems, whose virility and fierceness were so respected by Crowley. Thus many elements from all areas of his psyche have entered into the theocratic contents of this Book which became the center of Crowley's life.

So often, during the writing of this interpretation of Aleister Crowley, I have leaned over backwards trying to be fair. As I analyze this, it seems on occasion that this means I have been making concessions to his critics and to some of his enemies, placating them, as it were, so that my motives should not be impugned, in order that I should not be accused of fanaticism, of blind worship of an adolescent idol. It is thus a kind of ego-defense against possible attacks by critics. It could be argued then that my perception and description of his colossal egotism may—at least in part—be a projection of my own. If so, it behooves me to recognize this and to withdraw it, with the realization that in his own story and in his own life-long search for meaning, for God, he had no need for any fairness on my part. He does not need to be bowdlerized—nor defended.

He was obligated to regard every single event and every phenomenon of his life as a particular dealing of God with his own soul. Then, though periodically misled by his own Shadow, at the same time, since *Demon Est Deus Inversus,* he was nonetheless guided throughout by—what shall I say, his Angel? This is the simple language he was able to use unashamedly. A golden thread of illumination and glory runs through all his writing and the dramatic, adventurous story of his life.

If this interpretation is to be a valid objective one, it must emphasize a point which is implicit in the man's search for meaning. From the moment of his Golden Dawn initiation in 1898 to the time of his death in 1947, Crowley had concentrated all his energies on a single divine theme. Certainly there were times when he wavered—and wandered. He was but human. "Behold," he wrote in 1907, "I am a man. Even a little child might not endure Thee!"

His ego occasionally got in the way. Everyman's story is depicted here. This is almost what makes his story epic. There were affairs with all sorts of women, some sordid, some far different. Yet when he did not complicate the picture by stressing their inferiority, he never ceased to express how greatly he was indebted to his women. His love affairs taught him how to feel in a feminine way. He was able to say that at the outset of his spiritual life three men played an important role in his growth to spiritual maturity, but in the American episode of his life and afterwards, women, and only women, were his initiators. His wide erotic experience, unusual though it was, and differing quantitatively only from that of most men, nonetheless was dedicated wholeheartedly to the noblest quest of them all.

But what really characterized this man, stamping him as far different from all other men, elevating him wholly beyond most, was his unswerving devotion to the Great Work. There can be little question about the uncompromising nature of his love for God, even if he has not always stated it simply and clearly in those specific words. To quote one of his own neologisms, he was a HIMOG—a holy illuminated man of God. And we would do well never to forget what he had to say in *The Book of Lies* about such a person:

> A red rose absorbs all colours but red; red is therefore the one colour that it is not.
> This Law, Reason, Time Space, all Limitation blinds us to Truth.

All that we know of Man, Nature, God, is just that
which they are not; it is that which they throw off as
repugnant.

The HIMOG is only visible insofar as He is imperfect.

Then are they all glorious who seem not to be
glorious, as the HIMOG is All-Glorious Within?

It may be so.

How then distinguish the inglorious and perfect
HIMOG from the inglorious man of earth?

Distinguish not!

But thyself Ex-tinguish: HIMOG art thou, and
HIMOG shalt thou be.

That flame burned in him at all times, regardless of the
seeming perversity of the more human, frail part of him.
Despite the excesses of his picturesque life, and what I have
assumed to be his psychopathology, his devotion and love
persisted throughout all vicissitudes. We must take him
seriously and literally when he cried:

O my God, but the love in Me bursts over the bonds
of Space and Time; the love in me is spilt among them
that love not love.

He persisted in that love, as he further wrote:

Thou hast fastened the fangs of Eternity in my soul,
and the Poison of the Infinite hath consumed me
utterly.

Time and space were never limitations for the dedication
of his love; their restricting bonds had been dissolved by
Eternity and Infinity. And to these he was the confirmed,
committed and consecrated devotee. He may have slipped at
times, being a rebel, and by his egotism he may have
been driven in strange neurotic ways. But his love and
dedication were never eclipsed. There are not many, I am
certain, who could have been as patient, as enduring, as

determined as he was in all the multifarious practices and exercises that he used as stepping stones to the great goal—Self-realization. This alone stamps him of a different breed from most of us, and demonstrates the clarity and purity of his Devotion to the Light.

This was no metaphysical preacher who pretentiously let it be known that sugar would not melt in his mouth, or that he was too pure for words. Nor was he a fanciful Master of the Far East, who purported to fast a great deal of time but who otherwise lived on fruit and cereals, maintaining a stolid pseudo-silence, only broken by pointing to letters on an alphabet-board. His motto was "Be strong! Then canst thou bear more joy!" He pretended to be nothing more than a man. But what a man!

That he has behaved stupidly and rottenly at times is indubitable. But to state this is merely testimony to the fact that he was a human being just like any of us, no matter how sublime and ineffable were the high mystic states that he experienced. That he rebelled against being guided and led gently by the hand, is evidenced by the whole of his personal history. Yet this is not to condemn him by any means. The vanity and conceit and presumption of the human state were parts of his birthright, and they were amply represented in him. Against this old Adam he struggled valiantly. Sometimes he failed; at other times there were some glorious successes. Because of this, his is the story of every man who has been blessed with creativity, the surging of the spirit within. We can see ourselves clearly in him.

But there was always something more. He possessed an indomitable courage, he had perseverance, and he loved his Angel. How else could he have been the scribe to the first chapter of the Book and have been the oracle of the Star-goddess with her ecstatic rhapsody:

I love you! I yearn to you! Pale or purple, veiled or

voluptuous, I who am all pleasure and purple, and drunkenness of the innermost sense, desire you . . . . Come unto me!

It really makes little difference in the long run whether the Book was dictated by a praeterhuman intelligence named Aiwass or whether it stemmed from the creative deeps of Aleister Crowley. The Book was written. And he became the mouthpiece for the *Zeitgeist,* accurately expressing the intrinsic nature of our time as no one else has done to date. So his failures and excesses and stupidities are simply the hall-mark of his humanity. Was he not, by his own admission, the Beast, whose number is 666, which is the number of Man?

To close this chapter, I can do no better than to quote *The Summons,* one of Crowley's last statements concerning *Liber Legis.* He wrote:

The book announces a New Law for mankind.

It replaces the moral and religious sanctions of the past, which have everywhere broken down, by a principle valid for each man and woman in the world, and self-evidently indefeasible . . . . I summon, therefore, by the power and authority entrusted to me, every great spirit and mind now on this planet incarnate to take effective hold of this transcendent force, and apply it to the advancement of the welfare of the human race.

For as the experience of these two and thirty years has shown too terribly, the book cannot be ignored. It has leavened Mankind unaware: and Man must make thereof the Bread of Life. Its ferment has begun to work on the grape of thought: Man must obtain therefrom the Wine of Ecstasy.

NOTES

[1] *The Equinox of the Gods,* O.T.O., London, 1936, p. 13.

[2] I would like to insert this parenthetical demurrer about the conventional occult identification of the Holy Guardian Angel with the so-called Higher Self. Crowley considered this identification a heresy and an abomination, and he expressed himself in no uncertain terms about it. For example, in *Magick Without Tears,* he wrote:

> We can readily concur that the Augoeides, the "Genius" of Socrates, and the "Holy Guardian Angel" of Abramelin the Mage, are identical. But we cannot include this "Higher Self"; for the Angel is an actual Individual, with his own Universe, exactly as man is; or, for the matter of that, a bluebottle. He is not a mere abstraction, a selection from, and exaltation of, one's own favourite qualities, as the "Higher Self" seems to me . . . .
> I can, for instance, work myself up to a "Divine Consciousness", in which I can understand, and act, as I cannot in my normal state. I become "inspired"; I feel, and I express, ideas of almost illimitable exaltation. But this is *totally* different from the "Knowledge and Conversation of the Holy Guardian Angel", which is the special aim of the Adeptus Minor. It is ruin to that Work if one deceives oneself by mistaking one's own 'energized enthusiasm' for external communication. The parallel on the physical plane is the difference between Onanism and sexual intercourse . . . .
> I believe that the Holy Guardian Angel is a Being of this (angelic) order. He is something more than a man, possibly a being who has already passed through the stage of humanity, and his peculiarly intimate relationship with his client is that of friendship, of community, of brotherhood, or fatherhood.

[3] This and the following few quotations were written by Crowley, and are extracted from *The Equinox of the Gods,* London, 1936.

[4] *The Equinox of the Gods,* p. 68.

[5] There appears to be however another diary kept at about the same period of time; it was called *The Book of Results,* in which there is also an entry for March 17th. I quote it verbatim:

> It is 'all about the child'. Also 'All Osiris.' (Note the cynic and sceptic tone of this entry. How different it appears in the light of Liber 418!)
> Thoth, invoked with great success, indwells us. (Yes; but what happened? Fra. P. has no sort of idea.)
>
> *A.C.*

[6] Charles R. Cammell, *op. cit.,* p. 107.

APPENDICES

APPENDIX I

In his book *The Great Beast,* John Symonds included an appendix which gave a horoscope of Aleister Crowley with a brief reading by Robert Gleadow. This chart and reading delineated a rather fatuous and insignificant person of no outstanding ability, one doomed to failure and poor choices. This chart is based upon his birth at Leamington, at 11:16 p.m., October 12, 1875.

Feeling that this genethliacal chart in no way did justice to Crowley, and certainly did not coincide with what I knew about the man and his work, I consulted a friend of mine who is, among other things, a shrewd student of Astrology. After discussing the above concepts, we agreed that the above-mentioned chart seemed to invalidate the empirical validity we felt was inherent in astrology.

My friend, Louis T. Culling, then outlined for me the thesis laid down many years ago by E.H. Bailey that it is possible to erect a so-called "lunar epoch" chart, for the probable moment of conception, and that this chart might delineate more accurately the potentialities and destiny of the individual. A chart is erected for approximately 273 days before birth, following well-defined rules and regulations with which I am not at all familiar, and so will not describe at second hand. But on the basis of these rules, Culling erected a prenatal chart, which I give on the next page.

The delineations are not mine. I merely reproduce them as I have obtained them from Mr. Culling. But it is clear that this prenatal chart depicts a character-structure that is far

511

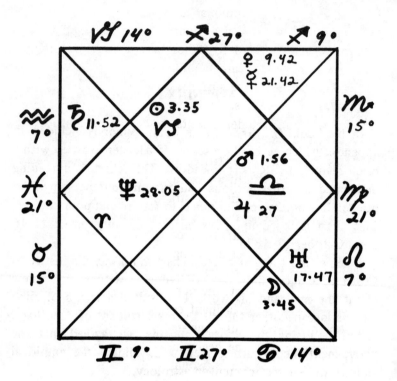

different from that described by Gleadow. At the same time it appears to be far more accurate in its description of the man Crowley. Perhaps the most noticeable feature of this chart is its rough division into two separate hemispheres. One contains all the planets but one. This planet is found all by itself in the intercepted first house in Aries. The inference is that Crowley was "far out" and these drives and interests alienated him from himself, and isolated him from his environment as well.

Pisces is on the Ascendant. It is a watery, emotional and intuitional sign, characterized by the desire to attain to distant ideals rather than to achieve practical ends. It is a Mutable sign, signifying the ability to make changes without feeling too much annoyance, adaptability. It implies a negativity that leads to an indrawnness, a hiddenness and a depth which are hard to fathom. As the astrologers put it, this Water is the ocean, boundless, infinitely deep, calm at times, but only on the surface, capable of sudden change to the wildest of storms. At first glance, it is inoffensive, but there are hidden undercurrents which can be subversive and dangerous.

Its ruler is Neptune, representing expansiveness, extremism, a bountifulness, a lack of putting limits to anything. It often gives a strange sense of humor, never dormant, but always active and ebullient. Neptune is the dreamer, the idealist, the reacher for the intangible. It dissolves and corrodes anything that tends to restrict or put bonds or bounds to structures. It may represent the genius—or the escapist; the dope addict or the creative artist, the wastrel and the brilliant confidence man. This planet is found in the first house, the stamp of the personality, and in Aries, representing the beginning, energy, and aggressiveness. So whatever Neptune is, would be bountifully energized by Aries, the pioneer.

Culling prefers to limit his description of this map to a very brief discussion of the 1st, 5th and 9th houses. The first house represents the beginning, the basic personality, where we find Neptune—representing his aspiration to the highest. The second house to be considered, the 5th, usually concerns pleasure, children, creativity—or, as Culling prefers to put it—attaining full autonomy in one's own sphere of endeavour. The 9th house represents transcendence, going beyond; and this certainly is very true of Crowley's entire life activity.

The conjunction of Jupiter to Mars in the 7th house is indicative of his thoughtless extravagance and expansiveness both in the field of human relationships, and in the sphere of finances. It is essentially a "bad" aspect.

Taking the chart as a whole, there is represented a genius

of tremendous energy who, though at odds with himself and with the world at large, sought out his own destiny, the fulfilment of his True Will, and to achieve individuation.

APPENDIX II

Since this book was completed, my attention has often been directed to the recent publication of Jean Overton Fuller's book *The Magical Dilemma of Victor Neuburg* (W. H. Allen, London, 1965). The usual malignant Crowley legend runs through the entire work like a dark-hued ribbon. It gets to be frightfully monotonous.

The quality of Miss Fuller's scholarship can best be measured by one of her assumptions—that Dion Fortune took over the Golden Dawn. Evidently Miss Fuller has not read Dion Fortune's historical account of both her own organization and the Golden Dawn published in *The Occult Review* sometime in 1933. In this article, Dion Fortune narrated how she was expelled from the Order by Mrs. Mathers but was later accepted as a member by the Bristol Temple of the Stella Matutina. With the permission of one of the Chiefs of the latter organization, she formulated her own Order in London, the Fraternity of the Inner Light. There was no take-over in any sense of the term.

There are a dozen other similar errors!

I was aghast at the remark alleged to have been made to her by Sir Gerald Kelly. Among other things, he is alleged to have said that Crowley was not a gentleman—that is, of the British landed gentry—and that he had some vulgarisms. That the British aristocracy is heavily loaded with vulgarisms does not need to be labored here. It is too well known. That Gerald Kelly is a rank snob and a vulgar hypocrite is also self-evident. His is the class-conscious attitude that altogether

515

justified Crowley's total contempt of him, as I have indicated on an earlier page. It is worth noting that in the essay Crowley wrote about him in *Equinox IX,* there appears this comment:

> He set seriously to work to obtain commissions, through the social influence of his family and his friends. The seats of the mighty, he learnt, were amicably stirred by the titillation of a tongue; the brush became a secondary instrument in his armory. His very conversation forgot art; he began to prate of "gentlemen" and "his social position." He began to reproach me one day for knowing painters who could paint. "There are bad painters who are gentlemen," he said, "and there are bad painters who are not gentlemen. Now *my* friends are gentlemen." I had humbly to confess that I did not know one bad painter who was not a gentleman!

Kelly's attitude had not changed in fifty years. And if his attitude is characteristic of today's England, the opening lines of Crowley's poem of some sixty years ago are still relevant:

> O England! England, mighty England, falls!
> None shall lament her lamentable end!

Miss Fuller also describes an initiatory ritual supposedly undergone by Neuburg. I have the gravest doubts that Crowley ever employed in the A∴A∴ rituals of the kind that Miss Fuller describes. There is intrinsic evidence that she has merely borrowed from, or assumed that Crowley used, the Golden Dawn Neophyte Ritual in the mangled form given in *Equinox II.* The fact is that the *Equinox* version consists of a merger of the Golden Dawn Neophyte Ritual and another set of documents called Z-1 and Z-2, both of which describe the inner workings or rubric of the ritual. They were all kept distinct and separate in the Golden Dawn. Crowley or Captain Fuller, or whoever wrote that part of the serial called

"The Temple of King Solomon" in *Equinox II,* thought that inserting parts of the rubric into the ritual proper would make the latter more intelligible. I have my serious doubts. But the manner in which Miss Fuller dramatizes that initiation ceremony forces me to suspect that my worst doubts were fulfilled. She is merely guessing.

For the rest, there is only the repetition of the old canards, some considerable misinformation, and the inclusion of her own special brand of hypocrisy. She appears not to mind discussing the homosexual relationship between Neuburg and Crowley. She even quotes from a Crowley letter to Fuller about Neuburg's pederastic preoccupations with the brown bottoms of Arab boys. But then, very much like Charles R. Cammell, she balks at quoting "blasphemies" from *The Book of the Law.* It makes very little sense. And I must say I find it a bit sickening!

Apart from a few fascinating excerpts from Neuburg's magical diary, which give Miss Fuller's book its sole value (and which I would like to see published *in toto* without her comments) this book has minimal value.

Beyond agreeing with Miss Fuller that much of Neuburg's poetry is very good, and that he did in fact encourage some of the younger budding poets in England, I find absolutely nothing here to warrant the slightest modification of my own contribution to Aleister Crowley's spiritual odyssey.

THE CAMEL'S EYE

Of what window,
of what house,
Do you see the Serpent's Cross?

By what eye,
or what mime,
Does the Priestess turn to Faust?

With moon as Amoun Ra's Sword

whirling high at Fortune's gate.

The shining star of the Emperor's heart,

turning life at a foolish rate.

A stormy sea with burrowed eyes,

crying out for tempered Fate.

All men are fools -- behind a Camel's eye.
Seeking smiles from the Devil's Plate.
His crown of thorns,
his feet of clay,
bearing gifts for his godless mate.

All men are fools -- behind a Camel's eye,
Seeking God -- Tempting Fate.

For Israel Regardie
— In His 75th Year —

By Christopher S. Hyatt
Los Angeles
April 9, 1982